From Exile to Washington

From EXILE *to* WASHINGTON

A *Memoir of Leadership in the Twentieth Century*

W. MICHAEL BLUMENTHAL

THE OVERLOOK PRESS
NEW YORK, NY

This edition first published in hardcover in the United States in 2013 by
The Overlook Press, Peter Mayer Publishers, Inc.

141 Wooster Street
New York, NY 10012
www.overlookpress.com
For bulk and special sales, please contact sales@overlookny.com,
or write us at the address above.

Library of Congress Cataloging-in-Publication Data

Blumenthal, W. Michael, 1926-
From exile to Washington : a memoir of leadership in the twentieth century
/ W. Michael Blumenthal. — First edition.
pages cm
Includes bibliographical references and index.
Summary: "Born in Weimar Germany, W. Michael Blumenthal grew up during the ascent of the
Third Reich. He and his family fled from the Nazis to the other side of the world—first to Shanghai,
then to America. There, he made a career in business and politics, as an adviser to President Kennedy
and as the Secretary of the Treasury under President Carter. In 1997, after a half century as an American,
he did what many German Jews would never consider: He returned to Berlin. In *From Exile to
Washington*, Blumenthal explains how his life experiences led him to reaccept his German homeland.
He vividly describes his youth in Berlin during Nazi rule, his dramatic escape to Japanese occupied
China, and the life he made in the United States. Whether as a professor of economics, a business
leader, or a presidential adviser, Blumenthal has always been keenly attuned to current events. With
the authority of an elder statesman, Blumenthal presents a compelling view of a new Germany—
one that has been forced to confront its own dark past and become a world leader once again."
—Provided by publisher.

1. Blumenthal, W. Michael, 1926- 2. Cabinet officers—United States—Biography. 3. United
States. Office of the Treasurer—Biography. 4. United States—Politics and government—20th
century. 5. Germany—History—20th century. I. Title.
E840.8.B59A3 2013   943.087092—dc23   [B]   2013027572

Book design and type formatting by Bernard Schleifer
Manufactured in the United States of America
ISBN: 978-1-4683-0729-0

FIRST EDITION
1 3 5 7 9 10 8 6 4 2

For Barbara

History is the essence of innumerable biographies.
—Thomas Carlyle

CONTENTS

PREFACE

The twentieth century was a period of enormous material progress, but also of regression into the worst kind of barbarism. Throughout recorded human history, mankind has always been at war with itself in a conflict between two sets of antipodal elements of the human spirit: on the one hand, cognitive brilliance, inventiveness, cultural accomplishment, courage, and concern for the individual and the common good; on the other, cruelty, cowardice, indifference to human life, greed, and the lust for power.

At no time was this contrast between beauty and brutishness, and progress and regression, as evident as in the last century. In the brief space of a hundred years, a mere wink of the eye of recorded history, our lives and the very planet we inhabit changed dramatically, often for the better and sometimes for the worse, but no one on this earth was left untouched. For those of us who lived through it, it was a fascinating if sometimes frightening time to be alive.

There were great discoveries in the basic sciences, pathbreaking new technologies, and the development of a wide array of new sources of energy. Man harnessed the atom, walked on the moon and probed the outer reaches of the universe. Rapid dissemination of human knowledge left few parts of the world untouched. A revolution in electronics gave us instant worldwide communication and the jet engine brought the furthest corners of the earth into reach in less than twenty-four hours. A large number of diseases, little understood when the century began, were conquered, and within the span of three generations greater medical advances were achieved than in all of previously recorded history. Life expectancy increased dramatically in many parts of the world, and as the twentieth century came to an end, the new science of genetics had begun to unlock the mysteries of life and death itself.

Far-reaching developments also fundamentally reshaped political relationships and the world economy. Colonialism, still a major world force at the century's beginning, was swept away virtually overnight and scores of newly independent nations emerged in Africa and Asia. It had been more than a hundred years since the French Revolution's battle cry for liberty, equality and fraternity, but at the beginning of the twentieth century true democratic government was still uncommon in Europe and, except in North America, virtually nonexistent anywhere else. In fact, in the early decades, it was democracy that was under pressure, while totalitarianism was in the ascendancy, and on the eve of the Second World War constitutional government in Europe had become the exception rather than the rule. Yet fifty years later, following a long and dangerous confrontation between these two political philosophies, democracy rather than totalitarianism had prevailed. Even in hindsight, the sudden disintegration of the Soviet Union and speedy disappearance of Communism as a world force were among the most astonishing events in modern history.

For a long time, Europe had looked with admiration and envy at the economic and political benefits Americans derive from their union, but her own continental integration had remained an impossible dream. Yet this seemingly unreachable ideal was brought much closer to reality as the century was drawing to a close. European economic and political unity made greater strides over the last several decades than anyone had believed possible, and though a lot remained to be done, by the year 2000 national boundaries in Europe had lost much of their meaning.

Yet there is the other side to consider—the twentieth century's dismal record of aggression, wars, and violation of human rights. Hundreds of millions of lives were lost in two great world wars and in many lesser ones, in regional conflicts, and in ethnic, racial, and religious strife. The disintegration of colonial empires did not occur smoothly, and in newly emerging nations long-standing ethnic and religious divisions erupted in bloody rivalries once the colonial masters had disappeared.

In the Western world, far-reaching technological and political changes led to major societal upheavals, and with new uncertainties came new fears. As great opportunities arose for some, the changes produced a real or imagined loss of established status and position for others, and to cater to these insecurities there appeared those who offered seductively simple but flawed remedies.

Jews had been traditional victims of prejudice and blame, particularly in troubled times. At the beginning of the century, however, Jew-hatred had seemed on the wane, only to intensify again after the First World War in much of the Western world, culminating in great violence with tragic consequences for European Jewry at mid-century. Utilizing emotional anti-Jewish appeals as one of their weapons, reactionary, xenophobic, and radical political leaders seized power by force or deception, promising people liberty even as they disenfranchised them, and drawing the world into decades of hot and cold wars in attempts to shape the century to their own ends.

The result was two of the most destructive wars in human history, fought with unparalleled ferocity and cruelty against soldiers and civilians alike, a seemingly never-ending string of postcolonial conflicts, violent revolutions, and regional strife, and nearly four decades of tense and dangerous cold-war confrontations. As the twentieth century was ending, rogue states and cross-border terrorist groups created new insecurities and posed entirely novel threats to the established order.

It is one of the basic premises of this book that history is made by people and that it is always subject to the vagaries of circumstance and chance, depending on who has their hands on the levers of power at critical turning points, which choices they make and what their relationships are to one another.[1] As the historian Fritz Stern has aptly put it, "in history nothing is certain until it happens." Thus, few of the twentieth century's major developments were unavoidable or inevitable, and there are many instances when the course of events might easily have moved in a different direction.

Would the First World War have occurred if the relatively moderate Emperor Frederick III, Germany's absolute monarch, had not succumbed to cancer in 1888 only 99 days after ascending the throne, and if his rash and imprudent son, Wilhelm II, had not succeeded him? What if the Treaty of Versailles following the First World War had read differently because leaders less bent on retribution and revenge had been in charge in France after 1918, and less feckless ones in Britain, or if America had not turned inward in the twenties under the unimpressive Harding and Coolidge Presidencies? Or what, we may ask, if during its first abortive experiment with parliamentary democracy in Germany, the Weimar Republic had been blessed with stronger, more effective leaders during those critical interwar years (as Germany would be after 1945): would that have kept Hitler from seizing power and changing history? If, at the last moment, an attempt on Hitler's life in '38 had succeeded, as it almost did, could the Second World War still have been prevented and the events of the half century thereafter taken a very different course?

On the other hand, if the United States had not learned from its past mistakes and if its accidental, inexperienced yet resolute President Harry Truman had not had the courage to invest heavily to rebuild Europe after the Second World War, or had failed to support European economic integration and not rallied Western Europe to build the institutions for a strong Western Alliance of free nations, might the Cold War have ended quite differently? What if wisdom had not prevailed on both sides when Soviet missiles were detected in Cuba in 1962?

The point is this: the history of the last century is replete with seminal events, some that served the cause of peace and advanced the condition of humankind. Yet others that also were the consequence of human decision making reflect baser instincts of a lust for power, immorality, disrespect for human life, and—yes—enormous foolishness.

On balance, we were lucky. The Cold War ended peacefully and nuclear catastrophe was avoided. The dictators who waged war and deprived millions of their liberties and lives disappeared. Yet, in the twenty-first century new dangers confront the world, new challenges and risks to freedom and democracy must be faced. The question is whether we will have learned from the past, can rise to the task, and will be as fortunate to survive intact as we were in the previous century.

In many respects my life has mirrored the twentieth century's crises and good times. I was born in Germany during that brief period in the 1920s when the future on both sides of the Atlantic looked reasonably hopeful. Yet not many years later, as the Second World War began and Hitler's crimes inflamed the world, I was confined to a far-away corner of Asia, so destitute that newspapers were stuffed into my shoes to cover up the holes.

I began life as a German and I have been an American for over sixty years, but during the upheaval years of economic turmoil, dictatorships, and war, I had no passport at all, while some years later no fewer than four different nations were willing to issue me theirs.[2] For two and a half years I was a prisoner of the Japanese, and later not even the most junior American consular official would have given me the time of day. Yet at another time, when America had emerged from the war as the leader of the West, I would, as his ambassador, represent the U.S. president abroad in the sixties, and as secretary of the treasury in the seventies I was nominally fifth in line to succeed him in an emergency.[3]

Once, no one would hire me, and I could find no job at all. Later, when standards of living had risen and economies were booming, I headed first one and then another major multi-billion-dollar corporation, each an instrument and symbol of the century's technological and economic progress. And in the eighties, as the electronics revolution ushered in globalism and changed the world, I had an inside view of this momentous turning point in human affairs while leading one of the world's great computer companies.

That I would become a privileged observer of a few of the century's milestone events, and very occasionally even a minor participant, certainly was not preordained, and is largely due to an accident of birth and to fortuitous circumstances that put me into places and positions where I met some of the key decision-makers and saw them in action. Thus it was happenstance that cast me alternatively as victim, witness, or bit actor into the middle of the action and at the side of world leaders and decision-makers during key twentieth-century moments.

My earliest memories are of Berlin under Hitler in the thirties. I expected never to return to Berlin, but by a quirk of fate I would become closely involved there again in the nineties, when a very different Germany had evolved as a strong democracy. I saw the old China in its dying days and left it with few regrets. Yet in the seventies, I would get to know its top leadership, find myself playing a role in the reestablishment of Sino-U.S. relations, and be an inside witness to the changes that had transformed China into a major world power by the end of the century. The dramatic changes in the Middle East and a few of the events that defined them I saw at first hand, dealing with Menachem Begin, Israel's ideologically rigid prime minister, at critical moments when the process of peace might have been advanced but was not, and dealing with the Shah of Iran at a fateful time when a popular uprising cost him his throne and turned his country from ally to enemy of the United States. From the fifties to the seventies, in business and in government service, I became closely involved with the path-breaking developments leading to economic unification in Europe and with the major decision-makers on both sides of the Atlantic who were its architects. Most importantly, I had at various times the good fortune to work directly for three presidents of the United States, in close proximity to them in the White House.

This book tells the story of the century's ups and downs as I experienced them, close to some of the major decision makers. It is intended as a history of the fateful years, told from the vantage point of actor and observer. It is, however, neither a history of the twentieth century as a historian would tell it, nor a normal autobiography, but somewhat of a hybrid, a book that lies, as Eric Hobsbawm once described such efforts, "in a twilight zone between history and memory, between the past as a generalized record . . . and as a remembered part of one's own life."[4] It is therefore a necessarily subjective account, one that I realize has risks.

The reader will recognize a few recurring themes that have impressed me as I have reflected on the last century's events. One, already mentioned, is that how history evolves is impossible to predict but depends on the people who make the decisions and on the accidental events that put them into positions of power. Another is that, therefore, the individual decision-maker matters a great deal in shaping historical events, especially at the top where the right combination of temperament and personal leadership qualities is critical. And, finally, that infrequently there can arise exogenous events that lie beyond the power of anyone to control, developments that can determine the course of history as much as the decision of any leader. In the twentieth century, the electronic revolution that ushered in the present era of globalism was one such event.

The twentieth century should teach us that wisdom does not necessarily triumph over foolishness, and that respect for human life does not always carry the day. Yet it also shows that there is reason for the more optimistic view that with a modicum of luck and common sense it often enough does.

The era of globalism confronts us with as many new dangers and risks, but also with more great opportunities for progress and the continued betterment of the human condition. How things will evolve cannot be known. The question is not only whether good fortune will smile on us, but whether there will be leaders who apply the lessons of the last century to shape the new one in a positive way.

From Exile to Washington

THE THIRTIES
Germany in Trouble:
In Nazi Berlin

Roots

I was born on January 3, 1926, in the small town of Oranienburg, near Berlin, into a comfortably affluent Jewish family of country bankers who had lived in Germany for as long as anyone could remember. Before long, it would become evident that it had been a fateful time to have come into the world.

When the new century dawned, life had still been orderly and predictable. The great European powers—Great Britain, France, and Germany—their colonial empires intact, remained at the center of the international economic and political system. War between them was considered remote if for no other reason than that military technology had advanced so far as to render such foolishness self-defeating and suicidal. Across the Atlantic, America was booming, world trade was expanding, and in many places living standards were on the rise. The universal assumption was that the good times were here to stay and that the future looked bright.

Germany's long-established Jewish citizens, the Blumenthals of Oranienburg among them, had shared such optimism. Once they had faced the perils of a second-class status as a disenfranchised, distrusted minority subject to discrimination and periodic waves of repression. But those days were since long ago a thing of the past. In the previous century, German Jews had been granted full civil rights, and many had prospered in business or moved into the professions. Though anti-Semitism was certainly not yet a spent force, at the turn of the century it seemed to be waning, and many Jews confidently believed that it was only a question of time before progress and enlightenment would wipe away what barriers against them still prevailed.

In Oranienburg, my great-grandfather had been the first among the town's small Jewish community to be elected to the Town Council, and my grandfather had followed in his footsteps as one of the town's most respected citizens. At the turn of the century, the Blumenthals were doing well financially and felt comfortable and secure. Many years later, in a less happy time, my father, born in 1889 as a loyal Prussian subject of the Hohenzollerns, would nostalgically look back on those early years of the new century as the best—"the good old times," he called them, and sometimes simply, "Kaiser's times."

The outbreak of the Great War in 1914 was the turning point when many illusions were shattered and when it became clear that the optimism of prior years had been misplaced. The war no one had anticipated and few had wanted lasted four years and proved one of the costliest in human history. Thereafter, the twentieth century would follow a very different course from that once expected.

An entire generation of young European men had been decimated on the battlefield, and large parts of the European continent, particularly in France, lay in ruins. The Russian Tsar and the Emperors of Austria-Hungary and Germany had disappeared from the scene, and politically weak and unstable governments had taken their place. Years of hard economic times and political uncertainty followed. In Germany, in particular, the horrendous inflation of the early postwar years, unprecedented in severity, had impoverished the middle class, nurtured extremist, reactionary sentiments, and put the socio-political fabric of the nation under extraordinary stress.

The effects of the war had been highly damaging, but the twenties were also impacted by changed realities that had been germinating below the surface but whose significance few prewar observers had recognized. Many of these were now out in the open: the new discoveries and scientific advances and the benefits, as well as upheavals, that resulted from them; the internationalization of the world economy and its impact on individual nations; the disintegration of anachronistic empires in Europe, and the ending of colonialism overseas; the decline of Europe as the world's dominant force and the rise of America; and, finally, the effects of the growing political consciousness of the masses and the clash of competing ideologies about how best to organize modern life.

The search for answers would dominate world affairs for much of the twentieth century and would be the cause for many of its upheavals and armed conflicts. Marxism, nostalgia for the old, combined with radical ideas about how to turn back the clock, the rise of fascism, ethnic conflicts, big and little wars, the misuses of science and the popularity of pseudo-scientific solutions to complex problems, intolerance, racism, and murderous forms of anti-Semitism were some of the consequences. Ultimately, it is the search for answers that gave rise to the twentieth century's prolonged Cold War and nuclear stand-off, to its many dangers and setbacks, but also to the century's amazing intellectual feats and progress.

In some countries, Germany included, economic conditions had substantially improved in 1926—the year of my birth—and some Germans would later call this period their Golden Years. After a grim beginning for the Weimar Republic in 1919, when the very survival of Germany's first experiment with parliamentary democracy had been much in doubt, this was a second, more hopeful, albeit brief phase in its short fourteen-year life.

The harsh terms of the Versailles Treaty and the crushing burden it imposed on the traumatized defeated German nation had created enormous and lasting internal tensions, and the impact of the ruinous inflation on the middle class had further exacerbated them. There had been frequent changes of government, repeated attempts by left- and right-wing extremists to overthrow the young Republic, constant unrest in the streets, and virtually daily political assassinations. Almost miraculously, however, the middle years of the twenties brought consolidation and greater calm. The German economy improved, buttressed by foreign credits, mostly from America. Unemployment was low, prices relatively stable, and shelves were once more amply stocked with food. No one as yet realized, however, that this happier phase would prove quite brief and would soon be followed by the young Weimar Republic's final years when, under the impact of a world depression, its disintegration would usher in a twelve-year descent into catastrophe.

No nation was as deeply affected by the collapse of the world financial system as Germany, which had relied heavily on the inflow of American funds in its postwar reconstruction efforts. When these ceased in 1928 to 1929, suddenly and completely, the whole system came crashing down. Hundreds of German banks—including the Blumenthal bank in Oranienburg—failed, and Germany was plunged into an economic crisis worse even than that of the United States. Between 1928 and 1932, German National Income declined by a staggering 62 percent and exports were cut in half. Every third worker was unemployed, and poverty and despair were widespread and far worse than in the terrible first postwar years. What confidence in Weimar democracy had remained was totally destroyed. The beginning of the end of German democracy was at hand.

In 1929, the year of the Blumenthal bank's collapse, I was three years old. To escape the shame and ignominy of the failure, my parents had packed up their belongings and fled Oranienburg for Berlin. My earliest childhood memories are of those years.

Oranienburg to Berlin

We arrived in Berlin sometime toward the end of 1929. Germany was sliding rapidly into a deep economic crisis, while my parents were seeking the anonymity of the capital to hide from the shame of the collapse of the family's bank, a victim of bad management and the world economic crisis. Their savings were gone, they were utterly broke, and neither of them had any readily marketable skills for earning a living.

The timing could not have been worse. Over two million Germans were already on the dole. Berlin was in chaos and unemployment was growing, from three hundred thousand in January to over twice that number after the New York stock market crash in October. One hundred fifty thousand Berlin metalworkers were out on a prolonged strike to protest a 15 percent cut in pay, and in the streets Communists and Hitler's Storm Troopers were locked in bloody battles. Marauding Nazi gangs roamed Berlin, assaulting their opponents, roughing up Jews, and brawling in movie houses against films they didn't like. When the showing of Erich Maria Remarque's antiwar *All Quiet on the Western Front* had to be suspended because of Nazi threats, the Communists retaliated against one of Hitler's favorites, *The Flute Concert of Sans-Souci*, glorifying Frederick the Great.

Meanwhile, Berlin City Hall was awash in confusion and barely able to function. In the latest election a dispirited electorate had voted heavily for extremists on both the left and right, the ruling Social Democrats had retained power by a hair, and openly antidemocratic parties occupied a plurality of the seats. As always in times of distress, anti-Semitism was predictably on the rise again, and the poisonous Joseph Goebbels, Berlin Gauleiter (provincial leader) of the growing Nazi party, was stoking the fires of anti-Jewish bigotry and hate.

The city was a dangerous and troubled place, and my parents were facing a particularly traumatic and difficult time. To begin with, there was no money for a place of our own, forcing us to crowd into my maternal grandmother's apartment, a less than satisfactory arrangement for all concerned. I have only a hazy memory of an old-fashioned, high-ceilinged and dark apartment at Kantstrasse 134a in the Charlottenburg district of West Berlin.

I was just about to turn four, and our next two years at Kantstrasse coincide with my earliest memories, of which only the recollection of a vague sense of sour moods, tension, and unfamiliarity with new surroundings remain. I do however recall being bundled off almost at once to a very "German" Kindergarten, where I was placed in the care of a formidable "Tante," who, for whatever childish reason, scared me half to death. I have forgotten her name but a surviving photograph shows her as an elderly lady with thick glasses and a stern mien, sitting stiffly on the grass surrounded by a dozen or so of her young charges. I think it was mainly her glasses and unusually deep voice that frightened me. I also remember her as a stern disciplinarian, protective and not unkind, but imbued with an irresistible need to expose us to the essential virtues of order, discipline, and obedience. In the Germany of the day, the proverbial rule that children are best seen but not heard was still much in vogue, and most grownups treated children accordingly. The atmosphere at Tante's was certainly a far cry from that of the Princeton nursery schools to which my wife and I would some twenty-five years later entrust our own kids in America. A warm and nourishing environment, with an emphasis on giving us free rein to develop our individual personalities, my Berlin "Kita" definitely was not.

Those first months in the turmoil of the German capital, suddenly dependent on the good graces of my somewhat misanthropic grandmother, a woman afflicted by bouts of depression and not blessed with a cheerful disposition or given to generous hospitality, must have been a deeply traumatic experience for my parents. The change in circumstance from comfortably fixed and settled citizens to homeless near-paupers had come as an unexpected shock. In Oranienburg, they had been respected pillars of the community and one of the first families among the town's Jews. There had been a large and impressive house in a prestigious part of the town and—as was not uncommon in those days—enough servants to relieve them from the more tedious chores of daily living: a full-time cook, a maid and once-a-week *Waschfrau* for the laundry, a chauffeur for the family car, and a live-in nanny for my sister, Stefanie, who was five years older than I was, and me. Neither by temperament nor experience were they at all prepared for the sudden and complete reversal of fortune they now faced.

Certainly not Ewald, my father, his mother's pampered and insecure eldest son, whose personality was poorly suited to taking initiatives or to dealing resolutely with sudden adversity. As to my mother, she had grown up in much more modest circumstances, the Markts having come to Berlin from the Eastern province of Posen less than a generation before her birth. Her marriage had been a decided step up in lifestyle and status, though one to which she had had no difficulty becoming accustomed. Unlike her husband, she was by nature a person of great energy and strength—assets upon which she would have ample need to draw in the years to come. She too, however, needed time to come to terms with what had happened.

My father had just turned forty when the crisis hit. In the late eighteenth century, his great-grandfather, Israel, had still been a devout Jew, close to his roots and his synagogue, and relatively unconnected to the German environment around him. Israel's son, my great-grandfather, had carried the process of cultural assimilation forward, changed his given name from Levin to Louis and risen to the lofty height of Oranienburg's town elite. With my mid-nineteenthth century grandfather's generation, the process of the Blumenthals' assimilation as Germans had been completed. The children had been given quintessentially German names at birth—Hans for a deceased firstborn, Ewald for my father, and Helmut, Edith, and Theodor for his younger siblings. They were now Germans first—proud nationalists and loyal subjects of the Kaiser. They knew they were Jews—nor would their neighbors have let them forget it—but the bonds to their religion and Jewish culture had grown weak. My father was a thoroughly secular Jew, did not know Hebrew or go to the synagogue, and, except on infrequent ceremonial occasions, practically no one in our family did. He had been raised as a Prussian German; Jewishness was now a secondary fact.

His best times, he was fond of recalling, were the years before the war, the sweet years. He had spent them in Berlin in comfortable bachelor quarters during his one-year military service and banking apprenticeship, liberally endowed with family funds. He had been placed in a small private bank on Behrenstrasse near the Gendarmenmarkt whose owners were his father's friends, the idea being that he would learn there the rudiments of a business he would one day run at home.

Contemporary photographs show him as an agreeable-looking young man of medium height, with already thinning dark hair and an attractive face with pleasant brown eyes. My grandmother Ida Eloesser adored him and, after the childhood death of her eldest, had showered all of her love and affection on him, there being a fair gap between my father's birth and that of his younger brother Helmut. As he liked to tell it with evident relish, tangible proof of Ida's devotion and indulgence had taken the form of a secret financial arrangement between mother and son, designed to assure him a pleasant life in Berlin with ample cash to enjoy the big city's manifold attractions. The idea was that his father would provide a not ungenerous monthly stipend for his upkeep—which she would clandestinely match, thereby doubling it. It left him with warm memories of his years as a free-spending twenty-something in prewar Berlin!

My father was intelligent, but neither brilliant nor particularly well educated. As was common in his day, he had left school at the age of sixteen with merely an average formal education. Besides his native German, he had learned a little Latin and spoke only a smattering of English and French. Intellectual stimulation at home had been limited and the life of the mind did not greatly interest him, but he was fundamentally honest, gentle, and, by nature, kind and placid. I cannot recall any great displays of emotion from him, whether in joy or anger or, for that matter, strong words of any kind toward his wife, children, or anyone else. He had, I suspect, deep feelings of insecurity and a strong sense of his limitations, which translated into a certain passivity and tendency to seek the path of least resistance, leaving it to others to make the hard decisions he could not himself face.

Basically he was happiest when spared complications of any kind and left free to enjoy the little pleasures of life—good food, personal comfort, and enough folding money for the occasional, discreet extramarital tryst. All his life, it seems, women had found him attractive, and he had never been averse to responding to them when opportunity beckoned.

Had he lived at another time, none of this might have mattered much, but, as with many assimilated German Jews, it equipped him poorly for the crises he would face in later life. In exile, the loss of a settled identity would hit him particularly hard. With no religious faith to fall back on and few other sources of comfort such as professional status or outside interests, he never again achieved the sense of security he had known as a young man.

My parents were married after a brief courtship in the fall of 1920. My mother, Valerie, was barely twenty-two at the time, nine years his junior, an attractive and bright young woman with blond hair, blue eyes, and a fetching shape. The younger of two sisters, she came from a Berlin Jewish family of modest financial means and social standing. If the Blumenthals were somewhere between well off and wealthy, the Markts were firmly lodged at the petit-bourgeois lower end of the social scale. Neither they nor their two daughters had benefited from particularly good schooling. My mother's education had ended when she was sixteen with secretarial training, and when she met her future husband she was holding down a junior office job. But she was by nature a hard-driving and ambitious woman, blessed with a high native intelligence.

Husband and wife clearly had very different personalities and were not particularly well suited to one another, yet it is not difficult to understand what brought them together. My father had an eye for attractive women—it would later be one of the problems between them—and was probably attracted by her good looks. Possibly he had also been impressed by the qualities he most lacked—her ambition, energy, and drive. For her part, she would have had no difficulty falling for the good-looking, friendly man, some years her senior, who was the eldest son and heir of a leading family in their town. I suspect that the idea of marrying "up," and its possibilities, had not been lost on her. In one respect, there was, however, no difference between them at all. Both came from thoroughly secular German-Jewish families. Both had been raised under the Christmas tree, so to speak, rather than with the traditional Chanukah menorah. Neither was a practicing Jew.

Their marriage was one of opposites, but in more settled times it might well have survived. Under the difficult circumstances they would face as outcast emigrants, the marriage lasted for twenty-two years, finally collapsing under the cumulative effect of my father's proclivity for occasional extramarital philandering, my mother's long memory of past resentments, and the heavy pressures of the refugee years in the Far East. For a long time, there had been an unspoken rule between them that helped keep the peace: she decided, and he followed. It was in her nature to take charge, just as he was most comfortable to sail in her wake. It made for unexpressed feelings and a shallow relationship but rarely for open controversy, and for a good many years it kept them together.

As a young woman of twenty-two, my mother faced her first great challenge: to master the transition into the unfamiliar environment of the upper-middle bourgeois orbit of the Blumenthals. The leap must have been daunting, but she learned quickly, and even before my birth in 1926 she had discovered her husband's weakness and passivity and moved in to fill the vacuum. Ida, her mother-in-law, had prematurely and suddenly died, not long after my mother came to Oranienburg. So, well before the bank's collapse, she had assumed the central position of authority in family affairs. In Berlin, she would quickly take charge of the finances and become our sole breadwinner under the most stringent and difficult conditions.

By any measure, she was a formidable woman. She held the family together in the darkest days, and it is no exaggeration to say that we owe her our lives. But she was not a particularly warm or affectionate mother for me. She cared for us and no doubt she loved me, but her style was to announce her decisions and expect us to follow them. Her capacity to tolerate alternate viewpoints was limited, and sensitivity to the feelings of others not one of her greater strengths. Many years later, she observed to me ruefully in San Francisco that unfortunately what Americans called "human relations" "hadn't existed" when she was growing up. ("*Zu meiner Zeit hat es das nicht gegeben.*") I did not have a close relationship with her any more than

I did with my father, and the more she attempted to control me, the more I clashed with her and resisted. But I missed her greatly once she was gone, and still do. Perhaps we were more similar than I realized, and her influence on me greater than I had allowed myself to admit.

For her, as for all German Jews, the years under the boot of Nazism and in exile would be extremely trying, but whatever the obstacles, she attacked them obstinately and never flinched. I greatly admire her for that. But I also missed an atmosphere of warmth, and felt the absence of an open sharing of feelings and of family cohesiveness. When the times were darkest, there wasn't much among us to fall back on—only the force of her character and her unrelenting will.

She had just turned thirty when we arrived in Berlin. The capital was in crisis and she had two small children and a largely helpless husband on her hands, no money, and few prospects. But she lost no time in embarking on a sustained quest for a new source of income that would allow us to escape the stifling atmosphere of our temporary cramped shelter at her mother's apartment.

Her first venture involved a quickly abandoned attempt at a career in motion pictures. Someone had introduced her to the friend of a friend connected with the film studios at Neubabelsberg outside Berlin, where an impressive group of talented young producers and directors had established Germany's reputation as one of the most innovative and successful production centers of the new world industry of "talking pictures." Ernst Lubitsch, Billy Wilder, Fritz Lang, Erich Pommer, and Robert Siodmak, among others, all got their start there. As Jews, they were quickly driven out by the Nazis after 1933— mostly to Hollywood—where they became even more successful household names, while the German film industry never recovered from the loss.[5] My mother, however, never made it past a few stints as an extra or with tiny speaking roles, and had little prospect of either financial or artistic rewards.

Further abortive efforts to earn enough money to support us followed. Ironically, success arrived just months before the Nazi takeover in 1933 when, after seeing her struggle in the prevailing deep depression environment, a friend agreed to stake her to the limited capital needed to open a small retail store of her own. She had seen enough such stores in her daily rounds, my mother assured him, to be certain she could do it better than most. Which was how, in the summer of 1932, we moved into a cramped apartment of our own, behind her small shop for ladies fashion accessories, opposite a leafy park complete with playground and water fountain. Olivaer Platz 10 was in a solid middle-class neighborhood near Berlin's best-known major avenue, the Kurfürstendamm, commonly known as Ku'damm. There I would spend several contented childhood years in the park across from the store, racing my scooter and honing my limited skills for competing in complex games of marbles.

My father was stationed behind the cash register awaiting customers and my mother took charge of everything else. Later, when business grew, Fräulein Dora Hahn, a young woman in her mid-twenties, was added as the shop's staff of one. My mother worked hard and had high hopes. She called her store Wallys, coopting the popular form of her first name.[6] The Christmas business exceeded expectations and in the very first year, she had netted a profit of RM 8,000, a respectable result. The future looked promising. But then, Adolf Hitler was named chancellor of Germany, and nothing would ever be the same again for Wallys' owner, or for any other German Jew. Losing no time in implementing the anti-Jewish policies he had promised, he announced a national boycott against Jews. So, on April 1, 1933, Nazi storm troopers took up position in front of my mother's store and urged the customers to stay out. It is one of my earliest and most frightening memories. The signs they carried read JEW STORE. GERMANS DON'T BUY HERE!

My Childhood Berlin

Nothing so much illustrates the enormous changes in twentieth century lifestyles than to cast a backward look at the Berlin of my childhood.

With more than four million inhabitants spread out over a vast area of some 900 square kilometers, Berlin was a great European metropolis, architecturally not the most beautiful, but technologically as advanced as Paris or London, and superior to most other cities. Prior to the Nazi takeover, Berlin had become renowned as a major center of industry, science, culture, and learning, the home of one of the world's great universities, with scores of lively theaters, famous museums, and world-class opera houses and concert halls hosting the great performing artists of the day.

Today's Berliners would hardly recognize the street scenes of the early thirties as they remain etched in my memory. Horses, for one thing, were still in evidence. The last horse-drawn buses had in fact only been withdrawn a few years before,[7] and such everyday staples as coal, beer, and ice—refrigerators in private homes were still a rare luxury—were usually delivered to stores and homes by horse-drawn carts. For some reason, even bulky furniture vans were almost exclusively powered by the large and powerful draft horses, who left their visiting cards on the streets for the city sweepers. *Pferdeäpfel*, or "horse apples," we children called them. Automobiles were a luxury and beyond the reach of the middle class. Traffic was on the rise, but except for a few main thoroughfares the streets were not nearly as congested as today. Only a few people in my parents' circle of friends owned cars, and those who did were either quite well off, or they were the occasional bachelors out to impress the ladies. Automobile taxis had become common, but on Olivaer Platz there was still a stand for horse-drawn *Droschken*, and even today I can hear the coachmen, enthroned atop their carriage boxes, bantering with passersby in their earthy Berlin slang.

Bicycles were everywhere and Berlin's impressive network of subways and elevated trains, built around the turn of the century, was one of Europe's most modern. The preferred mode of public surface transport, however, was the now largely extinct streetcar, the Berlin *Elektrische*,[8] whose clanging was an ubiquitous background traffic noise. Berlin is dotted with greenery and surrounded by lovely lakes, but a million or more of the city's lower income groups lived in drab tenements, the *Mietskasernen*, some with multiple dark and unhealthy inner courtyards. Telephones numbers had six digits and many poorer Berliners still made do without them.

The street scene reflected traditional social conventions that have long since disappeared, and the wounds of the lost Great War were still much in evidence. Here and there, one-legged veterans stood at street corners selling pencils, flowers, or assorted trinkets. Nannies wore nurse-like uniforms with veils draped over their backs, and traveling craftsmen, the *Wanderburschen*, could be seen in the distinctive garb of their craft. Chimney sweeps, their faces covered in black soot, were a common sight, and meeting one was said to bring good luck. Widows wore black for a full year and were easily recognizable by the black veils partially covering their heads and faces. For men, a black armband was expected after a death in the family. University students proudly sported their visored fraternity caps, though these were soon replaced by the less colorful brown uniforms of the Hitler Youth. Uniforms, a long-standing German specialty, were an integral part of the city scene. In Nazi Berlin post-1933, there was a plethora of these, brown ones for the SA, black for the SS—especially feared by Jews—distinct variations for members of the Party's motorized formations, for Labor Service members, Hitler Youth, Wehrmacht soldiers and countless others. For little boys too young yet for the Nazi party, the sailor suit made popular under the Kaiser was still a first "uniform" of choice.

Until boys were well into their teens, the dress code was short pants and knee socks, while Knickerbockers, the "almost" long pants tied at mid-calf, were a popular sporty halfway alternative even for adults. I recall my mother outfitting me with several pairs, even spending some of our last Marks on them just prior to our leaving for China—where I refused to wear them because they were the source of much amusement there in my British school. American-style jeans, the ubiquitous world apparel of the late twentieth century, were as yet totally unknown.

The average German lived a relatively insular life and his first-hand knowledge of foreign countries was much more limited than is the case today. My parents, for example, always recalled as very special that rare trip taken outside of Germany—a honeymoon in Italy. Our summers were spent on the beaches of the Baltic or North Sea, less than 150 miles from Berlin. Heringsdorf on the Baltic was a family favorite.

My parents were proudly German and deeply hurt that the Nazis had stamped them as alien and inferior. Yet as much as they insisted that they were Germans "just like everyone else," the truth was more nuanced and ambiguous. They were, of course, thoroughly German in their values and demeanor, but the distinction between German Jews and non-Jews—a legacy of centuries of separation and prejudice on both sides—had never been fully bridged, and even my parents knew it. Casual relations with non-Jewish neighbors and business acquaintances were open and friendly, though less and less so under the Nazis. Herr Kettler and Herr Jehle, the co-owners of the corner barbershop, would drop in at Wallys for a chat, or to make purchases for their wives; the corner greengrocer and the butcher saved "specials" my mother liked, and my father regularly stopped in for light-hearted banter and the occasional beer at the Mehlgarten Kneipe (pub) on Olivaer Platz, where news about families was exchanged. After the Nazi takeover, some neighbors joined the Party, but only a few were fundamentally anti-Semitic. Some now passed their Jewish neighbors in the street and studiously looked the other way, but they were in the minority. Most others, even those who had something good to say about "Adolf"—a not insignificant number contrary to later claims—were more embarrassed than convinced by the Party's vicious anti-Jewish propaganda. "They don't mean people like you" was a common sotto-voce refrain.

The truth remains, however, that long before Hitler came on the scene, and certainly thereafter, my parents' social life evolved primarily around other assimilated Jews. Close friendships between Jews and non-Jews existed but were rarer, and I cannot recall a single exception in my parents' circle.

Only some 5 percent of Berlin's pre-Hitler population was Jewish, but in the Wilmersdorf and Charlottenburg districts—our part of town—there was a much larger concentration, and in some of the comfortable old apartment houses of the area as many as a third of the tenants were Jews. There were ample opportunities there to socialize with people of similar backgrounds—to the exclusion not only of gentiles but equally so of recently arrived coreligionists from Poland, the so-called Ostjuden with whom my parents and their friends professed to have little in common and considered not German enough—too "Jewish," if truth be told. Their greater attachment to Judaism, and the public evidence of it in dress and language, made my parents uncomfortable and struck them as dangerous fodder for anti-Semites. The reality was that, unconsciously or not, assimilated German Jews had absorbed some of the prejudices of the wider non-Jewish German world to which they aspired to belong. Later on, I believe, many became embarrassed and regretted this attitude. It took my parents' own exclusion by the Nazis and displacement to the refugee ghetto of Shanghai to finally drive the point home for them.

Our family was neither large nor particularly close. My mother's eldest sister, my aunt Grete Levy, and her husband, Siegfried, lived nearby. My father's siblings, Theo and Edith, lived farther away and by 1937 they had actually taken the plunge and emigrated to Brazil. Another brother, Helmut, moved in his own orbit and came to visit infrequently. The Tarlows, my mother's two elderly spinster aunts, sisters of Grandmother Markt, lived in that eastern section of Berlin heavily populated by the less assimilated Jews my parents considered déclassé, and were visited by us only rarely.

By far the most admired and distinguished members of the family were Arthur Eloesser, my paternal grandmother's brother, and his wife Margarete. Arthur was a well-known critic of literature and the stage and the author of a number of scholarly books, who in the twenties, had risen to the top ranks of his profession, including the presidency of the German Federation of Writers. Occasionally we would be invited for tea at the Eloessers' spacious apartment near the Lietzensee, my sister and I well scrubbed and appropriately dressed in our Sunday best. I remember being duly impressed by the book- lined study where the famous Onkel Arthur received us for what my respectful parents always considered a very special occasion. After 1933, Arthur was fired from all his positions and could publish only in the Jewish press. He died in 1938. His widow stayed behind in Berlin and was murdered.[9]

Aunt Grete Levy and husband, Siegfried, lived two blocks from Olivaer Platz at Duisburger Strasse, one of our many quiet neighborhood streets. In a way, I had more intimate contact with them than with the rest of the family. While still quite young, I had accepted the twice-weekly chore—for a 5 Pfennig fee—of climbing the back stairs to their apartment to fetch Tante Grete's garbage and dispose of it in the basement—an arrangement that kept me flush with cash for candy, marbles and lead soldiers. My mother held me on a short leash where pocket money was concerned. Wrangling permission—and the money—for a Sunday afternoon movie usually required an extended tearful begging campaign, earning me the unenviable title of *Nervtöter*, or simply put—a pest.

Of my mother's aunts, Tante Gustel Tarlow and her sister, Johanna, who died when I was still quite young, we saw very little. We paid them a visit only once a year, trekking to their boarding house near the old Bahnhof Börse for the annual Seder Passover dinner—the one true Jewish occasion to which I was exposed in those days. For some reason, my mother felt some deep obligation to do this year after year, though neither of my parents made an effort to hide their discomfort at having to travel to an undesirable neighborhood for a ceremony that meant little to them. Their attitude wasn't lost on my sister and me, and I remember the visit primarily as a boring annual chore anticipated with little pleasure. There was always a lot of praying in a language I didn't understand and—worst of all—a seemingly interminable delay before the food was served.

Twice each year, at most, my father's brother Helmut would be invited for dinner, a burden borne by my mother with stoic, though barely concealed, distaste. Her brother-in-law offended her sense of propriety, and she disliked him intensely. The problem was that he was an open and ostentatious homosexual at a time when, as far as my parents were concerned, such proclivities were best hidden or at least handled with great discretion. Helmut, however, made no secret of his sexual preference and enjoyed reporting in detail on his latest conquests among the colorful, ever-changing cast of characters in his group of like-minded companions. He was a different Blumenthal altogether, a drummer and vocalist of sorts in a dance band, with a thoroughly bohemian lifestyle and the language and personal habits to match. He must have known how my mother felt, and it has occurred to me that he may have enjoyed taunting her and deriving special pleasure in her discomfort.

Helmut's life was anything but easy, and I am afraid she did him a considerable injustice. At age eighteen, in the last days of the Great War, he had been severely wounded, lost a leg, and spent a year or more convalescing in various military hospitals. The prosthesis he wore was awkward and painful, and he walked with great difficulty. In much pain for a long time, he had become habituated to powerful painkillers and struggled with a morphine addiction for years. I recall that he played in a downtown café with a band of musicians, dressed as pseudo-Mexicans, which I found very exciting. For my mother, he was the family's black sheep, and she simply couldn't abide his "differentness." Ironically, it would be his musical talents which eventually saved his life. Left behind in Germany as a wounded war veteran, he was shipped by the Nazis to their Theresienstadt camp for "special cases," where he survived by playing the drums in the prisoner band.

In sum, I suppose it could be said that I grew up in a mildly dysfunctional family setting. My strong and determined mother held us together, but it was not a particularly close and nurturing environment. Open signs of love and affection were not her style, and just as lacking in my father's distant and self-absorbed indifference. In the tense Nazi years of the thirties, all her energies were focused on survival and on her store, where she spent long hours every day. Coupled with a dearth of other sources of intellectual stimulation in the home, it might well have been a ready-made formula for a troubled childhood.

That I nevertheless escaped relatively unscathed into reasonably well-adjusted adulthood I owe, I believe, to the good fortune of my attachment to a nanny—a *Kinderfräulein*—who provided a full measure of the warmth, love, and positive attention that were lacking for me elsewhere. She had come into the Blumenthal household in Oranienburg in 1922 when my sister was a year old, and she was there four years later at my birth. She stayed with us in Berlin through all the ups and downs until that gray and rainy night on April 7, 1939, when she and the Levys saw us off at the train station on our way to China. I never saw my uncle and aunt again—both were killed in Poland. She, however, wasn't Jewish, and I would rediscover her in East Berlin after the war in 1953, on my first return visit to Germany. Fourteen years after she had tearfully seen us off on our flight from the Nazis, I had an emotional reunion with her. As it happened, I had overslept after a long and tiring overnight flight and was late for our appointment. I arrived breathlessly at her door some thirty minutes too late, while she stood there and gazed at me with stern unconcealed disapproval. "Na, weisst Du, Werner . . .! (Really!)" were the first words out of her mouth, accompanied by an accusing glance at her watch. Only then, but with tears in her eyes, did she embrace me. Being unpunctual was not what she had drilled into me. She was quite ill by then, barely surviving in those difficult early postwar years, and I was able to supply her with food packages for a while before her death.

To my parents, she was Fräulein Else, the quintessential German nanny: professional, competent, utterly reliable, and deeply devoted to the children. Along with loving attention to our needs, the responsibility to teach us proper manners was also deeply ingrained in her. With her warm affection came a firm insistence on cleanliness, neatness, punctuality, obedience, and respect for elders. These were the virtues she was trained to impart to her charges, and this she did with kind but unrelenting persistence. Her kind has long ago ceased to exist, but in the Germany of the twenties and thirties she was one of many.

Her full aristocratic name was Else von Willmans, Edle von Wildenkron, which no doubt had impressed my parents. She was the descendant of a long ago ennobled but impoverished government bureaucrat in the eastern part of Germany, and being hired out as a *Kinderfräulein* was, in those lean days of the early twenties, a common fate for the large surplus of postwar marriageable women in Germany's war-depleted population. Like many, she would remain a spinster all her life.

I adored her, and I believe the feeling was mutual. She provided plenty of love and attention and knew my needs and foibles better than anyone. Yet she was also an insistent disciplinarian with a firm sense of right and wrong who took a dim view of breaking the rules. Unlike my mother's occasional *Backpfeife*—a hard slap on the cheek—I do not recall her ever resorting to physical punishment. But violating my mother's rules was far less traumatic for me than disobeying else's. A scolding or a stern look of disapproval from her was all that was necessary to bring me back into line.

School Days

I grew up in troubled times, but I can't say that my Berlin childhood was especially unhappy. Young children move in their own orbit, trusting their elders and lacking the political sophistication to grasp the full meaning of events in the world around them. In the first years under Hitler, that was how it was with me, even as my parents struggled to cope with the insane environment of Nazi Germany. Hitler's brown Berlin with its flags, uniforms, songs, and slogans was all I knew. I understood that we Jews weren't a part of it, wondered why, but accepted this as a fact of life. Meanwhile, Berlin was that throbbing, energetic metropolis with its exciting sights and sounds, and I was just a normal kid growing up there and, in my childish way, having a good time. Of course, once the synagogues were burned, Jewish stores lay in ruins, and the terror of concentration camp arrests was upon us, even we children couldn't escape the pressures and the fear. But that came later.

At age six, a few months before the Nazi takeover, I was enrolled at the local elementary school, an ugly red-brick building that somehow survived the war and still stands today. The German educational system of my day was rigid and far from democratic. After the first four years, at age ten, a fateful lifetime decision had to be made. Those slated for better schooling and perhaps the universities transferred to eight or nine years at a "higher" school, the *Gymnasium* for boys, and *Lyceum* for girls. The rest, typically working-class children, stayed behind for four more years of classes, usually followed by an apprenticeship or vocational training. Switching from one school track to the other after the fourth year was well-nigh impossible.

There were several Jewish children in my class, and except for our exclusion from the junior Hitler Youth, we were treated like everyone else. While my parents made sour faces at home, we learned the same Nazi songs and listened to stories glorifying Germany's national-socialist rebirth. The teachers were stern disciplinarians of the old school, but discrimination against Jewish children was the exception. Punishment for infraction of rules may have lacked subtlety, but it was straightforward and ecumenical as far as Jews and non-Jews were concerned. For more serious offenses, corporal punishment was the accepted form of retribution, swift and to the point, ranging from a scuff on the back of the head to a painful smack across the fingers with a ruler or, in extremis, a public caning in front of the class, administered on the offender's backside with the dread *Rohrstock*, a special cane kept in the teacher's desk for the worst culprits. It was a punishment as humiliating as it was painful, and I suffered it only once. I will never forget my mortified embarrassment when the telltale signs were discovered on my posterior during the evening bath.

Occasionally, there was some bullying and shoving by classmates, some verbal insults, the pointing of fingers and anti-Jewish slurs mirroring largely what my classmates were hearing on the radio, in the streets, or at home. In those early years, however, I do not remember much of that; we had been strongly warned by our parents to avoid confrontations and never to fight back, and the teachers generally disapproved of taunting as an unwelcome break of discipline.

Mostly, the Jewish children associated freely with their classmates on the playground—cowboys and Indians was one of our consuming passions. We competed at marbles, kicked a soccer ball, avidly followed the fortunes of Berlin soccer teams, and argued about our favorite race car champions. The glamorous Mercedes driver Rudolf Caracciola was my particular idol.

In sum, it was a normal Berlin childhood, but one that ended abruptly in 1936 with the completion of my four years at elementary school and transfer to a Gymnasium. This occurred just as the downward spiral of the exclusion of Jewish citizens from more and more facets of normal German life accelerated. Jewish children now had to go to Jewish schools and were allowed in Berlin's regular Gymnasia only in rare instances. The school to which I was sent turned out to be a wonderfully happy choice and a major turning point in my life.

The Jewish Kaliski School in the Dahlem district of West Berlin was a Gymnasium unlike any other, and very much a product of its time: organized in an emergency, coeducational, full of improvisation, perennially short of funds, harassed by its neighbors, struggling against the daily chicanery of a hostile environment, and faced with myriads of restrictions and challenges. And yet my Kaliski School was a truly unique and remarkably effective institution.[10] Organized in 1932, it existed for only seven years until the Nazis shut it down for good in 1939. At its peak, some 400 Jewish boys and girls studied there, cared for by a dedicated teaching staff passionate about their mission to provide a progressive education, demanding and of the highest standard, yet specially tailored to the times and special needs of the students.

In the outside world, life was more and more difficult for the grownups, but within the school we were drawn together by a shared fate into a close community of students and teachers determined to make the best of our uncertain situation. Our teachers were committed to preparing us as best they could for what was by then the certainty of a precarious refugee future across the far corners of the world, perhaps in the United States for a lucky few, or elsewhere in Europe, or in some South American country, in Palestine, Africa or even in Shanghai, that dreaded last resort for those no one else wanted.

My three years at the Kaliski School were the most important, satisfying, and significant educational experience of my life. "Study hard," my mother was fond of preaching to me, "what you have once learned, no one—not even the Nazis—can take away from you." That was also what our teachers expected of us, it was serious business and we probably worked harder and grew up and matured faster there than kids our age under more normal conditions. If hard times are an inducement to good performance, the teachers and students of the Kaliski School proved the point.

There were three distinct elements to the curriculum. The basic academic program was intensive, with special emphasis on foreign languages, mathematics, and, of course, geography. We were made to read voraciously, a lifelong habit that has never left me. In three years, I learned spoken and written French and I had enough English so that I felt quite comfortable in it as we left Berlin—a big help at my British school and for life in the French part of Shanghai. A second major focus involved drilling us each afternoon in "practical" skills considered useful for our refugee future—cooking and general kitchen work, gardening so we could grow our own food, woodworking and general familiarity with tools, even needlework useful for taking care of our own clothes and darning our socks. In all this, the constant emphasis was on a spirit of community, cooperation, and mutual help. Life will be tough, we were told, and you must learn to help each other.

There were also sports, music, and theatrical performances, but the single most significant element of the Kaliski experience was undoubtedly the third: the effort to instill in this highly secularized and German-acculturated group of children a novel sense of Jewish consciousness. For the first time in my life I began to learn Hebrew. Not much has stuck with me over the years, but, instead of Nazi marching songs, I was now taught Jewish hymns and the folk songs of the Kibbutz. At Friday night services we lit candles and took turns reciting the traditional blessing over bread and wine.

For the first time in my life, I was a part of an entirely Jewish community, and without fully realizing it, my German identity became submerged in that awareness of my Jewishness that has remained a part of me for the remainder of my life. It was a wondrous development, not the least for my astonished parents. I can still recall their bemused, not entirely comfortable reaction when I reported proudly that I had been selected to lead the singing of the Friday night blessing at the school, and even more so when I pressed them to emulate the practice at home.

The world around us was growing more threatening by the day. Isolated, excluded, and threatened, we were now outcasts, second-class Germans at best. For the grownups it was a new reality hard to accept. How could the Jews not be full Germans in a land where they had lived for generations? But at least our oppressors had achieved this: more and more, the Jews began to learn something of their forgotten heritage and, however reluctantly, to return to it. It was through their children in the newly established Jewish schools that the point was being driven home.

Hitler

If learning about the meaning of being a Jew was a central element of my 1930s childhood in Berlin, the other overriding reality was the Nazis—and Adolf Hitler, the Führer, who dominated every aspect of our lives. Many Germans had never actually seen him in the flesh, but he was everywhere in newsreels, on the radio, and his photograph was on every wall. "Heil Hitler" was now the official greeting, and more and more people were using it.

I saw him only once, fleetingly, when his motorcade passed

unexpectedly in front of me on the Ku'damm. He sat in an open Mercedes limousine, the biggest in a caravan of cars speeding past us, going I know not where. For a brief moment I thought he looked right at me, but no doubt I just imagined it. Then he was gone, the crowd around me still waving and shouting their "Heil Hitlers." I have never forgotten my chance encounter with him. Even today, over seventy years later, the occasion remains etched in my mind. Hitler wanted to kill me for no other reason than because I was a Jew and part of a people he variously called "humanity's destructive mold," the "incarnation of blood defilement" or "bloodsucking spiders." I was a young child when he came to power and would have been only fifteen or sixteen years old when, if not for happenstance and good fortune, his agents would have carried out his wishes and starved, shot, or gassed me, which is how my best Kaliski School friend Helmut Strauch died (probably in Auschwitz at age sixteen), and my aunt and uncle (killed the same year). So, I must be excused for having Hitler on my mind. In a much wider sense, he affected the twentieth century as no one else did, and changed the lives of millions far beyond Germany's borders. His rise to power is one of the century's most fateful seminal political events. Without him, all would have been different. Because of him, nothing remained the same.

It is an irony of history, that the century in which parliamentary democracy triumphed would be most profoundly influenced not by the statesmen of the great democracies, but by their four most fanatical and determined enemies who opposed them—and especially by Adolf Hitler, the most ruthless and implacable foe of democracy of them all. Among the great political figures opposing the democracies in the twentieth century, Lenin has his place in history as the founder of Communism who transformed Tsarist semi-feudal Russia; Stalin for his reign of terror at home and his efforts at Communist subversion abroad; and Mao Tse-tung as the revolutionary leader who united the most populous nation on earth. But it was Adolf Hitler—the Austrian who imagined himself more German than the Germans—who left the deepest imprint on the world and did the most to change the course of history. It is he alone, who was the twentieth century's unique "terrible historic phenomenon, and who gave the world a new face,"[11] as the historian Hugh Trevor-Roper has observed.

It was Hitler who thrust the world into the bloodiest war in history, who caused untold misery and destruction, ordered the murder of millions of Jews, and is responsible for the death of fifty to sixty million or more soldiers and civilians. We do not have precise numbers, because there simply were too many. None of the other dictators equaled him in the extremity of his politics, the violence of his racism, and the cynical brutality of his conquests. It is he who came closest to bringing Europe and much of the rest of the world to its knees and who left unimaginable devastation and ruin behind. He ruled for only twelve years, but his legacy was felt for decades and still rests heavily on Germany's shoulders. Of Hitler alone it can be said that he made the history of the twentieth century. Is it right to call it "Hitler's century," as the historian Ian Kershaw has suggested?[12] Quite probably it is. At any rate, as regards my own life, no one affected its future course more than he did.

For me, Hitler defies full understanding and transcends my imagination. I have read a great deal about him—several large shelves in my Princeton library are filled with Hitleriana—yet much about him remains inexplicable. What is the explanation for his monumental hatreds and crimes? How could this poorly educated and twisted upstart rise from nothing and rule a people who prided themselves on their culture, inducing them to stand by him until the last moment, when all lay in ruins and he himself was gone? Was this perverted. amoral man sane or mad, merely an opportunist without principle, an accident allowed to stumble across the world stage wreaking havoc, or a diabolically clever manipulator of men and events with a clear world view and a coherent plan?

Two generations of historians have tried to answer these questions, and their literature is as extensive as the variety of their interpretations. According to a survey in the nineties's, over 1,500 titles and 120,000 individual articles and works had then already appeared, and their number continues to grow.[13] Yet the more we know, the more incomprehensible he is, the harder to understand and to explain. He dominated the world of the thirties and forties, and the history of the twentieth century without Adolf Hitler would lack its central core.

Throughout his life, Hitler clung to his obsession about a Jewish conspiracy for world domination and the responsibility of Jews for every major world problem. In public and private, this remained at the center of his thinking until the last day of his life. In seeking an explanation for his abiding hatred of Jews, scholars have long debated when and why it first seized him.

Whenever it began, it is clear that as of 1919, his oft-repeated view of a conspiratorial "world Jewry" was fully formed. Whether this was merely a tactical ploy or deeply felt is a more important question and on that, I believe, the evidence is clear, though not all Hitler scholars would agree. To be sure, Hitler was a consummate actor who took pride in his capacity to hide his true feelings, and he probably recognized the usefulness of anti-Semitism as a tactical device and made ample use of it, tailoring it to the occasion.[14] In his public statements and actions there were many tactical twists and turns, contradictions and inconsistencies in detail. But for me, there can be no doubt that his Jew-hatred was much more than tactical; it was a central theme of his world view from which he never deviated, the core of his beliefs, and a key motivating factor for all his actions. Even as he faced imminent death and sat down to dictate his political testament to his secretary, barricaded deep within his Reich Chancellery bunker, Jews remained uppermost in his mind. Tactical considerations no longer mattered, as he expressed his thoughts at this final moment: "Above all, I pledge the leadership of this nation and its followers to the painstaking observance of the racial laws and the pitiless resistance against the world's poisoner of all people, international Jewry."[15]

Hitler did have a clear worldview. As he wrote in *Mein Kampf*, he saw himself as ordained by Providence to lead the German people to a place of dominance in the world, to eradicate the shame of Versailles, to gain living space at the expense of the eastern Slavs, and to deliver the world from communism, liberalism, democracy, and—above all—from the plots of world Jewry, which, he believed, was intent on the destruction of all that is fair and honorable in the world.

All this was tied together, and in his mind his hatred for Jews justified all his endeavors. Jews had to be eliminated because they were "vermin"[16] and because they had stabbed Germany in the back and conspired to impose the Versailles Treaty on her. Weimar culture was a Jewish plot to corrupt the moral fiber of the Aryan race, and the work of Jewish intellectuals was "Jewish pestilence."[17] Jews were inferior, yet devilishly clever in camouflaging themselves in various guises. He justified his war of conquest for living space and Slavic lands as a crusade against "Jewish" bolshevism, just as it was Jews who were inciting the capitalist Western democracies into the war. His archenemies, Roosevelt and Churchill, were front men for "Jewish" capitalists, while bolshevism was a Jewish plot to dominate the world by different means.

He saw his mission as leading the Manichean struggle of a noble Germanic Reich against the Jewish Antichrist to the east and west in an apocalyptic confrontation of power and will. For him, it was a struggle which warranted all means—total state repression and control at home, cynical manipulation and subterfuge in international relations, amorality and ruthlessness at home and abroad, unrestrained sacrifices by soldiers, and pitiless brutality of conquest. In all this, Hitler evoked a utopian view of national redemption with himself as the leader of an idealized super race, a Germanic community of Volk more akin to the mythical, fictionalized world of Wagnerian opera he adored than to reality.

It was a delusionary, distorted view of the world that nevertheless reflected the fundamental traits of his character. Foremost among them were his pathological egomania and his insatiable need for power. He believed himself a genius chosen by the Creator and Providence, who was always right, needing "no experts and no brain trust (like Roosevelt). For me, my head suffices."[18] His egomania rendered him incapable of any self-criticism, doubt, or objectivity. Only what he believed was true. He could tolerate no disagreement and whoever dared to disagree was quickly banished from his presence, or worse. Even when everything was lost, Hitler was incapable of admitting any personal responsibility for the disaster over which he had presided. The failure of the war was not his fault, he told his assistant, Bormann, shortly before his death, but everyone else's—the treason of Spain, the weakness of Italy, the duplicity of the French, and the stupidity of the English and Americans, who, under the thumb of the Jews, had been unable to understand the wisdom of his policies.[19] The German people were also to blame, because it was "my fateful undoing to be called upon to lead a people more fickle and easily impressionable than any other."[20]

Linked to his extreme egotism were his narcissism and vanity, the intoxication with his own voice, his overriding need to dominate those around him, and the desire for constant flattery and adulation. The more successful he became, the greater the banality of the sycophantic praise heaped upon him by his entourage and those who depended on him, and the greater his insatiability for more. In time, their praise of his own brilliance and infallibility became an impregnable wall behind which he hid and which shielded him from the reality of the outside world and his own mistakes and errors of judgment. At his military headquarters in East Prussia and Eagle's Nest retreat in the Bavarian Alps, he subjected a captive audience of his ministers, generals, secretaries, assistants, staff, and assorted sycophantic retainers to endless monologues, boring them to tears with his sermons on women, marriage, diets, dogs, the rise and fall of the Greek and Roman empires, Charlemagne, architecture, art, music— even his insights into the habits of bees and ants.[21]

Hitler was a political romantic, a prisoner of his own fantasies and fables. To feed his inordinate need for self-dramatization, he created his own reality in a fictional world in which he saw himself as a great Wagnerian figure battling for Germanic greatness and racial purity, performing heroic deeds in apocalyptic struggles. "Whoever wishes to understand National Socialism must first know Richard Wagner," he once said.[22] He worshiped power and believed that the world belonged to the strongest, those with the most dominant will. He idealized the "eternal law of the stronger." War is "the father of all things," he proclaimed, and "bravery is more important than wisdom or reason. Only those who prevail in war have the right to live."[23] He thought and spoke in extremes. In his Darwinian world, moderation was not a virtue, kindness was a sign of weakness. He bluffed and he gambled, counting on his own steely will and guile, and the surprise, gullibility, and weakness of his opponents. As he was about to invade Poland, Hermann Göring once dared to suggest tactical caution, but Hitler airily brushed him aside: "In my life I have always gone for broke," he told Göring.[24]

He pulled his inner circle with him, because, in a strange way none could explain fully, Hitler exuded a demonic energy that had a mesmerizing effect on its members. Two of his closest associates, Hermann Göring, his designated successor, and Albert Speer, his protégé and favorite architect, both intelligent and strong personalities, later confessed that, once they were in his presence, he cast an irresistible spell over them. Yet Germans appear to have responded to his spell more than did those from abroad. It was Germans who frequently remarked on the hypnotic effect of the searching gaze of his blue eyes with which he liked to intimidate them, but on some foreign visitors it made quite the contrary impression. After his first personal interview with Hitler, André François-Poncet, the French ambassador, was decidedly unimpressed and noted only "his pale face, protruding eyes, and the distant gaze of a sleepwalker."[25] Anthony Eden, who first called on him in 1934, similarly remembered Hitler as staring at him with eyes that were "pale and glaucous."[26] François-Poncet thought the fixating look was a studied act meant to put his visitor off guard, as was the practice of veering, in one conversation, from periods of passive listening and easy merriment with a slapping of thighs, to excited, bold, and passionate monologues "with the facial expression of a lunatic."

Either way, he was an unusual and riveting figure. Yet as a person he was, at the same time, extraordinarily shallow, often indolent and passive, an emotional basket-case who lacked many of the basic human emotions, secretive, without friends, and incapable of a normal relationship with women. Some have speculated that he may have been a secret homosexual, though there is no evidence of that. By nature he was certainly a prude, and perhaps merely indifferent in matters of sex. He could be charming, thoughtful, courteous and even flirtatious toward his female staff, the wives of some of his ministers, and the occasional smitten "grande dame" drawn into his orbit. Yet at other times, the views he expressed about women were anything but flattering. A wife on the stupid side was preferable, he instructed his dutiful circle of sycophant listeners, because smart ones took up too much time in a busy man's life. Very young women were best because one could "mold" them better, and the personality of Eva Braun, the woman he married just before his suicide, seemed to conform to these criteria. By all accounts a cheerful lightweight, Braun was kept around by Hitler for years but always relegated to a secondary, background status.

He had read widely in his early years and had a good retentive memory, but, on the whole, Hitler was poorly educated. He claimed to have an infallible musical ear, but apart from Richard Wagner, his taste in music was quite ordinary. At the Berghof, his retreat in the Alps, his favorites were Lehár operettas, Richard Strauss waltzes, the Baden-weiler march—and Donkey Serenade, that great American classic!

It is one of history's sad questions, and tragedies: how this abnormal, ghastly man with his distorted worldview, could come to power, and how, though he caused untold distress, he could maintain himself for so long. How was it possible, one must ask, that this odd, banal, tedious, friendless, deluded, semi-educated misfit could for years command the slavish obedience and adulation of a nation and strike fear into the hearts of the entire world?

A part of the answer is that Hitler was a fateful accident of history. He was the product of a special time, and his road to power was the result of unusual circumstances, the weakness and irresolution of his opponents, accident, and—for Germany and the world—a big dose of very bad luck.

Rise to Power

The Germany of the early thirties in which I grew up was a troubled nation in the depth of economic misery. Its people had been traumatized by a lost war, hyperinflation, and a harsh peace treaty, and they faced mass unemployment and were angry and dispirited. The Weimar Republic was their first experience with parliamentary democracy, and it had failed them even before Hitler came to power. There was a dearth of effective leaders to champion democratic government, the left-of-center parties were deeply divided amongst themselves, and the public was tired of political confusion and longed for law and order and a strong hand at the top. Under the Constitution, Field Marshal von Hindenburg, the president, was the supreme authority, but he was old and in decline, and his monarchist and reactionary advisors who exercised the real power were plotting to subvert the very Republic they were sworn to uphold.

The story of how Hitler managed to outwit them has been told in detail many times. Suffice it to say that the power elite had never taken him seriously enough because his views seemed grotesquely outrageous and extreme. Contemptuous of his person, they underestimated him greatly and thought they could control him and use his chancellorship as a front for their own objectives. But they were incompetent, cowardly, and ineffective, while Hitler risked all and outmaneuvered them at a moment when his own star was actually in decline. Once in office, he quickly turned the tables on those who had put him there, employed thinly-disguised pretexts and pseudo-legal means to seize absolute power "temporarily," suspended civil rights, arrested the opposition, and used street violence, brutality, and fear to install his dictatorship.

It was to his great benefit that he had frequently been underestimated. Most people never expected him to reach power and when on January 30, 1933, he did, the early speculation was that he was unlikely to last long. Germany had seen eleven chancellors come and go in thirteen years, and almost twice as many cabinets. The internal situation remained highly unstable, and there were good reasons to believe that this improbable extreme right-winger wouldn't fare any better. Only two members of Hitler's cabinet were members of his Nazi party and reports from Berlin speculated that the real power was held by others. The *New York Times's* Emil Lengyel emphasized that Alfred Hugenberg, the powerful industrialist, leader of the German People's Party and new minister of economy and agriculture, was a "giant shadow" over Hitler and the man to watch. Others thought that the key was Hermann Göring, the famous air ace. Reports from London had it that with four separate government positions, it was Göring who had his hands on the main levers of power, and that it was "being whispered in Berlin's private places that Hitler is merely window dressing."[27]

Few people had read *Mein Kampf,* and those who had ridiculed it as so much gibberish. "It's 140,000 words long and has 140,000 errors in it," a large New York audience was told dismissively by the German writer Lion Feuchtwanger in February of '33. Feuchtwanger was a Jew and announced blithely that he had every intention of returning to Germany at the end of the month. The prevailing opinion was that Hitler would either fail, or that his extreme views and actions would quickly be tempered by reality and that those who had put him in power with the backing of President von Hindenburg were fully capable of holding him in check. The day after Hitler was sworn in, the *New York Times's* confident headline from Berlin was that "Hitler puts aside aim to be dictator," and its report assured readers that there was really "no warrant for immediate concern."[28]

That these views were greatly in error, and that Adolf Hitler was a man very much to be reckoned with, soon became apparent, though it would take a while for the full significance to sink in. Far from being under the thumb of those who had put him into office, Hitler proved the cannier, stronger, and more ruthless. Within months, Hugenberg was pushed aside, his supporters were solidly lined up behind Hitler, and Göring emerged as one of the Führer's most devoted satraps. Hitler, the Führer, had quickly made himself the undisputed dictator of a resurgent Germany, outlawed Communists, suppressed Socialists and all opposition parties, unleashed a brutal reign of street terror, imprisoned and murdered thousands of his opponents in concentration camps, and begun to harass the helpless Jewish minority with discriminatory laws, threats, humiliation, and economic chicanery in an orgy of aggression that shocked the world.

All this he had done in little more than a year, and still there was no slowdown in the fast and furious pace of his dictatorial regime, which increasingly revealed itself as a blatantly lawless and criminal enterprise. Yet the German people, grateful for jobs and impressed by his international successes, supported him more than ever before.

Hitler had been greatly helped by favorable economic developments, the nadir of Germany's deep economic depression having been reached not after he came into office, but a year before he took over. At its worst, in February 1932, staggering unemployment had affected almost two-thirds of the entire labor force. But as the year progressed, a slow recovery of world markets finally got underway and German exports gradually increased. By the end of 1933, the Nazis' first year in power, unemployment had already dropped back.

Quick to claim the credit, Hitler followed this up with a series of large domestic-spending programs that fit his longer term military and political goals, and were carefully designed to please key elements of the population. It is this that led to the complete elimination of unemployment in Germany within three years—for which the people would forever remain grateful to their Führer. Foreign observers, not looking too closely, were equally impressed, and noted that Mussolini, the Italian dictator, had accomplished the seemingly impossible by making the trains run on time, Hitler had succeeded in putting an entire nation back to work in three years, but that recovery from the depression in democratic countries was proceeding at a much slower pace. Could it be, some asked, that the planned and autarkic economies of authoritarian fascist regimes and Communist Russia were inherently superior to laissez-faire capitalism in matters of economic management and performance?

In reality, the rapid upswing of the German economy in the first years under Hitler had little to do with significant structural changes or the nationalization of major parts of the economy. He had been prudently cautious to avoid rocking the boat, and instead had chosen to win the quick cooperation of business and labor by buying them off with a range of expensive targeted programs beneficial to them. For industry, he lowered business taxes, subsidized strategic plant and investment spending, launched a major public works and Autobahn construction initiative, and disbanded independent trade unions. To offset the loss of their unions, workers were kept content with a massive government-financed public employment program which created a million new jobs in a single year, state-paid "Strength through Joy" vacation trips, and assorted other party-sponsored fringe benefits underpinned by an incessant drumbeat of nationalist propaganda skillfully orchestrated by Goebbels. The institution of a compulsory National Labor Service and the reintroduction of military conscription in March 1935 absorbed what remained of the idle manpower pool.

For the military, finally, there was satisfaction over Hitler's unilateral abrogation of the hated Versailles Treaty and the launching of a secret—and eventually quite open—aggressive program of rearmament, including the previously prohibited rebuilding of the German navy and air force. The Versailles Treaty had limited Germany to an army of 100,000 men and seven divisions, but Hitler had given secret orders to disregard these limits as early as 1933. Eighteen months later, he directed the creation of thirty-six divisions and eventually total prewar military spending would reach a staggering RM 60 billion. By then, Germany had become by far the strongest military power in Europe and had upwards of 600,000 men under arms, and many others organized in parallel semi-military units.

If not for war, all this would have been unsustainable and fraught with great risk, because Hitler financed it largely with heavy borrowing and significant increases in public debt, while his reserves of foreign exchange quickly ran dry. But he cared little about such matters, and blithely assured his worried economic experts that his plans for the acquisition of German Lebensraum would eventually resolve matters quite satisfactorily.

Internationally, having abrogated the Versailles Treaty, Hitler also scored a string of impressive successes with daring gambles in his first three years in office. The world watched all this with astonishment and growing concern, but at home his people were grateful and his popularity soared to greater heights than for any German leader since Bismarck. Yet none of this would have been possible if his domestic adversaries had been willing to act against him once his reign of terror got underway, or if the world had more quickly realized the danger he posed, and had more resolutely and effectively opposed his violation of treaty obligations.

It is these failures, and the aura of unimpeded successes at home and abroad they earned him, which fed his egotism, strengthened his belief in his infallibility, encouraged him to intensify his domestic and international aggressions, and gave him the time to develop Germany's overwhelming military strength. Emboldened by the weak reaction of France and England to his violation of the Versailles Treaty and rearmament, he quickly reoccupied the Rhineland in March of 1936, his most dangerous and daring gamble yet. Under the Treaty, the Rhineland had been designated as a demilitarized zone in which Germany was to have no armed forces and to engage in no military activity. The Locarno Treaty of 1925, to which Germany was a signatory, had solemnly guaranteed these territorial obligations, yet Hitler chose to ignore them and sent his troops into the Rhineland with two hours' notice. His own generals had warned him that France had the military strength to turn him back, but Hitler insisted on risking it, and when neither France nor England moved to stop him, his popularity at home soared and his image as a dangerous international tactician was further enhanced.

The Rhineland venture was perhaps the best chance to stop him. Germany's rearmament program was still in its early stages and lacked the kind of overwhelming force of later years. The operation was, in fact, undertaken with only four battalions, and Hitler himself had issued standing orders to pull back in the face of a military countermove from the French. The mere mobilization of a few French divisions would have been sufficient, and Hitler himself later gleefully admitted it.

Yet the march into the Rhineland became a watershed event. The French were deeply shocked, there were urgent calls between London and Paris but in the end, nothing was done. England was loath to engage in strong action, let alone to risk another war, and the French were unwilling to move alone. There were protests and remonstrations, much talk of blockades and sanctions, but in the end nothing happened, and a remilitarized German Rhineland became a fait accompli. Hitler could chalk up a big victory, set about to build up his West-wall fortifications, and turn his attention to the seizure of Austria. The dismantling of Czechoslovakia, and ultimately the invasion of Poland followed, and the die for World War II was cast.

Appeasement

The world followed the developments in Germany closely, and whatever hopes for Nazi moderation in domestic policies and international relations had existed soon yielded to revulsion over the assaults on freedom and world peace, though not to effective action to counter the slide into disaster.

For U.S. diplomats stationed in Germany, the change took longer than it should have. In early 1933, they had adopted a wait-and-see posture and rationalized Hitler's attacks on Jews as early aberrations and the result of excess revolutionary zeal. Even the scandalous anti-

Jewish boycott of April 1 did not greatly impress George A. Gordon, the U.S. chargé d'affaires in Berlin, who saw fit to report to Washington that "it had done Jewish businessmen little harm, and perhaps was a useful safety valve for the enthusiastic rank and file, at not much cost to anybody."[29] From Stuttgart, U.S. Consul General Leon Dominian, chimed in that excesses "are unknown in this consular district" and that "it is believed unlikely that persecution of Jews will be undertaken on a large scale [here] . . ."[30] In May, a lengthy Embassy report addressed to Secretary of State Cordell Hull, emphasized that "foreign travelers in Germany upon their return home have stated that they saw no atrocities."[31]

By the fall, however, even the more naïve U.S. diplomats had shed their illusions. At the end of September, George S. Messersmith, the U.S. Consul General in Berlin, noted "a complete absence of any humanitarian principles and extreme brutality" as the now unmistakable hallmark of Hitlerism, and quoted an English correspondent's assessment of Hitler's government: "The motto of the French revolution was Liberty, Equality and Fraternity; the motto of this revolution could very properly be Brutality, Mendacity and Loquacity."

"I concur," Messersmith wrote, "and I would add to it 'Duplicity.'" Germans support their Führer, he continued, because their stomachs are full, they admire him because a cult of personality has virtually deified him, and because they are constantly being lied to and have little knowledge about the outside world under a barrage of propaganda and misinformation orchestrated cleverly by Josef Goebbels. Nothing in social history, Messersmith concluded, has ever been more heartless and devastating than Nazi anti-Jewish policies. As to Germany's new foreign policy, "they don't want war yet . . . but they are getting ready for war, and we must definitely reckon that the protestations of the leaders of Germany concerning their love of peace and their desire for peace are not sincere."[32] His boss, U.S. Ambassador William E. Dodd, writing directly to the president, concurred. Hitler and the top leaders, he informed Roosevelt, have all "been more or less connected with murderous undertakings," the Führer himself had a semi-criminal record, and Göring and Goebbels, the two most important Nazis next to him, are all "animated by intense class and foreign hatreds and are both willing to resort to most ruthless arbitrary methods."[33]

In the U.S. media and amongst the public, the mood concerning the Nazis had changed much more quickly. In the first few days, the *New York Times* had still told its readers not to worry, *Time* had put Hitler on its cover, and the *Chicago Tribune* had approvingly noted "the fascist hostility to Communism" and speculated that Hitler's surprising rise to power was the result of German youth's "pride and passionate will to recover past freedom and honor."[34] But less than two months later, well ahead of the diplomats, the media radically changed their tune. Reporting on the brutal lynching of a Jewish lawyer in Kiel, and the shock and humiliation of harassed German Jews taking flight—events that had apparently escaped the attention of the U.S. Embassy and its consulates—the *Tribune* now deplored the terror and suppression of freedom and civil rights, while the *Times* was conjuring up the collective moral sentiment of the modern world against Nazi Germany's "brute exaltation of mere strength."[35]

In New York, the governor and leaders of all faiths addressed tens of thousands of protesters gathered in Madison Square Garden to voice their indignation at Nazi actions, and more than a million Jews, according to the *Times*, held rallies throughout the United States to protest the atrocities of April 1.

Already there were those still isolated voices sounding clear warnings that Hitler's true intentions were a clear menace to world peace. In a prominently reported speech in March, John Hibben, Princeton's president emeritus, flatly predicted that Hitler's policies were bound to lead to war.[36] From London, *New York Times* reporter Wickham Steed agreed that Hitler's aim was conquest, pure and simple, and warned American isolationists and others whose instincts were to stand aside. The world had smiled about the risk of war in 1914, he cautioned them, and in view of what was taking place in Germany, it would be a grave mistake to do so again."[37]

These were prescient insights and should have been heeded. But they were not. Throughout the first years of the thirties, there were plenty of commentators and political leaders in all capitals who warned of the dangers of a nationalistic, resurgent Germany under Hitler and urged military strength and clear action to counter the threat, but they remained lonely voices in the wilderness.

One of them was Winston Churchill, but he was out of power and neither the British government nor the majority of the House of Commons were in a mood to listen. "We read all the news which accumulates of the (German) military spirit," he told the House in November of '33, "we see that a philosophy of bloodlust is being inculcated into their youth to which no parallel can be found in the days of barbarism . . ."[38] Time and again between 1933 and 1935 he repeated his remonstrations that Germany's aggressive regime required resolution and a strong response, that England needed to rearm, that this was a far surer guarantee for peace than appeasement, and that the very act would more effectively restrain German ambitions."[39] Anthony Eden, Lord Privy Seal and under-secretary in the foreign office, was another political leader in favor of a stronger response, and two visits to Hitler only confirmed his gloomy view of the Führer's mendacity and protestations of peaceful intent in the face of aggressive rhetoric and actions. But Eden's too was a minority view and could not move Britain's weak McDonald coalition government from its dogged pursuit of peace through universal disarmament, well after Germany had left the League's Disarmament Conference and was openly pursuing a contrary path.

Thus the descent into disaster continued, and no one stood up to halt it. Everywhere Hitler was stirring the pot, and agitating German minorities in Czechoslovakia and Poland. The German reoccupation of the Ruhr had caused great excitement and dismay and earned Germany an official League condemnation—but in the absence of England's willingness to make common cause with France and risk a military confrontation, nothing further was done. Within days, in fact, English officials had approached the Germans to explore the feasibility of new negotiations for a peace treaty and alternative ways to redress their grievances. Even the German side was astounded at the ease of Hitler's victory and the lack of forceful resistance.[40]

As to his continuing assault on freedom at home, and the mounting persecution of the Jewish minority, these were roundly deplored and condemned in Europe and the United States, but nothing else was done. Contrary to the U.S. Embassy's earlier reports, forty-five Jews had been murdered in the first year of Nazi power, 26,000 opponents (Jewish and non-Jewish) had been put into "protective custody" within the first six months, and an estimated 100,000 alleged enemies were languishing in Hitler's concentration camps by the end of the year.[41] A steady exodus of Jewish refugees from Germany was underway, but universal expressions of sympathy rarely meant that doors were being opened to them, or that pressure was put on Hitler to moderate his policies. What was happening inside Germany was considered regrettable, but nevertheless a domestic affair.

In his postwar memoirs, Churchill aptly entitled the history of this period of the thirties as the "Darkening Scene."[42] The League's Disarmament Conference had gone nowhere and Japan and Germany had left it. Fascist Italy's "Duce" defied the League and in 1935 embarked on a war of conquest in Abyssinia. In Spain, General Francisco Franco moved against the republican government unleashing a civil war, and in Portugal another dictator, the former professor of economics António Salazar, was in control. In Soviet Russia, Stalin's reign of terror was in full swing, and in Asia the Japanese, having previously conquered Manchuria, were advancing on the Chinese Mainland. Everywhere parliamentary democracy was in retreat, and authoritarianism on the rise.

Why did the three greatest democracies, England, France, and the United States fail to act against these threats to world peace from the dictators?

The reasons, regrettably, are plain enough. In Britain in 1933, the Oxford Union debated the resolution "that this House refuses to fight for King and country." It passed. In no other country was the spirit of pacifism as strong as in Britain, and two years later eleven million British voters went to the polls to back an antiwar "peace ballot." Strengthening the country's defenses was strongly resisted even as Germany openly moved in a contrary direction. Britain actually reduced its expenditures for arms. Balancing the budget to fight the financial crisis of '31 was accorded a higher priority, and it was argued that armaments might in themselves be a cause for war. Disillusioned with Europe, reluctant to back France with guarantees against Germany, preoccupied with its colonies and doggedly committed to the pursuit of the illusory goal of universal disarmament through negotiation, Britain did not heed warnings of danger from Germany, British defenses deteriorated, weapons became obsolete, naval construction slowed, and the air force declined to fifth place in the world. It was a mix of failures and delusions that led to pervasive weakness in Britain's international posture and, for too long, to a futile policy of appeasing Nazi ambitions.

As to France, no country felt more threatened by Germany, but France was too timid and divided to act alone. In Eugen Weber's words, the thirties were her "hollow years," when ineffective politicians grappled with insoluble problems in a country devastated by four years of war fought on her soil, paralyzed by scandal, its national spirit sapped by the cynicism and decadence of her elite.[43]

"Victory was to be bought so dear as to be almost indistinguishable from defeat," Churchill wrote, and nowhere was this observation more apt than in regard to the French. With 1.4 million killed and another million gassed and wounded in the Great War, France's manpower losses had been greater than those of Germany—23 percent of all those mobilized, and 27 percent of all young men between the ages of eighteen and twenty-seven. Her richest regions had been ruined and many thousands of miles of roads and railroad tracks destroyed.

The Third French Republic was as much a failed democracy as

the Weimar Republic, bedeviled by constant political turmoil—there had been nineteen governments and eleven prime ministers in eight years. Communists battled Socialists, anti-militarism and a pervasive pacifism as strong as in Britain was led by such influential intellectual and literary figures as, among others, André Gide, Louis Aragon, and Romain Rolland. Thus, in a message not lost on Hitler, and not to be outdone by their Oxonian counterparts, French students at the elite École Normale Supérieure had, in early 1935, strongly voted against the reintroduction of conscription at the precise moment when that very step had just been taken in Germany.

Aware of these weaknesses, France had clung for too long to her own set of illusions. One was that Germany could be made to meet her reparations obligations in full, the other that her wartime allies could be relied upon to stand by her side. Both assumptions proved to be false. Germany wasn't paying, America had withdrawn into isolation, and Britain was an unreliable ally unwilling to guarantee French security against the Germans. British lack of support had been a strong factor in the French decision not to mobilize and confront Germany in the Rhineland. But it had also been a wakeup call, albeit a belated one, and it led to the first serious efforts to strengthen French defenses in the following years, when enormous resources were expended on building a static line of fortifications, the Maginot Line. Unfortunately this was as flawed an effort as it was late, devised by a military devoid of ideas and more focused on fighting the last war than on taking account of the critical new technologies of warfare likely to determine the next. When war came, it proved to be no impediment to Hitler and his generals, spelling the doom of the Third Republic in France when German tanks began to roll.

Hitler's assumption that neither England nor France, each for her own domestic reasons, had the capability and will to oppose him with strength had proved correct. But what about America? Was there a threat to his ambitions from across the Atlantic? In 1937, Hans-Heinrich Dieckhoff, the German ambassador in Washington, assured him that he had nothing to fear from an isolationist America either. "From the

German standpoint," he informed Berlin, "the position and the activity of the supporters of isolationism are to be welcomed."[44] The Americans might express their disapproval, especially about Nazi Jewish policies, but direct action was unlikely because American isolationists could be relied upon to prevent that. For a long time, Dieckhoff's assessment proved correct and it took years for U.S. policy to change course. Meanwhile, Hitler had accepted his ambassador's judgment and discounted any American threat. He had only the sketchiest knowledge of the United States, and in this instance his demented race theories blinded him to any realistic view of America's vast human and material resources. He thought little of Roosevelt, whom he considered to be under the thumb of the Jews and the leader of a nation made up of a polyglot racial stock, soft and unwilling to fight.

True enough, those demanding a strong American response to Hitler remained in the minority for a long time. America's isolationist sentiment had taken deep root in the twenties and remained firmly entrenched in the next decade. Ninety-five percent of all Americans, reported the Institute of Public Opinion in 1935, agreed that the United States should never again under any circumstances participate in a European war. In Congress, there were powerful forces among the senior chairmen of committees who zealously watched over the slightest evidence of a change toward a more internationalist policy and busied themselves to erect additional barriers against foreign involvement.

Some of the staunchest isolationists were also deeply reactionary opponents of the president, suspicious of his domestic programs, fanatical anti-Communists, and not altogether unsympathetic to anti-Semitic prejudice. They liked Hitler's anti-Communist rhetoric, while his assault on the Jews and on civil liberties was of less concern to them. On the question of opposing internationalism, they were joined by elements of the President's more liberal supporters and midwestern progressives, who had bought the proposition that it was big business and arms merchants who entangled the country overseas, fostered wars and enriched themselves in them. A policy of distance from Europe appealed to them as assurance to keep

America out of another war, and Roosevelt needed their support for his domestic programs.

Persecuting the Jews

Once Hitler was in power, my parents' concerns were the most immediate and personal ones of adjusting to everyday living under the Nazis. They had been utterly stunned when the unthinkable happened and the Nazi firebrand had actually been appointed chancellor. What now? They had no great illusions about Jewish prospects under his rule, yet like the rest of the world they were uncertain about what would follow and hoped against hope that in spite of his extreme anti-Semitic rhetoric, the realities of governing and the need to accommodate his coalition partners would temper his actions. The *Central-Verein Zeitung*, official organ of the Federation of German Jewry, advised putting one's trust in President von Hindenburg, counseled a low profile and quiet dignity, and emphasized the Jewish commitment to the fatherland in peace and in war.

Almost at once, however, it became clear that such protestations of loyalty would fall on deaf ears. The reality within days of the takeover was a frightening climate of lawlessness and unrestrained assaults by Nazi storm troopers against erstwhile political adversaries and individual Jews, exceeding my parents' worst fears. Dozens of Jewish lives were lost and hopes for moderation gave way to helpless confusion and the shock of the anti-Jewish boycott on April 1, 1933. It brought the indiscriminate street violence of the first weeks to an end and the day itself was generally peaceful, but as an officially sponsored initiative, it added more reasons to worry about what lay ahead. I was only seven years old at the time, a little blond tousle-haired boy in short pants with perennially scuffed knees, more concerned about my bike than the boycott. I do remember, however, the two scary-looking storm troopers posted in front of our store across the street on Olivaer Platz, while my parents cowered inside. I guess I knew somehow that it was a "bad" day, but not even the grownups yet realized its full significance.

It was, in fact, an ominous omen of things to come, the first in a stream of official anti-Jewish measures steadily escalating in scope and severity. Over the next half dozen years, my parents would have to suffer through a torrent of over 140 discriminatory laws and decrees imposed on Jews, making their lives progressively more unbearable.[45] Much of this was deeply harmful, some merely petty and vindictive. One day, broad and sweeping legislation deprived all those in the professions—lawyers, doctors, accountants—of their livelihood, excluded Jews from the military, journalism and the public service, and announced special taxes for Jews only. The next week, Nazi attention would focus on small irritations to complicate our everyday lives, with a ban on driver's licenses, on the ownership of pets, on listing Jewish holidays in pocket calendars; there was even a special rule against the keeping of carrier pigeons by Jews.

Periods of escalating pressure would be interspersed with shorter phases of a tactically motivated easing. In the first year, thirty-one separate anti-Jewish laws and regulations were imposed. In 1934, when the economy was still weak and Hitler was preoccupied with eliminating his party competitors, only eight new measures were announced, and only eleven during the Berlin Olympic Games, when the emphasis was on presenting a more benign image to the outside world. But thereafter the pace accelerated again to a peak of thirty-seven laws and regulations, with the worst and most extreme ones in 1938, the year of the November pogroms. During each slowdown, hopes would briefly rise that the worst had passed, only to be quickly dashed again with the next onslaught.

Had Jews been privy to the Nazis' secret plans, even the optimists would have understood that the end goal was never in doubt. Allowing them their own cultural life, sparing small shops and businesses for a time, exempting war veterans, and allowing Jewish children to remain in regular schools in the early years, had given comfort to some that there were limits to anti-Jewish discrimination. But these had only been temporary moves, deliberately false signals to be reversed as it suited the oppressors. The fundamental aim had always been clear. "Our goal is to deprive all Jews of their livelihood, and to increase the pressure on them and to intimidate them by whatever means necessary to drive them out,"[46] a secret memorandum of the SD, the feared security arm of the SS, had stated in January 1937 when the Olympic Games were over. "We'll proceed at our own pace, as serves our needs, but the guideline is this: the Jewish question cannot be solved until there are no more Jews in Germany."[47]

The problem the Nazis faced was that most of Germany's 520,000 Jews, my parents among them, didn't respond quickly enough. Less than a quarter of them left in the first four years. Most of the others stayed, in part because finding a haven anywhere was very difficult, but mostly because no one could believe that forcing all Jews out of Germany was Hitler's real policy and that he would use the most brutal means to achieve it. So for four years, my parents were among those who tried to adjust to each new chicanery hoping it was the last, and waiting for better days. Only in 1937 did they too begin to think seriously about where we might go, but the turning point, when the last illusions vanished, came a year later.

Hitler was reaching the peak of his power. Austria had been taken in March. In the fall, the Munich agreement had dismembered neighboring Czechoslovakia, and he had moved in to occupy a large portion of it. His secret preparations for an attack in the East were well under way. Germany had become the strongest military power in the world, and he was certain that no one could stop him now. As to the hated Jews, there was no longer any need to tread cautiously. He felt invulnerable to the criticism of the outside world and the time had come to take the final steps: to "aryanize" the shops Jews still owned, strip all Jews of their remaining possessions, deprive them of whatever means of livelihood remained, isolate them from society and make life unbearable for them. All he needed was a suitable pretext, and in November 1938, it fell into his lap. Eyewitnesses later reported that when Hitler was told on the evening of the 9th that the junior

German diplomat Ernst vom Rath, shot in Paris by the young Jewish exile Herschel Grynszpan had died, he huddled in earnest conversation with Josef Goebbels, and at one point was heard to tell him, to "let the SA have their fun." Goebbels, one of the most rabid anti-Semites of Hitler's underlings, gladly obliged. What ensued over the next forty-eight hours through the breadth and length of the Third Reich was the most unrestrained, savage, and deadly pogrom in the entire twelve years of Nazi rule.

Goebbels later asserted to a disbelieving public and shocked world that it was a spontaneous outburst of public indignation over a deliberate provocation by world Jewry. But there was nothing spontaneous about it. He had sent Nazi storm troopers into the streets at night throughout Germany, ordered them to leave their uniforms at home, and to destroy, burn, and pillage against the Jews at will. So much glass was broken that night that the pogroms of November 9 to November 10 would become known as *Kristallnacht*, the night of broken glass, but that hardly conveys the deadly nature of what occurred. Thousands of stores and homes were smashed and looted, 195 synagogues throughout Germany were torched and desecrated, 36 Jews were murdered and their murderers never prosecuted. Over 20,000 Jews were arrested and badly mistreated in concentration camps where dozens more would die in the ensuing weeks.[48]

The world was stunned and horrified. To David Buffum, the outraged U.S. consul in Leipzig, it was "a flagitious attack upon a helpless minority that very probably has no counterpart in the course of the civilized world."[49] His colleague in Stuttgart described Jews suffering "vicissitudes . . . that would sound unreal to one living in an enlightened country during the twentieth century."[50] London's *Daily Telegraph*'s Hugh Carleton Greene reported that for a time mob law ruled Berlin, adding, "I have seen several anti-Jewish outbreaks in Germany during the last five years, but never anything as nauseating as this."[51] In England the archbishop of Canterbury issued a letter in the name of all English Christians, "to give immediate expression to the feeling of indignation . . . at the deeds of cruelty and destruction."[52] The

United States recalled its ambassador, and the *Washington Post* observed that only the St. Bartholomew's massacre in 1572 had equaled Kristallnacht in ferocity and blood."[53, 54]

The violence and brutality of the November pogroms and the arbitrary mass arrests of Jewish men deeply demoralized German Jews. No one could still hope to wait out the bad times; everyone now wanted to get out.

The year 1938 was the end for us as well. Two men came for my father in the early morning, sometime before 6 A.M. They were detectives from the local police station and reasonably polite but otherwise uncommunicative as they waited for him to get dressed and took him away. The commotion had woken me, and I can still hear my mother's insistent questions as she asked what it was all about, the note of panic and helpless frustration in her voice, and my father's frightened last look back at us as he was being led away. He barely survived the dreadful Buchenwald camp and returned six weeks later, his head shaved, sixty pounds lighter and in a pitiful state. He never spoke about Buchenwald again, but it left him with a deep psychological trauma from which he never fully recovered.

Flight

It is difficult to describe the atmosphere of fear and nervous tension in the weeks and months between his release and our final flight. The herculean task of surmounting the innumerable obstacles in the way of our escape had fallen to my mother. Her husband had been arrested and her store smashed and ordered "aryanized," which involved hours of strained negotiations and meetings late into the night, with Dora Hahn, her longtime sales assistant, now a delighted "purchaser" on the cheap and nothing to show for us in the end.

Once there had been 50,000 Jewish-owned retail shops in Germany, and now the Nazis decreed that the last 9,000 to be "aryanized," an often corrupt, quasi-legal process for transferring the properties from Jews to specially favored party members, with much intrigue and maneuvering over the choicest morsels. This is what my mother now faced. For the Jews, it was all simple enough: they would receive next to nothing, and whatever they had left another government agency would find ways to take. So more laws were passed to ensure that nothing was forgotten. If fired from their jobs, Jews would be forbidden to receive pensions or final compensation. Whatever valuables they still possessed—gold, silver, jewels, art—had to be turned in; only a wedding ring and one pocket watch were excluded. Savings accounts were assessed with an "atonement" charge, and a 20 percent "emigration tax" was imposed on the remaining balance. For each new regulation, there had to be proof of compliance and one more time-consuming document to be obtained, one more hurdle in the way of gaining permission to leave.

By 1939, this systematic robbing of the Jews was actually reorganized into a kind of seamless conveyer-belt process—a product of the fertile mind of the German bureaucracy intended to "shear the sheep" more efficiently. As one writer has described it,

> when the prospective Jewish emigrant entered the hall, he was confronted by ten or twelve stations at a long table, at each of which a Gestapo officer was seated. Arriving there, he was still a German national, owner of an apartment, or perhaps a store, a bank account, a few savings. As he went—or rather was pressed along—from station to station, he was progressively relieved of each of these possessions. By the time he exited the hall at the other end, he was a stateless beggar, the owner of only a single object: a one-way passport out.[55]

In Berlin, it was instituted only after our departure, too late for my mother's "enjoyment." She had joined the thousands of other women without husbands and sons, besieging foreign consulates and embassies for a visa, while cajoling, bribing, and pleading with travel agents for passages on overbooked steamers and battling with German bureaucrats for the myriad of documents required before we could leave. The mad scramble for the precious papers was beyond belief. Just to get in the door was a victory, and *Newsweek* magazine reported from Berlin that the onslaught of the women there had produced 2,800 visa requests at the U.S. consulate in a single day.[56]

Yet most doors across the world remained closed. There was no effective international structure to care for refugees, there were no resources to ease their plight, and few if any countries were willing to offer more than a handful of them asylum. Broad worldwide condemnation of Hitler's inhuman treatment of the Jews was rarely matched by constructive action to help. That so little was done, and that so few countries were willing to open their doors and provide sanctuary for these hapless Jews, is one of the great tragedies of that unhappy period. The excuses were many. Recovery from the severe depression of the early thirties had been slow, and unemployment in many places was still high. That was one of the explanations, particularly in the United States, though there was plenty of evidence that many potential immigrants were children and seniors not entering the workforce and that, in general, those who did enter tended to stimulate and generate employment rather than preempting it. A rarely openly stated though widespread reason for keeping the doors shut was that in the thirties, anti-Semitism was still a potent force in many parts of the world. When, after the November pogroms, an outraged President Roosevelt wanted to know what success there had been in finding safe havens for German Jews around the world, a memorandum of the Department of State put the matter succinctly: "It is easy to dismiss the whole problem by saying 'Nobody wants more Jews!' That is undoubtedly true."[57]

In the summer of 1938, proof that effective help for German Jews was not to be became abundantly clear. An international conference had been convened in the French resort town of Évian to see what might be done. Twenty-nine countries and thirty-nine private organizations had responded to the call, and in Germany the Jews had watched and waited with high hopes, but after a week of sterile speeches and haggling, the Conference adjourned in failure. As the delegates dined in style on the terrace of the posh Hotel Royal overlooking Lake Geneva, one country after another put forward the reasons for its unwillingness to help. The countries nearest Germany—France, Belgium, the Netherlands and Switzerland—said they were saturated with illegal immigrants. The Canadian delegate, with vast empty spaces in the West, pleaded high unemployment, and all other English-speaking countries of the Empire refused to relax their severe restrictions against the immigration of German Jews. Britain declared Palestine off-limits to appease the Arabs. In Brazil, Argentina, and Chile, pro-Nazi German minorities successfully beat the opposition drums, Venezuela being one of the few countries to state openly that Jews simply were not wanted. The Trinidadians made the same point more elegantly by explaining that immigrants could not be considered from "nations south of Belgium and east of France."[58]

With no conference participant willing to help, much time was taken up with the discussion of thoroughly impractical and quickly discarded ideas for sending the refugees to exotic places like British Guiana, Madagascar, Tanganyika, Alaska, or Mindanao, whereupon one delegate was heard to observe that such suggestions reminded him that Évian was "naïve" spelled backwards. The Jews themselves later wryly observed that the world, according to Évian, seemed to be made of two types of countries: the kind where Jews couldn't live and survive, and the ones they weren't allowed to enter.

As to the United States, the traditional country of immigrants, the situation was not much more hopeful. Throughout the thirties, an unsympathetic Congress and State Department bureaucracy, using subterfuge, delay, and red tape, had done their best to inhibit the entry of even the limited quota of immigrants from Germany allowed by law. Once as many as a million new immigrants had come in a single year. In the Depression years, however, the number had declined steadily from 242,000 in 1930, to a nadir of 23,000 in 1933. During the subsequent four years, 1933 to 1937, more people actually left the country than were newly admitted.

Labor unions feared unemployment and were strongly opposed. Anti-Semitism was a fact of life in many places, stoked by Nazi sympathizers, reactionaries in Congress, and a thinly veiled anti-Jewish attitude in the department of state. Assistant Secretary Breckinridge Long, in charge of such matters, used every conceivable subterfuge to keep the number of Jewish immigrants down. His staff, including his personal assistant and his legal advisor, were open anti-Semites, and in the consulates of several European cities, notably Zürich and Berlin, there were others with similar views.[59]

The sad result was that nothing was done to ease up on U.S. immigration restrictions, and during the entire critical years of the thirties, except for a single year, the German immigration quota was never filled.

Two statistics illustrate this tragedy. One is that the number of German Jews killed by the Nazis, approximately 150,000, happens to equal almost precisely that part of the German quota available under existing law, that wasn't filled. The other is even more telling. During the ten-year period 1921 to 1930, 4.1 million new immigrants were allowed into the United States. In the critical next ten years from 1931 to 1940, only 508,000 were admitted, while during 1991 to 2000, 7.6 million came—over 800,000 in the single year of 1996. In the Germany and Austria of the thirties, the combined total of all Jews desperate to leave was almost precisely that number admitted in the single year of 1996! How many of them might have been saved if U.S. policy had been more liberal will never be known.

We were among the last lucky ones, and by April 1939, my mother had managed to surmount all the hurdles, allowing us, finally, to escape. Our destination was the international city of Shanghai, a dreaded place of crime, poverty, and disease at the other end of the world, the last resort for those who had found no other place to go.

The Nazis officially decreed the loss of our nationality in 1941, but in my mind I stopped being a German—or wanting to be one— the moment we crossed the border into Italy. I had no regrets at all to be leaving and was too young to have left anything of value behind. Nor did I share my parents' fear of Shanghai, but looked forward with pleasurable anticipation to an exciting journey halfway around the world and to what awaited me in the mysterious Orient. Because of all that had happened, my years growing up in Berlin quickly receded into the background and soon became an eminently forgettable closed chapter, with no relevance to the future. An accident of birth, so to speak.

It would be many years before it dawned on me that in this instance the reality was more complex. It is true that my being a German was never an issue again, certainly not in my more than sixty years as a citizen of the United States. Yet it took advancing years and the perspective of a full and varied life, to understand that by growing up as a Jew in the Germany of the thirties, I had been a witness to events that had deeply influenced my outlook on life. Unconscious or not, some lessons were learned that permanently shaped my attitudes, actions and character.

An illustrative early childhood experience in Berlin comes to mind. I have always been afraid of water and when I was seven, my mother sent me off to swimming lessons in the hope of curing me of my fears. I remember being, to put it mildly, highly unenthusiastic and scared half out of my wits. Yet once she decided on something, that was how it had to be. My class met in an indoor pool at a police athletic facility used by the public. Our instructor was a stern disciplinarian. Having demonstrated the rudiments of the breaststroke and after a quick session at the pool's shallow end, including the command to dip our faces into the water (which I successfully faked), he lined us up at the deeper end and told us to jump in. *Eins, Zwei, Drei*— everyone jumped, but I alone remained standing, frozen in fear. "Jump!" he ordered me sternly. "I'm scared," I wailed. "Coward! A German boy isn't scared," he bellowed and unceremoniously threw me in. No doubt he thought it was the quickest solution to my un-German problem, but his pedagogic theory proved a disastrous failure. To this day, I cannot forget the sense of helplessness as he sent me flying and the water enveloped me, the closed-in sensation of swallowing water, and being unable to breathe until he pulled me out.

Most of all, what has stayed with me is the feeling of a loss of dignity, of violence in a situation in which I had no defenses, of impotence against the arbitrary action of a superior force.

Just as with my failed swimming lesson, the strongest feeling left from the Berlin of the thirties, and especially of the last six months after the pogroms, is the memory of that same sense of helplessness, impotence, and outrage. An abiding aversion to arbitrary and unfair acts by those with superior power has strongly influenced me at many stages of my life. It was, I believe, one of the fundamental motivations for government service and my desire to do it better, and for the policies for which I would later fight in public companies under my charge.

It started with my father's sudden arrest without explanation, the witnessing of my mother's frantic search for him over several days, and the *Angst*, without daring to ask, that perhaps he would never come back.

I had been told to stay indoors after the night of the November pogroms but curiosity had won out and I had sneaked into the streets to see it all for myself—our smashed store, the devastation everywhere and the smoldering ruin of the Fasanenstrasse Synagogue a few blocks away. Then followed the long months of travail and uncertainty with constant new rules and chicanery to complicate our lives, the hopes and defeats in the search for a place to go, the hunt for a berth on a ship that often seemed hopeless, the clearances interminably delayed, and the atmosphere of disintegration among teachers and school friends frozen into the same state of helpless confusion and fear. I recall the last two Sundays in Berlin, and the trauma of my parents when eager buyers filed through our apartment in search of bargains among our household effects, wich were being dumped at distress prices to raise the last money needed to leave. Many years later, hoping for some restitution after the war, my mother would list them all in excruciating detail: her combination buffet and liquor cabinet inlaid in marble, a large round table and eight upholstered chairs, two easy chairs, a large (modern) rug, the Rosenthal china for twelve, crystal, the silver inherited from her mother, linen, towels, blankets, and plates.[60] It must have been terribly painful for her to see it all go in this way, eagerly scooped up by the beneficiaries of our misery in those last agonizing days. And finally, there was that moment on the morning of April 8, 1939, after a long night on the train, as we crossed the frontier into Italy and the last moment of doubt was gone that something might still go wrong. It seemed an interminable time, as I was left to guard our possessions while my parents and sister were strip-searched by the SS—and then the lifting of the veil of terror and threat as the train began to move and the frontier was crossed.

The emotions of those last months have remained, but so have lessons learned in those final weeks and months in Nazi Berlin, lessons that would serve me well in later life. I had discovered that moral courage is a commodity in short supply, that civic cowardice and the temptation to tolerate injustice against others runs deep in us. I had been taught a valuable lesson about the transitory nature of one's existence, the ephemerality of status and material possessions.

Adversity can be a great leveler. As refugee in exile, the rich man in Germany was no better off than his servant, the one with the important job no more favorably placed than the clerk outside his door, and German honors and titles counted for nothing in another place. "How would you have fared, crossing the Brenner Pass with 10 Marks," I often would ask myself when faced with the self-satisfied airs of the egotist "big shot" encountered in other phases of my life.

The most valuable lesson was to see that when things go wrong, it is not titles and possessions that count, but the inner strength on which we must draw, and the courage to carry on when the odds against us are great. Those strengths are sometimes far greater than we ourselves suspect. It is this that my mother taught me above all.

In the decade of the thirties, Adolf Hitler put his indelible stamp on the history of the twentieth century and on the lives of countless millions, including my own. Yet his rise to power, his ability to consolidate it, his violation of treaty commitments and his multiple assaults on neighboring countries were neither unstoppable nor inevitable.

Rather, they are a dramatic object lesson in how accident, good or bad luck, and the strengths and weaknesses of individual leadership personalities—in this instance, their miscalculations, incompetence, and lack of will—can shape history with long-lasting and fatal consequences. Stronger and more courageous leaders in France and England might well have succeeded in putting a halt to Hitler's international adventurism before it was too late, beginning with his reoccupation of the Rhineland, and put a halt to the forbidden rearmament and expansion of his armed forces. It was the world's misfortune that at the critical moment, such far-sighted leaders with the power and willingness to act did not appear.

Even within Germany itself, this "luck of the draw" played a determining role. Almost from the start, there were those who plotted to bring Hitler down, legally or violently. They too failed, either through indecision or plain bad luck. A lowly carpenter almost succeeded in removing him from the world stage in a failed assassination attempt in 1938. Had that man succeeded—it was a matter of thirty minutes of timing—the history of the twentieth century would surely have been different.

Hitler's rise and impact on history are perhaps the single most dramatic example of how individual leaders and fortuitous circumstance can shape the course of world events. In later years I would be a witness to that lesson being repeated over and over again.

THE FORTIES
The War Years:
Shanghai

The End of Appeasement

Berlin was once home to several impressive train stations, and Berliners were particularly proud of their Anhalter Bahnhof. Built during the nineteenth century railroad boom and considered a masterpiece of renaissance architecture by its designer, Franz Heinrich Schwechten, it was noted for the harmony of its vast façade, with an impressive portal ringed by a dozen segmented arches and flanked by two large square towers. Behind it stood what was hailed as the largest station hall in the world, "second to none in its monumentality,"[61] housing six major platforms and several additional switching tracks. The entire complex, with freight and repair yards, extended five kilometers from the entrance toward the south.[62]

Nothing is left of the Anhalter Bahnhof today. Virtually demolished in one of the Allied raids on Berlin, it stood in ruin for fifteen years, until the authorities carted away the remains in the late fifties over the nostalgic protests of the population. Only a small section of the central portal was left as a somber reminder of the wartime disaster, and behind it, a small park now occupies the area of the erstwhile station itself.[63] When I passed there recently, people were viewing an outdoor exhibit of photographs depicting the fate of various Berlin victims of Nazi persecution including, curiously enough, two or three who had made their escape to Shanghai. I don't know whether the exhibit's organizers realized that their final glimpse of Berlin had probably been from this very spot and that it was at the Anhalter Bahnhof that they had boarded their train into exile.

Seventy years later, there is much I have forgotten or recall only dimly about those long-ago times. But among the few special moments etched in my mind, leaving Berlin on the evening of April 6, 1939, from the Anhalter stands out. It was well after dark; we were waiting quietly and saying our good-byes, our few remaining possessions already stored on board, and my parents were nervous and tense. Several small clusters of other departing Jews waited nearby, each similarly engaged and hoping to attract as little attention as possible.

Though aware of my parents' anxiety, I was mostly excited about the impending journey and the adventures ahead. How my mother and father must have felt, standing there amidst the boisterous crowds, I can only surmise. Exhausted from the preceding weeks when all their energies had been devoted to negotiating the hurdles and bureaucratic chicanery of Nazi officialdom, they must have experienced a measure of relief that we would soon be beyond the Nazis' reach. But this would have been tempered with sadness at the finality of leaving and fear of the unknowable ahead. What awaited us in Shanghai was still beyond anything they could have imagined. Nor could they have known that nearly all of the relatives they were leaving behind would perish.

That evening Anhalter Bahnhof was a beehive of activity, our own subdued mood in sharp contrast to the festive atmosphere around us. Easter was only days away, and the train station was filling with noisy vacationers heading south. As always in Berlin, there were uniforms galore, but this time the ones most in evidence were of Wehrmacht soldiers on Easter leave or en route to their units in Czechoslovakia, recently seized by Hitler in yet another bloodless adventure, and in clear violation of solemn commitments made just six months earlier to the British and French at Munich.

The Führer was riding high, and among his people his prestige had never been higher. With each daring move he had steadily enlarged the reach and power of the Reich. Each crisis had turned in his favor, with either acquiescence or no more than toothless protests from the outside world. The dismemberment of Czechoslovakia appeared to have been no different. Adolf Hitler seemed unstoppable and Goebbels's propaganda machine was hailing him as the greatest German of all time. His self-confident soldiers thronging the station were clearly in a buoyant mood and happy to believe him.

Ironically, had the future been known on that April night, the sentiments might well have been reversed. The happy vacationers and young soldiers would have realized that the faith in their Führer and their optimism about Germany's future was misplaced and that very hard times lay ahead. The miserable departing Jews, on the other hand, would have been entitled to a sense of relief—if not elation. Though they didn't yet know it, war was imminent, and they were departing just before the doors out of Germany would close, sparing them the sad fate of those they were leaving behind.

In time it would become clear that, appearances to the contrary, Hitler's brutal seizure of Czechoslovakia did not, after all, go down as just another in his long string of successful territorial expansions, another fait accompli accepted by the feckless West. Convinced of his own infallible judgment and the weakness of France and England, and ignoring the warnings of his diplomats and generals, Hitler had finally overplayed his hand. Czechoslovakia was a major turning point, and five months later it would lead directly to the war with the West he had hoped to avoid.

Ever since assuming power, Hitler had had his way. With little or no opposition, he had taken back the Saar, marched into the Rhineland, abrogated the restrictions of the Versailles Treaty, and begun to rearm and rebuild the Luftwaffe and the Navy. Then, in early 1938, using a combination of threats of force and blackmail, he had successfully engineered the anschluss of Austria.

But for Hitler it was never enough. Within weeks of marching into Austria, he had begun to agitate for the annexation of the Sudetenland from Czechoslovakia, provoking there what trouble and unrest he could through Konrad Henlein, the subservient local Nazi Sudeten leader. In the ensuing crisis, Hitler had solemnly assured England and France that his only interest was to bring home those Sudeten-Germans and their lands lost in the unfair Versailles Treaty. Once more, England and France had given in, and Neville Chamberlain, England's premier, had triumphantly returned home and proclaimed "peace in our time" to a grateful nation. Deeply averse to the risk of war, the British public still supported Chamberlain's policy of humoring Hitler, but the settlement of the Sudeten question at Munich nevertheless had been a great betrayal of one of the last democracies in central Europe. Many people knew it, and the very name of "Munich" would later become synonymous with betrayal of principle and political sellout.

In any case, the hopes for a dependable peace with Hitler did not last long and the final disillusionment came quickly. At the very same time he was assuring Chamberlain at Munich that the Sudeten question involved the last of his territorial demands, Hitler had secretly ordered his generals to plan for precisely what he had foresworn there. The code name for this betrayal was "Operation Green": the conquest by force of all of Czechoslovakia. In March of 1939, a scant six months later, Germany suddenly and without provocation had invaded what was left of Czechoslovakia and swallowed up the country by dividing it into the German Protectorates of Bohemia and Moravia, and a puppet Slovak state. Brushing aside the doubts in his own ranks, Hitler had broken his word and then gone yet further, demanding the return to Germany of Memel, a German-populated town under Polish control, commenced agitation against that eastern neighbor, and, once again in secret, commanded the Wehrmacht to prepare for "Case White," the conquest of Poland itself.

In the West, there had always been distaste and dismay over Nazi brutalities at home and blackmail abroad, even while its leaders were appeasing the German Führer. This time, however, the sense of betrayal and the shock over another cynical violation of solemn commitments recently given was so deep and complete that it led to dramatic consequences, which came as an unexpected and shocking surprise to Hitler. Even those previously willing to give him the benefit of the doubt were now convinced that his word could never again be trusted, that nothing would stop him and that buying him off did not work. Pacifist sentiments in Europe took a nosedive and public opinion in England and France swung sharply against the Nazi government. In England, conscription was reintroduced and volunteer recruitment shot up.

The attack on Czechoslovakia brought Britain's appeasement of Hitler to an end and gave way to a policy of deterrence, even at the risk of war. Chamberlain recalled his ambassador from Berlin and signaled the dramatic change in an uncompromising speech on March 18, 1939, showing, as William Shirer put it, that "the scales had fallen from his eyes."[64] In France, Prime Minister Daladier ordered a speed-up of rearmament, and in an unmistakable message that the Allies now were serious, England signed treaties guaranteeing the integrity of Poland, Greece, and Romania. Hitler was stunned and furious. This was not at all what he had expected, even though he remained certain that, when the chips were down, England and France would not actually move.

In the United States, the isolationist mood reflected in the Neutrality Acts also began to weaken. Refusing to give official recognition to the dismemberment of Czechoslovakia, the State Department issued a stern public condemnation, calling it a "temporary extinguishment of the liberties of a free and independent people," and President Roosevelt himself minced no words in dressing down the German ambassador.[65] On both sides of the Atlantic the realization took hold that Europe was quite possibly moving toward war. From London, German Ambassador Herbert von Dirksen sent this sober warning: "It would be wrong," he wrote Berlin, "to cherish any illusion that a fundamental change has not taken place in Britain's attitude to Germany."[66]

In truth, with his seizure of Czechoslovakia, Hitler had made war virtually inevitable. With the perspective of time, it is now plain that his decision to break his word and to dismember Czechoslovakia was dramatic evidence of fatal flaws in his character, which became more and more obvious with time, and which would lead him to the repeated miscalculations that eventually brought him down. His worldview was clear enough. He wanted the German Reich to be the master of continental Europe, seize Lebensraum in the east, and by one means or another eliminate the hated Jews from German life and eventually from all of Europe. In the early years he had shrewdly calculated his tactics, always the daring gambler yet maintaining a sense for timing and an appreciation for the limits of the moment. But deep down it was in his nature that each success made him more reckless and drove him to ever quicker action and, in the end, to what Joachim Fest has called "a neurasthenic craving for sheer movement."[67] It is this that led him to his first far-reaching mistake en route to a losing world war.

Shanghai

Over the years, I have often been asked why, of all places, we chose to go to Shanghai. The answer is distressingly simple: we were fleeing for our lives, and no other country would let us in. Thus we were going to Shanghai, everyone's least favored destination. It had a frightful reputation as a lawless, wild city in war-torn China, with a bad climate, tropical diseases, and no jobs, but between 1938 and 1941, some 18,000 German and Austrian Jews nevertheless fought, bribed and scrambled for a berth on a Shanghai-bound ship or seat on the Trans-Siberian train, and all for the same reason: they were fleeing to the one place in the world that would have them.

Shanghai, the sprawling East Asian metropolis near the mouth of the Yangtze River, owed its fame to its longstanding reputation for intrigue, oriental mystery, opaque legalities, unconventional living—and unrestricted exuberant vice. However, in the history of the Second World War, the city hardly deserves mention. The major battles were fought elsewhere, and little of wider significance happened there. On the morning of December 6, 1941, Pearl Harbor day, the Japanese military simply marched in and occupied Shanghai without major incident until V-J Day. Only in the final weeks of the Pacific War did the Allies take any notice by unloading some bombs near the waterfront during two or three brief daytime raids. Though these surprise attacks inevitably cost lives in the heavily overcrowded city, they were at best perfunctory affairs, a mere sideshow hardly worth mentioning in wartime dispatches.

Until the final days of the war, Shanghai remained a distant spot in the world conflict. Yet in its own way, it was nevertheless for me an excellent place from which to witness the impact of war on ordinary people whose lives are disrupted and changed forever, and to learn how they cope with the stress and hardship for which nothing has prepared them. My childhood years in Hitler's Germany and reaching adulthood in Shanghai were the two defining experiences of my early life, which shaped my outlook and fundamental values for what came later. In Berlin I was too young for personal suffering, but old enough nonetheless to feel its impact on those around me. But Shanghai was different. There the impact on me was much more personal and direct, and what I saw and learned impressed me deeply. I never forgot it, or tried to—neither behind a corporate desk, nor even as an advisor to the president of the United States.

In Shanghai, I often cursed my cruel fate and chafed at being a virtual prisoner with nowhere to go and with highly uncertain future prospects. I was already a young adult, impatient, ready to do things, and angry at being treated like an outcast. I thought life was passing me by and that these were wasted years. Yet I now realize that I was wrong. The tough refugee war years were precious lessons for the future; I lived them intensely, and they taught me much that was valuable and that I might never have learned in normal circumstances. Today I am grateful for that—which is not to deny that there were experiences I would just as happily have been spared.

In Shanghai I learned what it means to be hungry, poor, and forgotten for no fault of one's own, and what people will do when their backs are up against the wall. I saw that life can be unfair, that titles, possessions, and all the trappings of position and status are transitory, that they are not as important as one's own inner resources in the face of hard times, personal setbacks, and defeats. In Shanghai I was exposed as nowhere else to the effect of arbitrary government actions on ordinary people, and it is there that I was first confronted with the evils of crude racism, discrimination, and egregious intolerance. The city was also an excellent place to get a thorough lesson in the propensity of those on top to be uncaring and indifferent toward the plight of the less fortunate and the weak.

However, I also learned in Shanghai that there is a brighter element in the human condition and that it can show up even in the worst of times, such as the capacity of those under stress to overcome great odds and to marshal remarkable courage and creativity in the midst of chaos. It was in Shanghai that I was first exposed to the benefits of community action, to the good things that can happen when people pull together in times of need, to the comfort of a rich cultural life, to literature, music, and the performing arts, to inspiring examples of selfless help to others, to tolerance and grace under pressure, and to how much can be accomplished through self-help and cooperation, even in the worst of times.

As a young adult in Shanghai, I discovered more about being human, about the capacity for evil and the potential for good, than most people in more settled times might experience in a lifetime. The Shanghai of the late 1930s was home to the most diverse group of peoples, races, religions, cultures, and languages imaginable, and the meeting place of an extraordinary cast of diverse and unusual characters. Businessman, missionary, refugee, adventurer, spy, or agent provocateur, rich or poor, saint, sinner, snob, genius, or fool—in Shanghai one could meet them all, and if one kept one's eyes and ears open, there was something to be learned from all of them. The city by the Huangpu River, a tributary of the Yangtze, was my proverbial "School of Hard Knocks." I graduated from it a kind of optimistic cynic, which sounds like a contradiction but really isn't. On the one hand, it shattered many youthful illusions: when the worst is possible, don't think it can't happen—that was one of the enduring lessons. But a certain lifelong optimism tempering this somber view came from seeing what love, family, character, courage, and perseverance can nevertheless accomplish when things are tough, and that this too is an ever-present potential in many of us. Even while still a teenager in Shanghai, I concluded that what I can do in life depends primarily on me—partly on luck but always on trying and pushing ahead, and that if I don't look out for myself, nobody else will.

The Shanghai years are also the source of many of my later political convictions and my lifelong interest in public affairs. Having been victimized by bad governments and by ineffective and indifferent ones, I wanted to get involved and to do better, to help shape public policies focused on the least advantaged. Exposure to widespread poverty kindled my interest in the social sciences, particularly economics, and is the reason why I became a lifelong social liberal. In the United States, it would lead directly to the choice of my profession, politics, and to the Democratic Party of Franklin Roosevelt, Harry Truman, John Kennedy, and Barack Obama. But that came much later.

Extraterritoriality

The first European traders had settled in Shanghai in the 1840s after taking control of the city by force, soon to be followed by Christian missionaries and a motley assortment of others in search of adventure and wealth. From the beginning, the principal commodity the uninvited foreign guests offered for sale was Western religions and vice—specifically opium—and it had made those dealing in the latter, and a few Chinese middlemen, extraordinarily rich. A century later, vice was still a Shanghai staple. Opium was nominally illegal but easily obtainable by the city's thousands of addicts, and I soon began to recognize their languid faces, seemingly oblivious to their surroundings whether supine on crude bunks in squalid hovels or reposing comfortably in more elegant quarters. In modern Shanghai, vice came in many forms: a great variety of drugs, gambling, prostitution, child pornography, kidnapping, murder for hire, and more. The rule was free enterprise, entrepreneurship, and unbridled capitalism, conducted in an atmosphere of callousness, frivolity, and the hedonistic pursuit of pleasure.

Shanghai's unique feature was "extraterritoriality," a wondrous relic of the colonial age which granted the Europeans who ran the city immunity from Chinese law and empowered them to do pretty much as they pleased, subject only to the laws of their own countries administered by their own officials in their own courts.[68] If a French citizen broke the law he answered for it before a French *juge*, an American appeared before a U.S. Federal District Court judge "just like at home," an Englishman was subject to H.M.'s Crown, and so forth. Only the Chinese were dealt with in Chinese courts.

"Extrality," as the 1842 Treaty of Nanking forced on the Chinese by a British invasion force called it, was the price the defeated Chinese had paid for steadfast refusal to open their northern ports to trade with the outside world. Not taking "no" for an answer, the British had eventually dispatched 4,000 men aboard a small flotilla, who quickly overwhelmed the outmoded army and ancient defenses of the Chinese. Tea and silk were precious commodities much in demand at home, and Britain refused to be denied them. Nor did the professed lack of Chinese interest in manufactures prove an insurmountable obstacle to profitable business. Opium, from India, was an even better quid pro quo, and for that a ready Chinese market was developed without much resistance.

The Treaty of Nanking and others that followed—for a hundred years the aggrieved Chinese would refer to them as the "unequal treaties"—had also forced the Chinese to cede to Britain control of Hong Kong outright, had guaranteed a favorably low tariff on foreign imports, and had extended extraterritorial privileges in Shanghai to other European signatories allowing them, as a British historian put it "to share the fruits of England's victories."[69] Two years later, the French and Americans came for their shares, and subsequently other nations were also allowed in.

Under the original treaties, the British had staked out a small area of twenty-three acres for purchase and residence, eventually merging it with the Americans' into a single unit they called the International Settlement. The French had chosen to go it alone and had taken over an adjoining area, the "Concession Française." ("*Die French*," most German-speaking refugees would call this section of town, an early example of "Genglish," and a modest concession to what little English they had begun to learn.) In time, taking advantage of subsequent periods of chaos and war, the areas of extraterritoriality had steadily grown in size. As of World War I, the International Settlement had ballooned to some 5,500 acres, while the French Concession covered roughly half that size.[70]

It was within these areas that foreigners had set up their system of government independent of Chinese authority. In the Settlement, a Municipal Council (the SMC), in which even in the late thirties the majority were still non-Chinese, held sway and ran the police, fire department, post office, customs, and other municipal services. A similar system prevailed in the French Concession next door. Nothing in the original treaties had specifically authorized this precise arrangement: it had just "happened." The foreigners had interpreted the treaties to include the right to extraterritorial rule in those parts of the city they had taken for themselves, and the Chinese had acquiesced. What had emerged was a unique and peculiar arrangement, not quite a colony but close to it. A British officer once charmingly characterized it as simply "a fortuitous aggregate of self-governing English merchants."[71]

By the late thirties, the system had evolved and been modified a number of times, but its essentials remained unchanged. In the Concession, the French were still in charge, answering directly to superiors in their colony of Indochina. In the Settlement, some Japanese, Chinese, and other nationals had been added to the SMC, though the British remained in control. Yet extraterritoriality was now in its twilight days and the city was an island living on borrowed time, under pressure from surrounding Japanese military forces who had defeated Chiang Kai-Shek's Kuomintang (KMT) Nationalists in 1937 and installed a puppet regime in Nanjing under the renegade ex-KMT collaborator Wang Jingwei. The result was a bewildering array of uncertain and conflicting jurisdictions within a single city—the French Concession, the International Settlement, the Honkou area where the Japanese military were in charge, several traditionally Chinese districts where the puppet regime of Wang held sway, and—for good measure—Huxi, a wild no-man's land in a disputed western part of the Settlement, popularly known as the Badlands, where no one was in charge and the Settlement's police and Wang's men perennially battled for control.

To maintain law and order in this crazy quilt pattern of politically antagonistic areas would have been difficult even in times more normal than the late thirties. Already the world's fifth largest city, Shanghai was overcrowded and bursting at the seams with additional millions of Chinese war refugees seeking its international protection. The majority were utterly destitute and without shelter, and many were dying each day from hunger and disease. According to one report, as many as 100,000 dead bodies had been picked up in the streets in the single year of 1938 alone![72]

With the Sino-Japanese conflict still raging in the countryside and the outbreak of war in Europe, the city had also become a haven for spies, collaborators, and political provocateurs of every kind, a shadowy battlefield where the KMT underground fought the Chinese puppet city government and vice versa, where assassinations and kidnappings were common, and where rival criminal gangs struggled in shifting alliances with city officials to control the rich spoils from Shanghai's rackets and industries of vice.

Shanghai was a city of enormous contrasts, deeply divided between the very rich and the wretchedly poor, "a city of 48-story skyscrapers built on 24 layers of hell," as one writer put it."[73] Appearances to the contrary, it was very much a Chinese city with only a thin Western veneer, but for both sides it was a place for high living amid great human misery, a sort of Sino-Western capitalist heaven and corner of hell, all wrapped in one.

From afar, the first impression was that of a great European metropolis. The Bund, its famous broad avenue along the river, was impressive with tall buildings, fancy hotels, clubs, and banks bathed in bright neon lights at night. A closer look revealed, however, that behind it the city was intensely Chinese, a place of narrow streets and dirty lanes with the smells of the Orient to match, choked with carts, rickshaws, bicycles, and sweating "coolies" struggling under super-human loads. Hawkers noisily offered their wares, pickpockets of incredible skill preyed on the unwary, and swarms of beggars aggressively accosted foreigners and finely clad Chinese ladies for alms, the latter hobbling by on bound feet and oblivious to the misery of the less fortunate. Far away, behind tall walls on the outskirts of Shanghai, stood the mansions of the ruling expatriates and rich Chinese, who partied extravagantly and lived an abundant life waited on by small armies of house boys, amahs, cooks, nannies, gardeners, watchmen, and any number of other servants. In Shanghai, the few—expatriates, deal makers, assorted gamblers, and adventurers, and the handful of very rich Chinese—could live very well indeed.

Shanghai, one might say, was at once Casablanca and Las Vegas, which is why it attracted an extraordinarily diverse range of residents, visitors, and others in a mad jumble of nationalities and tongues. Among the U.S. visitors, there were the famous and the merely curious and an assortment of authors, actors, and filmmakers who dropped in to play or in search of exotic material—Noël Coward, Douglas Fairbanks, Charlie Chaplin, Vicki Baum, Josef von Sternberg, among them—and those who came to stay longer, in search of adventure or quick riches, or to do drugs, or for the women. A few, on the lam, simply came to hide. Christian missionaries found Shanghai irresistible and arrived to run schools, orphanages, and hospitals, and to proselytize among the Western educated and the poor.

The prominent and the well-heeled checked in at the luxurious Cathay Hotel on the Bund and savored the extravagance of its Lalique lamps, art deco furnishings, and mixture of Western and Oriental kitsch. They attended lavish parties, went slumming in the casinos, nightclubs, and dancehalls, sampled its upwards of 700 bordellos, and in calmer moments perhaps dropped in at the American Jimmy's Kitchen for lunch, or the fancy Russian DD's Café for chocolate cake and afternoon tea. Those who came with empty pockets took up residence in one of the fleabag hotels, or, if a bit squeamish about vermin and bugs, checked into the Foreign YMCA. But not all stayed there for long. In Shanghai fortunes were as quickly lost as made.

Shanghai was a gambler's paradise and its dozens of casinos attracted its share of adventurers, confidence men, and sharpsters from all over the world. For several years, one of the best-known and most talked about was Jack Riley, an American whose rags-to-riches-to-rags story deserves mention as vintage "Shanghai."

I remember seeing him occasionally around town—tall, good looking, gregarious, and popular. It was said that one day he had surfaced as if out of nowhere, unknown and without funds, running a penny-ante open-air dice game on the Bund. He must have been very lucky—or perhaps just a very deft cheat—for in rather little time he was the proprietor of his own bar, soon thereafter had won control of slot machines all over town, and eventually advanced to running the crap tables at the top casino of the Badlands, Joe Farren's luxurious place on Yu Yuen Road. Riley was also a talented athlete, with baseball his special passion but, alas, his undoing as well. He was a high-living and famous Shanghai figure one day, but the jig was up the next, and Shanghai good-naturedly took it in stride when the popular American was forced to quit town a lot less unobtrusively than he had arrived—in shackles aboard the SS *President Cleveland* bound for the United States in the personal care of Sam Teitelbaum, a U.S. marshal, there to serve out the remainder of a lengthy prison term.

Riley, it developed, had honed his athletic skills neither in college nor on the diamonds of the Minor Leagues, but rather on the Oklahoma State Penitentiary's "resident" team, an institution where at the time he was doing ten to twenty years for armed robbery. The story was that he had one day simply walked off during a game against convicts at a sister institution, surfacing in Shanghai shortly afterward to begin his glamorous if short-lived new life.

Jack Riley was a prototypical Shanghai figure, in his day among the most prominent and colorful of the adventurers, lost souls, and outright crooks who sought out the Shanghai environment as temporary refuge, hiding place, or permanent home. The strangest and most puzzling character of all, however, was also the most unforgettable, a veritable poster boy for the special ambience of international Shanghai in its final days.

His real name was Ignácz Trebitsch, a Hungarian Jew and arguably one of the twentieth century's most notorious frauds and confidence men who appeared in Shanghai, where he eventually died in 1944. In the course of a colorful life, he had gone by many names, though history remembers him best as Ignatius Trebitsch Lincoln. In Shanghai, he was the Venerable Chao Kung, an arresting figure in the flowing garb of a Buddhist monk, his head shaved and forehead branded, majestically walking the streets while fingering his prayer beads.[74] Occasionally I saw him around town, and once he sat down next to me in the coffee shop of the YMCA and wanted to know from where I had come. "Ah yes, yes," I recall his reply, switching to fluent though accented German, "Berlin, I have known it well." Which, for once, was the truth, Trebitsch having played a short but central role in support of the extreme rightists' failed attempt in 1920 to topple the Weimar Republic during the so-called Kapp Putsch.

In the course of his extraordinary life, Trebitsch had appeared and vanished in many places, and at various times had been Anglican curate, Christian missionary, failed oil company magnate, journalist, spy, and even—briefly—a British M.P.! He was also a convicted embezzler and thief, had bankrupted a business and served three years in an English jail for fraud. Trebitsch merits mention for two reasons. First, he fit Shanghai like a glove—and vice versa. If there is any single figure who best symbolizes the city's unorthodox ambiance of fraud, mystery, and color, it is he. The second reason—not known to us at the time— is the more ominous and important. Trebitsch loved international espionage and intrigue, and even as the outwardly benign Buddhist monk Chao Kung, he had been in touch with the Gestapo in Shanghai, offering to further the Nazi cause among the Buddhists of Tibet—

and had half convinced them that he could. It took a stern cable from Berlin to the SS's infamous representative in the Far East, Josef Meisinger, to abort the affair. It was Heydrich himself, Heinrich Himmler's deputy, who ordered Meisinger to desist: "In the matter of Trebitsch Lincoln, therefore, you are not to proceed. Surely you are aware that he is a Jew."[75]

Refugee Life

Daniel Libeskind's extraordinary design of today's Jewish Museum Berlin, which established his fame as one of the world's foremost contemporary avant-garde architects, incorporates as a central element an "axis of exile," intended to remind visitors of the fate of German Jews expelled to the far corners of the earth and forced to make a new beginning in unfamiliar surroundings. A long, upward-sloping walkway takes the visitor to a unique garden of stone pillars standing on an uneven surface, and creating for many an eerie sensation of physical imbalance and emotional confusion. It is the architect's way of symbolizing the experience of a refugee lost in an alien environment far from home—and it works. Most visitors feel a distinct sense of disorientation, a few even become physically ill.

I don't know whether Libeskind had Shanghai in mind when he conceived his stone garden, but he might well have. For the 18,000 frightened and penniless refugees from Nazi Germany, to be thrust into this witches' brew of alien confusion during the decade of Shanghai's worst years required a wrenching and painful reorientation. Some could never really adjust to it, and a few it destroyed. In virtually every respect, what the refugees encountered in Shanghai was the antithesis of their prior experience in Europe.

Instead of the temperate climate of Berlin or Vienna, Shanghai lies at a tropical latitude akin to Cairo or New Orleans. Summers are hot and humid, winters uncomfortably cold and clammy. Sanitation was minimal, the sewers grossly inadequate, tap water dangerously undrinkable, electricity uncertain and housing standards abominable.

"Night soil buckets" instead of flush toilets were common. Diseases—cholera, smallpox, typhoid, amoebic dysentery, and any number of intestinal and parasitic infections—were a constant threat.

Equally as jarring as the physical challenges was Shanghai's lawlessness—the free-for-all, dog-eat-dog environment of pervasive corruption without reliable rules, in stark contrast to the certainty of a law-based, highly regulated environment that these Central Europeans had heretofore taken for granted. Extraterritorial Shanghai was in its waning days, but it was still Sin City, where laws could be bent and rules ignored, where anything was possible and nothing worked quite as it did anywhere else. As the confused refugees walked ashore, Shanghai was quite unprepared for them—and they were anything but ready for what they found there.

On board the *Haruna Maru*, the Japanese ship taking us to China, two books were making the rounds. Our group of anxious travelers considered them required reading, and I recall my parents studying them with earnest attention. One was a small English primer for German speakers called *A Thousand Words of English*; the other a collection of stories about doing business with the Chinese entitled *Four Hundred Million Customers*.[76] Its author was Carl Crow, an American advertising executive and longtime resident of Shanghai. His main theme was that there were incredibly many Chinese in China, that all were potential customers, and that they were a charming people but wedded to peculiar customs not easily understood by Westerners.

The importance of learning English, the lingua franca of the roughly fifty separate national resident groups in Shanghai, was indisputable. It was also true, however, that it hadn't occurred to anyone on board the *Haruna Maru* that learning Chinese—the language of 99 percent of Shanghainese—might actually have been another extremely useful preparation for their new life. As it turned out, most of them never did learn the language, though in that respect the new arrivals would merely conform to the prevailing view of all Europeans that to take the trouble of acquiring a decent knowledge of the local language and culture was a charming eccentricity for those so inclined, but as a practical matter an unnecessary burden.

As to Crow's anecdotes about a foreigner's business dealings with the Chinese, no one on our ship had the slightest idea that the vast gulf in status and business opportunity between an established American expatriate and a penniless refugee coming to wartime Shanghai rendered much of what he had to say irrelevant for their purposes. In Shanghai there were few firmly enforced official limits, but the city's foreign community was snobbishly hierarchical and exclusionary. People moved in their own orbits and the social and business lines were rarely crossed. The English and Americans held the key positions of power, and enjoyed the greatest privileges and prestige. Crow was almost certainly a member of the elite Shanghai Club on the Bund, where deals were made with expatriate counterparts over leisurely "tiffin" lunches, or over drinks by the fabled Long Bar. A stateless refugee could hardly hope to be admitted into this exclusive expatriate shrine. Crow's principal clients were the big American and British tobacco companies and import houses, whose products he helped pitch to big Chinese "compradores"[77] or to other top western-educated local merchants. For this he was certain to be paid in dollars, and could afford to live in a large house in the tony Western part of town, waited on by a small army of servants. The refugees would have to adjust to an entirely different world, one where their daily interaction with the Chinese bore little resemblance to that of Carl Crow. No club where useful contacts were made would be open to them, and the odds that an American or British company would employ them in even the lowest capacity were as long as the likelihood of contacts with Shanghai's key Chinese tycoons.

The reality was that the practical and emotional challenges for which the refugees had to prepare were of quite a different kind, ones for which Daniel Libeskind's upward sloping and uneven Exile Garden is an infinitely more fitting paradigm. Even that ex post symbol of refugee disorientation conveys, however, only an imperfect sense of the depth of the existential crisis that awaited the *Haruna Maru*'s China-bound refugee travelers.

Beyond the brutal climate,[78] they had to absorb the full force of an immediate, drastic reduction to a rock-bottom standard of living in an Asian context, the implications of which would hit these middle class Germans and Austrians with unexpected suddenness. For those with access to "real" money—dollars, sterling, or Swiss francs—income- and excise-tax-free, Shanghai was actually a bargain basement, where a pack of imported Lucky Strikes or Camels could be bought for two-thirds of the price in the home market, the same being true for most other imported goods. Even a modest monthly salary paid in a hard currency went a lot further in Shanghai than at home, and the lowest paid expatriate could live extremely well. But for a refugee without funds, largely dependent on charity and with little prospect of hard-currency earnings, the issue was how to get by on a local budget equivalent to ten U.S. dollars or less. The moment after leaving the protective cocoon of his ship, he would be confronted by this painful reality at the most elementary level—coping with primitive shelter and earning enough money for basic food.

The responsibility of caring for the refugees was borne in the first instance by a few overseas charities and by the two established Jewish communities of Shanghai who took up the challenge as best they could. The smaller of these communities consisted of Sephardic Jews originally from Iraq, many of modest means but including a few of the city's super-rich—the Sassoons, Kadoories, Hardoons, Ezras, and a handful of others. The second was a larger community of Russian Jews, more recent arrivals from Harbin and the Russian Far East, themselves refugees who had come to Shanghai to escape Communism and the endemic anti-Semitism of their home country.

Feeding and housing their newly arrived coreligionists began as a manageable task. At the end of 1938, only about 1,400 refugees had arrived, but what had begun as a trickle soon became a steady stream and then a veritable flood threatening to overwhelm the frantic efforts of the receiving groups. By May of 1939, 7,000 more had arrived; eventually the refugee community would grow to almost 18,000.

In the spring of 1939, 2,000 utterly destitute refugees had already been lodged in emergency camps donated by wealthy local Jews. These were the primitive *Heime* (shelters), where a total of 4,800 residents and others would eventually be fed from community kitchens at a cost of thirty-three cents per day, while those not in the camps had to get by on a monthly stipend of as little as fifty Chinese dollars, the equivalent of about five U.S. dollars. "Can anyone live on that?" Sir David Sassoon, a major Jewish benefactor and one of Shanghai's richest residents, had wondered in an interview in the *North China Daily News*.[79]

The *Heime* had been set up in abandoned properties in Honkou, the Japanese-occupied part of town near the docks and one of Shanghai's worst districts, heavily damaged in the 1931 and 1937 Sino-Japanese fighting. Few Westerners ventured into this uninviting bombed out area, inhabited mainly by poorer Chinese, where the Japanese military was calling the shots and extraterritoriality no longer counted. They had, however, agreed to let the refugees live there, and that was where they were taken. Contemporary photographs show the arriving refugees, still dressed in soon-discarded, highly impractical clothes for the Shanghai climate, transferring from ships up a wooden plank into crude open trucks that took them to their new homes. There they were placed into dormitories, issued bed clothes, a blanket, tin plate, cutlery and a cup, and armed with a bit of useful advice for survival in Shanghai: "Don't drink the water, don't drink milk or eat raw food, stay away from the Japanese military, and don't trust policemen."[80] Goodbye Carl Crow, and welcome to a refugee's Shanghai!

Our own situation was less desperate, but though we were among those spared the *Heime*, facing the multiple jarring realities of our new life was traumatic enough. Relatives in Brazil had scraped together a little money for us—about a hundred English pounds, I believe—which placed us among the minority of refugees with "means." My parents had rushed off to a bank in Naples to pick up the cash, and throughout the voyage I recall them nervously guarding our precious nest egg, alternately counting and re-counting it, and then hiding it in yet another secret place. It was the only thing that stood between us and total disaster, and not a penny of it could be spent during our month-long journey. So when we arrived on May 10, 1939, we were among the lucky few who could bypass the trucks to Honkou, heading instead to a single room in a fleabag hotel in the less depressing International Settlement.

A few days later—my seventeen-year old sister having been sent off as a nanny to an English family in Shanghai, thus saving us one mouth to feed—we rented our first permanent quarters across the border in the French Concession. Home now was a single room in a small house inside a narrow lane of very modest row homes, grandly named Erin Villas, at 51 route de Grouchy. Our landlords at House #8 were poor White Russians. "Colonel" Kichigin, the impressive looking man of the house, seriously addicted to his vodka bottle and without any visible occupation, claimed to have been a high officer with the White Russian army fighting the Reds. My father, drawing on his Prussian military background and remembering battles against the Russians in Galicia, quickly concluded contemptuously that Kichigin could have been no more than a sergeant. Refugees tend to have inflated memories of their erstwhile status in life, he observed. He had noticed this among our own shipboard refugees, many of whom loudly claimed to have lived in ample surroundings while holding down important positions in Berlin or Vienna with sizeable incomes and solid bank accounts. The Russians, he was sure, suffered from the same delusions. It made one's reduced state more bearable and less demeaning.

Madame Kichigina, the lady of the house, supported the family as a masseuse to expatriates, and the two young daughters, I overheard from my parents' mumbled allusions, had "night jobs"—one plying her trade as an outright prostitute, while the other labored as a hairdresser during the day and supplemented her income at night in a small Russian bar that, given the seemingly endless string of her "gentleman callers," appeared to amount to roughly the same thing.

The house was small, crowded and primitive, the Kichigins loud and impulsive, forever quarreling, always broke but otherwise good natured and generous. When it came to feasting at Russian Easter and Christmas, vodka flowed freely and the downstairs table would groan under the weight of Russian delicacies elegantly prepared by "Grischa," a Chinese cookboy who swore like a Cossack in fractured Russian and slept on the kitchen floor, sometimes alone and sometimes in the company of one of Erin Villas ample supply of wash and baby amahs. To this day, my limited vocabulary of Russian derives primarily from Grischa's colorful imprecations concerning the mothers of the subjects of his wrath, their low morals, intimate anatomy, and devious sexual practices. For an impressionable young boy just into puberty, there was much to learn at the Kichigins. The most fascinating part of the scene—and the subject of many a heated dream—unquestionably was the two daughters and their blithe habit of wandering around the house in various states of undress, while calling to Grischa for food and drink.

Getting used to the primitive living conditions at the Kichigins— a far cry from our Kurfürstendamm apartment—was only slightly less disconcerting than being lodged in a Honkou *Heim*. My mother had banished me to a rickety folding cot placed behind a large steamer trunk in our single room. Worse, however, was the adjustment to Shanghai's inhospitable climate and to the infestation of Erin Villas— a common Shanghai affliction—with bedbugs, giant cockroaches, and the occasional rat—from which there was no effective escape.

The climate alone was bad enough. "One never feels happy away from the climate into which one is born," Vicki Baum has her Chinese protagonist observe, as he watches his foreign friends suffer in Shanghai's summer heat."[81] Eventually we learned to accept the Shanghai weather stoically, but the misery of it never quite ceased. Even in May, the temperature regularly climbed to 90°F with levels of humidity that left one drenched in sweat within minutes of stepping outside, and tormented by irksome heat rashes on unaccustomed

European skins. In July, there were days when the temperature would top out at over 104° with little nighttime relief, the oppressive heat occasionally interrupted only by torrential monsoon rains, with which the inadequate sewers could not cope and which inundated the streets in a deadly mix of two or more feet of polluted water.

The main question for all refugees, however, was how to earn enough money to stay alive. Jobs were hard to get and paid very little. For Westerners, manual labor was not an option—the Chinese did that for next to nothing; and only those few with unique skills—a chemist with specialized experience, a former musician from the Berlin or Vienna Philharmonic, or perhaps a renowned physician—stood a chance. For the great majority of the others, finding any kind of gainful employment was a matter of luck and rarity much talked about and envied.

What was left was what Jews have been forced to do over the centuries—sell, trade, hustle, and improvise. In Shanghai this also involved attempting to convert odd skills and hobbies into moneymaking schemes. Recreational musicians sought gigs in nightclubs or bars, housewives baked Viennese or Berlin specialties for sale, and those skilled with their hands knocked on office doors and offered to repair typewriters and such. The inventiveness of the refugees was astounding, and though many failed, the success of at least some was remarkable. The Eisfelders opened a small café, little more than a hole in the wall, and soon became famous for German-style cakes and Torten of a quality previously unknown in Shanghai. Another refugee opened an "Emigrant Thrift Shop" where expatriates came to browse and bargain-hunt for personal possessions the new arrivals put up for sale, and Herr Tarrasch, who knew a lot about good German Wurst and Schinken, quickly became a favorite supplier to expatriate households in the privileged parts of town. In the resident Nazi German community, his success proved so great, in fact, that the local Gauleiter soon felt compelled to issue an official warning that, even in China, buying from Jews was forbidden.

Some of the refugees' schemes and ventures succeeded, many others did not, but before long Shanghai's Western community began to notice them. The refugees were making an impact. It was hard work with frequent failure, made all the more difficult by the flexible ethics and outright dishonesty and corruption presenting the new arrivals with unaccustomed challenges. Shanghai was a haven for practitioners of the art of the flim-flam, and many a refugee paid the price. Customers did not pay, promises were broken, and always there was "squeeze," the ubiquitous bribe that needed to be paid to get anything done.

My mother, who had plunged into this scene with her indomitable determination and energy, was also not spared the obligatory Shanghai lesson. Within days of having settled in at the Kichigins, she had convinced the Russian owner of a piece goods store on Avenue Joffre (now Huaihai Lu), the French Concession's main artery, to let her try selling his wares directly to the chic little boutiques and dressmakers catering to expatriate ladies, that dotted the area near the French Club on rue Cardinal Mercier.[82] Her problem was that the load she was toting from place to place was far too heavy to carry, but public rickshaws were unreliable, and the pullers difficult to instruct in a language she neither spoke nor understood.

After much agonizing debate, a decision had therefore been taken for a major investment in a private rickshaw of her own, a sleek and shiny black affair and a distinct step up from the generally dirty and uncomfortable public ones. The idea was to ease her travels with the inventory of cloth, while at the same time impressing customers with so luxurious a mode of transport. Along with her fancy rickshaw, a personal coolie puller had been duly engaged, an elderly type named Foo who, having been outfitted with a clean pair of pants, Chinese-style jacket, and straw sandals, was expected to "drive her" on her daily rounds. Foo understood rudimentary instructions—in pidgin English, of course—a not difficult to master Shanghai vernacular for which her study of *Tausend Worte Englisch* had however left her quite unprepared.[83]

It wasn't long before she was relegated back to the public rickshaws after all. Within two weeks or less, Foo—the rickshaw, pants, jacket, sandals and all—had been swallowed up in Chinese Shanghai, never to be seen again, the investment in elegance irretrievably lost. As for my father, never much of a businessman even in more settled times, the analogous lesson was learned almost as quickly. A small part of our £100 capital had been invested in a joint venture with a Chinese partner and another refugee in an abortive manufacturing venture of sorts, which quickly collapsed, the investment gone and the Chinese partner lost in the zigzag of Shanghai's streets with the remaining cash.

These early lessons in Shanghai business life, which many refugees learned, had their roots in the city's long tradition as a place where everyone was "on the take" and where, as Crow described it with a touch of admiration, "racketeering flourishes with a velvety smoothness that makes Chicago gangsters seem like noisy play-boys."[84] At the top, there was a long-standing unofficial alliance between Shanghai's foreign and Chinese leadership and its big criminal gangs, enabling the latter to protect their territories and enrich themselves from drugs, gambling, prostitution, and other assorted rackets, while ensuring that foreign and Chinese tycoons were left in peace and matters did not get out of hand.

In the twenties, this system had produced such colorful characters as "Big-eared Tu" and "Pockmarked Huang," both leaders of the Green Gang and associated criminal triads. Tu had helped finance General Chiang Kai-shek's political machine, for which he had been made an honorary Major-General in the Nationalist army. Huang was the undisputed boss of the underworld in the French Concession while conveniently holding down the simultaneous position of Chief of Chinese detectives in that part of town. A third underworld boss, one Chang Hsiao-lin, was head of the French Opium Suppression Bureau, allowing him to control the illegal trade and to split the proceeds between his gang and his government partners. In the Settlement, yet another Green Gang chieftain named Sheng-Shinlung enjoyed the same kind of arrangement as simultaneous head of a detective squad as did his successor, a certain Loh, who however was finally assassinated in 1938 for the political sin of collaborating with the hated Japanese. Such conflicts of interest and egregious corruption at the top of Chiang Kai-shek's government eventually contributed significantly to the decline and collapse of the Nationalists in a sea of public disgust, by handing a powerful weapon of propaganda to the more puritanical Communists of Mao Tse-tung. Chiang's brothers-in-law, H H Kung and TV Soong, both immensely wealthy but greedy to a fault, took turns for years as ministers of finance of the KMT government and enriched themselves even as they mismanaged the country's financial affairs.

The corrosive effect of so much corruption, graft and criminality at the top invariably permeated down to the lowest levels. On the street its manifestations were everywhere. The cop on the beat, in plain sight, "squeezed" the hapless rickshaw coolies, laborers and the public in general. Carrying their meat to market in the summer heat, farmers would be stopped, the sun beating down on their wares and threatening imminent spoilage, until they had paid up. Each policeman passed a share of the daily take on to his sergeant, and he to his boss and boss's boss, everyone taking his bite along the way. Especially in the environment of war and distress of the late thirties, with so many unemployed, underpaid, exploited, and starving, some of this was soon accepted as almost one's rightful due—the only way in which a small employee could hope to feed his family and get by.

Exploitation and need are great dissolvers of moral dilemmas—as I would also discover. The war ended my schooling at age sixteen, and I landed a job as an errand boy in a chemical factory owned by a firm of Swiss entrepreneurs hoping to make a killing by taking advantage of their unique position of neutrality. The year was 1942, the Pacific War had just begun, the Japanese were in control, and times were hard. To say that we were grossly underpaid and exploited by our war-profiteering owners is putting the situation mildly. One of my tasks involved occasional bicycle errands to purchase odds and ends—special nails and screws, sticks of lubricants, and the like. I recall my initial puzzlement when first, at the Chinese shop in town, I was handed a receipt—with a courteous bow—for an amount some 20 percent in excess of the price I had actually paid. It was simply how business was done and the shopkeeper took it for granted that I expected no less. Keeping the difference was to ensure that I would favor the store for future business, and to cement a profitable arrangement for both sides. I confess that whatever moral compunctions may first have assailed me did not survive long. Soon, like everyone else in Shanghai, I was collecting my "squeeze" to supplement my starvation wages, and positively vied for yet another errand to my friendly supplier in town.

And so it went, from top to bottom. Grischa, the Kichigins' cook, collected his commission from the greengrocer at the corner, the fire brigade appeared only when "squeezed," the hospital nurse properly attended to patients only after her palm was greased, and at our chemical plant, Mr. Yik, the compradore, let no consignment pass through the doors without collecting his rightful due. I played the game like everyone else, but a lifelong lesson was learned nevertheless. In the absence of a culture of elementary honesty and law and order, life corrupts all and becomes intolerable, and no governmental authority, whether in a police state or a democracy, can indefinitely expect to function and survive.

Temptation

I can lay claim to an excellent education in China, though not of the formal kind. What schooling I had wasn't particularly impressive, and my most valuable learning was in the streets.

Outside, there was the overcrowded Shanghai with its kaleidoscopic sights, sounds, and smells—chaotic, sometimes dangerous, full of temptations but always exciting.

Shanghai life was lived in the streets, where anything could be bought and sold, an infinite variety of food was cooked and consumed, fortunes were told, pockets picked, faces shaved, illnesses treated, teeth pulled, and ears cleaned. In the streets the homeless and poor attended to their most elementary needs, babies were born, and the destitute died. There one rubbed shoulders with hawkers and hucksters, with Scottish soldiers in kilts, Italian sailors, and U.S. Marines, with Annamite and turbaned Sikh policemen, with hustlers and whores, story-tellers, beggars, and pimps, young boys and girls available for sale or rent, nuns in black habits, and Buddhist monks with shaved heads in flowing saffron robes. In the streets there were innocent pleasures to be had, and others less so and best kept to oneself.

Almost from the first day we arrived, I began to escape into the street as often as I could in search of adventure in Shanghai's twisted alleys and busy lanes. I wanted to see it all, and before long I had found the spots where the greatest excitement was to be had. Soon I bargained and cursed in street Chinese as if I had been doing so all my life. I picked up scraps of Russian from the neighbors on Route Grouchy, babbled in ridiculous pidgin English like everyone else, and, living in the Concession Française, achieved fair fluency in French. Multilinguistic acrobatics were common and considered no great achievement among the youngsters of polyglot Shanghai.

Best of all: for the first time of my life I was on my own, and virtually free of effective parental control. In Nazi Berlin, my life had been heavily constrained; at home I had been protected and closely watched, and there had been any number of rules and restrictions to observe. Shanghai was different. I was a teenager now and growing up fast. All around, life pulsated with few fixed rules, wild and anything but orderly. It did not take me long to discover that there were now possibilities—previously undreamed of—for getting a taste of what was going on, with no one to rein me in.

My parents worried about Shanghai's temptations and about my growing up unsupervised and wild, "like one of the Hottentots," as my mother often sighed. Overwhelmed by daily problems and rarely at home, she still made valiant efforts to keep me in check, but it was a losing battle even for someone as determined as she. On the move from morning till night in the debilitating summer heat or clammy, bone-chilling winter cold, toting her bolts of cloth from place to place, she would return at night exhausted and thoroughly drained, with little energy left for anything beyond stern lectures and dire warnings about the risks of the fleshpots of Shanghai and its climate of debauchery and danger.

I'm afraid I rarely listened. Dividing my life neatly between the official and the forbidden parts, I became quite skilled at weaving the web of obfuscation and pretense needed to keep the two apart. On the former—school, scouts, and whatever "healthy" chores and activities she had devised—I would cheerfully report at the end of each day. The rest I kept strictly to myself, and although my mother probably suspected a lot, neither she nor anyone else knew the extent to which I was learning to taste forbidden fruit.

Often I merely roamed. I loved observing the public scribes—elderly gentlemen with wispy beards and erudite mien, their brushes and ink pads neatly laid out, with a rooster nearby chained to its perch and imperiously standing guard. Illiteracy among the country folk refugees and the poor was high, and the scribes did double duty reading them their mail and composing replies, while telling them their fortunes on the side. For this the rooster was trained to extract one of many tiny scrolls out of a bowl, from which the soothsayer would cite with much ceremony and in a sing-song voice whatever mysteries of the future it revealed. Next to it might be a traveling library of picture books, where for a copper or two a passerby could squat and lose himself in a fantasy world of Chinese history with tales of dragons, warriors, and intrigue. Elsewhere there were kids with crickets, birds in cages, kittens on strings, cardsharks promoting crooked games of chance, and everywhere folk carrying baskets suspended on bamboo poles, selling, bargaining, shoving, and shouting amid thousands of food stalls, each with its distinctive smells. There were doughy concoctions, hot sesame rolls, soy cakes bubbling in an acrid vile brownish sauce, chestnuts, yams, fish, and meat, lychees, melons, cheap ices in summer, and roast sweet potatoes in the winter's cold—and around them, Chinese sitting or squatting and forever eating, burping, spitting, shouting, laughing, or quarreling.

A greater temptation—and a riskier one—was to venture to places where I wasn't supposed to be and where, generally for good reasons, few foreigners were seen. At Thibet Road and Avenue Edward VII, I would occasionally crash the giant multistory Great World, a wondrous emporium of entertainment catering to every pleasure of the senses and the flesh for the broad masses of Chinese. Josef von Sternberg, the filmmaker, had seen it earlier in the thirties and pronounced it unlike any other place on earth, with "gambling tables, sing-song girls, magicians, pickpockets, slot machines, fireworks, bird cages, fans, stick incense, acrobats and singers" on one floor, and "restaurants, actors, crickets in cages, barbers and midwives" on another.[85] Badly damaged by bombs in the 1937 war, the Great World was well past its prime in my day, its offerings much reduced but in its essentials still largely the same—floors with Chinese theaters and the clanging of cymbals and drums, several Buddhist shrines, innumerable places to eat, tricksters of all types—and girls, lots of girls of every age and type. My teenage hormones were raging, and the aura of erotic excitement of the Great World is hard to convey. Slim Chinese girls in gowns, sometimes with high, revealing slits firing my pubescent imagination, could be seen all over town, but in the Great World the girls were there for a purpose. Alas, I was almost always broke, and thus mostly reduced to observing and to dreaming, rather than sampling the offerings. A lucky star must have watched over me, because the skin trade was closely linked to crime and disease. Somehow I never came to serious harm.

But Shanghai was also home to even less innocent pursuits: in dance halls and nightclubs where opium was smoked, and in casinos and places for betting on every conceivable game of chance. The variety of gambling establishments catering to every wish and whim, many with lavish offerings to lure customers, was an irresistible magnet for me, even though I quickly developed a visceral aversion to the gambling itself (which has stayed with me throughout my life). What attracted me were the free gifts, the gamblers' faces, the stacks of money being won and lost, the tension and atmosphere of danger, mystery, decadence, and dissipation. Once I had learned how to get by the guards at the door, the casinos became one of my favorite clandestine destinations.

Horse racing on the race course in the center of town, frequented by an upscale crowd of foreigners and well-heeled Chinese, was hard to crash and dull besides.[86] The dog races at the Canidrome and jai alai at a giant fronton in the heart of the Conçession Française, where mostly Chinese gambled, were a lot more fun, and I spent as much time there as I could, happily accepting the free cigarettes and soft drinks being passed around, while watching agile Basque players climb the walls to chase the balls in what appeared to be near impossible acrobatic feats. Rumor had it that most of their games were fixed, but the gamblers didn't seem to mind and for me it was all a lot of fun.

By far the most exciting, however, were the dozens of large and smaller casinos of Huxi, the area of town popularly known as the Badlands. This was the lawless district where in the timeless Shanghai tradition various political factions exerted control in ever-shifting alliances with the underworld. In the Badlands, Wang-Jingwei's puppets competed with the Settlement police, the Japanese pulled strings behind the scenes, Chiang's agents waylaid their enemies, and kidnappings and political assassination were the order of the day.

The allure of the dens of vice in the Badlands was irresistible. Hanging around there, where opium was smoked and occasional shootings and police raids briefly disturbed the concentrated quiet of the gamblers at work, was not a very smart thing to do. No one ever quite knew who was in control and who was being paid off, but for the clients gambling was serious business and most of them didn't really care, and, prudently or not, neither did I.

War

We had settled as best we could into our upstairs room at the Kichigins, but watched anxiously as the Europe we had left behind went up in flames. Within a few months of our departure, Hitler's string of aggressions had finally led to war and though my parents and their friends were homesick and miserable in our uncomfortable exile, they realized how fortunate we were to have escaped. For the moment, though, the war in Europe was only a distant rumble. The more immediate issue for us was day-to-day survival in Shanghai.

Certain negative implications of the outbreak of war in Europe were however inescapable. Shanghai was to have been merely our temporary refuge while waiting for admission to some better country, but the war was now making an early departure unlikely. There was also growing concern about friends and relatives left behind, and their mail was becoming sparse and filled with dark hints. It worried us, but otherwise we welcomed the turn of events in Europe and took an optimistic view. A few incorrigibles even began to speculate about the possibility of going home someday. Germany was now opposed by England and France, the two great powers who had defeated her once before, and the hope was that Hitler's six-year tyranny might now be brought to an end. Since the Germans hadn't done it from within, the refugees argued, the British and French would now do the job from the outside. Meanwhile we cheered Shanghai's small Allied military garrisons—East Surreys and Seaforth Highlanders from Britain and a regiment of French soldiers—and admired the small contingent of friendly and strapping U.S. Marines, hoping that President Roosevelt would soon lead America to join the anti-German cause. The strongly pro-Allied English language press became required reading.

Throughout the spring and summer of 1939, Hitler had steadily increased the pressure on Poland, ignoring all warnings that one more aggressive act might lead to armed conflict with the West. The real surprise, however, had been his astounding about-face in relations with his arch foe, the Soviet Union, and the signing of a Nazi–Soviet Non-Aggression Pact in mid-August. In Nazi ideology, Communists were the principal enemy, closely linked and on a par with the hated Jews. Now all that had suddenly changed, and even the glib and cynical Goebbels had struggled mightily to explain this stunning reversal to an astonished German public, presenting it as the Führer's brilliant diplomatic coup against Poland's Western allies.

It has been Poland's historical misfortune to be a victim of its own geography, uncomfortably lodged between two great powers who have coveted parts of Polish territory while jockeying against each other for advantage. When Russians and Germans suddenly joined hands, the Polish fate was sealed, and all the frantic last minute maneuvering of the desperate Poles to avoid their country's dismemberment had proved to be of no avail. The signatures on the Nazi–Soviet Pact were barely dry before the impatient Führer launched his invasion in the small hours of September 1, on the pretext of Polish incursions on German soil, a sham organized on Hitler's orders by the SS and Secret Police. Two days later England and France, though still woefully unprepared for a major struggle against the powerful Germans, declared war. A new world conflict, the twentieth century's second, longest, and deadliest, was underway.

Hitler's ultimate goals lay in the East, and not in war with the West. After Czechoslovakia, attacking Poland would, however, prove his second fateful miscalculation. Though he had little empathy or respect for the French, he had always grudgingly admired England and her colonial Empire. In his eyes her people were, after all, racially acceptable Anglo-Saxons and until the last moment he had firmly believed that when the chips were down neither England nor France would stand by their commitment to the Poles. "What now, Ribbentrop?" the shocked Führer is said to have asked his foreign minister who had repeatedly assured him that the West had no stomach for war. For a long moment the two sat in stunned silence, but the die was cast and German Panzers were already on the move.

The deal with the Russians and the speed of Poland's collapse had shocked us in Shanghai, but during the following months of inactivity we convinced ourselves that the real battles lay ahead and that when they came, the war would surely take a different turn. But we were wrong, and like much of the world we watched in dismay as, the following May, German armies easily circumvented the defenses of the French, rolled over neutral Belgium and Holland, and forced France to surrender in little more than a month. Everything seemed to be going Hitler's way. In the summer, Italy entered the war on the

German side, and Japan signed a Tripartite Pact that, Hitler hoped, would keep the United States at bay. Yugoslavia was occupied in April of 1941, Crete fell to the Germans in May, and Norway and Denmark were firmly under Hitler's control. In North Africa his best general, Erwin Rommel, was chasing the British across the desert and even Cairo was at risk.

In Shanghai, the optimists were hard pressed to find a silver lining amid so much unmitigated bad news, but strangely I cannot recall that anyone truly believed that Hitler might actually win the war. That was too awful to contemplate. Perhaps our fervent wishes had merely become father to our thoughts, but if there were true, unwavering believers in Britain's beleaguered cause anywhere, it most certainly must have been we refugees in Shanghai. Britain's miraculous escape from Dunkirk was widely welcomed as a critical success for our side, and when the defiant Churchill took over as prime minister and the RAF held off the Germans in the air, the optimists were back to insist that all would still turn out well.

The invasion of Russia in June of 1941 was the cause for a brief moment of euphoric hope that a major change was finally at hand, but we were plunged back into the depths of disappointment and near-despair when Russian defeats turned into a sustained rout along the entire eastern front. The Soviet alliance had been revealed as a temporary tactical diversion and Hitler had finally embarked on his long-cherished crusade for Lebensraum in the East. With a massed army 3.5 million strong, he had unleashed his Blitzkrieg against his Soviet partners, intent on defeating them with lightning strikes and overwhelming force.

Thus he drove forward throughout the fall of 1941, deeper and deeper into the vastness of Russia, unprepared for the snow and ice, his supply lines stretched thin but scoring success upon success over the Soviet enemy, which was fighting heroically but unprepared for the force of his attack.

These were dramatic and frightening events and they would finally have a major effect even in our distant part of the world, none of it good. War in the Pacific was now looming as an ominous possibility as well.

In the United States, Japan had never been particularly popular, while China's defense against the Japanese invaders had evoked much sympathy. When Japan had occupied France's Indochinese colonies, attitudes hardened perceptively on both sides and U.S.–Japanese tensions escalated. Japan was dependent on imports for nearly 90 percent of its oil and many other vital raw materials, but the United States had imposed an embargo against their export and attempted to use a combination of persuasion and pressure to induce the Japanese to pull back in China. Japan, however, refused to yield, because the real issue was a fundamental difference of attitudes and worldviews between the two countries. America remained wedded to Wilsonian concepts of territorial integrity, open markets, commercial opportunity, and the rule of international law. To an aggressive, militaristic, and expansionary Japan intent on a dominant role in the Far East, this implied frustration of fundamental goals and maintenance of a status quo favoring the West. Neither side was yet ready to go to war, but the standoff continued throughout 1941. By fall, rumors of an inevitable armed conflict could no longer be ignored, and we watched anxiously as Western consulates —the ultimate symbols of our protection—reduced their staffs, and expatriates were urged to go home. By October, even the small Allied military garrisons were being withdrawn, with only two tiny gunboats, one British and one American, left behind as a symbolic force.

Shortly after our arrival, my ever-law-abiding parents had dutifully checked in at the German Consulate of Shanghai and presented their passports, emblazoned with the red J (for "Jew"). They believed they were still German citizens and assumed that it was the proper thing to do. Thankfully, the Consulate had reported this orderly initiative back home, informing Gestapo headquarters in Berlin that "the Jew Ewald Israel Blumenthal and his family, erstwhile of Berlin" had arrived in Shanghai.

Two years later, the long since expired passports were still in our hands—but only as a reminder of a closed chapter. By then, the Nazis had officially decreed that we were Germans no more. Now we were stateless, and with our protectors heading for home, we were isolated, helpless, and afraid. If war came to our part of the world, how would we—abandoned to the control of Germany's ally in the Far East—survive?

The Honkou Ghetto

"*Shanghai Ghetto*: Back by popular demand." Almost sixty-five years later, in California, the local Palm Springs *Desert Sun*, is advertising another week's run of "a great film about a life you never knew existed." During the last year or two, this one-and-a-half-hour documentary has played to large audiences in movie theaters across the United States. Now the film is back in this small resort town for the second or third time, and again I am puzzled and surprised that so many turn out to see it, even on this weekday afternoon.

I have often wondered why the Shanghai refugee community's brief life in the Honkou ghetto—no more than a footnote in the history of Nazi crimes and Holocaust survival—should hold so much fascination for others. Surely none of us confined there would have dreamed that we would one day be so interesting to the outside world and that we would generate a veritable flood of articles, books, exhibitions, academic conferences, and even a full-length documentary film. Is it because ours is one of the more unlikely stories of survival in an especially exotic place, or is there another explanation?

On the screen appear the familiar images of old Shanghai, and the faces of seventy-year-olds I knew when they were young two generations ago, telling their stories to an engrossed American audience. One of them is Betty Grebenschikoff, one of my neighbors on Chusan Road, the "Broadway" of the ghetto and heart of the area some called Little Vienna. Now well past middle age, she takes us on a personal tour behind the façade of twenty-first-century Shanghai's gleaming skyscrapers to her dilapidated old house, still standing in all its decaying glory, and into the small, squalid room where she spent the war years with her parents. Betty and the others on the screen are getting along in years but they are remarkably lively and animated as they recall the poverty, bad food, and hunger, vermin, and illness, being stateless and forsaken, the unpredictability of the Japanese, and the occasional kindnesses of our long-suffering Chinese neighbors. Suddenly I realize that in their stories about life in a strange, unhealthy and inhospitable place, what comes through is not just the deprivation but something stronger and surprisingly positive, a certain nostalgia, an undertone of warmth and pride in the schools and sports, the religious life, hospitals, soup kitchens, cafés, theaters, cabarets, and all the other makeshift institutions of self-help in our improbable Far East ghetto community. And I ask myself whether the audience senses it, as well—if, perhaps, this is the real explanation for the continuing appeal of our story.

The worst phase of our Shanghai exile began when, in 1943, the Japanese military ordered all Jewish refugees to move to Honkou. Honkou bore little resemblance to the ghettos of old Europe or to the lethal Nazi ones in Poland. Rather, it was a more benign but unique Japanese creation blandly called a "Designated Area." For us it was simply "the District." It existed only for twenty-seven months, had no walls, no barbed wire or other barriers around it, and one had to look closely on a map to find its exact boundaries (although we "inmates" certainly knew them well!).

Nor were we tightly sealed off from the rest of Shanghai. For one thing, there were few Japanese guards, and evading our less-than-stalwart Auxiliary charged with keeping us inside was not difficult. Furthermore, a lot more Chinese than Jews continued to live in Honkou; they could come and go as they pleased, and we intermingled freely with them. And, at least in theory, it was possible to get permission to leave the District for work or some other purpose deemed "legitimate" by our Japanese masters though, in practice, this eventually became so capricious and time-consuming that many never tried and the others threw in the towel sooner or later. As to sneaking out illegally, surprisingly few did so. The refugees, after all, were Central Europeans and remained ridiculously law-abiding even under unjust and degrading conditions. "The law is the law" my Prussian father would observe with a shrug, reflecting a widely held view. The punishment, moreover, meant confinement in polluted cells where infection with life-threatening illnesses was a high probability and which few were willing to risk. When all is said and done, it was a miserable ghetto all the same.

It hit us suddenly. At first, after the outbreak of war in the Pacific, nothing much had changed except that economic conditions worsened and life generally became more difficult. International businesses closed and jobs disappeared, rice and basic foodstuffs grew scarce, and prices escalated. During 1942 some British, American, and other enemy nationals were repatriated and the rest interned. The war news was anything but encouraging. In Europe, the Germans had resumed their advance along the entire Russian front and penetrated deep into the Caucasus. In Asia, Japan had followed up the attack on Pearl Harbor by quickly seizing Hong Kong and Singapore, driving the Americans out of the Philippines, occupying Malaysia and parts of the Dutch East Indies, and in the first great sea battle appeared to have won a victory over the U.S. Navy in the Java Sea. There was precious little for us to cheer about, except that at least we felt reassured that our personal situation under Japanese occupation was relatively stable and that neutrals and stateless Westerners like ourselves would be left alone.

That, however, proved a painful illusion. Toward the end of 1942, the first disquieting rumors of ominous developments had begun to circulate, but rumors were common in wartime Shanghai and little attention had been paid to them. All the more reason, therefore, that the short Proclamation concerning stateless refugees that suddenly descended on us through the newspapers and over the radio on February 18, 1943, would hit us like a bolt out of the blue. Signed by the Shanghai commanders of the Japanese Army and Navy, it ordered all refugees—those who had come to Shanghai after 1937—to move their businesses and residences into a "designated area" in Honkou within ninety days, and thereafter to leave the area only with the express prior permission of the authorities.

The Proclamation was a devastating bombshell: short, its language cool and unemotional, and the word *Jew* never mentioned. The reason given was "military necessity," without further explanation, and violators were to be subject to "severe punishment." Hardly anyone believed that there wasn't more to the story. What military necessity could possibly require segregating only the Jewish refugees? There was much anxious speculation about the real plans and motives of the Japanese, but no one could come up with plausible answers.[87] For the moment, there was nothing to do but obey. A few refugees panicked, but most took the news with fatalistic calm, though no one doubted that the effect on us would be severe.

Roughly half the refugees already lived within the borders of the designated area, but for the other half, like us, there were serious practical and financial implications. Apart from the loss of businesses and jobs, the biggest problem was the relocation itself. The area into which we were ordered to move was small—no more than a mile or two of a few dozen run-down city blocks in the least appealing part of town, drab and already overcrowded with Chinese residents and Jewish refugees. Where we'd find shelter there was left up to us, and everyone scrambled frantically to comply. In most instances relocation meant "exchanging" a reasonable apartment in a decent part of town for a squalid, much inferior single room in some overcrowded and primitive house inside the District. Sometimes even this required bribes or usurious commissions to agents and go-betweens. But with our backs against the wall, choices were few. The *Heime* were overfilled, and the pressure on the existing fragile refugee infrastructure that had evolved there since 1938 was overwhelming.

For us, the forced move came at a bad time. My mother's textile sales had gradually evolved into a tolerable small business and after two uncomfortable years at the Kichigins, we had only recently taken the plunge and rented a small apartment of our own. Then came the war, which damaged her business severely, one consequence being the end of my schooling so that I could take a job as an errand boy for the munificent weekly wage of twenty Chinese dollars, the equivalent of roughly two dollars U.S. It was a pittance, but it helped with the grocery bills.

Then, in the spring of 1942, my parents' troubled marriage had dramatically collapsed. One day, without warning, my mother simply announced that she was leaving to move in with another man—a friend of the family, no less. My father, who had continued his discreet meanderings through the bedrooms of willing refugee ladies in the neighborhood, a not unusual situation in the unstable refugee environment, was nevertheless stunned and dismayed. For me it was a disheartening emotional shock as well. I was barely sixteen years old, and henceforth I was forced to make my way pretty much on my own.

It was in this highly unsettled situation that our transfer into the ghetto had to be faced. After much negotiating and many anxious moments, our apartment was exchanged for one tiny room for my father, sister, and myself, no more than a sort of wooden box stuck on the back of an uninviting Chusan Road house, into which some ten separate families were now crowded. There was no private bath for us and only one outside cold-water tap, but—luxury of luxuries—a real W.C. toilet, albeit shared by several families, and a small dark kitchen where we took turns cooking our meals. It was a miserable existence—our living standard dropped to rock bottom—yet we were still better off than some, and we had been spared the ignominy of the dormitories and communal kitchens of the *Heime*.

Fifty-nine Chusan Road would be my home for four years, and when I left this slum en route to San Francisco I hoped never to see it again. Little did I dream then that the house (it still stands there in all its squalid glory) would one day become a minor tourist attraction for the many visitors who come to view our erstwhile ghetto: today, a plaque affixed to its front by the authorities proudly notes that this is the place where the former U.S. Secretary of the Treasury W. Michael Blumenthal "resided" during the war.

In May 1942 I applied for my first pass, and for a while I continued to travel to my job as errand boy in a Swiss-owned chemical laboratory on the outside, negotiating each day what was now a lengthy one-hour commute, mainly on foot.

The Japanese Proclamation confronted our stunned community leaders with monumental problems for which they were ill prepared, and in 1942, after the outbreak of the Pacific War, the minutes of an emergency meeting of refugees and Russian Jewish leaders make somber reading.[88] Until the prior December, up to 8,000 refugees had been totally or in part dependent on assistance financed mainly through monthly transfers of U.S. $30,000 from the Jewish Joint Distribution Committee in New York.[89] According to the report, with nothing coming in, only enough money for four days of operations was left as of January 10. Daily rations had been curtailed to one bowl of soup and nine ounces of bread for each of the 4,000 neediest, while the rest had been cut off completely. The doctors were warning that this was a starvation diet and that unless improved, a large number of deaths were to be expected within a year. Five hundred local staff members could no longer be paid and were being asked to continue without salaries.

In the camps there was a severe shortage of soap and usable clothes, several inhabitants no longer washed or changed underwear, and lice were everywhere. Some unfortunates' clothes, hopelessly infested, had had to be burned and they could now be seen wandering around the Honkou streets stigmatized in garments made from old jute bags. Their self-respect gone, a few had even resorted to begging, with an attendant risk of deep psychological problems. Some children were no longer coming to school because they lacked suitable shoes and clothing.

Eventually the crisis had been eased somewhat when an emergency temporary relief plan was approved by the Japanese. It involved borrowing locally from private sources against a guarantee of repayment from New York after the war. Supplemented with other self-help measures and stringent savings, this had allowed Honkou to survive from month to month, but the fundamental issue of a critical lack of resources, and a decline of living standards to rock-bottom levels remained unresolved.

A year later, with the impending influx of additional thousands into Honkou, an already serious situation now threatened to become desperate. The refugees were expected to administer their own affairs, but without money and critical resources in an overcrowded unhealthy place subject to the whims of the Japanese, the obstacles were enormous. The 18,000 refugees being crowded into this narrow area were anything but a homogenous group, but comprised a wide spectrum of social, cultural, educational, and religious backgrounds. Some were devoutly orthodox, many were not; others had moved far away from their nominal religion, and a few weren't even Jewish at all. They came from diverse countries—Germany, Austria, Poland, Hungary, and Czechoslovakia—and ranged from highly trained professionals to those with limited education and working-class backgrounds. Smooth self-governance of so complex a mixture at extremely close quarters became a formidable challenge. A few refugees had personal savings, and access to better food and basic amenities considered "luxuries" out of reach of most others, thus raising the specter of internal tensions bred by envy, jealousies, or worse. Even before the influx of additional thousands, there had been a lot of in-fighting and political dissension in Honkou, and it could now be expected to get a lot worse.

Survival

Looking back on the next two and a half ghetto years, it is remarkable that so diverse a group of poor and bedraggled European Jews, cast adrift in China under tough conditions in the midst of war, nevertheless succeeded in establishing a viable, self-sufficient and reasonably well-functioning community with institutions and facilities that bear comparison to those even of larger towns in Europe and America. When the war came to an end, the Honkou refugees were running decent schools, there were active sports facilities for the young, religious institutions flourished, doctors took care of the sick, a hospital functioned adequately, and even the poorest had enough food to survive. There was music and theater, there were cabarets, lending libraries thrived, and hundreds of small shops, restaurants, and cafés made life tolerable and kept the community together.

Not all had gone smoothly, of course, and not everyone had coped well. Along with dedication, commitment, and constructive community action, there had also been selfishness, betrayal, venality, and failures. Honkou had brought out the best—and the worst—but in the end the better had prevailed. There were no mass suicides, there was no mass starvation, no major criminality, and no general breakdown of manners and morals. The dignity of the community had been preserved and we emerged thin and undernourished but otherwise in good spirits, physically and emotionally intact.[90]

The details of this remarkably successful response to great challenges under emergency conditions in a hostile environment have been told (and studied) many times.[91] It was the product of a wide range of individual reactions and strategies for personal survival, and in many ways these were the key to our group's perseverance. Each of us had to confront the same problems of daily life in the District—to deal with the holes in our stomachs, our shoes, and our lives, to tackle the many small indignities of a marginal ghetto existence, and confront the ever present nagging fears and uncertainties about the future. We had to do things we'd never dreamed of and for which many were neither prepared nor equipped. Mostly everyone was on his own in coping with these challenges, but sometimes only community support and group cooperation were the answer. None of it came easily, and it was always necessary to draw on inner resources and to never lose the will to make it.

The functioning of a viable economic and social community infrastructure depended on those who had the imagination, talents, strengths, and community commitment to carry the less well equipped along, and Honkou was fortunate that there were a sufficient number of talented people who rose to the occasion. Even a rudimentary ghetto economy required enough people contributing some value-added, and entrepreneurs, risk takers, and traders who could make the money "go round" and attract some from outside. Wartime support for the neediest funded by outside aid wouldn't have sufficed without supplemental self-help measures from within. Religious and cultural institutions as emotional support systems in a time of need couldn't have functioned without pooled efforts.

In Honkou we had our share of the weak and helpless and of others too selfish to play a part. But special circumstances can also bring out the unexpected best in ordinary people. At various times in my later life, in business and in politics, I would make that discovery time and again. The experience of the ghetto was the first and most noteworthy example of this.

Among the many memorable people I met there, one man in particular impressed me deeply. Eli was only a few years older than I and much of our time together was spent around the dormitory in one of the *Heime* he called home. The room was small and cramped with only enough space for thirty-six double-decker bunks around a large wooden table. The men who lived there were a highly diverse group. In their prior lives some had been professionals with academic degrees, others had been business people or lower level employees, and some had working class backgrounds like Eli, a waiter who had left school in Berlin at age fifteen.

What united these men living in that dingy Wayside Road *Heim* was the one thing they now had in common: all were single, without families, penniless in Shanghai, and among the least well placed. As different as their education and status had been in their previous lives, as different now were their responses to the challenges of their reduced state. Some took care of themselves and worked every day; others grew indolent, let themselves go, and spent their time mainly cadging for money, cigarettes, and food. A handful hardly got out of their beds at all. Dirty, unkempt, and apathetic, they lived mainly on handouts of leftovers from their roommates.

My friend Eli was one of the youngest in that room, but he had become their undisputed de facto leader who kept them going. He had arrived in Shanghai still in his teens, inexperienced and destitute, without a word of English, speaking only the distinctive argot of East Berlin laced with generous portions of robust Yiddish slang. His parents had expected to follow him but never made it. Though he didn't know it then, he would never see them again.

He lacked the formal resources of some in the community, but he had something a great deal more precious—resourcefulness, physical and mental toughness, personal discipline, and an exuberant will to live and to succeed. He was brash, cynical, sometimes ruthless, but mostly kind, cheerful, and occasionally very funny, and I never ceased marveling at how many balls he was able to juggle at the same time. When he could, he worked as a waiter, and when he couldn't, he found other means to earn his way. Ranging all over the District, he would ferret out the cheapest supplies of cigarettes, toiletries, and items of scarce food, and "retail" them—a single cigarette or half ounce of sausage at a time.

The two of us could not have been more different, but I admired him enormously for his spirit, inner toughness, strength, and the example he set for others. He impressed me all the more, because I had also seen in that room the broken men who hadn't been able to cope. For them, education, status, titles, and prior honors had meant nothing when the going got tough—another valuable lesson I would never forget.

It was men and women like Eli who made our little community a functioning success, who maintained their dignity and their spirits, who kept trying, helped others and never gave up. They are the ones who kept our economy alive. Rereading our newspaper of those years, the *Shanghai Jewish Chronicle*, I marvel at the variety and ingenuity of what they did. "I buy and repair old zippers," announced one. "Defective lighters repaired, neckties 'refreshed,' old shoes bought and sold, English lessons given, learn Esperanto from me for a brighter future," advertised others.[92]

Those with a little capital opened stores and cafés where one could pass the afternoons, keep warm in winter, and gossip about the war over a single glass of tea. Sixty separate operettas and plays were produced, at least eight separate newspapers were published at various times, and possibly more. There were benefits for the "Kitchen Fund," to help the poorest, and there were those who worked in the hospital for little or nothing and ran the sports events for the young.

That is how the 18,000 refugees lived and survived. Two and a half years were not a long time, but for us they often seemed like a lifetime, and without our everyday heroes Honkou might have turned out a great deal worse.

Rescue

We were isolated and cut off from reliable information, but by the spring of 1945 we knew that after victory in Europe, the defeat of Japan was only a question of time. That, however, was the critical issue: how long would it take, and with how much more fighting before the inevitable surrender? Would we be caught up in the final struggle if the still largely intact Japanese military in China refused to lay down their arms when the order was given? What would happen if Shanghai became a battleground at the last moment, or if rioting broke out once the occupying troops withdrew?

What we knew was spotty and ambiguous, and in the early summer months of 1945 tensions in the ghetto were on the rise. By July, military activity around Shanghai had visibly increased, and it did not improve our state of mind that thirty-one refugees had been killed in one of the American air raids over Honkou, along with many Japanese and untold numbers of Chinese.

No one fully realized how hopeless Japan's situation had become and how near we were to the end. The Japanese-controlled media were no help. There was no mention that American planes were daily bombing Japan virtually at will, or that 800 Superfortresses had done major damage on a single day, August 2. What they did report that day was that Japan still insisted that all of East Asia had to be "free of Anglo-American colonial exploitation" before the war was ended, quoting Premier Suzuki's statement that "Japan will take no notice of Allied surrender terms." Even the dropping of atomic bombs over Hiroshima and Nagasaki on August 6 to 8 was passed over blandly in the press as a mere firebombing, and no one realized the enormous significance. Only the startling news on August 8 that Russia too had entered the war against Japan and begun operations with a giant pincer movement from the east, north, and west against Japanese forces in Manchuria, provided the first tangible hint of dramatic new developments, though for the moment it further increased our uncertainty about what lay ahead.

When the end came, it therefore came with a dramatic suddenness. On August 15, the first rumors of a Japanese surrender swept through the ghetto like wildfire but for many it still seemed too good to be true, just another Honkou "canard." A day later, however, all Japanese soldiers and civilians suddenly disappeared from the streets, the media were silent, and an eerie quiet enveloped us. Then the confirmation came, pandemonium broke out, and the real celebrating began.

It was true: Japan had surrendered, the war was over, and we were free! Two days later the first Allied rescue planes landed on a military airfield near the city, and the strong, healthy American soldiers who descended from them were worshipped and welcomed as emissaries from that other world of our dreams, with an awe difficult to convey.

Soon our thoughts turned to the fate of those left behind in Europe, and to our own chances of leaving Shanghai. Surely all doors would now be opened to us, we assured ourselves. But the reality was somber. The news of the deaths in Europe came quickly; finding a country to admit us would take a great deal longer.

Not surprisingly, the question the Shanghai survivors (and subsequent historians) have continued to ask is, What was the real explanation for Japan's special treatment of the Jewish refugees from Hitler's Germany? To this day no fully satisfactory explanation has ever been given. With so many diverse groups of non-enemy nationals under their control in Shanghai, why did they imprison only the 18,000 powerless refugees from Europe? And why did they then leave us to fend for ourselves, do us no further harm, and treat us with relative indifference? Tokyo professes no longer to know, has refused access to its archives, and claims that nothing of relevance exists in Japanese files. But it is doubtful that this is the full story. One reason for Japan's reluctance to come clean may simply be understandable embarrassment over what, with hindsight, were probably irrational decisions made in the context of confused wartime thinking and the shifting fortunes of war.

Much remains conjecture, but enough evidence has emerged from postwar recollections and testimony of individual actors to provide fairly solid circumstantial insights into what happened. In sum, as a result of the interplay of many forces, what the Japanese military did—and did not do—appears to have been the result of at least three principal factors: a unique, if distorted Japanese view of Jews in general, attempts at once to appease and resist Nazi pressures, and, finally, the changing fortunes of the war itself.

Japan's peculiar attitude toward Jews explains much. Most Japanese were never anti-Semites; until the early years of the century they had rarely encountered Jews, and few Jews had lived in their country. In Japanese eyes, Jews—like non-Jews—were Europeans, and the difference was poorly understood. Their first significant exposure to a "Jewish issue" was, if anything, highly favorable. In the Russo-Japanese War of 1904 to 1905, it had been Jacob Schiff, the senior partner of New York's Jewish investment banking firm Kuhn Loeb, and a Jew, who had stepped forward and alone floated large war loans to finance Japan's war debts. Tokyo had been grateful, had never forgotten it, and had drawn the exaggerated conclusion that Jewish finance was all-powerful, and that it was to Japan's advantage to court rather than to offend Jews. Even during World War II there were those in Tokyo who held firmly to the myth of Jewish power. That, in the end, may have saved us.

But that was only one side of the story. A significant Jewish population had come under the control of the Japanese military in Manchuria during the twenties and thirties. It is there that a small number of intensely nationalistic younger officers became self-styled "Jewish experts" and were first exposed to and infected by the virulent anti-Semitism of local White Russians. They studied anti-Semitic literature and translated it into Japanese, including notably the *Protocols of the Elders of Zion*, the fraudulent tract manufactured by the Czarist secret police alleging a Jewish conspiracy for world domination. Though professing to be "anti-Semites," these officers, who wielded great independent power, nevertheless concluded that rather than oppressing the dangerous Jews, they should be watched, controlled, and utilized for Japan's benefit in the development of Manchuria, and as hostages to exert influence on worldwide Jewry in favor of Japan.

It was a different view from Tokyo's, though the conclusion these officers drew was not altogether dissimilar. In China they encountered the wealth and power of the great Sephardic financiers of Hong Kong and Shanghai, and that only strengthened their view of Jewish financial power. The result, at least for a while, was a puzzling juxtaposition of increasingly anti-Semitic sentiments expressed by some of the Japanese military in China on the one hand, and on the other their simultaneous policy favoring our admission into Shanghai, and their decision to let us settle in the Honkou area under their control.

The outbreak of war in the Pacific changed all that. Now Jews had lost their value, whether as hostages or as bridge builders to powerful Jewish financiers, perhaps even to the U.S. Secretary of the Treasury, Henry Morgenthau himself. Moreover, while the policy regarding Jews was accordingly being reexamined in the spring and summer of 1942, Japan was also reaching the high-water mark of her advances in Asia. It was a time when the Germans seemed unstoppable, and from Tokyo and Shanghai it appeared to many Japanese that the Axis was on the way to winning the war. As far as Japan's military in China was concerned, the issue was no longer how to use the Jews, but rather how best to neutralize and control them. Harsher treatment could now be meted out with relative impunity. And finally, with the prestige of their German Axis partners and respect for their power and successes running high, the so-called "Jewish experts" were now more willing recipients of eager advice on the matter from Gestapo agents specially dispatched by Himmler to Shanghai. Postwar testimony leaves little doubt that in 1942 this was another significant factor affecting the internal debate about our fate.[93]

The German influence mattered. Since the middle of the nineteenth century, there had always been a sizable German community in Shanghai, and during the war it numbered some 2,500 persons. Most were businessmen and traders, and in their outlook they did not differ greatly from others in the expatriate community. A Shanghai Nazi Party had been organized even before Hitler came to power, but the number of true believers and active supporters had always remained small.

The Party leadership made strenuous efforts to discourage contact with Jews, and there were strict orders to stay away from Honkou and not to buy from them. Compliance, however, had always been spotty. Even party members frequented Jewish shops when it suited them, and some refugees peddling goods outside the ghetto counted Germans among their best customers. When the wife of one of the Nazi leaders was denounced for having been observed shopping in Honkou stores, her laconic reply was revealing: "Would you like me to list the wives of other Party members who have also been buying there?" she asked.[94]

Yet though the relationship of Shanghai's Germans to the refugees was mixed, that of the top Nazi leadership and the scores of Gestapo officials, agents, spies, and propagandists dispatched to wartime Shanghai decidedly was not. It is telling testimony to the determined fanaticism of Himmler and the long arms of the Gestapo, that they saw fit in the middle of their life-or-death struggle in Europe to invest substantial resources pursuing us even to this far corner of the earth. Postwar testimony showed that liaising with the Japanese, spying on them, and propagandizing for Germany was only a part of their assigned mission, and that disseminating anti-Semitism, observing the refugees, and seeking to influence Japanese policy against them was very much another.

The key actors, reporting directly to Himmler in Berlin, were two SS officers—first Gerhard Kahner and later Fritz Huber and, to a lesser extent, Baron Jesco von Puttkammer, another high-ranking Nazi. A particularly ominous role seems to have been played by the more deadly and notorious Josef Meisinger, an SS Colonel and long-time Nazi attached to the Tokyo Embassy, who made several visits to Shanghai beyween 1941 and 1942 apparently to pressure the local Japanese to single us out for "special treatment."[95]

The full story of Meisinger's activities in Shanghai remains murky and unsubstantiated to this day, but the fate of refugees appears to have been one of his special interests. Some months before the Honkou Proclamation, Shanghai's Jewish leaders had been secretly warned that deadly steps against the refugees were being considered and a sympathetic Japanese official present at these meetings later testified that Meisinger's suggestions included surrounding the Honkou ghetto on the day of Rosh Hashanah, the Jewish New Year, and deporting the Jews en masse—on ships to be sunk in the China Sea, or to be left in abandoned salt mines to starve to death, or placed in concentration camps on the Yangtze River island of Chongming. The Germans, Meisinger is said to have assured the Japanese, would be glad to take care of the details.[96] Whether the Japanese officers seriously considered such drastic actions is not known; that they gave a polite hearing to these ideas appears not unlikely.

The reality is that none of it happened (and that, fortunately, none of it was known to us at the time). The Japanese were not fanatical Jew-haters like their German partners, and the likelihood that they would have agreed to murder us in cold blood may always have been low. No doubt to the chagrin of the Nazi zealots, the lesser decision merely to segregate the refugees from Europe in the Honkou ghetto, leaving the rest of Shanghai's Russian Jewish and Sephardic communities alone, appears to have been their compromise solution.

By then the fortunes of war had decidedly turned against both

Germany and Japan. At Stalingrad, the Germans had suffered a major defeat. Neither Moscow nor Leningrad had been taken, and along the entire Russian front the Germans had been thrown on the defensive. Rommel's advance had been reversed at El Alamein, and with the Allied landing in French northwest Africa, final German defeat in North Africa was only a matter of time. Germany's situation was growing more precarious everywhere. On February 18, 1943—the very day of the Stateless Refugee Proclamation—Goebbels had declared "total war," thereby acknowledging the reversal of German fortunes.

In Asia, there had been reversals as well. Japan had lost two great naval battles at Midway and the Coral Sea, and the United States had gone on the offensive, invading Guadalcanal and attacking in New Guinea and the Solomon Islands. The prospect of an Axis victory was receding, and the Japanese knew it. Once again it seemed the better part of wisdom not to risk offending world Jewry in a postwar world. From Tokyo, still in part under the spell of their belief in Jewish power, the Japanese order to their officers in China was to be cautious in whatever measures against us were taken: "You should be careful," Tokyo instructed, "that the measure should be carried out in no unnecessarily provocative manner . . ."[97]

For a while, the "Jewish experts" in Shanghai had largely been given a free hand. The order from Tokyo reining them in had come just in time. The final decision had been merely to segregate the refugees. Our subsequent careful treatment no doubt was a related consequence as well.

Stateless

When the Japanese left Shanghai, it was a time both of great sadness and of hope for a quick new beginning. The town, full of American soldiers and sailors, was booming again. Dollars were flowing, shelves were restocked with food, representatives from the United Nations and Jewish Relief organizations flew in to care for us, and many refugees found employment with the U.S. Armed Forces.

Life had become a great deal more tolerable, yet there was indescribable sadness when the terrible news emerged that only a small handful of friends and relatives had survived the Nazi Holocaust in Europe. No one had expected the dimensions of the disaster of the gas chambers and Hitler's machinery of death that were being revealed day after day, and the impact on the Shanghai ghetto of learning the full tragedy was devastating. Day after day, anxious crowds would gather around the United Nations lists that showed the names of the few found alive, who were anxiously searching for parents, siblings, and other loved ones. Virtually everyone was gone, and the prevailing mood was one of unmitigated hatred, fury, and despair. The very words *Germany* and *Germans* had become curse words. No one could bear the thought of going back to Europe. Now everyone, whether young or old, wanted to make a new beginning elsewhere—in Palestine, America, Australia, or South America—but not in Europe. Before the war, most of the doors had been closed to us, but now hope ran high that lessons had been learned and that the sheer number of victims would induce the Free World to help the survivors.

Yet the confident hope for prompt action would prove overly optimistic and for some it would take another four years before their exile in China ended. Even with the best of intentions, the reluctance to change laws and bureaucratic inertia against more liberal immigration policies continued for years, even in the postwar era, much as they had in the years before the war.

Late in 1945, I think it was in December, some four months after V-J Day, the issue was brought home to me in a very personal way. I was working for the U.S. Air Force at the time—as a warehouseman at seventy-five dollars a month—but all my thoughts were on leaving China, getting away and settling down somewhere to begin a new life. One day the newspaper carried an interview with a Canadian diplomat who had recently arrived in Shanghai to open the consulate there. "Canada is a vast and rich country," he was quoted as saying, "slightly larger than the United States and with a total population roughly that of the Greater New York City area." There were big postwar development plans, he said, and the doors were open for healthy young immigrants eager to help.

That got my attention in a hurry, and my imagination was set ablaze. Here, at last, was my chance, I thought. The very next day, I put on a clean shirt and my one good pair of shoes and presented myself at the Canadian consulate. I had carefully rehearsed my speech, and now I told the Consul how impressed I was with Canada—its size, vast sparsely populated spaces, and future prospects—and about my own ambitions and willingness to roll up my sleeves as a good Canadian. I was, I assured him, healthy and unencumbered, and exactly the kind of immigrant Canada seemed to want.

The conversation was going swimmingly, and the Consul seemed impressed. He wanted to know when I thought I might wish to leave, and I assured him that the sooner was the better, as far as I was concerned. The exact wording of his next question has stayed with me for the rest of my life: "May I inquire under what passport you intend to travel?" he asked. "I am a stateless refugee, a Displaced Person from Nazi Germany, and I have no passport," I explained. The United Nations would issue me a travel document, and with a Canadian visa, I added hopefully, traveling to Canada shouldn't be a problem.

I spoke virtually flawless English at the time, still with the slight British accent I had acquired in school. That seemed to have confused him. His attitude had now visibly changed, though it continued to be friendly. Being a stateless DP complicated matters just a bit, he informed me, but he urged me not to give up hope. Matters of this kind had to be referred to the Embassy at Chongqing. "Write them a letter and tell them your story, just as you have presented it to me. I am sure," he added hopefully, "for a young fellow like you it will receive the most careful attention."

Within days, and several drafts later, I had composed and mailed an impressive plea to Chongqing for admission to Canada, listing all the reasons why I thought Canada and I were a perfect match—and in less than a week a brief reply from the embassy was in my hands.

It came on beautiful blue paper emblazoned with the seal of Canada. My letter had greatly impressed the embassy, it said, and been—I remember these words exactly—"forwarded by diplomatic bag to Ottawa." An answer should be forthcoming within a month. By "diplomatic bag," no less! No question, I told my friends, for me Shanghai would soon be history. I was off to Canada.

Promptly a month later, the eagerly awaited letter arrived from Chongqing on the same impressive letterhead. "We regret to inform you," the short reply read, "that under present laws you are ineligible for admission to Canada." Had I been the holder of a British passport, the answer would have been different. Even at the end of 1945, admitting a stateless DP was a different story.[98]

It would take another twenty months of disappointment, frustration, and anxious waiting before a door would finally open to me, and then it would be the United States that let me in.

On December 22, 1945, President Truman signed a Refugee Admission Order to "facilitate full immigration [for qualified DPs] to the United Staters under existing laws." The bureaucracy was being ordered to remove the old roadblocks forthwith, and "to speed and simplify the issuance of visas." Bureaucratic wheels turn slowly even in the best of times. It took another year and a half before a young U.S. vice counsel put his stamp on my UN travel document, a thrilling moment I can never forget. In September 1947, my sister Stefanie and I left Shanghai for San Francisco on the S.S. *Marine Adder*, a converted U.S. troop transport.

THE FIFTIES
Postwar USA:
Apprenticeship Years

San Francisco

In the thirties, the event that changed history was the rise of Adolf Hitler, and the forties were dominated by the Second World War. In the fifties the Cold War and the nuclear stand-off between East and West would set the course of the twentieth century for years to come.

The fifties were years of transition from a world at war to one dominated by the confrontation between two competing power blocs and ideologies, from a colonial to a postcolonial world, and for the testing of the newly established United Nations and its affiliated institutions. Among the Western powers, it was a time when a network of institutional arrangements was put in place to manage their alliance, rebuild Europe, and take the first steps toward European economic integration.

It was a decade of rebuilding, of progress and big changes, of important discoveries and great initiatives like the Marshall Plan, but also of multiple challenges and crises. The Cold War intensified, and with a Communist coup in Czechoslovakia, a revolt in Hungary, and the creation of two Germanys, the division of Europe became complete. Armed conflicts on the peninsula of Korea, in Southeast Asia, and in the Middle East cost many lives. Elsewhere there was the rise of Communist China, Sputnik, and space, Soviet challenges and Western counter moves, espionage maneuverings, and East–West competition in Africa, Asia, and Latin America.

The fifties were also major transition years in the United States. The war had greatly altered American life and the transformation continued at a rapid pace under the impact of fast-moving domestic and international events. It was a time of unprecedented affluence and rising living standards, and of profound changes in the way Americans lived and played, in their relations to one another, and in what they expected from life and from their government.

Periods of fundamental change, however positive, always cause uncertainty and often result in intense political controversy, for even with economic prosperity there are bound to be winners and losers. The fifties in America were no different, and fierce partisan battles were fought almost continuously between liberals and conservatives, North and South, and within and between the two major parties over economic and social policy and civil rights. The confrontation with Communism at home and abroad inflamed partisan spirits and gave rise to emotional battles over protection against internal subversion on the one hand, and the preservation of civil liberties on the other.

In the fifties I became an American. After stepping ashore in San Francisco on September 24, 1947, I at once plunged deeply into American life and began my own personal transformation. I had come with only about sixty-five dollars in my pocket, but I was young, confident, and optimistic. Encumbered by neither fear nor doubt, my state of mind matched that of the country. I had arrived in the United States at a particularly dynamic and exciting time when much was in flux, progress and prosperity were in the air, and lots of returning veterans about my age were making a new start just as I was.

For me, it was an unforgettable time of education, discovery, and personal growth during which I became a citizen, married, and started a family. Eager to know the United States, I took every opportunity to travel and explore my adopted country. During the fifties I lived on the East and West coasts, traversed the continent several times, attended three very different universities, became involved in politics, and had my first real experience with American corporate life.

I had come to America at a moment when the country was growing and changing, when much was in flux and when there was plenty of opportunity for my own personal development. I felt deeply about the issues of the day and eagerly participated in the political debates. Thus I plunged into the academic and business worlds, soon felt a part of them, and became actively involved in politics at the local level—never expecting that before long I would have the opportunity to play a larger role on a wider stage.

During this period I also returned to Germany for what would be the first of many postwar visits. The brown uniforms and Nazi flags were gone, and the country was very different from the one I had left, but I now felt detached and alienated from it. Germany had become a foreign land. Many things felt distant at one level, even while eerily familiar at another, and I returned with a better understanding of how firm my commitment to America had already become.

Postwar Boom Years

The late forties marked the beginning of a decade of dynamic U.S. growth. Not just industry but policy makers and most others were initially surprised by the strength of the postwar economy. At the end of the war, the challenge of shifting to peacetime conditions had loomed large, and the two most hotly debated issues—jobs for returning veterans and how to substitute civilian demand for the falloff in defense expenditures—had been viewed with apprehension. Could wartime full employment survive the return to peace?

Of the more than 12 million men and women in uniform at the end of the war, all but a million and a half were subject to rapid demobilization, and the main concern was finding enough employment opportunities for all. Many believed that rising unemployment and an early recession were a real possibility. At the peak of the war, government spending for goods and services had reached $89 billion and accounted for 42 percent of the GNP, but on a single day after the defeat of Japan, war contracts worth $23 billion were cancelled overnight, and by 1947 the share of defense spending in the GNP had dropped to less than 10 percent. It was hard to see how so large a cut could be absorbed quickly or smoothly, and the conventional wisdom had it that a possibly painful and prolonged period of transition lay ahead. A few contrarians disagreed—former Vice President Henry Wallace predicted 60 million jobs by 1950—but this was not in line with mainstream thinking and had been dismissed as excessively optimistic.

Much like forecasting the weather, predicting economic trends remains as much art as science, even in today's world of sophisticated mathematical modeling and supercomputers. That would prove very much the case in the late forties. As the ample columns of "Help Wanted" ads greeting me in San Francisco showed, the experts were wrong and their fears unwarranted. The conventional wisdom of a slow adjustment was off the mark, and Wallace's seat-of-the-pants buoyant prediction came true in 1948, two years ahead of schedule. Private investment readily filled the gap of declining government expenditures, and if there was an issue with consumer demand it was that there was too much of it. The problem was not a lack of jobs but rising wages and prices. Even as millions of veterans reentered the labor force, unemployment stayed below 4 percent, except for the brief recession year of 1958. During the entire decade of the fifties, it would never rise above 5.5 percent.[99]

The prognosticators had failed to foresee several factors that combined to produce the economic good times of the postwar years: large wartime savings accounts waiting to be spent, a population boom, easy credit, government spending for veterans, highways, and education, and the stimulative effects of the Marshall Plan and European reconstruction. The returning soldiers and sailors were starting new families and wanted to enjoy the good life. During the war, $37 billion in personal savings had been accumulated, and now this money was flooding into housing, cars, refrigerators, clothing, new gadgets of all kinds including the novel TV sets, fancy food, travel, and vacations. And when the ready cash ran out, Americans bought on the cuff, and the banks were eager to accommodate them.

Entirely new industries sprang up overnight, and old ones

boomed. Prefabricated housing came into its own, and in the suburbs large tracts of new houses—the Levittowns—mushroomed. The builders were getting rich but couldn't keep up with the demand stimulated by liberal government-guaranteed loans for veterans. New housing starts in 1939 had reached their hitherto highest level in history with 515,000 units, but for much of the fifties they rarely dipped below 2,000,000.

During the war Detroit had turned from making passenger cars to the manufacture of trucks, jeeps, and tanks. But now the traditional love affair of Americans with the automobile was back, the open road beckoned, and everyone wanted new wheels. In the boom year of 1929, just before the Great Crash, there had been record new car sales of 4.4 million, a number never again equaled over the entire decade of the thirties, and some had said that it would never be. Yet by 1950, the old record was easily surpassed as Americans bought 6.6 million cars in a single year. This in turn stimulated the demand for new and better roads, and a construction boom ensued when the government, after several years of planning, launched a national Interstate Highway building program in the mid-fifties of unprecedented size and scope.[100] In time, the ten-year, $100 billion initiative would spawn tens of thousands of miles of new roads and superhighways, creating many new businesses and jobs, and contributing powerfully to postwar growth.

The boom of the postwar years was changing the face of the nation, and what had been a longterm trend toward declining population growth was sharply reversed. When I arrived in 1947, there were 144 million Americans; at the end of the fifties, partly due to an unprecedented postwar "baby boom," and partly to a liberalized policy of immigration that brought more than 3.5 million new Americans into the country by 1960, there were 180 million of them. Urbanization was the other big demographic change, with almost 70 percent of Americans living in urban areas at the end of the fifties, compared to only 56 percent before the war.

Economic growth and well-paying jobs were improving American living standards as never before. Total industrial production grew by almost 50 percent between 1950 and 1960, but prices rose only half as fast and average real weekly wages were twice as high as before the war. For the first time, more Americans were employed in service industries than in factories, where automation was substituting for unskilled labor and scoring major improvements in productivity.

A veritable revolution was also underway in education. Before the war many Americans still had only an elementary school education. Now most were at least high-school graduates, and enrollment in colleges and universities, spurred by the government-financed GI Bill of Rights, more than tripled from 1.5 million before the war to almost 5 million in 1965.

The effect of these remarkable developments on the pattern of American life was profound. The main issue now was no longer how to get a job, but how to sustain one's increased standard of living and enjoy its fruits. Unemployment and poverty had ceased to be the threat they had been in the thirties, and the preoccupation now was with consumption. Americans flocked to the burgeoning suburbia and sparkling new shopping malls, frequented chain restaurants and drive-in movies, and spent weekends shopping for new-fangled appliances, mowing their lawns, polishing the recently bought family car, and watching their favorite programs on TV.

Their values and habits were changing in many ways. Religion was still important, and church membership was high, but so was a record divorce rate. As the Kinsey Report, a much-discussed, path-breaking 50's study tackling a daring, heretofore unmentionable, subject matter showed, even American sexual mores—though never quite as conservative as had been believed—were loosening under the impact of the postwar consumer society. The role of women in American society was in flux, and, by the end of the decade, the availability of the birth control pill would prove another powerful factor in changing sexual mores. During the war, millions of women had entered the labor force for the first time, and now they were no longer content to return to their restricted traditional role of housewife and homemaker.

As one observer put it: "'Rosie the Riveter' isn't going back to emptying slop jars."[101]

In the fifties the United States was by far the richest country on earth. With only 6 percent of the world's population, Americans were producing one-third of its goods and services, and their standard of living was the envy of the world. Yet, though America was a prosperous nation, the country wasn't necessarily a universally happy one. Exuberance and optimism were mixed in equal parts with anxiety, political conflict, and racial strife. The war had transformed many aspects of American life for the better but had also created many new problems, and the rapid pace of change, together with challenges abroad, led to major disagreements about where the country was headed and what the right policies and priorities ought to be.

Enormous gaps remained between the rich and the poor, and not everyone was benefitting equally from the new affluence. In the cities there were still massive slums and substandard housing, and in the hills of Appalachia and the dustbowls of the Midwest, there remained major pockets of poverty and under-development. Furthermore, while President Roosevelt's New Deal had redressed the worst deficiencies and provided a minimal level of protection against the risks of unemployment, illness, and old age, the social safety net remained highly inadequate. As prices rose, labor unions clamored for higher wages, while industry adamantly opposed them, and powerful conservative forces fought most proposals to meet the grievances of those least able to fend for themselves.

The most glaring blot on American life, however, was the persistence of pervasive racial discrimination. During the war, many blacks[102] had moved north to work in the defense plants of Pittsburgh, Detroit, Chicago, and the West coast, and others had served honorably in the armed forces. Now their demands for more equal treatment were growing insistent, and larger numbers of whites were beginning to listen to them, but powerful elements continued to resist them fiercely.

When I arrived in San Francisco, postwar America was still a White Man's country and blacks remained largely disenfranchised. Only a small number voted or were allowed a part in the political process, and most were still rigidly excluded from major institutions of power and influence, including the better colleges and universities. Many intellectuals were anything but satisfied with American postwar society, and, paradoxically, it was the very affluence of the country and its side effects that worried them. They deplored the blind consumerism, and what they considered the drift toward a mass culture dedicated to unfettered material pursuit, rootlessness, self-satisfied conformity, and a lack of concern about race discrimination and the American underclass. Many in America were celebrating fifties affluence, but there were liberals and social critics who saw in its banality and injustices a "dismal decade."

Thus, the mood in America was far from uniformly happy. Exuberance and self-satisfaction on the one hand were mixed with dissatisfaction and anxiety on the other. And if the domestic situation had elements of both, the international environment had its own risks and problems and contributed additional fears about where the country was headed.

Americans had waged war with single-minded determination, hoping that victory against the aggressors in Europe and Asia would lead to a peace in which the wartime allies would work together in harmony. As early as 1941 in the Atlantic Charter, and on various occasions thereafter, President Roosevelt had laid out the American vision of an open postwar world devoid of power blocs or competing spheres of influence, and based on international cooperation, the right of self-determination, an end to colonialism, and the rule of international law under the new United Nations.

Yet most of the specifics had been left to be decided later. Under the pressure of more immediate wartime priorities, the British had reluctantly acquiesced to FDR's ideas, other colonial powers hadn't been asked, and the Soviet dictator, Stalin, had signaled from the beginning that he had his own ideas on the subject. Thus just as the hopes of an earlier U.S. president for a more just and orderly world had come to naught after the First World War, so Roosevelt's ideals quickly proved illusory after the second. By 1947, there was little doubt that what he had bequeathed to his successor was not a community of views about the shape of a peaceful postwar world, but the starkly different reality of conflict and confrontation, and a dangerous Cold War between the Soviet Union and the West. International cooperation among equals in an open world, self-determination, democracy, and freedom of choice were not Stalin's priorities, but expanding the Soviet sphere of influence and creating a large bloc of Communist satellite buffer states on his borders was.

Within a year after the end of hostilities in Europe, the world looked very different from the one envisaged by Roosevelt. In his historic speech in Fulton, Missouri, in 1946, with President Truman sitting at his side, Winston Churchill had eloquently acknowledged this and denounced Soviet Russia's "expansive and proselytizing tendencies" and the establishment of undemocratic police states in East Europe behind what he said was "an Iron Curtain across the Continent." By 1947, Soviet domination over Poland and Eastern Europe had become a fact of life. The Soviets and the United States disagreed on virtually everything, and "containment"—the Western response to Soviet ambitions, and keeping Western Europe, China, Japan, and the Middle East outside the Soviet sphere—became the central element of U.S. foreign policy. To counter Soviet pressure on Greece and Turkey, an emergency aid program was put in place, and the vastly more ambitious Marshall Plan for the rebuilding of the Western European economies was announced just before I arrived in California.

In China, Mao Tse-tung's Communists were steadily extending their control, and in Indochina and elsewhere in Asia and Africa anticolonial nationalism became a factor in the Cold War. The United States still maintained its uneasy nuclear monopoly, though most realized that this was unlikely to be other than a temporary advantage. When the Soviet Union exploded its first hydrogen bomb in 1955, the risks of Cold War confrontations in a nuclear world had become a reality.

Over the next decade, before and after Stalin's death in 1953, crisis followed crisis, and with the creation of the NATO military alliance, the division of Europe into opposing camps became complete. A West German state in which Allied forces were permanently stationed was a fact of life, as was active U.S. support for Western European economic integration, as another bulwark against Soviet pressure followed. East–West disagreements evolved into often dangerous confrontations, sometimes with armed conflict by proxies, and on the Korean peninsula in a bloody war with direct American participation. In the 1948 Berlin airlift, Soviet efforts to dislodge the Western Allies from the erstwhile German capital were successfully countered, but China fell to the Communists a year later. In a divided Vietnam the two opposing sides coexisted in uneasy confrontation after the ouster of the French colonials, and all across the globe direct and proxy contests between the Western and Communist sides continued, and an arms race with no apparent letup grew ever more expensive.

For the United States, the fifties were a watershed period marking its end of innocence in world affairs. The old debates about internationalism versus isolation—so often the source of domestic political controversy—ceased to be an issue. To contain the Soviet Union and counter the spread of Communism involved confrontation and challenge in many places at once, and the United States became deeply involved in virtually every corner of the globe.

Nevertheless, the new American internationalism—the Marshall Plan, support for European unification, economic aid for developing countries in Africa, Asia, and Latin America, military alliances, and Cold War confrontations—had as profound an impact on the domestic debate and the American political scene of the fifties as the old struggles between the isolationists and others ever had. To the battles over domestic social and economic policies now was added a sharp division of views over how to deal with friends and foes abroad, as well as the severe strains from a fanatical domestic anti-communist crusade by right-wing radicals against real or suspected subversives, spies, and their alleged fellow travelers. In the trading of accusations of insufficient vigilance and arguments about who was "soft" on Communists and who the patriot, basic notions of fairness and civil liberties came up against severe challenges.

Truman and Eisenhower

Three fundamental conflicts dominated U.S. politics throughout the late forties and fifties, under two presidents and two very different administrations: differing views about the role of government in dealing with economic and social problems; a bitter struggle over civil rights; and fierce controversy over protection against internal subversion.

Democrat Harry Truman and Republican Dwight Eisenhower, each occupied the White House for roughly the same length of time during this period and helped shape the debate. By family background and in their bedrock values they were remarkably alike. Yet in their personalities and outlook and the policies they pursued, they differed substantially.

Unlike Roosevelt, an Eastern blueblood with family wealth and a famous name, both Truman and Eisenhower were Midwesterners who had grown up not far from each other, one in Missouri and the other in Kansas. Both came from modest pioneering families who were no strangers to financial adversity[103] and both had spent years in relative obscurity on the public payroll.

Neither was an intellectual nor had much use for them, Ike once having defined one as "a man who takes more words than is necessary to say more than he knows,"[104] while Truman—the last president of the twentieth century not to have a college degree—was more comfortable with his poker-playing cronies than with Roosevelt's educated Ivy Leaguers. For both men, the move into the big time had come unexpectedly during the war. In Truman's case it was as a compromise choice for vice president in '44, while Eisenhower had been jumped over dozens of more senior officers as commander of U.S. forces in Europe. Neither had expected nor sought the move to the top, but both were smart and ambitious and hadn't hesitated to seize the opportunity when it came their way.

Yet it is the differences between them that mattered most. Though he had only a high-school education, Truman had read voraciously and was an avid autodidactic student of American history, who believed that the presidency was a place for active decision making to advance the welfare of the nation and its citizens. A lifelong partisan Democrat by conviction, he had an instinctive sympathy for the underdog, "for those that have been kicked around all their lives," as he once put it. Eisenhower, on the other hand, a graduate of West Point, had done little reading beyond military manuals and escapist fare, such as cowboy novels and magazines. Unlike Truman's strong partisan attachments, there had been no analogous commitment for him. The Democrats, not knowing to which party he belonged, had actually attempted to draft him as their own presidential nominee before he opted for the Republicans. And while not unfeeling about those at the bottom, there is little evidence that he cared as deeply about relieving their lot as Truman did. In the choice of his friends, Eisenhower had a greater affinity for wealthy business tycoons, and the cabinet he chose consisted, as one critic observed caustically, of "eight millionaires and one plumber."[105]

Truman was a doer, a Midwestern progressive with a manner that roiled emotions and provoked his enemies. He knew what he wanted, had the courage to push the controversial agenda he believed in, didn't shy away from tough choices and relished battling his opponents. He made decisions crisply—sometimes impulsively and not always wisely—but once made he stuck to them and never looked back. "The Buck Stops Here!" read a sign on his desk.

For Eisenhower the presidency was not so much a place for leadership and action as it was one of three coequal branches of government, and he was less prone to do battle with the Congress and much more willing to share power with it. By instinct conservative, he was by temperament more the conciliator and "Chairman of the Board" and believed that Americans should be allowed to live their lives without too much outside interference and that the government's role should in most instances be restricted to providing the framework enabling them to do so.

Of the two, Truman came into office under much less favorable circumstances and faced the more difficult decisions at a particularly critical time. Roosevelt had been a towering figure, an immensely popular leader, and the only president many young Americans had ever known. "Who is Truman?" his Chief of Staff Admiral Leahy is quoted as having asked in 1944 when the name of the relatively obscure senator from Missouri was first put forward for the vice presidency, thereby echoing a question many Americans were then asking. A few months later, when Roosevelt's death had suddenly thrust Truman into the top job, another presidential assistant remarked how awfully "small" he seemed sitting in Roosevelt's seat.

Although ill-prepared and uninformed in many areas when he first took office, Truman over the next several years made one momentous decision after another—from dropping the atomic bomb to end the Pacific War, to building the institutions of the Western Alliance in the Cold War, including aid to Greece and Turkey, the Marshall Plan, NATO, the Berlin airlift, and war in Korea, to the reconstruction of Germany and Japan. At home, he laid before the bitterly opposed and hostile Congress a controversial twenty-one-point program for managing the transition to peace, and succeeded in winning a narrow reelection victory no one had expected, even in the face of a segregationist revolt in the South.

When Truman left office, many Americans breathed a sigh of relief. They were enjoying a period of unprecedented prosperity and they wanted quieter times. There was a yearning for stability and for a president they could admire—and in General Dwight D. "Ike" Eisenhower they got one. In 1952, they elected him by a decisive margin—and four years later voted for him by an even greater one. For the rest of the fifties this very different president would completely dominate American life.

Truman had been attacked for his "cronyism," while Ike was admired for his virtues. Playing golf with his wealthy friends was approved of as more appropriate for a president than were poker games over bourbon whiskey in back rooms. Truman had challenged the establishment with new initiatives. Ike was less inclined to launch economic reforms or attack social ills, content to defer to the Congress and the courts. He was neither particularly charismatic nor inspirational, but he exuded geniality, moderation, and common sense, and his quiet, steadfast, avuncular manner admirably fit the nation's prevailing mood.

Liberals and many intellectuals were dismayed by the lack of new initiatives under Ike. They wanted more done on the welfare state and on civil rights, and they lamented the president's willingness to stand pat, to pause, and to prefer generally to just hold the line. They deplored what they considered his abdication of presidential powers to the Congress and the courts, but theirs was not a majority view. Throughout the years of his presidency, Ike's prestige and popularity remained high and the public was content to enjoy its prosperity and to leave things largely as they were.

On balance, both men were probably right for their time, and the United States, spared social turmoil and upheaval, emerged from the fifties strong and secure. The mistakes of the twenties were not repeated, in favor of a prudent balancing of action and a time for pause and restraint. The nuclear threat was kept under control, and America entered the next decade well positioned to lead the West in the pursuit of shared goals.

From the first day of my arrival in the United States, I had been drawn to the party of Roosevelt and Truman, and there wasn't any question about my political allegiance. The Democrats were the traditional party of immigrants, underdogs, and minorities, and the simple fact that they were also the party of FDR and his wartime leadership against the Nazis, was good enough for me. In Harry Truman and the policies he advocated, I saw Roosevelt's worthy successor. Right from the start it was clear that I would be a Democrat.

Becoming an American

In Honolulu, the *Marine Adder*'s first American port of call, the drinking fountain at the Royal Hawaiian Hotel dispensed free pineapple juice, and in San Francisco I could consume buckets of fresh milk, which in China would have meant risking serious illness or worse. I could even buy fruit from outdoor vendors and eat it on the spot without having to fear swift intestinal retribution. These were small pleasures, but they were an unbelievable joy after the miseries of Shanghai.

During those first heady September days in San Francisco I was in a perpetually dreamlike state as I strolled through the streets, delighted that the police were not on the take, and that people were generally friendly and looked well fed. Life had never been better and I eagerly embraced even the little things encountered daily: clean streets, the cacophony of exciting new accents and sounds, and shopkeepers who smiled and said "thank you," "please," and "have a nice day." Cable cars clanked up and down Nob Hill, the music blared, Dr. "Painless" Parker's smiling face—a dentist with a self-selected first name—beckoned to his Market Street office from oversized billboards, and on Van Ness Avenue the exploits of automobile row's "flagpole-sitters"—a particular craze at the time—were avidly followed by large crowds. It was all quintessentially American. The pigeons feeding on Union Square seemed a superior sort and even with San Francisco's proverbial fog, it was all magical.

Above all, nothing could top the wonderful sense of empowerment I felt, with the right of permanent residence in a country I was determined to like even before I set foot in it. Almost seventy years later, to remember these first days in America still lifts my spirits. Perhaps only a refugee immigrant reaching the country under similar circumstances can fully understand such emotions.

For several days my sister Stefanie and I soaked up the atmosphere of what is surely one of America's most beautiful cities. On our first Saturday night we anxiously awaited the Sunday papers, and all through the next day we pored over the job ads and planned for the Monday that would be D-day in our quest to join the American labor force. My buoyant enthusiasm left no room for doubt about an early success, and in this I was not to be disappointed. On the very first day, my sister landed a secretarial job at fifty dollars a week and I could triumphantly report similar good fortune with a job as billing clerk at the National Biscuit Company, or Nabisco, an American household name and one of the country's corporate giants. No matter that I had only a hazy notion about my duties and that the modest forty-dollar weekly pay was barely above the legal minimum. I was proud to be joining so prestigious an enterprise, and, as far as I was concerned, I was on my way upward on the first rung of the ladder of success.

Perhaps it was natural that I would at first view my new surroundings through the rose-colored glasses of a grateful, uncritical immigrant. Yet it did not take long to discover a less glamorous reality as I punched the Nabisco time clock each morning for eight hours of utterly stupid and mind-numbing work, thereby greatly accelerating a more sobering coming down to Earth. Along the way, not only my initial euphoria, but also my uncritical admiration for American business efficiency were among the early victims.

As a Nabisco billing clerk, I had in fact enlisted for duty on an exceedingly busy ship, but not a particularly happy one. In a Dickensian setting reminiscent of a nineteenth-century sweatshop, I had become part of a motley assortment of bored and sullen clerks arrayed around several long wooden tables, tasked to perform repetitive arithmetic calculations on endless columns of figures—in our heads—and then to enter the results manually on invoices for the next day's deliveries of Lorna Doones, Animal Crackers, Oreo cookies, and assorted other Nabisco bestsellers. The stack of invoices awaiting us each morning seemed to grow ever higher, and often there would be anxious pleas for overtime volunteers. Thus we labored on in a tedious routine with thirty minutes off for lunch, day after day, watched over by Mr. Duff, our boss, a dour and humorless elderly man seated at a desk in the center of the room and sternly peering at us over old-fashioned rimless glasses. His principal duties, as far as I could tell, were twofold: to enforce strict discipline, which he did mostly by noisily clearing his throat and directing reproachful glances toward anyone whose diligence flagged or—worse yet—who committed the sin of whispering to his neighbor; and to engage in a nonstop recruiting effort to replace those who had thrown in the towel and left for greener pastures— under the circumstances a frequent occurrence. Getting hired into this dysfunctional merry-go-round was easy; marshaling the stamina to stay the course for any length of time was the greater challenge. With staff turnover high, Mr. Duff was a busy man.

As in much of postwar America, Nabisco's business was booming, but no one seemed to have expected it, and the result was a mess. For the millions of returned war veterans, starting families and eager to enjoy the peace, the good life apparently included the consumption of enough Nabisco cookies, crackers, and cupcakes to strain the company's capacity to cope. Even a few simple changes in the office's routine would have worked wonders, but apparently no one had gotten around to thinking about them. In today's world, a single desktop computer would surely have obsoleted all of us overnight, but even in those pre-electronic days, enough electromechanical adding machines of the kind my future employer, Burroughs, was producing would have eliminated many of our jobs and saved Nabisco lots of money. If memory serves me right, we had a grand total of two rickety clunkers at our disposal, but one had to line up for them, and the whole procedure was time-consuming and hopeless.

I lasted two months at Nabisco, which was about the average, and departed just before the onslaught of Christmas orders threatened to drown poor Duff and his unhappy charges in a sea of paper. Still, though billing cookies at Nabisco was one of the less inspiring jobs I have held, it has remained an unforgettable one, not only because it was my first gainful employment in America but because it was instrumental in putting me back in touch with reality and in forcing me to do some hard thinking about my future. It is said that "the sight of the gallows clears one's mind," and that is what my stint at Nabisco did for me.

The monotony of adding, subtracting, and multiplying convinced me that there had to be more hopeful avenues for realizing my American dream and that at age twenty-two with a tenth-grade education and eight years in China, I was long on unusual experiences but woefully short on substantive knowledge. In America, after all, it was always possible to go back to school, and if there was no money, the answer was "to work one's way through." Spurred on by the mind-numbing Nabisco arithmetic exercises, I reached the conclusion that it was not too soon to set my sights higher and to give alternative roads to fame and fortune a try.

The Christmas boom was already under way when I marched up to Mr. Duff's desk, announced that I was switching careers, handed in my resignation and started working the swing shift at a local hospital. With a pay cut of ten cents an hour I was moving backwards financially, but the idea was that it would free up my mornings for freshman classes at the local City College. It meant living uncomfortably close to starvation, but I was familiar with that from Shanghai and consoled myself that this time it was an investment in my future. My daily routine now involved a full morning of classwork and lectures, followed by a mad dash downtown to run the hospital elevator till ten at night, burning the midnight oil to prepare for the next day, and gulping lots of coffee while trying to stay awake.

City College of San Francisco (CCSF), where I spent my first three hectic undergraduate semesters, was a unique institution. Organized in the mid-thirties and tuition-free, it catered to over 2,000 students of all ages, regardless of prior preparation or qualification. There were semi-professional and university level courses, anyone was admitted, and for those who did well there was the possibility to transfer across the bay to UC Berkeley—one of the nation's finest public universities. That was my own goal from the start, and having adequately acquitted myself, it is where I concluded my final undergraduate semesters.

With my deficient education at the advanced age of twenty-two, no other college would have admitted me, and I have always been grateful to CCSF—a true "people's college,"—for giving me the opportunity. When I was invited back almost forty years later to be honored as an alumnus "who made it," I was happy to express these sentiments very directly. It is not uncommon for cabinet members to be favored by any number of universities with an honorary degree but against the dozen or so I accepted, to be singled out by CCSF had special meaning for me. "This is the place that gave me my ticket to the future," I told the students, and I meant it.

This return to my first alma mater remains memorable for another, very different reason as well. The record shows that I shared the day's honors with another famous CCSF alumnus, one of the great running backs in the history of American football, and I confess that for the students gathered to witness the honors ceremony that day, he was the object of infinitely greater interest and admiration than the sixty-fourth secretary of the treasury of the United States. His name was O. J. Simpson, then much venerated, but today doing time in a Nevada penitentiary.

After CCSF, the University of California (UC) was a big step up. Berkeley, the crown jewel of UC's far-flung campuses, was bursting at the seams with over 30,000 students of all ages and ethnic backgrounds, including quite a few foreigners and many returning veterans. To study there was exciting—and a bargain: except for a nominal semester fee of thirty-five dollars—which even I could afford—it was free![106] Intellectual standards were high and challenging, and it was at Berkeley where my interest in international economics, politics, and public affairs was awakened and greatly stimulated by several remarkable scholars and teachers. Foremost among them were two fine economic theorists, Robert Aaron Gordon and Howard Ellis—both eventual presidents of the American Economic Association—and John Letiche, a younger scholar who brought international economic policy issues alive for me. Hans Kelsen, a critical positivist legal scholar who taught international law, had a worldwide reputation for, amongst other accomplishments, his authorship of the Austrian Constitution of 1920, Kenneth Stampp was a Pulitzer Prize–winning historian who kindled my lifelong fascination with the Civil War period of American history, and Andrew Jaszi was a young Hungarian professor of German who introduced me to the poetry of Heine, Rilke, Hofmannsthal, and classical German literature.

CCSF was a "streetcar campus" but at Berkeley I moved into International House, a residential facility specially tailored to the needs of older American and international students. Money continued to be a problem; I was perennially broke, and poorly paid, bottom-of-the-barrel jobs—toting mailbags at Christmas, factory work, or janitor and deliveryman—remained standbys while I gradually picked up campus tips about jobs with the best pay for the least hours worked. Eventually, I hit the jackpot with an early-morning dishwashing job at my "I House" residence, an excellent arrangement of three hours' labor in exchange for free room and board, which left me liberated for the rest of the day. I was one of a motley assortment of equally impecunious students in the kitchen crew, and we passed the time debating weighty intellectual issues or arguing about problems in postwar international relations, while scraping plates and stacking the large washing machines. My favorite coworker was a cheerful young Pakistani with whom I amused myself in the exchange of bawdy songs, he in Urdu and I with German and occasional Chinese offerings. That neither of us could understand the other's favorites didn't seem to matter. Ali Bhutto later went on to become the prime minister of Pakistan but ended his days prematurely on the gallows, the victim of a military coup. That he would rise to such heights only to come to so ignoble an end, certainly did not enter my mind as we whiled away our daily three hours of breakfast-cleanup chores.

On and off the campus my Americanization progressed quickly, and before long I was entertaining ambitious dreams about my future and spinning elaborate strategies of how to realize them.

In the classroom, I focused on history, economics, and international affairs and—on a parallel track—management and administration. I had seen horrible government in Nazi Germany, had been exposed in China to the corrupt and ineffective rule of Chiang Kai-shek, and had vivid memories of China's spectacularly failed economic policies, with millions suffering under hyperinflation while a few profited and got very rich. Time and again I had chafed against impenetrable walls of mindless rules and bureaucratic obfuscation. All this now shaped my intellectual interests. I wanted to know how economies worked and what, if anything, could be learned from the past. The process of policy formulation fascinated me, and with firsthand exposure to bureaucracy at its worst, I knew instinctively that what counted was not only the "what" but also the "how"—how to organize, lead, and translate policy initiatives into effective programs of action.

More than half a century later, the memory of what first possessed me at about this time to set my sights on the fanciful goal of becoming a senior U.S. government executive has grown dim. To aspire to a policy job in Washington was, under the circumstances, wildly ambitious. I hadn't even received my citizenship papers yet, and friends had counseled that, for a naturalized citizen, the prospects of a place in Washington's corridors of power were poor, especially in the elite Departments of Treasury and State on which my eyes were fixed. Yet, I clung to my decision stubbornly, driven by a mixture of youthful hubris and personal ambition.

Undoubtedly my refugee and immigrant experience must have been at the root of these dreams of glory. Having been a nobody, I wanted a career with a chance to be noticed. Frustrated by the rules and whims of others, I wanted the power to control my own destiny, and the memory of past slights and second-class status made it especially attractive to contemplate a position with recognized prestige. I was also pretty competitive by nature—perhaps those were my mother's genes—and I liked the idea of doing something others wouldn't dare to do, and the opportunity to prove that I was capable enough to succeed. The plan I hatched, therefore, involved trying for a graduate degree that might improve my chances. Princeton, Harvard, and Johns Hopkins had the best programs for public-affairs studies and could open doors for a Washington job, though whether I would be admitted and how to pay for the schooling remained a key question. Scholarships were harder to come by in those days than now, and being chosen for one was akin to winning the lottery. But if this was the land of unlimited opportunity, I decided it was worth a try.

Race Relations and Civil Rights

Meanwhile there was the excitement of the domestic political scene during Truman's first term, his miraculous reelection victory in 1948, and tense battles with Congress over economic policy, alleged domestic subversion, and civil rights. Part of the process of my assimilation into American life involved following those events closely, trying to understand how things worked, analyzing the politics of give and take, and rooting for the "good guys."

The war had created new realities, and American attitudes were gradually reshaping the political landscape. The South was industrializing and becoming more like the North. Many rural southern blacks had moved to the big cities of the North and West and had become more assertive. Elsewhere, the children of the ethnic immigrants of a previous generation—Poles, Irish, Italians, and Eastern European Jews—now constituted a majority in suburbia, less prone to bloc voting, more conservative and middle class.

The war experiences of GIs and the Cold War had ended isolationist sentiment in America as a political force. Widened horizons and the Holocaust in Europe had made many Americans more tolerant, more open to societal change, and more willing to end discrimination against minorities at home. In fact, though no one yet fully foresaw it, lasting changes in the relationships of all the various racial and ethnic groups to one another within the American melting pot were underway. In time these changes would totally remake the country's sociopolitical landscape and open doors that had once been firmly closed to African-Americans, non-white immigrants, and other minority groups. At the heart of this period stood the civil rights movement of the fifties and sixties, the struggle for racial justice and greater equality for African-Americans that lasted the better part of two decades and was rightfully called a second American Revolution.

In the beginning I had wanted to see only a perfect America and had been slow to recognize that racism and prejudice against various minorities were still a fact of life in American society. Southern segregation was the most blatant blot on American democracy, but though aware of this at one level, I had initially ignored it as remote and unreal. In San Francisco, it was easy to look the other way. There was no legally-sanctioned segregation, no separate water fountains, nor official exclusion of blacks from restaurants, theaters, and public facilities, and no sitting at the back of the bus. Yet by long-standing traditions, unofficial discrimination against African-Americans was real enough.

Part of my assimilation into American life involved having to come to terms with this reality, and also that anti-Semitism, though waning rapidly in the aftermath of the Holocaust, was by no means a spent force either. The fact was—as my Jewish friends would remind me—that as recently as the thirties there had been an upsurge of a crude kind of American anti-Semitism. In 1939, at least 800 unabashed anti-Semitic organizations with a combined membership of three million had still operated openly in the country. Even after the war, while a poll in *Fortune* had found in 1946 that only 8 percent of Americans admitted to being "strongly anti-Semitic," 64 percent had said in another survey that they had "heard" talk against Jews.[107] Elsewhere more genteel but equally harmful forms of discrimination were still in effect. Right up to the war, the existence of quotas to limit Jews at elite universities and professional schools had been an open secret, and no one could be sure that in the fifties it was really a thing of the past. Most Jews, in fact, doubted it. "Restricted" housing and discrimination in vacation communities and clubs were still common, major banks and corporations rarely promoted Jews into upper management, and in the Department of State, the Congress and the military, anti-Semitic sentiments were still a fact of life. No Jew and, for that matter, no Catholic had ever been elected president, and the conventional wisdom was that none ever would be.

Yet none of this compares to the situation facing blacks, nominally citizens but deprived of their civil rights quasi-legally and by intimidation in the South, and elsewhere by custom if not by law. In the southern states there was strict segregation on trains and boats, in hotels, restaurants, and every type of public accommodation. Black children attended separate and inferior schools—white colleges and universities refused to admit them—and their chances of voting in elections were slim. The legal basis for this outrage, *Plessy v. Ferguson*, an 1896 Supreme Court decision validating a "separate but equal" doctrine, was still in effect, even though it had long been clear that under prevailing circumstances, true equality was impossible.

Harry Truman had ended segregation in the military, and his twenty-one-point domestic action program had included some modest steps to combat job discrimination against minorities, especially blacks. But even if the country was willing to listen, key members of Congress as yet wanted none of it. A powerful coalition of Southern segregationists and Northern conservatives still controlled the major committees and was determined to use every possible parliamentary maneuver to preserve the status quo. These were men from another age, and many of them had served in the Congress for decades. Some were merely quaintly colorful, many were deeply conservative and wary of change, and a few were openly bigoted racists. One of them, Senator John Overton of Louisiana, so hated Daylight Saving Time that he refused to change his watch and insisted on staying with "God's time." Another, Senator Clyde Hoey of North Carolina, always appeared on the floor in a gray swallow-tailed coat reminiscent of nineteenth-century fashion, replete with a rose in his lapel. Senator James Eastland of Mississippi was an avowed racist determined to preserve the segregation of blacks at all costs. In the House, John Rankin, a fellow Mississippian, was an outright red-baiting anti-Semite and demagogue who thought Jews were subversives and blacks a mongrel race.

* * *

The struggle for civil rights was the dominant issue of the fifties and I had my crash course in the subject in the unlikely setting of the gambling casinos of Lake Tahoe, Nevada. The venue was special enough, but the circumstances were no less so and left me with the determination to join the fight against these evils.

Lake Tahoe, straddling the California–Nevada border at an altitude of over 6,000 feet, is surely one of the most stunning mountain lakes in the world. Located in the Sierra Nevada mountains and surrounded by spectacular scenery, its roughly 200 square miles of deep blue water shimmering in abundant year-round sunshine dazzle the visitor. Today the lake is one of the most visited resorts of the West and much of its incredible beauty has fortunately been preserved. I spent two extraordinary working summers there in 1950 and 1951, with "only-in-America" experiences that were a fitting chapter in my Americanization. One was an exciting romance with a young Shoshone Indian woman, a summer worker at the lake. The memory of this exotic adventure with a "real American" is enough to make that first Tahoe summer unforgettable, though it is not the only reason. I hadn't come, after all, in pursuit of love nor as a vacationer to enjoy Lake Tahoe's pristine allure. The real attraction—money—was less inspiring but equally compelling. According to campus wisdom, Tahoe was the place for summer work if one wanted to earn top dollar, and the reason was simple: in the unreal environment of a gambling casino, money tends to flow freely. In each of the two summers, working several jobs at once, I managed to accumulate savings of close to a thousand dollars, a truly princely nest egg at the time! Thus, in the summer of 1950, in pursuit of riches and adventure, I set out with Isaiah Zimmerman, a fellow student and friend from Shanghai, to follow the money trail. We made our way up to the lake, where we talked our way into dining room jobs at the Club Cal-Neva, and later the Cal-Vada.

Love affairs and money aside, the summers at Tahoe turned into a wild time of work, sleep deprivation, and nonstop excitement. At night we bused tables and doubled as stagehands for the nightclub's headliner acts; mornings we drove laundry trucks; and afternoons we took turns as casino shills. Shilling, for the uninitiated, was—and possibly still is—an established profession in the Nevada casinos, for which one had to be duly fingerprinted and licensed. (My shilling license from the Washoe County Sheriff's Office has remained a prized memento to this day.) Simply put, a shill's function is to play with house money and to simulate table action, thus to entice the "real" gambling public to step up and place their bets. Best of all, the custom is that big winners betting on the shill's roll of the dice tip them and—depending on the size of their winnings—sometimes do so quite liberally.

The clubs' modus operandi has remained the same time-tested formula for success. Top entertainers were booked to appear onstage on the California side of the club and packed in the crowds, hopefully putting them in the mood to leave their money at the casino tables on the Nevada side, where the house made its real profits. Among the biggest drawing cards were two famous strippers—euphemistically billed as "exotic dancers." One was the nationally renowned Sally Rand who danced with fans; the other, Lili St. Cyr, a younger "artiste" whose specialty was to languish sensuously in a bubble bath, undressing and dressing amidst lascivious undulations to the wild applause of an appreciative audience. Sally Rand was the more famous crowd-pleaser in those more innocent days when open sexuality was still taboo in America. She was by then well past her prime and comfortably on the north side of fifty, for which she compensated with provocative costumes and cunning peek-a-boo tricks coordinated with precise onstage lighting effects. For this, Isaiah and I—who doubled at working the spotlights—had been carefully coached, and were satisfactorily tipped by her stage manager. If all went well, the climax of her act involved a brief, final "revealing it all" moment, no more than a second or two, as she opened her fans under our discreetly dimmed lighting to heighten the mystery and illusion.

What I remember best about Ms. Rand is that for us "insiders" there was soon no mystery at all. Her act over, she would leave the stage to thunderous applause, and clad only in birthday suit and high heels, her fans dangling at her side, march the length of a hallway to her dressing room next to the kitchen. In the brighter light and in full view of waiters, cooks, bottle washers, and busboys, she appeared as she really was—an aging, well-worn and not overly attractive woman. It was a nightly "appearance and reality" lesson I would often later remember when listening to the rhetoric of Washington politicians.[108]

The best known entertainers at the clubs were the immensely popular black jazz singer and pianist, Nat King Cole, and the Mills Brothers, the no less famous black balladeers of pop and sweet and low classics. Cole was the best known and most visible black performer of the era, with a seductive voice that melded jazz and blues in the ballads that had made him famous. At the piano and with a single spotlight on him on an otherwise darkened stage, he would launch into his #1 hit, "Mona Lisa," or his just as popular "Route 66" and "Nature Boy" among others. John Mills and his three sons, accompanied by their guitarist, unfailingly brought down the house with their signature songs. "Paper Doll" would eventually sell some 6 million copies, "Glow Worm" was the nation's top song in 1952, and "Lazy River," "Till Then" and a dozen others regularly evoked thunderous ovations. Everyone knew the Mills Brothers' songs. They had been the first black artists allowed to cross rigid color lines and to perform in white venues, had appeared in a command performance for British royalty, and starred in their own national TV show and in many movies.

Nat Cole and the Mills Brothers were the first black Americans with whom I exchanged more than a few words. Cole was the more reserved, though friendly and always polite. Isaiah and I would push his piano on and off stage, run an occasional errand for him, and be rewarded with a smile and a tip. It was the Mills Brothers, however, who were especially friendly, and with whom we had long talks on the back porch during intermissions and late after the second show. In time, it was through them that I got my first real insights into what it meant in those days to be black in America.

They came from a small town in Ohio where, they said, race relations had been more relaxed but as separated as in any southern state. They were great storytellers, and I think they relished disillusioning their two well-meaning white student helpers by telling us of their more extreme discrimination experiences. Our ignorance about blacks amused rather than annoyed them, and what rancor they must have felt usually remained veiled behind a mix of good-natured gallows-humor and wry resignation. They strongly approved of Truman's civil rights initiatives and closely followed pending court actions, but remained a lot more skeptical than hopeful about the prospects for real change.

The guitarist—I think his name was Cliff White—however, was different. He was the first truly angry black American I had ever met. He was younger and had served in the army during the war. As a northern African-American, being stationed at southern army bases had clearly left a mark on him. He seethed with anger and frustration over his experiences and had developed a palpable dislike for most whites and white society. I think he had the makings of a real revolutionary and in another place he might well have been one. He made a lasting impression on me.

Around us, the political environment was heated. The bitter fight over a liberal civil-rights plank in the Democrats' party platform in 1948 had led to the segregationist, third-party Dixiecrats, in spite of which Truman had managed to pull out a narrow election victory with the support of 70 percent of the growing number of urban blacks in the North. In 1948, he had issued an executive order ending discrimination against blacks in the Armed Forces, and the Supreme Court had affirmed the right of blacks to attend public institutions of higher learning. These were signs that times were changing, but the Mills family saw it differently. In their eyes, such moves, however welcome, remained highly inadequate and unlikely to lead to fundamental changes as long as the "separate but equal" doctrine remained in effect, and no one thought that would change.

I had thought of race discrimination in America as primarily a problem of the South. Once, when I said that, I remember Harry Mills's simple question: how many blacks had lived on my San Francisco street, how many had worked at Nabisco, or attended my classes at UC Berkeley? It is odd and, looking back, embarrassing that I hadn't until that moment really noticed that I had never seen a black person on my middle class San Francisco street, nor given much thought to what was essentially a black ghetto in the Fillmore district, one of the worst parts of town. I also had to admit that there hadn't been any black Nabisco billing clerks and that I had seen few black students in any of my classes.

The Mills Brothers were forcing me to see my adopted country as it really was. They were privileged performers much applauded on stage by white audiences, yet blacks could rarely get a table where they appeared, they pointed out. Their accommodations at the club, they noted, were always at the edge of the property, so that no white had reason to complain about having them as neighbors, and they told stories about hotels and restaurants that had refused them, and that, even for them, getting a decent sleeping-car compartment was never a sure thing.

Segregation and racial discrimination, I was learning, were still very much a problem in the North as well as in the South. True enough, it was in the South that the most egregious patterns of holding blacks down were still in place, where Jim Crow laws, all-white primaries, poll taxes, and rigged literacy tests still deprived blacks of their political rights, and strict segregation and inferior education and housing marked them as a virtual pariah caste. Outside the South the situation was more mixed, but de facto segregation and discrimination in housing, education, and employment were no less harmful.

The civil rights movement was still in its infancy during my two Tahoe summers, in 1950 and 1951. The major battles still lay ahead and were fought over the next fifteen years, often against fierce resistance. The elder Mills and his sons can be forgiven for their skepticism in 1950, and their guitarist for his bitterness and anger, yet real change did occur, and once the dike burst that change came with unexpected speed.

It is remarkable, however, that when the time finally came in the later fifties and sixties it was accomplished with very little bloodshed and without the violent upheavals that similar changes in deeply ingrained customs and habits have caused in other societies. The changing attitudes of Americans in general made it possible. Much, however, was due to the enlightened leadership of Martin Luther King Jr. and others, and their effective strategy of nonviolent pressure for change.

The key milestone occurred on June 10, 1964, when the civil rights revolution was truly won. On that day, the Senate took an unprecedented step and defeated a coalition of Southerners and Western conservatives, broke their seventy-five-day filibuster and voted "cloture," ending debate and clearing the way for passage of an omnibus civil rights bill revolutionizing race relations in the United States. It was a moment of historic significance and all one hundred Senators were in attendance. Even Clair Engle of California, recovering from brain surgery, was brought into the chamber in a wheelchair and, though unable to speak, recorded his affirmative vote by pointing to his eye.

The Civil Rights Act of 1964 was only the third piece of civil rights legislation in over a hundred years. When it passed the Senate nine days later, on June 19th at 7:49 P.M. on the eighty-third day of debate, it ended the longest legislative debate in Senate history and marked the culmination of an intense effort stretching over virtually the entire first two postwar decades. For the first time in American history, legislation was on the books recognizing the unequivocal right of black Americans to full equality in all areas of American life.

That this legislation had passed in 1964 was a near miracle, and to make it happen it had taken a combination of a nation shocked by a presidential assassination, the unparalleled political skills of Lyndon Johnson, a Southerner, and, no less importantly, the tireless efforts of Hubert Horatio Humphrey, the populist prairie liberal from the American heartland and the floor manager of the bill. Humphrey, the Democratic Whip, had first made his mark as a fighter for racial justice at the contentious Democratic Party Convention of 1948, where he had led—and ultimately won—a seemingly hopeless drive for a strong and uncompromising civil rights plank in the Party's election platform.

At the 1948 Convention I had admired Hubert Humphrey's fiery oratory from afar; sixteen years later we had become personal friends. I was the U.S. ambassador in charge of trade negotiations in Geneva— another subject of keen interest to him—and on that memorable day I happened to be in Washington and telephoned him to offer my congratulations. Hubert was in full flight. "We did it, we did it," he exulted. "Come join us. Tonight we celebrate!" Which was how I was a witness to a memorable incident. I met Humphrey in downtown Washington, and we hailed a taxi to attend a reception at the British Embassy. Our driver was an elderly black man, and when he recognized Humphrey, he reached for his hand, held it a long time and only reluctantly let it go. "Thank you, Senator," he stammered with tears in his eyes, "thank you for cloture." Humphrey beamed—and I thought of the Mills Brothers and wondered what they were thinking on that day.

I have never forgotten that evening in 1964, and the long night of celebration lasting, in typical ebullient Hubert Humphrey fashion, till the small hours of the morning. Always the happy warrior, he was a man with a big heart who genuinely relished politics as a noble calling. Hubert had his faults. He was extroverted almost beyond endurance, and often a better talker than listener. But he was also exceedingly smart, warmhearted, and kind, fundamentally honest, and with a minimum of guile in a town where that can be a rarity. He was a leader who never gave up, and who made things happen: few people did more to advance the cause of civil rights than he did.

Princeton

I arrived in Princeton for graduate work in the fall of 1951. The university's program in Public Affairs studies had the reputation of being one of the best, and when they accepted me I was thrilled. The doubts of my more pessimistic friends notwithstanding, I had achieved my first objective. There was no scholarship, but I was determined to go, and, if all went well, to return to the West and, eventually, to a public affairs career.

None of this turned out quite as planned. My sister, Stefanie, made California her permanent home, married, and raised a wonderful family there. My parents, each with their respective new spouses, also lived there the rest of their lives. Yet for me life would take a different turn. For one thing, I never returned to live in California. For another, my two year M.A. evolved into several Princeton degrees and a lifetime of close association with the university. Last but not least, my first professional jobs were not in government but in academia and business, and the town of Princeton became my permanent home and has remained so ever since. So much for careful planning.

The biggest change, however, was that I did not go alone. Just before leaving Berkeley, Eileen Polley and I were married in a simple student ceremony. Appropriately enough, we had met in a class on international economics. The mutual attraction came quickly, and from the first date our relationship proceeded smoothly. We discovered common interests in domestic politics and world affairs, friendship blossomed into romance, and when the move to Princeton entered the picture, making the relationship permanent had a certain inevitability neither of us questioned.

We were both very young, though at twenty-five I considered myself a lot more grown up and world-wise than I probably was. Eileen was barely twenty-two, an attractive Southern Californian, intelligent, even-tempered, with an interest in the world at large. In spite of a typically middle-class, sheltered, and, to be honest, rather provincial upbringing, her independence, curiosity about the world, and taste for adventure impressed me. I liked that she had distinct goals of her own and had already taken some unconventional steps to realize them, including financing her own travels abroad and the decision to exchange the security of her small college for the more demanding environment of Berkeley with its wider horizons and greater personal challenges.

This was a felicitous combination of qualities from my point of view, and it probably explains her own daring decision to team up with a gangly and impecunious immigrant with big ideas. She later confessed that it was her weakness for unconventional, interesting foreigners that had first lit the flame. My colorful early life in far-away places had intrigued her, and romance had done the rest. Eileen wasn't Jewish; her father was an immigrant from England and her mother the descendant of Ohio homesteaders with roots in America going back as far as anyone could remember.

We had many good years together. In time she earned her Ph.D. in psychology and embarked on her own professional career. We produced three problem-free daughters, and today we share eight grandchildren of whom we are both very proud. As to her taste for politics, travel, and adventure, she certainly got as much of that, or more, than she may have bargained for. Together we traveled the world, lived in three different countries, and shared exciting and varied experiences in academia, international business, and during two tours of duty in Washington, D.C.

We stayed together for the better part of thirty years, comfortably and without serious problems. In time, as we grew older, we drifted apart until what differences in character and personality had always been there became more obvious, and divorce inevitable. As the flames abated, the comfort of the familiar and shared experiences was no longer enough. I admit that much of it was my fault, and this I regret. In more recent years, freed from me, Eileen has built an entirely new life for herself and has done wonderful work in the Peace Corps and as a volunteer worker in the challenging environments of Romania, Honduras, Nepal, and Kenya. I am happy to say that we are still friends. What remains are many good memories along with the inevitable regrets.

There are at least two dozen towns named Princeton spread across the United States, but the oldest and best-known is the one in New Jersey that is home to the university bearing its name.

Chartered in 1746 as the College of New Jersey, Princeton is one of the nation's oldest institutions of higher learning, the fourth established in British North America. John Witherspoon, one of its first Presidents, signed the Declaration of Independence; the Continental Congress met there at Nassau Hall in 1783 (still the main Administration building on campus); and two U.S. presidents, dozens of cabinet members, governors, and thousands of future legislators and cultural and business leaders were educated there. Princetonians have never hidden their pride in the university's place in U.S. history, nor their certainty that it has always been—and remains—one of the country's best.

For much of its existence, Princeton pursued an unabashedly elitist approach to education. Until about the Second World War, it remained a small, all male, all white institution of a few thousand undergraduates and a graduate school, in an environment that exuded privilege, exclusivity, wealth, high standards, and an aura of understated snobbish academic and sociopolitical "noblesse oblige." Until the war, no black students were admitted, informal quotas limited the number of Jews, and women were allowed in only after 1969. Today upwards of 7,000 students are enrolled there, and its endowment in 2008 of $16 billion—over $2 million per capita—makes it the wealthiest of any major university in the U.S.[109]

When the Continental Congress met there, its secretary, Charles Thomson, remarked, "I do not know of a more agreeable spot in America." A hundred years later, Mark Twain concurred that "Princeton would suit me as well as heaven," and after Albert Einstein had fled the Nazis and settled in Princeton in the thirties he confessed "to be almost ashamed to be living in such a place."[110] Most of today's residents would share these sentiments. Princeton remains an especially pleasant university town of about 30,000 inhabitants, and one of its special charms is that it has retained its agreeable character in spite of the many changes around it.

We arrived there in the last days of September, in the middle of a formidable spell of unpleasantly hot and muggy "Jersey weather."

Our honeymoon had been a leisurely trek across the United States in a 1940 Plymouth purchased with my Tahoe savings, a reasonably well-preserved if slightly fickle eleven-year-old car of which I was inordinately proud. Princeton became our first home in the East; later we returned there several times, our three daughters were born there, and I still live there today.

It was, however, not love at first sight, there was a lot to get used to, and not all of it at first easy or pleasant. Accustomed to the beautiful California sunshine, we had to adjust to the humid New Jersey weather, and then realized that minimally adequate affordable housing was hard to find. The university, attuned exclusively to single males, had little to offer for married graduate students, and the best we could do initially was to take two cramped furnished rooms in the modest house of a piano tuner on the "wrong" side of the railroad tracks several miles from campus.

Beyond these minor irritations, there was much else to absorb. The Princeton of the early fifties was at once intimidating and exhilarating intellectually, and the university's ways puzzling and contradictory. From the uninhibited melting pot campus of Berkeley and its tens of thousands of students with diverse backgrounds, ethnicities, and political leanings, we had suddenly been thrust into the polar opposite—a small, all-male institution of a few thousand in an environment in which we felt somewhat out of place.

Yet like much of the country, Princeton had actually undergone significant changes during the war, and was entering a period of many more far-reaching ones. Eventually these would alter the institution's character almost beyond recognition, but in the early fifties this was not yet widely apparent, and her traditional ways remained much in evidence. Though the university had long ago shed its formal links with the Presbyterian church, Harold Dodds, the university's president, was a Presbyterian in the traditional mold (no previous president ever having been anything else). The undergraduate college was still essentially lily-white, and the snooty, socially hierarchical eating clubs—Princeton's fraternities—dominated undergraduate life. Moreover, though admissions criteria were changing, the powerful board of trustees remained a self-perpetuating old boys club and perfect mirror of the traditionally homogenous and discriminatory makeup of the students.

At Berkeley, every conceivable political view had been in evidence, often noisily and in inverse proportion to the number of its adherents. Marxists rubbed shoulders with right-wingers, libertarians with anarchists, and traditional Democrats with hereditary Republicans. At Princeton there may also have been Marxists among the undergraduates, but, if so, they kept a low profile and, at best, were tolerated as eccentric and politically incorrect. Except for the secretarial and library staff, women—particularly young ones—were nowhere to be seen in what remained an exclusively male bastion. Eileen reported that walking across the campus was always an uncomfortable adventure involving turned heads and hungry stares.

At the last moment, the university had relented and come up with a small tuition grant; Eileen took an office job to support us, and I plunged in and hit the books. I was one of merely fifteen entering graduate students at the Woodrow Wilson School of Public and International Affairs, where we were drilled intensely and reminded often that we bore the responsibility to carry on a long tradition of Princeton "In the Nation's Service and in the Service of All Nations," the university's unofficial motto.

Many Princeton alumni have occupied senior government positions, and several of our faculty members had served in Washington during the war. To us they embodied the lesson that our mission was public service. We met in small seminars, often taught by teams of faculty members from the economics, politics, and sociology departments. We studied and read, debated, wrote innumerable "policy papers," practiced oral exposition, and covered vast quantities of material. The required preparation was seemingly never-ending, and most stimulating of all were the extraordinary men who taught us and the rich library and research facilities on which we could draw. My fellow students were, on the whole, a talented group and some have remained my lifelong friends. Many eventually went into the Foreign Service and key Washington departments and rose to senior levels as ambassadors and in other policymaking positions.

Thus the Public Affairs program at the Woodrow Wilson School was everything I had hoped for and more. Increasingly I was drawn to economic policy issues, stimulated by renowned scholars like the erudite Jacob Viner, who taught us international economics and the history of economic thought; Will Baumol, a brilliant young theorist; Richard Lester, a labor economist who knew how to combine theory with the politics of practical labor relations; Lester Chandler, an authority on banking and monetary theory; and Alpheus Mason, a scholar of jurisprudence. When exactly the thought took hold that a Public Affairs M.A. would not be enough and a doctorate in economics a more complete conclusion to my academic preparation, I can no longer recall.

For my dissertation topic I had chosen a project that would require a year of research on the German steel industry, for which I had been fortunate enough to win a traveling fellowship. I had recently become a U.S. citizen, and it had been fourteen years since I left Berlin as a German boy of thirteen. Now I would be returning as an adult American to a country from which I was largely estranged, and which I viewed with considerable distaste. Most Jews in those days had sworn never again to set foot on German soil, and some were incredulous that I would voluntarily go back to live there for the better part of a year. My answer was that my topic—the politics and economics of labor management "codetermination," in the coal and steel industry of the Ruhr after the war was important enough to justify my decision. The Allies had broken up the large interlocking mining combines that once controlled 40 percent of Europe's entire output and had been a vital part of Hitler's war machine. The new labor system in the dozens of smaller companies put in their place with Allied approval was supposed to promote industrial democracy in postwar West Germany, yet it was raising lots of questions much discussed but poorly understood in the American literature.

At least that was my rationale, though in truth, I was also intensely curious to see the defeated Germany for myself and to try to understand what had possessed the German people to support or tolerate the Hitler dictatorship until disaster engulfed them. Perhaps, however, I wasn't being totally honest with myself, for the true reasons for my choosing to go back were deeper and more complex than I was willing to admit until much later.

Postwar Germany

Thus began my first direct reexposure to the country of my birth. I arrived in Cologne in early August 1953 by rail from Paris, and Eileen and our daughter Ann Margaret, born earlier that year, followed a month later. Outside the Hauptbahnhof, the grand, partially damaged Cologne Cathedral—in urgent need of repair—loomed as a forlorn reminder of better days. All around it was the evidence of devastating destruction, 90 to 95 percent of all buildings in Cologne's center having been destroyed in the war and almost 80 percent in the city as a whole; the rubble was estimated to add up to staggering mountains totaling 30 million cubic meters. Even four years later, in 1957, only half of this detritus of war had been removed, and it would take at least a decade more to get rid of it all.

My fieldwork was to take me to the nearby areas of the industrial Ruhr. The DGB (Confederation of German Trade Unions) ran a research institute in Cologne, and Erich Potthoff, the director, had promised his support. So the plan was to make Cologne our home base, find living quarters for us, and get to work. A simple enough plan when conceived in Princeton but, as I soon discovered, impossible to execute against the realities of German postwar life. The vast physical destruction of the German cities had far exceeded my imagination, with Cologne a spectacular case in point. Though my dollar stipend was generous by local standards (at a Mark/dollar exchange rate of more than 4:1), even minimally acceptable housing was simply unavailable for either love or money.

Entirely unprepared for so much devastation, I scoured the city in search of shelter for an entire month, brushing up against throngs of local citizens on similar quests. Two years later, by the city's official count, more than 60,000 Cologne inhabitants were still in the same predicament, and some had no roof over their heads at all.[111] So, as my frustration mounted and the day of the arrival of my family drew closer, I reluctantly gave up on Cologne and tried my luck at the other end of the Ruhr district, in the Westphalian capital city of Münster. There fortune finally smiled on me, and I was able to sublet two primitive attic rooms, in a rundown former patrician villa on Wallgasse, close to the town center.

Compared to Cologne, Münster was slightly better off, but not by much. There had been over a hundred Allied raids, the last and heaviest just before the end in March 1945, and 61 percent of the city—somewhat less than Cologne's 78 percent—had been turned to rubble. Of a prewar total of 33,000 housing units, only about a third had been left inhabitable, and by the early fifties only half of the others had been repaired. Many people were still in emergency shelters and wartime bunkers, and though the situation was improving, the housing shortage was made worse with the addition of a quarter of the population who were refugees from the East.[112]

Living in Germany, we found, would require some major adjustments. Our Wallgasse quarters were tiny, the baby had to be changed on our one small table, we cooked in a corner of the room on a single burner stove, and the bathroom was shared with other renters. The owners, an elderly lady and her widowed daughter with two young sons, lived on a lower floor where the only adult male presence in evidence was in photographs of young men in Wehrmacht uniforms gracing their walls. What they thought of us, and especially of me and my German-Jewish background, I will never know. It was obvious that their finances were extremely tight and that our presence made them acutely uncomfortable. Throughout our stay they remained formal but distant, polite but easily aroused by small irritations, and the relationship was never easy.

Slowly it began to dawn on me how heavy a price not only their victims, but the Germans themselves had paid for the Nazis. West Germany had been reduced to half the Reich's prewar size. The population was overaged, and women substantially outnumbered men, particularly those aged twenty to forty-five. Almost every family had lost a father, brother or son.[113] Though conditions were improving, wages remained low, taxes were high, and living standards not yet back to prewar levels. Many people remained dependent on social support and fully one-third of the federal budget had to be paid for occupation costs.

Yet there was also evidence of a strong national determination to turn things around, proving that the German reputation for hard work was well deserved, at least in the early fifties. Nowadays Germans virtually consider the thirty-eight-hour, five-day work week their birthright, but then they were working on average more than a forty-five-hour, five-and-a-half-day week. Free Saturdays, taken for granted today, were but a distant dream and actual weekly hours worked in industry were close to fifty.[114]

The economy, rising phoenix-like from the ashes, was poised on the threshold of a prolonged period of rapid growth. With substantial help from the Marshall Fund, there had been major strides forward right after the currency reform of 1948, aided by an undervalued currency and strong export demand stimulated by the Korean War. Industrial production had already risen by one-third since 1950, the first trade surplus was achieved in 1951, and between 1955 and 1960 its share of the GNP would reach levels greater than any in German history.[115] Just as I was arriving in Cologne, the papers were celebrating the five hundred thousandth VW Beetle rolling off the assembly lines. Eventually the world would call it the "German economic miracle," but the national debate between those favoring Economic Minister Ludwig Erhard's immensely successful market-oriented approach, and the Social Democrats' argument for a degree of planning, controls, and public ownership of key industries, continued.

Shortly after I arrived, the second Bundestag election campaign was reaching its climax. The Federal Republic was a mere four years old, and Chancellor Konrad Adenauer had established himself as a strong leader committed to a strategy of German–French reconciliation and German integration into Europe, NATO, and the Western alliance. In the background, however, the question of German rearmament loomed large and his Social Democratic Party opponents argued that an even-handed approach and a neutral Germany gave greater promise of reunification with the Communist East.

De facto sovereignty, moreover, had not yet been fully restored and the occupation authorities remained much in evidence. Thus, in July 1953 Der Spiegel reported with evident irritation and disapproval on the British authorities' enforcement of a ban on military uniforms, on the grounds that even "ceremonial" ones were too "military" in nature.[116] And elsewhere, much to the resigned amusement of the public, the Berlin Allied military commander had recently seen fit to confiscate more than a hundred field glasses from the local police as forbidden "war material."[117] Ridiculing Allied occupation policies was a favorite pastime on which most Germans agreed.

It was a fascinating if unsettled time to be in Germany. The Cold War was heating up, the Eisenhower administration had taken office in the United States, the standoff with Communist East Germany was complete, the first steps toward European economic integration were under way, and a host of unresolved problems still weighed on the West German Republic's fledgling life. Millions of refugees had been displaced from lost German territories in the East and tens of thousands more were fleeing from East German Communism every month. (The Berlin Wall would not be built until eight years later.) Many former German soldiers were still being held prisoner in Russia, but every few weeks trainloads of them were arriving to an emotional, if unsettling, homecoming.

The Allies' de-Nazification program, pursued with vigor in the early years, had ended with mixed results, and except for a small number of the worst Nazis, most erstwhile supporters and party members were still—or again—holding leading positions in business and public life. In my travels I soon began to cross their paths and regularly had to remind myself that a social scientist researcher must remain clinical and eschew subjective feelings. This, I must confess, I managed to do only with difficulty and mixed emotions.

Once settled in Wallgasse and having armed Eileen with a German–English phrase book and useful hints about coping with the challenges of everyday German life, I launched my forays into the codetermination companies of the Ruhr. For logistical support, I had acquired a surplus VW from the British military, painted, in the style of its erstwhile owners, in ugly army olive-drab. The ancient "Beetle" could be temperamental at the wrong moments, but it was cheap and otherwise indestructible as we bumped along over the cobblestone back roads of the Ruhr district (most of them long since replaced by Germany's impressive network of postwar Autobahns). Occasionally I would be gone for several days and range far afield in Germany. My principal "beat" was the coal and steel towns—Dortmund, Duisburg, Essen, Gelsenkirchen, Bochum, Wuppertal, and a half dozen smaller ones. During the day I did archival research and interviewed executives, labor leaders, and workers in offices or on shop floors, and in the evenings I drank beer incognito in the local *Kneipen* (pubs), the better to gauge the mood of the locals.

In Münster we quickly became part of a wide circle of professionals, university people, union officials and British military stationed in the area, which exposed us to a kaleidoscope of facts, stories, and impressions of individual Germans and the issues of the day. Many new friends and acquaintances were open-minded and eager for a democratic Germany. Among them, the DGB's Erich Potthoff stood out as a steadfast democrat without illusions, and he and I spent many hours together discussing Germany under Hitler, and debating the rebuilding tasks facing the new West German Republic. The federal constitution had established the rule of law and guaranteed individual rights, and there was no question that under Chancellor Adenauer, the government was making progress to solidify the foundations of a democratic state. Yet the traditional and autocratic mood of some political parties and among some segments of the population was also a reality. There was plenty of evidence of it in my travels and industry interviews and it worried me.

Yet through Potthoff and other new friends I was gradually becoming aware of something I should have known—that there were many young and older Germans with attitudes and beliefs quite unlike my preconceived notions of the "typical Germanic" ones I instinctively disliked, and who had never been Nazis. Indeed, eight years after the war, many were now firmly committed to a democratic Germany anchored in Europe and the West. They looked to the United States not as a former enemy but as a country they admired for its democratic traditions and as the leader of the Western Alliance of which they wanted their country to be a part. U.S. prestige, I found, was inordinately high among them, in part due to gratitude for Marshall Plan aid. Especially with the new generation of young people, Americans were popular, and the reading rooms of USIA's America Houses were crowed with those eager for American books, magazines, music, and films. Lectures on U.S. affairs were always well attended, an extracurricular opportunity that took me to many German towns.

The USIA America House in Hamburg was among the most active, and it was while lecturing there that I first met Eric Warburg. Eric was that rare exception: a U.S. citizen but a former German Jew who had returned to live in Germany. His situation was a bit special, however. The Warburgs had for generations been among Hamburg's best known merchant bankers and respected members of the local elite. When the Nazis took the Warburgs' bank they had fled to the United States, and Eric, the eldest son, had returned to Germany after the war as a U.S. Lieutenant Colonel and interrogation chief of the 9th U.S. Air Force where, along with others, he had been assigned to interrogate the infamous Hermann Göring (who, according to Eric had never known his true identity). Returning to his native Hamburg—where the family name still carried great weight—to reclaim what was left of their bank, he had joined a small group of other anti-Nazi returnees, among them Mayor Max Brauer, a pre-Hitler Social Democrat politician, whose goal to restore decent government and rebuild Germany's most important port city. Eric had great charm and a delightful sense of humor, and was an optimist by nature but not one with many illusions. We got along well and his insights into the German situation from an American perspective were always interesting. I lost sight of him in his later years— he died in 1990—but as fate would have it, his American daughter, Marie, and her husband, Michael Naumann (Gerhard Schröder's Minister of Culture), would, much later, become my closest German friends.

The Germany of the early fifties surprised me. The country was still a work-in-progress, insecure about its place in the world, eager to win acceptance in the West but domestically with lots of reminders of its inglorious past intermingled with signs of promise for a more hopeful future. I met many Germans, young and old, committed to Western democracy and the rule of law, who reflected the prevailing sentiments of the majority. But I also listened to a significant number of others full of self-pity and resentment over the lost war with wildly contradictory and backward-looking ideas about the major issues of the day, and others prone to fall back on a mixture of arrogance and servility in their dealings with foreigners and each other, which irritated me intensely.

On the extreme right of the political spectrum, small, thinly veiled neo-Nazi parties were scoring limited successes in local elections, yet there was no doubt that Chancellor Konrad Adenauer was moving the country in the right direction. In the 1953 elections, his center-right Christian Democrats and the opposition Social Democrats had won a solid three-quarters of the Bundestag seats between them. But among the leadership of the smaller Free Democrats, supported mainly by business, were more than a few recently rehabilitated Nazis with backgrounds that repelled me. The so-called All-German Party, made up of refugees unreconciled to the loss of their homes in the east, weren't stellar democrats either and had won about 6 percent of Bundestag seats.

Opinion surveys revealed that a solid 57 percent of all Germans in 1953 expressed satisfaction with the Adenauer government. Nevertheless, a third still thought it would be nice to have their Kaiser back, and a full quarter of the population retained "a good opinion" of Hitler.[118] Most blamed Hitler and those at the top for German wartime atrocities and the crimes against the Jews, but also thought the war crimes trials had been a mistake, and that the continuing incarceration of the guilty was unjust, even though many of those previously convicted had already had their sentences shortened or been released.

The Holocaust clearly remained one of the most sensitive issues, but often a taboo topic. Few Germans were willing to face it openly, though the government had offered compensation to Israel and was—cautiously and slowly—making restitution payments to individual former German Jews for property and lives lost. By 1953, the DP camps had been emptied of Holocaust survivors, and most of the occupants had left Germany. Only a handful of Jews, 20,000 to 30,000 at most, had chosen to stay.

Today anything relating to Jews and Jewish affairs in Germany or abroad, is obsessively covered in the German media, and the Holocaust is incessantly debated in public. In the early fifties the very opposite was the case and few Germans were comfortable talking about such matters. The reality was that the horror of the crimes against the Jews was too great, and the wounds, guilt, and trauma among Jews and non-Jews alike apparently too fresh and deep. Both sides, it seemed, felt that the less said about the Holocaust in public the better. When the subject did come up—as it not infrequently did in conversations with me—it almost always involved embarrassed expressions of sorrow and pain, coupled with a ritualistic profession of warm memories of former Jewish friends and neighbors ("did you perhaps ever meet my good friend, Max Levi, in New York?"). No one, as far as I can recall, admitted to any prior knowledge of the fate of the Jews under the Nazis, and most Germans insisted that the terrible crimes had been carried out in secret.

I very rarely heard an anti-Semitic remark, certainly never in my presence. Yet with de-Nazification at an end, and many former party members and fellow travelers back in their jobs, no one was willing for an open confrontation with the past. That, as it turned out, would be left to another generation of Germans several decades later.

In the summer of 1954 my work was complete, and it was time to leave. I had learned a lot, and in many respects my views about Germany had changed for the better. I had seen encouraging evidence of a slow evolution to a democratic Germany, which was a hopeful development. Yet the West Germany of those days was a land full of contradictions, where I never felt really at ease. I had met many who were genuinely committed to building a different, more tolerant and open society, but I also felt the stolidity, the lack of laughter, and the servility and absence of civic courage of others, which I disliked and had long associated with the German national character. Germany then was a busy and hard-working country, but not a happy or particularly attractive one, and the constant reminders of the atmosphere that had once prevailed there and hadn't, as yet, entirely disappeared grated on me. Thus, though I was glad that I had come, better understanding had not really been matched by any feeling of closeness for the country of my birth, and, if anything, I felt even more attached to the United States. I left wishing the Germans well, but in many respects Germany had remained foreign to me.

Near East Travels

Back in Princeton, two more daughters, Jill and Jane, arrived during the fifties, and gradually we put down roots in the community. My doctorate in hand, I accepted a junior faculty job at Princeton, not because of a burning desire for an academic career, but mostly because I needed the money and was pleased with the implicit vote of confidence from my professors. Yet as luck would have it, along with routine teaching duties on the campus, I was almost immediately recruited to assist a consortium of prominent scholars in an ambitious, high-profile research project impressively entitled the "Inter-University Study of Labor Problems in Industrial Development," thereby exposing me to unusual "unacademic" adventures outside the United States during my faculty years.

The guiding spirit of the project was Fred "Fizz" Harbison, a well-known labor economist and respected scholar. He was also a prime example of that peculiar species of "academic entrepreneur" occasionally encountered on university campuses, who delights in organizing and running ambitious research projects almost more than doing scholarly work and who is endowed with a special talent for hustling up the funds for a far-flung network of young faculty to whom the actual work is subcontracted. Fizz was a particular fan of international projects—mainly, I suspect, because he was an inveterate traveler who delighted in making whirlwind airplane trips to exotic places between his more mundane campus responsibilities. The Inter-University Project was his most ambitious achievement, a vast undertaking for which the senior consortium leaders joined with him were Clark Kerr (later President of UC Berkeley), Harvard's John Dunlop (who would serve as President Ford's secretary of labor), and Charles Myers, a labor economist at MIT.

The research they had dreamed up spanned the globe and involved a series of case studies in various countries investigating the training of a skilled labor force in the course of industrial development. In the jaundiced view of some outside observers it was a giant boondoggle, but Harbison et al. had succeeded in persuading the Ford Foundation to underwrite this expensive undertaking with the then princely grant of a million dollars, thereby enabling them to engage a small army of researchers to travel to distant places for the leg work involved. As it happened, one of the more interesting projects was just then being launched in Iraq, and it was for this that I had been tapped. My assignment was to spend what turned out to be an action-packed several months, spread over the course of three separate field trips away from Princeton, to research the experience with training Iraqis to staff the country's burgeoning oil industry, which, in those pre-revolutionary days, still remained firmly in the controlling hands of the British.

This was exciting work in an entirely new and unfamiliar part of the world. I had expected to be teaching undergraduate economics to Princeton freshmen, and here I was, far away in the Middle East for weeks on end, living an adventurous life interviewing scholars, politicians, and businessmen in Beirut, Damascus, and Baghdad, roaming through the oil installations of Basra, Mosul, and Sulaymaniyah, and meeting with British executives, Texas roustabouts, and Iraqi staff in the British Petroleum Company (BP) headquarters town of Kirkuk. Occasionally, I would brave the brutal summer heat to delve into dusty personnel records at remote pumping stations reachable only by jeep or flimsy single-engine "puddle jumper," airplanes.

The early fifties was a watershed period in Iraqi history, a deceptive calm before impending storms. Iraq was still a backward, under-developed and sleepy place steeped in its tribal traditions, a twentieth century creation of the British ruled by a branch of Hashemite royalty, and of significance in world affairs only due to its large underground reserves of oil. Though an artificial amalgam of disparate ethnic, religious, and tribal groups, the surface appearance was one of relative stability, and I do not recall any serious predictions of big changes in the offing. The Iraqis were, of course, enemies of Israel, but so was every other Arab country, and the king and his government were basically friendly to the West and—what mattered most to the West at the time—successful in keeping local Communists under control and the Soviets on the outside looking in. No one thought of Iraq as having great geopolitical significance other than as a supplier of oil, and no one dreamed that this country would one day emerge as one of the world's big trouble spots. That an American president would declare this desert land a major threat to U.S. security and world peace, and that 150,000 U.S. troops would become dangerously embroiled in its towns and deserts, was most assuredly a prospect nowhere on the horizon.

Appearances can be deceiving. The country's surface calm turned out to be just that when, in 1958, the king and prime minister were murdered in a military revolt, followed by a decade of internal turmoil giving way to the bloody thirty-year rule of the Ba'athists under Saddam Hussein. What this shows perhaps, is that the Western intelligence services of the fifties were no better at predicting risks or understanding the political dynamics of an alien environment than they are today. Yet nations have trouble learning from the past. Having failed to understand domestic Iraqi developments then, perhaps we should have been more cautious forty years later and viewed with greater skepticism the notion that we, as outsiders, can control events there, or that installing a democratic government in a tribal culture is a promising undertaking.

Actually, the signs of trouble were already on the horizon, and the oil industry I was studying was as good a place as any for detecting the rumbles of future upheavals for those willing to listen. Yet though my studies showed that big changes were in the offing, the foreigners who still controlled the fields seemed blissfully unaware of it.

Iraq's oil industry had its inception in the 1920s, and thirty years later foreign companies led by the British were still running the show. The top technical and managerial jobs remained almost exclusively in the hands of expatriates, Iraqis did only the lesser clerical and manual work, and few "locals" had advanced much above the lower rungs of the managerial ladder. The expats lived the good life in protected enclaves, drew ample allowances, and went on extended home leaves to recover from the rigors of a hardship post. The atmosphere was distinctly anachronistic and colonial, and their attitudes toward local employees eerily stimulated my memory of prewar Shanghai. At the BP Club in Kirkuk one dressed for dinner on Saturday night and the gin and whiskey flowed freely. Outside the protected walls of such enclaves, the atmosphere had turned restless, the handwriting was on the wall that the good life of privileged outsiders would not go on forever, and the impatience of Iraqis to take control of their industry was hard to miss. It struck me almost at once, remembering the Chinese

Communist revolution and the foreigners' fool's paradise in Shanghai, which had existed until the very last moment, how odd it was that no one in the top ranks of BP seemed to notice these winds of change. The prevailing opinion toward Iraqi workers was not unfriendly, though self-serving and paternalistic. The standard line was that the oil business was demanding and technical and that it would take decades before Iraqis could handle such tasks. Arabs are Bedouins at heart, I was told repeatedly, unsuitable for industrial discipline and with tribal attitudes incompatible with rational management decision making.

The evidence from interviews and personnel files reflected a somewhat different reality. It was true that the first generation of local workers, limited by education and experience, had risen to only modest levels. It was also true, however, that some of their sons were even then studying engineering and management at European and American universities. Nationalism was on the rise, and it was already plain to see that it would be these sons who would sooner or later seize control and prove quite capable of running their own affairs.

This, indeed, was precisely what soon happened, and the propensity of the West for underestimating the adaptability of a foreign culture to the needs of a modern economy has always surprised me. In today's globalized world few should still doubt it. The speed with which this happened subsequently in countries such as China, India, Taiwan, and Brazil, was a surprise to many, but, for me, Iraq was an early lesson that it pays to look at the evidence and to question established thinking and tired clichés, regardless of how fervently believed and repeated they might be.

Leaving Academic Life

Back at Princeton, I liked my campus friends and the intellectual give and take, but academic life failed to satisfy me fully. I wanted to be part of the action, in public life if possible; the university's ivory-tower environment was a bit too detached for that. My goal remained public service, but the problem was that Republican Washington was not a congenial place, and after Ike's landslide victory in 1956 this would be true for at least four more years. Just then, however, fate intervened—as it would repeatedly in my life—and events took a decidedly unexpected turn. That this led to leaving the academy in search of excitement "on the outside" was perhaps preordained; that it involved international business rather than public service was not.

It began, improbably enough, on the Cunard liner *Queen Elizabeth*[119] over a game of chess. I was on my way home from a research trip to Europe; jet airplanes were not yet an option, and the more civilized way of crossing the Atlantic by ship was still the common mode of travel. My interests at the time—studying how U.S. multinationals organized abroad to maximize their competitive advantage—had involved interviewing a number of U.S. chief executives in their home offices. Among them had been a most unusual man with decidedly unorthodox views, completely self-educated but highly intelligent and successful, who ran a company manufacturing, of all things, "crown corks"—or bottle tops—in a dozen countries around the world. We had run into each other again on the boat train from London (itself pure accident—I had missed my connection and stumbled onto the wrong one), and on the first day at sea a surprise invitation had come down from his first-class quarters to join him for tea, followed by a challenge to what turned into a nonstop string of chess games stretching over the next several days.

Herman Ginsburg was chairman of Crown Cork International Corporation and a much better chess player than I—he took delight in beating me handily. Yet I noticed that between one-sided checkmates, he was a lot more skilled in delving into my past than I was in questioning him about his business philosophy. With Ginsburg, as I would later learn, little was left to chance. A canny negotiator with a sixth sense for the motivation of his interlocutors, he invariably planned his moves carefully, in business as in chess, and left little to chance. He enjoyed winning—but avoided frontal attacks and preferred to probe for weaknesses and to achieve his goals by indirection—an iron hand in a velvet glove, so to speak. The approach he used to lure me from Princeton to his company fit this pattern.

"Tell me, why would an ambitious young man like you prefer to sit on the university campus and study what others do, rather than testing his mettle by doing it himself?" he wondered innocently one day as if the thought had struck him suddenly. Given my frame of mind, he had hit on just the right question. A bottle top company might sound ordinary to a student of how things work in the real world, he pressed on, anticipating my thinking, but the product wasn't as important as the challenge of building a profitable worldwide organization and—incidentally—did I know about corporate pay—and what was the salary of a junior Princeton professor?

He later gleefully admitted that my initial praise of academic life had rung hollow, and, once he decided to hire me, the line of attack had become obvious. Thus one thing led to another, and this was how within a matter of weeks my brief university career came to an end, and I was launched on my first international business job.

My academic friends had been astonished and bemused when I decided to exchange Princeton for Crown Cork. To forego the chance of academic tenure in favor of—of all things—the manufacturing of bottle tops, struck them as bizarre. Yet I saw it as a chance for new adventure, and to try something entirely different. With three small children, the prospect of virtually tripling my modest Princeton salary loomed as a not unwelcome change as well.

I spent four intense and insane years at Crown Cork International (CCIC), in what proved anything but a normal entry-level corporate job. Ginsburg had revealed little of what awaited me, but had been correct that though manufacturing bottle tops might seem mundane, managing a big company had not much to do with the product itself. For me, the challenge was to learn to be an effective manager in a highly unusual operation, which reflected above all the unique style and personality of the aging tyrant who dominated it. To be part of such an organization and to succeed in it transcended the significance of the products we manufactured and sold.

My new boss was a self-made man who had left school at fourteen, started out as a factory worker, earned law and accounting degrees at night, and by virtue of persistence, brains, and hard work clawed his way to the top. Small in stature and unprepossessing in appearance, a Jew in a gentile company at a time when anti-Semitic prejudice in corporate America was still common, he had advanced up the corporate ladder because he was needed rather than liked, and respected for his achievements even as he was resented for his brains. Ginsburg knew this, and in no small measure, it had shaped his character and outlook. He had become a cynic who trusted no one, and was prone to suspect the motives of friends and competitors alike. Learning to get along with him became one of my toughest and most demanding challenges.

For all his many talents, Ginsburg was a man of towering contradictions. On the one hand, he was unusually smart, with one of the sharpest analytical minds I have ever encountered, indefatigable in his attention to detail and a gifted entrepreneur with a keen eye for a business opportunity. On the other hand, his suspicions made him a terrible manager—excessively wary of the motives of others, overly cautious and conservative at times, and highly emotional and impetuous at others. Trusting no one, he had trouble delegating even the smallest details and for years had virtually single-handedly built Crown Cork's small international operations into a substantial public holding company for a network of profitable manufacturing subsidiaries in a dozen countries. Assisted only by a few bookkeepers and clerks, without even a single junior executive to share the load, he had only recently woken up to the fact that he was sitting atop an empire that was a giant organizational mess.

For longer than was prudent he had resisted recruiting additional management help, before taking the curious step of settling on me— a thirty-one-year old academic without executive experience—as the chosen instrument for his version of "organizational change." What ensued was a peculiar, intense, and highly personalized relationship between us, more like that of a father and son than between superior and subordinate in a normal corporate setting. For him it was one to which he was neither accustomed nor emotionally attuned, and for me the four years under him were full of extraordinarily demanding, often frustrating, and always challenging work, but they were an intense learning experience of unusual scope.

No business school, nor ten years of "normal" experience could have prepared me for Ginsburg. From him I acquired his lawyer's penchant for "knowing your brief"—the importance of being better prepared in a negotiation than those on the other side of the table. If anything was his primary rule it was this, and in Washington I would come to be grateful for the lesson learned. He was tough, difficult, and often infuriating, but, when all was said and done, he taught me a lot. He handed me many assignments he should have done himself, and hounded me mercilessly and often irrationally, but in time this gave me a thorough grounding in the practicalities of international trade and finance, and the realities of the economics and business practices of the developing world. Through him I learned how to organize, set goals, recruit, motivate, and evaluate staff—often by observing his own mistakes and remembering what *not* to do. Crown Cork, in sum, was a tough assignment, but it taught me much about international affairs, and it was there that I first learned what it takes to be an effective manager, an international negotiator, and a leader.

The Eisenhower Fifties

Meanwhile throughout most of the fifties, Eisenhower had presided over an affluent America, even as major developments were changing American society and societal deficiencies were multiplying. Social Security payments were low, and social programs in health, housing, and education far from adequate. Race discrimination remained a major blot on America, and progress to end it agonizingly slow. The fear of internal subversion was being exploited by unscrupulous politicians who put civil liberties at risk. In the Cold War, the fronts between

East and West were essentially frozen, and amidst belligerent rhetoric on both sides, often more for home consumption than reflecting reality, events occasionally threatened to get dangerously out of hand.

In 1956, an anti-Communist revolt in Hungary was brutally suppressed, shattering the hope of a thaw after the death of Stalin. The French were defeated in Indochina, and Communists took over the north, and Fidel Castro came to power in Cuba cheered on by the Soviets. In the Far East, Taiwan and Korea remained nervous trouble spots, and John Foster Dulles, Eisenhower's talented but self-righteous and opinionated secretary of state, spoke of "agonizing reappraisal" and "rollback" replacing containment in U.S. foreign policy.

Along with these recurring foreign crises, American emotions were stirred and headlines dominated by major national trends—the struggle for civil rights and controversies over civil liberties, for example—whose longterm significance was not always well understood. The South continued to resist the Supreme Court's reversal of the "separate but equal" doctrine by any means possible. Three years after the landmark decision in 1954, only 12 percent of its school districts had been integrated, and in no fewer than seven states not a single black child had yet been admitted to a white high school. In the entire region, only a quarter of all eligible blacks had been successfully registered to vote.[120] The frustration of blacks and their sympathizers with such limited progress led in turn to ever larger and more spectacular peaceful protests under the leadership of Martin Luther King Jr. A boycott by 50,000 black residents of the segregated Montgomery, Alabama, bus system in 1955, mass rallies in Washington, and sit-ins at Southern lunch counters dramatically focused national attention on the race issue. Whereas Truman had openly sympathized with black demands and supported them actively, his successor had a more nuanced view. To Chief Justice Warren, Ike had once expressed his worries about the wisdom of mixing white girls and black boys in the classroom, and the military in which he had served all his life had been rigidly segregated.[121] Moreover, it was in his nature to counsel patience and to prefer a gradual approach. It showed in the vigor of his actions, yet, on the other hand, he also believed strongly in the Constitution and the rule of law. Thus, though he was often criticized for being too slow, when the Court's edict was openly defied by Orval Faubus, the governor of Arkansas, Eisenhower had seen no alternative but to order the military to escort black students into Little Rock's white high school, after a dramatic and highly emotional confrontation that held the nation's attention for days. For once the liberals had cheered him.

The movement to end racial discrimination was about securing the constitutional rights of one group of Americans. Fear of internal subversion—the other big issue of the fifties—involved a tense struggle to defend the civil rights of all. Both issues were highly emotional and both threatened to divide the nation, yet while the former eventually had a positive outcome, the latter's sometimes vicious controversies over how best to fight subversion while preserving individual civil rights poisoned the domestic atmosphere and left scars that took a long time to heal.

Even before World War II, the fear of Communism had gripped America and led to the creation of a so-called House Committee on Un-American Activities, charged with investigating alleged internal subversion. The Cold War, Communist China, and the war in Korea had intensified the zeal of this and similar investigative bodies that in the fifties became the meeting places for publicity-seeking politicians who resorted to bullying and intimidation of witnesses in their investigations of Hollywood, the media, education, and various government departments. Soon nobody and nothing was safe from them. Exposing spies, Communists, and true subversives was legitimate enough, but the bitter irony was that in the methods they used—guilt by association and infringement of the witnesses' constitutional rights—it was they who were being "Un-American."

In truth, ferreting out subversives was only part of their motivation. In a wider sense, they preached a bigoted pseudo-conservatism and used the hunt for "Reds" as an attack on the establishment by inveighing against a vague "socialism" in American society furthered, they claimed, by Eastern "Ivy Leaguers" in both parties, "young men with silver spoons in their mouths."[122] Time and again conservatives and liberals squared off on opposite sides, and for a long time few dared to oppose the zealots openly. Hunting "Reds" took on the characteristics of a national witch-hunt, while a frightened and confused public was split between those who believed the Red-hunters and those who feared and detested them but dared not speak out. Attempts under both Truman and Eisenhower to appease them with tightened security regulations not only failed but spurred them to ever greater excesses.

Their principal exponent was Joe McCarthy, the junior senator from Wisconsin who terrorized the country and rode the issue to brief fame until, discredited in 1954 when he overplayed his hand, he disappeared from the political limelight as suddenly as he had gained it. But not before "McCarthyism"—and all those who supported it—had done immense damage and become a distasteful part of the American vocabulary. McCarthy was a skillful demagogue, and his ever wilder accusations poisoned the national atmosphere, weakened the State Department, and damaged the U.S. reputation abroad. Loyalty oath requirements on college campuses roiled academic institutions, where they collided with established norms of academic freedom. What sustained McCarthy for too long was that, for a time at least, even more respectable conservatives had found him an effective ally in attacking liberal opponents, and had used him as a handy instrument for their political ends.

Most of his allegations were never proved, but many careers were ruined and much injustice was done. Only occasionally were real spies exposed, and then never by him.

As the fifties were ending, McCarthy was gone, but the battle against racial discrimination was not over and continued to gain strength as the Reverend King and his supporters adopted ever more dramatic means to press for action, and impatience grew. Even well-meaning people still counseled patience. William Faulkner, no segregationist himself, publicly warned against coercing his fellow Southerners to accept quick changes, and many others, while professing sympathy, were equally reluctant to force the pace.

Yet here and there breakthroughs began to occur. On June 22, 1955, Princeton University announced the appointment of Charles T. Davis, a thirty-seven-year old scholar from New York, as the first-ever black member to its faculty. The event made national headlines, as did the news that New York Airways had become the first airline to hire a black flight crew member, and that students at the University of Iowa had taken the unprecedented step of electing a seventeen-year old black girl as their "campus queen." Slowly more blacks were being admitted to all-white institutions, schools were integrated, better employment opportunities for blacks opened up, and housing discrimination succumbed to successful court challenges. Yet restrictive housing covenants remained common, and many otherwise well-intentioned whites, fearing for the value of their properties, continued to honor them. To his embarrassment, even the deed to Vice President Nixon's Washington home was revealed to have such a provision, though he hastened to let it be known that he considered it unenforceable.

Thanks to the Mills Brothers, the race question continued to have special meaning for me, and in the later fifties in Princeton—an enlightened community relatively free of bigotry—I had a very personal taste of how difficult changing deeply rooted attitudes could be. The town prided itself on a long history of what it considered harmonious race relations. 10 percent of its residents were blacks, most worked in white homes or held other low-level jobs, and as far back as anyone could remember they had lived quietly in a cluster of small streets near the center of town. The houses were small, some a little shabby but most well kept in what was—not by law but by custom and economics—a de facto black ghetto. There they attended their own churches, shopped in small stores catering exclusively to them, and their children attended a largely black elementary school. Occasionally, there were exchange visits with white churches, which made for all-round good feelings, and there was a degree of interaction on municipal matters, but otherwise black and white Princeton moved on parallel but separate tracks.

Blacks living next to whites in the "better" part of town had rarely been an issue. The prices were beyond the reach of blacks, restrictive covenants would have made it difficult, and real estate agents were skilled in preventing it. But times were changing. Princeton was becoming part of suburbia, commuters to jobs in New York and Philadelphia were moving in, and a small sprinkling of middle class blacks could now be seen on the station platform alongside whites waiting for the morning train. They were more educated and affluent than Princeton's long-time blacks, and the black part of town was not an option for them, but the problem was that availability of better housing was tight—and for blacks virtually unobtainable. The conventional wisdom was that when a black family moved in, whites would leave, and real estate values would plummet. Fearing financial losses, builders, owners, and brokers working together invariably found ways not to sell to blacks.

So in 1955 I joined a group of like-minded citizens determined to tackle this problem. The idea was that our group, Princeton Housing Associates (PHA), would take the initiative and actively recruit an "open housing" builder pledged to sell to all comers, while PHA would smooth the way in the community, encourage both races to buy, and thus give the lie to those arguing that mixed housing was not commercially viable.

Or so we thought—but this proved a vastly more complex undertaking than we had expected. More than once over the next five years, after each new disappointment and setback, the resigned cynicism of Harry Mills and the anger of Cliff White would flash before my eyes. It took two years and untold fruitless negotiations to find even a single "maverick" builder willing to take a chance. Bankers were reluctant to give loans and the real estate industry regarded us as idealistic fools. Most surprising of all, finding white and black families willing to risk living in integrated housing proved difficult once the homes were being built. Lip service aside, both were afraid of being part of a mixed community experiment, and it required painstaking negotiations and active recruiting to find enough volunteers. Even after the twenty-four houses had been built it took more than a year to sell them. In the end our experiment did work, but it had taken a half-mad, idealistic builder, lots of community effort, and even a "quota" of our own—making sure that a bit more than half of the houses were bought by willing whites ready to stay the course, while keeping black homeowners slightly in the minority.

I often pass those houses today. The original owners are long since gone and in the beginning of the twenty-first century the problems of the fifties are a distant memory. I have no idea who lives there now, and few Princetonians even remember that this was once a frontier experiment for breaking down racial housing barriers. Yet our PHA experience was, at the time, a perfect mirror of the national struggle against discrimination and my first real taste of how difficult it was to overcome long-standing practices and deep-seated prejudices. Years later, on that night in 1964 when I celebrated "cloture" with Hubert Humphrey, the Princeton experience wasn't far from my mind.

In the fifties, finally, I also joined the Princeton Democratic Club and had my first exposure to local partisan politics, with important lessons not taught in the classroom but useful for my later public service years. Among them were the validity of former House Speaker Tip O'Neill's often cited dictum that "all politics is local," and my future boss and mentor George Ball's favorite advice—cynical but true—that behind every position of principle usually hides a specific selfish interest, or as the late Senator Russell Long was fond of reminding me, that in politics "it all depends whose ox is being gored."

The Democratic Club's meetings at the local firehouse were a colorful amalgam of liberal activists, university intellectuals, working class "locals," and blacks—a perfect mirror of the coalition of voters that had kept the Democrats in power in Washington for many years under FDR and Truman. Democrats all, they had very different motivations and interests, and most of our time was spent balancing these concerns and finding enough common ground to advance Democratic Party interests.

The University crowd disliked Eisenhower's caution on matters of race and his go-slow appeasement of the red baiters, and lamented the aggressive rhetoric of John Foster Dulles. They were focused on national issues, and in the presidential reelection campaign of 1956 they had thrilled to the elegant rhetoric of Adlai Stevenson "talking sense" to the American people. His resounding defeat had greatly depressed them.

The town locals gave at best lip service to such matters. Their major interests were patronage jobs for friends and relatives at township or county levels, and matters such as liquor licenses and the decisions of municipal planning boards. Not a few were McCarthyites, and while the blacks were allied with the liberals on matters of race, the other whites were decidedly unsympathetic to integration in housing and jobs and, if anything, considered black demands in these areas a personal threat. Winning elections at the local level was what mattered to them because it brought them small but tangible benefits. As we worked together to get out the vote for local and national elections, not a few of the "townies" probably voted for Ike but rarely admitted this, to ensure that the "gown" Democrats would help them and stay on their side.

As is true everywhere in the American two-party system, tenacious internal battles were fought to accommodate each group, and slates for club officers and candidates at local levels had to be carefully balanced—so many Irish, Italians, and an occasional "egghead" or black. At Crown Cork, Herman Ginsburg had taught me the art of negotiation, and in the firehouse, I would find ample opportunity to apply these skills in arbitrating disputes and accommodating conflicting interests. Learning "whose ox is being gored" helped to make the system work. I enjoyed the challenges, and gradually found that I could handle them pretty well. But I never stopped dreaming of the day when I could test myself on a wider stage.

THE SIXTIES
Washington

"The White House is Calling"

With the election of John F. Kennedy in November 1960, the American political scene was dramatically transformed. The Democrats were back in power, led by a charismatic new president—at forty-three the youngest ever elected to the White House, succeeding Eisenhower, who had been one of the oldest.[123]

I had followed these developments with great excitement, inspired by Kennedy's eloquent rhetoric and the prospect of an activist administration with a Democrat at the helm. As far as my friends and I were concerned, under Eisenhower the United States had been standing still for too long in the face of major domestic and international challenges requiring urgent attention, with too many problems left unresolved and too many new opportunities missed.

The U.S. population had grown by over 50 million during the fifties, a veritable demographic explosion with far-reaching changes in postwar American society. Inner cities and rural areas were in decline and suburbia was bursting at the seams as whites had moved out of the cities and blacks from the South moved in. In Washington, D.C., blacks now accounted for more than half the population, and for a third in Detroit and other big Northern cities like Philadelphia, Chicago, and St. Louis.

Living standards had risen substantially, but the gains were unevenly distributed, and large pockets of poverty remained in inner cities where blacks faced poor housing, a lack of jobs, and discrimination in education and employment. In the booming suburbs, on the other hand, there was a need for better roads, schools, and improved ways of dealing with the effects of technological unemployment. Supermarkets and big chains were displacing mom-and-pop stores. Self-employment—a traditional backbone of American society—was in decline, and more Americans than ever were working for large companies.

This was the inchoate mix of domestic problems awaiting the new president, but international issues were no less urgent. Cold War frontlines were dangerously frozen, and the launching of Sputnik had dramatized what appeared as a loss of U.S. technological leadership. The rise of Japan as an economic force had to be reckoned with, and the evolving European Common Market was a historic development that called for new initiatives to counteract powerful protectionist forces never far below the surface on both sides of the Atlantic. Many newly independent nations in Africa and Asia were flirting with Marxism and had become ideological battlegrounds between East and West. Closer to home, Castro had just taken over in Cuba, and throughout Latin America the pressure for economic development assistance and better trade opportunities was strong.

So here now was a dynamic new president who exuded energy, enthusiasm, and confidence and who promised to make the White House "a vital center for action" to meet the full range of domestic and global challenges. For this he had recruited the youngest cabinet in twenty years—all but one of its members were born in the twentieth century, and most had come of age during World War II. This was *my* generation, and the media featured reports of an ambitious talent hunt to recruit the brightest and the best for the sub-cabinet, White House staff, and key overseas assignments. Ted Sorensen, Kennedy's principal assistant, would later describe it as a true "ministry of talent."[124] The roster of well-known names with national reputations from academia, business, and public life joining JFK's administration was dazzling—Adlai Stevenson, George Kennan, Edward R. Murrow, Chester Bowles, John Kenneth Galbraith, Arthur Schlesinger, Eleanor Roosevelt, among others, and no fewer than fifteen Rhodes scholars spread through the Washington departments and overseas posts. At the Department of State, the talent was so deep that even such luminaries as Averell Harriman and G. Mennen "Soapy" Williams, ex-governors of major states and Harriman a long-time senior advisor to FDR and Truman, had agreed to accept third-level jobs. Everyone, it seemed, was eager to answer JFK's call to the New Frontier.

I had never met JFK, yet well before the election I had made up my mind that—come what may—I too wanted to be a New Frontiersman. When in a campaign speech Kennedy had appealed to "all those who believe, who want to join our government . . . not because of what we are going to do for them, but for the opportunity . . . to serve our country," I heard it as a personal call to duty; and when in another speech in Oklahoma he said that the New Frontier was "the opportunity for all of us to be of service . . . in difficult and dangerous times," it had further kindled my imagination. Here was a chance for the kind of idealistic public service that had brought me to the Woodrow Wilson School in the first place, and now I couldn't wait to seize it.

There were thousands like me whose language Kennedy spoke and who were responding to his rhetoric combining idealism and sacrifice. I was earning good money at Crown Cork and switching to a government job meant cutting my income in half, but in the excitement of the moment that seemed almost like a badge of honor. The competition for jobs was great and the odds of being chosen long, yet well before the inauguration, I had launched my quest for a government job—almost any job would do. Success was uncertain, and what actually happened surpassed anything I had dared to hope.

"The White House is calling you," my secretary at Crown Cork announced one morning in February of 1961 with evident excitement.

I had awaited those magic words for weeks, hardly daring to hope that I would hear them. "The White House" in this instance was Ralph Dungan, a Princeton classmate now installed as one of JFK's assistants at a desk close to the Oval Office. It was my good fortune that this cheerful, bright, and deeply committed Irishman had been put in charge of sifting candidates for the several hundred lesser sub-cabinet jobs each new administration fills with its own political appointees.[125]

From the beginning I had left Ralph in no doubt that I was an eager prospect for almost any assignment, and now he was suggesting that there actually might be a spot for me. "I can't make any promises," he cautioned, "but let's see where you might fit in. Come to my office in the morning. They will have your name at the East Gate entrance."

The next day, following a restless night, I passed the gate of the White House for the first time to Ralph's office and from there to an exhilarating two days of job interviews with senior members of JFK's new team, names I knew only from afar. According to Dungan, JFK wanted "new blood" to work on the foreign economic policy initiatives of the new administration. This is where he thought I might fit in. Strengthening the Western alliance with vigorous steps to expand world trade was one of these initiatives. Another big issue was Kennedy's call in his Inaugural Address for an Alliance for Progress with Latin America, and for U.S. aid and trade initiatives to benefit the newly independent ex-colonies of Africa and Asia. A new approach to foreign aid was to be a critical part of his program, with significant political implications in the Third World, where the old order was breaking up and becoming a battleground for influence between the Soviets and the West. Finally, there was the chronic deficit in the U.S. balance of payments—more dollars going out than coming in. The president was worried that it was draining our gold reserves, and wanted fresh thinking and new ideas.

Dean Rusk had been appointed secretary of state, and Chester Bowles deputy secretary. Adlai Stevenson's friend and law partner, George Ball, had moved into State's top economic job, and foreign aid was being reorganized by Harry Labouisse in a new Agency for International Development. According to Dungan, a few outsiders were wanted to interact with the often hidebound Foreign Service professionals, whose loyalties were less to JFK than to the Service itself, and who were prone to see two problems for every novel solution. Having made appointments for me with these three leaders of the new international economic team, Dungan wished me luck and sent me on my way.

Not long before, I had cooled my heels outside the U.S. Consulate of Shanghai, where merely to be admitted into the presence of the junior vice consul issuing visas had been a major feat. Now here I was, in a state of nervous exhilaration, awaiting my third interview in two days on the seventh floor of the Department of State, the inner sanctum of U.S. foreign policy, and about to be received by George Ball, the department's third highest official.

A day earlier, I had been interviewed by Labouisse and Bowles. The former had been pleasant though vague and unspecific. Bowles, however, had devoted over an hour to me. After a few initial perfunctory questions, he had treated me to an airy tour d'horizon of worldwide problems, with special emphasis on the plight of the less developed world and what he called the "revolution of rising expectations" in Asia and Africa. A suitable offer to work on these problems would be forthcoming, he had implied.

I had left heartened at the prospect of a job, but somewhat bemused nonetheless. Bowles was the most important national figure I had yet met, a senior executive in wartime Washington, former governor and member of Congress, whose appointment as deputy at State had been widely applauded. With so many major foreign policy issues facing the United States in Europe and elsewhere, his lengthy lecture on the Third World had struck me as odd.

In time, I would discover that Bowles had been true to form, and the more cynical members of JFK's inner circle, who prided themselves on being hard-headed realists, would soon write him off as the typical fuzzy liberal, more idealistic than practical, given to clichés, and more at home with lofty principles than tough action and decision making in the real world. Later on, once we had come to know each other,

George Ball, who hated clichés and had a wicked sense of humor, would refer to Bowles' favorite "rising expectations," as his "revolution of rising expectoration" and say of him that he was "a man too noble for life in the bureaucratic jungle."[126]

As it turned out, I was fortunate not to go to work for him. His tenure as deputy secretary was brief and before the year was out, Ball had replaced him.[127] Months before, I had accepted an assignment from Ball, an extraordinary man who became my boss and mentor in Washington, and eventually my neighbor in Princeton and a close friend. No man taught me more about public service and no one influenced my political attitudes and professional philosophy more than he.

George Wildman Ball had only recently been installed in the magisterial seventh-floor office into which I had been summoned that February morning. Over six feet tall, broadly framed, and elegantly tailored, the new undersecretary for economic affairs was a big man. His office was one of the largest I had ever seen, yet he filled it with his presence as if he belonged in it and had been there all his life. That it was a working office was plain enough. In the anteroom three secretaries worked the typewriters and manned a battery of phones. Inside, stacks of papers, books, and files were piled high on a massive desk, and more lay strewn over the floor around it. A stickler for neatness and order, the economic undersecretary decidedly was not. Meanwhile, assistants were scurrying in and out—to every appearance a small army of them—and several times I had to be excused while phone calls had to be taken or made.

I no longer remember the details of the interview, except that Ball had done his homework about me, that we hit it off from the start, and that he offered me a job on the spot—or rather a choice of two. I could be a staff assistant directly under him, or go to work two layers down as a deputy assistant secretary working on international commodity policy in the Bureau of Economic Affairs. The problem, he explained, was that Latin American and other developing countries depended heavily on the export of commodities in chronic oversupply and subject to wildly fluctuating and perennially depressed prices. The president wanted more aid channeled to Latin America, but a few cents less in world coffee prices could offset whatever was sent. My assignment would be to figure out what could be done to solve this problem.

Had I come straight from a university campus where everyone fends for himself and hierarchical lines are fuzzy and few, perhaps I might have opted for a spot on the undersecretary's staff on the seventh floor, the nerve center at State where the top people sat. But Crown Cork had given me an appreciation for the difference between line authority, even at lower levels, and a staff assignment nearer the top. I had, moreover, noted that the undersecretary already could draw on a fairly large number of such aides. I knew that I liked to run things—and that's how I chose.

Thus, within two months, in more dramatic fashion than I could have imagined, my dream came true. Ball and I shook hands, and on April 3, 1961, I was sworn in as a deputy assistant secretary of state for economic affairs. I was thirty-five years old, one of the youngest people appointed at that level. It had been a mere thirteen years since I had first set foot on American soil as a stateless refugee.

A Great American

In my time in the government, stretching over ten years and three administrations, I met any number of unusually talented men and women, but without question George Ball—a towering figure of the U.S. foreign policy establishment in the sixties—was the most remarkable of them all. He showed me what working on public policy issues is all about and to this day remains my model for probity, pragmatic idealism, effectiveness, and courage in the public service.

Beginning in 1961 he would, over the course of the next seven years, render outstanding service to the country as a prescient and courageous counselor in the inner circle of advisors to Presidents Kennedy and Johnson. Often he succeeded, and sometimes he fought the good fight and failed. Occasionally he was wrong, but far more often he was not and subsequent events would bear him out even when his advice was not heeded. In 1976, Jimmy Carter seriously considered appointing him secretary of state and, for sadly the wrong reasons, did not do so. That is a great pity. He would have been an outstanding secretary and served the country and the president well.[128]

Ball's great strengths were his sharply analytical mind, his literacy and deep knowledge of history, his ability to look beyond the conventional wisdom of the moment, and his rare gift of foreseeing where particular policies would lead and how to measure them against fundamental U.S. interests over the longer run.

His opposition, from the very beginning, to the U.S. military involvement in Vietnam—for which he is best remembered—is the most dramatic example. On November 7, 1961, when JFK was about to commit the first U.S. troops, Ball cautioned that it would be a tragic error. Having closely studied the disastrous experience of the French military in Indochina, he warned JFK that day—with prescient foresight, as it turned out—that once started there would be no turning back and that "within five years we'll have 300,000 men in the paddies and jungles," with no chance of victory. To which the president had replied with asperity, "George, you're crazier than hell. That just isn't going to happen."[129]

Unfortunately, of course, it did—except that the number of troops eventually committed by Kennedy's successor would far exceed George Ball's prediction, and 60,000 of them would die there.

From the beginning, Ball had seen the folly of Vietnam. His knowledge of history had convinced him of the risks of a U.S. military entanglement in an unwinnable war. His distaste for empty slogans and suspicion of the conventional wisdom had led him to reject "domino theories"—the then fashionable justification for U.S.-Vietnam policy—as a factually dubious phrase without historical precedent or substance. His clear sense of U.S. foreign policy priorities had persuaded him that Vietnam was in any case not an area of prime U.S. strategic interest.

It is ironic that it was his steadfast dissent on Vietnam for which he became best known. Vietnam, after all, was an exercise in futility and failure, and there was so much else of lasting importance in which he succeeded and where his contributions and counsel made a critical difference. No single American, for example, contributed more to generating U.S. support for the creation of a European Common Market. It was he who first saw the inherent logic of one of the most positive developments of the postwar era and that for the U.S. the short-term costs of economic integration in Europe were worth the longer-run prize of prosperity and peace based on a strong Atlantic partnership.

In the shaping of an immensely successful new U.S. trade policy in the sixties (on which I worked with him), as a member of the Executive Committee advising JFK in the successful handling of the Cuban missile crisis, and in leading the development of U.S. policies toward the Congo, Cyprus, and a host of other countries during the sixties, he consistently called the right shots and played a critical role in the inner councils of government.

In 1972, when we were both back in private life, I told him one day—"George, you have never been to the Soviet Union. You have intimate knowledge of Western Europe, but you have not been east of the Elbe River. You should go." He agreed—and so the two of us with our wives made the trip. In Moscow, we visited ministers, assorted Central Committee functionaries and Gosplanners, and crossed verbal swords in a lengthy private discussion with Alexei Kosygin, the Soviet prime minister. There were tough words and acrimony back and forth; George gave as good as he got and was both amused and slightly bemused by it all. What did he think of his first exposure to the mighty Soviets on their home ground, I wondered?

Late one night, when we had finally bribed our way to a table, some food, and a bottle of vodka, he utterly astonished me. "You know," he said, "we have grossly overrated these people. They'll never make it. Sooner or later this place will blow apart or simply collapse."

"What do you mean?" I asked somewhat dubiously. And then George, who had evidently done his homework more thoroughly than I realized, laid out in precise detail the facts and figures that he thought would ultimately cause the Soviet Union's collapse: the demographics, the ethnic tensions, the inherent inefficiencies of the system, the unsustainable strain of military expenditures, the growing impact of rapid technological change, and all the rest. This almost two decades before events would prove him uncannily right. No one else— Sovietologists or the CIA—had come close to discerning these trends so clearly. It had taken George all of four days!

He was, I believe, that particular human species Horace calls *Abnormis Sapiens*—the abnormally wise man, blessed with a felicitous combination of unusual gifts: a restlessly analytical and unconventional mind, a way with the English language, a wicked sense of humor, seemingly boundless reservoirs of energy and stamina, and the courage and moral integrity to say what he thought. His innate optimism was one of his great strengths. As he told it, it was Jean Monnet, the great Frenchman who was the father of the Common Market and Ball's close friend, who had taught him that "optimism is the only serviceable hypothesis of the practical man or woman in the pursuit of a great objective."

Yet he was neither a fool nor a dreamer. He knew how the bureaucracy worked and how to get things done, and had what is indispensable for success in Washington: a sense of power. He knew who counted in the decision-making process, and he understood the importance of defending one's "turf"—what he called "the territorial imperative."[130] He could be hard-headed and realistic in his approach to foreign policy issues, and he understood the need for compromise and political give and take. At heart, however, he was an idealist and patriot determined to defend vital U.S. interests on the great issues of the day. Quintessentially American in his view of the world, he remained a committed internationalist who believed in the importance of alliances and U.S. moral leadership in world affairs, and was deeply critical of the historical U.S. inclination toward isolationism and unilateral action. He understood as clearly as anyone the difference between "hard" and "soft" power in world affairs: the power to coerce based on military and economic might, versus the force of moral leadership that derives from American cultural and political traditions as the land of freedom, democracy, and equality of opportunity for all.

"What is American exceptionalism?" he asked his friends who had gathered to honor him on the occasion of his eightieth birthday in January 1990. "There is little exceptional," he continued, "about military strength or economic weight; other nations have also gone far in that direction. What is truly exceptional is moral leadership, which means a firm adherence to certain principles and the firm rejection of arrogant practices that have become almost automatic in our political life."[131]

He spoke these words over a decade before the George W. Bush presidency and our entanglement in Iraq. Their wisdom and clarity remain valid to this day.

The "New Frontier"

A half century later, it is hard to convey the sense of excitement that gripped Washington in those early months of JFK's New Frontier. The town was full of new faces and fascinated observers of the charismatic young president and his stylish wife in the White House, and the media were having a field day with admiring reports of their every move. The *New Republic* said Washington was "crackling, rocking, jumping,"[132] and two of the town's most influential pundits, Walter Lippmann and James Reston, noted approvingly that with all that "vigor" there was no doubt that "the torch has been passed to a new generation."[133]

Our group of eager new frontiersmen was in high spirits. We were young, optimistic, true believers, and certain that we were part of the single greatest historical adventure of our time. JFK's eloquence had inspired us, and no one questioned the practicality of his lofty goals. We worked in an atmosphere of highly infectious enthusiasm, and thought nothing of putting in long hours, far into the night. The president had told us that we could—literally—shoot for the moon, and each in his own area was committed to doing just that.

True, the world out there was dangerous and selfish, there were long-standing problems at home and abroad, and reactionaries opposing JFK dominated the Congress. But we believed with him that much was possible if confronted with courage, energy, and hard-headed realism. A subsequent candidate for president would, many years later, run on the slogan "Yes, We Can" at another time of ferment and challenge. Barack Obama has often been compared to JFK, which may be only partially correct. Yet in the spirit of optimism mixed with realism both believed in, and were uniquely able to convey to voters, they are remarkably alike.

Washington can be intoxicating for the newcomer who feels the special thrill of being "on the inside" and close to the seat of power. At the White House there were glittering parties, and though we were too junior to be included, we watched from afar, swapped stories about who was up or down, and felt immensely privileged to be there and "in the know." At embassy receptions, dinners, and private parties where insiders, journalists and diplomats mingled, we felt important —we gossiped, dropped hints about the significance of our own work, and opined knowingly about the president's programs.

It was all exhilarating, a wonderful time to be alive and among the many talented men and women the New Frontier had attracted. Each of us was fully absorbed in working on what he believed to be a vital part of JFK's agenda, whether domestic programs like housing, area development, medical care for the aged, the drive to raise the minimum wage, or international: creating a Peace Corps, launching his promised Alliance for Progress in Latin America, negotiating with Congress for new legislation on international trade, containing Castro, or plotting Cold War skirmishes with the Soviets in far corners of the globe.

I will always cherish the memory of those early days of the Kennedy administration, and I remain grateful that my initial exposure to government service occurred in that wonderful atmosphere of idealism, energy, and hope. It was a great beginning, even if I would eventually come to recognize a more nuanced reality.

Anyone who works in politics soon learns that campaign rhetoric and lofty goals are one thing, but that achieving them in the real world is quite another. Progress in a democracy is at best only gradual and incremental, and rarely—except at moments of national emergency—fast, far-reaching, and fundamental. Old habits and practices are deeply ingrained, and conflicting interests can be a powerful brake on change and reforms. The entrenched positions of those on the losing side are often excruciatingly hard to overcome, however justified the effort.

We overestimated what flair, vigor, courage, and commitment alone could achieve, and did not see that Kennedy's lofty oratory obscured some hard realities. For one thing, his mandate for fundamental change was quite limited. As he took office, the Democrats had lost seats in both Houses of a narrowly divided Congress under the control of the same coalition of Southern Democrats and conservative Republicans that had historically resisted many of the changes he advocated. And in the Cold War confrontation with the Soviets, the key problems were a great deal more intractable than his campaign speeches had suggested.

In hindsight, the achievements of the Kennedy administration were mixed. John F. Kennedy had entered the White House at a time of public doubt about America's will, and, initially at least, he succeeded brilliantly in restoring confidence and rekindling faith in American vitality and progress. Sometimes, as in his "Ich bin ein Berliner" speech in Berlin, his sense of the public mood and talent for appealing to it had been impressive and there certainly were several important accomplishments. The Peace Corps has remained a notable achievement to this day. In Europe, Soviet pressure was successfully resisted, even if the building of the Berlin Wall was not. The Alliance for Progress initially created valuable goodwill. His judicious handling of the Cuban Missile Crisis in 1962 successfully defused the most dangerous nuclear confrontation of the Cold War. Congressional passage of the Trade Expansion Act in the same year set the stage for the most far-reaching trade negotiation of the postwar period, and the space race he initiated ended in American victory only a few years later, when an American astronaut was the first to set foot on the moon.

There was, however, also the spectacular failure of the Bay of Pigs invasion of Cuba. The high hopes of the Alliance for Progress were never fully realized. The Cold War and the confrontation with Russia and Communist China grew more rather than less intense for most of the decade. Finally, sending the first substantial contingent of combat troops to Vietnam was arguably his worst mistake and led to an entanglement there that would ultimately cost tens of thousands of American lives.

Domestically, the record of the New Frontier was equally mixed. Only a limited part of JFK's priority legislation on the minimum wage, education, area development, and medical care for the aged actually passed, and that only in substantially watered down form. On civil rights, the single most urgent issue of the period, little of substance was done.

What had gone wrong? Some of it was simply trying to do too much. Fundamental societal changes were underway at home, and powerful realities characterized the world abroad. No presidential initiatives, however firm the commitment or judicious the execution, could have successfully affected these quickly, and sometimes the activism we so admired probably did more harm than good. There was altogether too much emphasis on ad hoc action and not enough on reflection; too much sloganeering and not enough analysis of the underlying assumptions on which all this policy activism was based.

The idea behind the Alliance for Progress, for example, was commendable, but overblown claims for it set up expectations that were bound to remain unfulfilled. Proclamation of a "historic decade of democratic progress" in Latin America, or of an effort "unparalleled in magnitude and nobility of purpose" were ringing words but they promised altogether too much. With hindsight, it was presumptuous to have expected—and so stated—that the Alliance could truly go far in solving Latin America's deep-seated economic problems in a single decade and create strong and vital democracies in societies where few of the prerequisites for it existed.

Even the emphasis on political courage—a constant in Kennedy's writings and speeches—proved more rhetoric than reality. He was, in fact, often overly cautious when bold action was sorely needed, and never more so than in his hesitation to deal forcefully with the urgent issue of civil rights. When he did so belatedly, it was only after 200,000 people, mostly blacks, had marched to Washington in silent protest to hear the Reverend King call for decisive new steps in his "I Have a Dream" speech. Kennedy's reluctance to tackle this politically charged issue was not an example of political courage exactly where it was needed most.

At any rate, with Kennedy's murder in Dallas, the heady times abruptly came to an end, though for some of us, the sober lessons of government decision making in the real world had already been learned. The magic had begun to wear off amid the reality of constant battles, small advances along with defeats, and a lot of hard work. Still, while after November 22, 1963, our innocence was irretrievably lost, the beginning had been a wonderful time.

"Diplomatists" and the "E" Bureau

I reported to the Bureau of Economic Affairs (the "E" Bureau) and was sworn in on April 3, 1961, a decisive turning point in my life, when the door opened for me to the world of politics and international affairs in which I would remain engaged on and off for the next two decades.

When first thrust into this unfamiliar environment, I was as broadly unprepared for it as I was ignorant of the inner workings of the federal government, or the arcane ways of the formidable State Department bureaucracy. I had a lot to learn, I had to do it in a hurry, and there was no grace period to ease the transition. Political appointees are received with a "wait and see" attitude by career professionals, but not taken seriously or trusted until they have proved themselves.

I remember the first days and weeks as an intimidating experience. My initial inclination was to wrap myself in silence and to hide my befuddlement by feigning weighty thoughts when gaping mental blanks were nearer the truth. Soon it dawned on me, however, that the better tactic was to swallow my pride, confess my ignorance, and plead for elementary explanations—interlaced with liberal resort to the "why?" question. As it turned out, this approach, though humbling, was more respected than disdained by my subordinates and helped me to learn more quickly. Asking "why" had the further benefit of uncovering the fact that sometimes even the most self-assured expert has trouble providing a reasonable justification for accepted truths and shibboleths firmly believed.[134]

My arrival coincided with the E Bureau's being in the midst of a whirl of activity. The New Frontier was reviewing many established policies and initiating a multiplicity of new ones, twelve-hour days were common, and the pace was intense.

The Cold War was at its height, and by the summer of 1961, the building of the Berlin Wall and Kennedy's fractious first encounter with Soviet Premier Khrushchev in Vienna had created a climate of hostility and bluster in U.S.–Soviet relations that did not bode well for an early easing of East–West tensions. Dozens of newly independent former colonies in Africa and Asia had become battlegrounds for power and influence between east and west. Some of these "new starters" were openly flirting with the other side, and the E Bureau was busy devising economic strategies for keeping them in the western camp. In Latin America, the official launching of the Alliance for Progress was slated for the summer and the preparations were getting lots of attention. Presidential power to negotiate trade agreements was due to expire, and in view of the growing weight of the European Common Market and the rise of Japan as a major trading power, to convince Congress to grant the president wider latitude for trade deals was an urgent matter, with protectionists and free traders lined up on opposite sides and furiously lobbying the Congress.

My new colleagues in E were an impressive group and, on the whole, smarter and more sophisticated than any I had ever worked with—though an entirely different breed that took some getting used to. To win their respect and acceptance was a critical first requirement, and for that one had to understand their unique culture.

The State Department is the oldest of the federal departments, the secretary of state is the senior cabinet officer, fourth in the line of presidential succession, and the department is envied for its career service, whose members man prestigious posts abroad. Yet, because they had traditionally been narrowly recruited from a limited segment of American society, foreign service professionals also acquired a less flattering reputation, particularly in the Congress, of being snobs and elitists unrepresentative of the American public, more attuned to the opinions of foreigners than to U.S. interests.

In the past there had been some truth to this, even though by the sixties the situation was beginning to change. For many years, the Foreign Service had consisted of a small and homogenous group of officers with similar backgrounds and skills. Yet as the major superpower and leader in the Cold War, the United States needed a much larger postwar Foreign Service, staffed with people with a more diverse mix of skills.

Though long overdue, it was a wrenching transformation unwelcomed by many, and to appreciate the depth of their feeling a little historical background is needed. American diplomats originally learned their craft from European colleagues whose customs they had tried to emulate. A common code of behavior prevailed, rank and protocol were important, and much business was done at dinners, receptions, and similar occasions. Manners and good breeding were highly valued, and the emphasis was on "style, grace, poise and above all, birth."[135] The ideal was that of the generalist diplomat schooled to deal with all manner of political matters, wherever he was posted.

Narrow specialization, such as expertise in economics, let alone in technical or consular matters, had less prestige; was frowned upon with snobbish disdain; and was considered a sure way of limiting one's career prospects. Diplomacy was seen as a special craft best left to those carefully chosen, trained and tested by their peers and possessing what George Kennan once called a certain "*habitude du monde.*"[136]

The process of selecting new recruits perpetuated this system through an anachronistic examination, rigged to reduce the number of successful entrants and—as importantly—to weed out "undesirables." Even in 1947, fewer than 10 percent of almost 1,300 applicants had managed to pass both the written and oral parts of the tests. Keeping out women had deep roots based on quaint notions like those of Assistant Solicitor to the State Department Frederick Van Dyne who warned in the early 1900s of "female diplomatists," well-known inability to keep a secret."[137] The result was that even as late as 1948, among 1,332 successful recruits, only sixteen had been women.[138]

Anti-Semitism, whether crude and open or of the more subtle social variety, also had a long history in the Department of State. Since until at least the thirties, not many Jews made it into the elite Eastern prep schools or the Ivy League, even well-meaning non-Jewish graduates of those institutions had little personal contact with them, and had internalized the prevailing negative stereotypical view of Jews. For that reason, and less perhaps because of a smaller number of open Jew-haters, there had been a paucity of Jewish Foreign Service officers. "Jews lack the grace and manner required for diplomacy,"[139] German Chancellor von Bismarck had opined a long time ago, an attitude perhaps not unrelated to George Kennan's insistence on a certain *habitude du monde*. Ethnic diversity was in any case not a priority in the Eastern establishment, and in the context of the anti-immigrant nativism of key congressional committees shared by many Foreign Service officers during the interwar years, it goes a long way in explaining the opposition to Jews in their ranks, the indifference of many U.S. consuls to the plight of Germany's Jews, and their frequent outright obstructionism in issuing immigration visas to Jews during the thirties.

As to African-Americans, they were even rarer in the Foreign Service until well into the fifties. Few blacks bothered to apply, and the occasional tokens admitted had little chance of rising to the top and were likely to be shunted off to places like Liberia or similar career dead-end postings.

There were still traces of this culture of exclusivity in the State Department in which I landed in 1961, but it had already evolved into a much changed organization. If once the generalist political officers had been at the top of the heap, now economic, military, scientific, and public affairs specialists, as well as UN and international organization experts, were rising to leading positions alongside them, the total now numbering about 20,000 Americans and Foreign Service staff worldwide.

In time I came to appreciate and respect some extraordinarily able senior officers of the old school—men like Charles "Chip" Bohlen, Llewellyn Thompson, H. Freeman Matthews, Douglas MacArthur II, and a half dozen others. They held many of the key departmental and ambassadorial posts, and without their knowledge and experience, the foreign policy establishment would have been much the poorer. We worked well together, even if I observed with bemused detachment their measuring me as outside their traditions and concerned with economic issues for which they could work up little enthusiasm.

I recall especially one memorable meeting with Chip Bohlen, at the time the U.S. ambassador to France. I had come to see him on a diplomatic matter concerning—of all things—chickens. The Common Market had virtually shut its borders to U.S. poultry exports, which, in turn, triggered what the media had dubbed a trans-Atlantic "chicken war." Enlisting Bohlen to lend a hand in this "war" was, I soon discovered, no easy task.

In the broad sweep of international relations during the Cold War, the Chicken War had the ring of silliness hardly worthy of the attention of a senior diplomat accustomed to dealing with prime ministers on questions war and peace. Yet in the relations between nations there are occasions when the seemingly frivolous can rise to an importance meriting the attention of the highest levels of government. Such was the case with American chickens being, as it happened, the major export product of Arkansas, at the time the home state of two of the most powerful chairmen in the U.S. Congress—Wilbur Mills of the House Ways and Means Committee, and William Fulbright of the Senate Committee on Foreign Relations. Which was how market access for Arkansas chickens had become the key to tax and trade legislation and the ratification of international treaties in the Congress, and why top ambassadors were instructed to present urgent aide-mémoires to senior ministers explaining to them the critical importance the United States attached to the exports of fryers, broilers, and cut-up "backs and necks."[140]

I cannot forget the face of the elegant Bohlen dolefully regarding me from behind his impressive desk at the Place de la Concorde, as he received my request of a personal intervention on the poultry question "at the ministerial level." Pensively inhaling smoke through a long cigarette holder, he listened in shocked silence, his face a study of amusement mixed with deep distaste. Was it really the White House view, he inquired sorrowfully, that this was a matter requiring his personal call on a busy French minister of state? Having been assured that indeed it was, he resigned himself to his fate and, always the professional, did his duty, yet undoubtedly with a nostalgic backward glance to happier days when such business was left to lesser breeds.

Atlantic Strategy

In his run for the White House, John F. Kennedy had held out hope for a shining new era of peace and prosperity, with the United States boldly leading the way. The reality was, however, that the environment for U.S. leadership was a lot more complex, the problems more intractable, and the resistance to new ideas and meaningful change more formidable than had been assumed.

The Berlin Wall was the source of much nervous tension. Popular revolts roiled East Germany and Czechoslovakia, and the Vietnam War was beginning to add to the bickering within the Alliance over nuclear policy and the U.S. defensive shield in Europe. Building an effective Atlantic partnership was not proving a simple matter. The Europeans quarrelled among themselves and were split into two trade blocs with competing visions of how best to align their economies—the European Free Trade Association (EFTA) of seven countries led by Great Britain on the one hand, and the Common Market of six continental nations, clustered around Germany and France, on the other. Meanwhile General de Gaulle, with vainglorious posturing and pretentions of French "grandeur," resisted U.S. leadership on military matters, and complicated the development of common defense policies in NATO.

Elsewhere, the colonial system was breaking up, and a great many small, economically underdeveloped and politically unprepared nations had emerged. Among them, military dictatorships and authoritarian regimes were a lot more common than functioning democracies, entrenched oligarchies were resisting change, and many new nations had become battlegrounds for power and influence between East and West.

The fundamental U.S. strategic response under JFK was two-fold. In Western Europe, the key idea was to push for the creation of a strong Atlantic Alliance to counter Soviet ambitions. Its twin thrusts were building up the military shield of NATO on the one hand, and U.S. support for European economic integration on the other. Elsewhere in the world, to keep Latin America, Africa, and Asia free of Communism, the emphasis was on supporting democratic change through accelerated economic and technical assistance, the Peace Corps, and new initiatives to improve access for their products to the U.S., Japanese, and European markets.

This was the context in which I was assigned to work on a variety of economic issues over the course of the six years, 1961 to 1967. In essence, I was given responsibility for two programs. The first was to develop and implement a new U.S. commodity trade policy intended to help stabilize the export earnings of developing countries heavily dependent on such raw material exports as coffee, cocoa, sugar, tin, lead, and zinc. Eventually, this led to my second major assignment of chairing the U.S. delegation to the largest postwar trade negotiations under the General Agreement on Tariffs and Trade (the GATT, now known as the WTO), which would occupy me for the full four years from 1963 to 1967. This was the so-called Kennedy Round (KR), a multi-year nonstop bargaining marathon over tariffs and trade among the world's principal trading nations and dozens of smaller ones at the United Nations in Geneva.

A new commodity policy for less developed countries was one of the economic strategies relevant to the Alliance for Progress—but the aims of the Alliance were equally political. 2 percent of the people owned 50 percent of Latin American wealth, and 70 percent of the population still lived in poverty. As JFK had put it, improved economic opportunity would lead to changes in the political status quo by allying the United States with the forces working for democratic change. More trade and aid, produced by improving living standards and providing a better life for all, would accelerate the break with a feudal past and the domination of generals and oligarchs, strengthen democratic institutions, and build a dyke against the inroads of communism and the attraction of Castro-style revolutions.

The goals of the Kennedy Round were also as much political as economic. The thinking was that lower trade barriers would have beneficial economic consequences for all, would accelerate worldwide economic growth, and raise living standards—"the rising tide that lifts all the boats," Kennedy had called it. More important, U.S. leadership on lowering trade barriers for the free world would provide some of the glue for the Atlantic partnership, the prominent Washington columnist Joseph Kraft having christened this twin thrust of NATO defense and economic initiatives as the administration's "Grand Design"[141] for organizing the power of the free world.

JFK, in turn, had called the idea a "Declaration of Interdependence." The Atlantic partnership of a strong Europe in alliance with the United States was to be a major bulwark in defense of Western values, with Europe as a natural U.S. partner by virtue of a common heritage and common democratic ideals. As Europe gained in strength, the disparity in economic weight on both sides of the Atlantic would be reduced, leading to a collaboration between equals, impossible if Europe remained fragmented. Yet the Common Market, by eliminating barriers internally while retaining a common external tariff, would by definition be discriminatory toward outsiders, including the United States. A reciprocal lowering of tariffs was to be the answer and its political dimension was well appreciated on both sides of the Atlantic. The president and his principal advisors had repeatedly made the point, and in Europe Walter Hallstein, the president of the Common Market Commission, had also acknowledged it. The Kennedy Round, Hallstein said, was "a foreign policy issue in the widest sense," and would give "specific content to the general concept of the Atlantic Community."[142]

Because economic integration and political unity in Europe excluded the United States, there were those who from the beginning opposed it on narrow trade grounds. At the same time, there were European cynics who questioned our sincerity, and outright protectionists who disliked trade liberalization on principle. During the Cold War, the counterargument that, nevertheless, an economically and politically unified Europe was in the larger U.S. interest because it strengthened the alliance against the Communists, had stilled some of the doubters.

Commodity Policy

Each of my government years had its own challenges and excitement, but the first two years, between 1961 and 1963, working on commodity policy, were among the most satisfying. That only became clear to me when, in the late seventies, I returned to the government after an extended absence and was startled to discover that the major economic issues being worked on had changed surprisingly little. A full decade had passed and three administrations had come and gone, yet many of the trade and finance issues of the sixties were still on the table, the same bureaucratic turf wars were being fought, and congressional hearings and negotiations with foreign governments all sounded eerily familiar. Even the lobbyists were pretty much the same. The explanation lies in the fundamental Washington fact of life that few issues ever get settled permanently and that the bureaucracy always lives to fight another day. Tax reform, for example, was on the table in the sixties, Jimmy Carter pushed it in the seventies, George W. Bush returned to the same issue (albeit with different prescriptions) a full thirty years later, and Barack Obama is at it again. Yet the commodities question was that rare exception to the rule: an assignment with a recognizable beginning and a measurable end. It is this that made my work over the first two years of government service especially rewarding.

To find a workable solution to the commodities question was difficult, but understanding the problem was not. Dozens of countries in Latin America, Africa, and Asia depended on one or two primary products for the bulk of their export earnings. Many were desperately poor, and everywhere the story was the same: chronic overproduction, unpredictable price swings, and a longterm trend toward deteriorating "terms of trade"—the ratio between the prices received for their raw material exports and the manufactured goods they imported from abroad. The UN index had dropped by 10 percent within a few years, stalling economic development and leading to further impoverishment. Many raw material–exporting countries were thus caught in a vicious circle, frustrating any hope for improved living standards and threatening to dissipate whatever economic aid they received.

Most observers agreed that this was a big barrier to improving these countries' economic well-being (and in many cases it has remained so to this day), but from Washington's viewpoint it was also an urgent political problem. For JFK, American leadership on alleviating their economic misery and strengthening their democratic institutions was a key element of the policy to counter Communist encroachments, and Castro's rise in Cuba had intensified the urgency of this effort in

Latin America,[143] a major idea behind the Alliance for Progress. "Frequent violent changes in commodity prices," JFK had told a gathering of Latin American diplomats, "seriously injure the economies of many Latin American countries, draining their resources and stultifying their growth. Together we must cooperate . . . to find practical methods for bringing an end to this pattern."[144]

Previous administrations had been long on expressions of sympathy for the plight of primary product producers, but short on joining in practical measures to alleviate it. The president's statement now signaled a new direction. My job, as George Ball had instructed me, was to put flesh on the bare bones of JFK's mandate and to lead State's development of steps to translate it into reality. In practical terms this meant examining each situation on its merits, and proposing specific programs to promote more orderly world markets by aligning world production more closely with demand including, in some cases, a willingness to become an active participant in producer– consumer agreements.

The first challenge was figuring out where and how to begin implementing this new approach. Each case was different. The lead and zinc exporters of the world were engaged in a desperate effort to stave off a damaging price war, but only a few countries were affected. For the natural rubber producers the threat was synthetics being dumped on world markets and ruining their economies, while African cocoa exporters clamored for help with an export-import control mechanism. The most urgent and obvious candidate for priority action, however, was coffee—after petroleum the most important primary product in world trade. Coffee was produced in some seventy countries and impacted the lives of many millions of people. In at least a dozen Latin American countries coffee accounted for 30 to 80 percent of total export earnings, 70 percent for Colombia, Guatemala, and El Salvador, and for at least 50 percent of the export income of Brazil, the country producing half of the entire world's coffee.

Producers in different parts of the world had been fighting each other for many years; their separate interests were often in conflict and there was no agreement among importing countries on what should be done. In the world market, all the classic problems were present: an inelastic supply, perennial overproduction, low and unstable prices, and lack of finances to store excess stocks and manage seasonal marketing patterns. Prices had fallen by half in a decade, and while the volume of Latin American exports had increased, the revenue it generated had actually declined. A further complication was that Germany, Italy, and France levied heavy taxes and tariffs on Latin American coffee as a way to secure preferred market access and better prices for the newly independent former colonies of French-speaking Africa.

Prior attempts by the coffee countries to work out an exporters' agreement had foundered on their inability to enforce export quotas and the lack of financial resources to manage stocks. Now the Latin Americans, having heard JFK's promise, were clamoring for U.S. help in bringing the rest of the importing countries into a workable arrangement. No such producer–consumer agreement had ever been tried successfully. The experts were skeptical that it could be negotiated, and, in any case, doubted that it could work.

Sometimes, however, it pays to be unencumbered by the experience of past failures. I well understood the skepticism of the economics profession to commodity agreements on theoretical grounds—they interfered with free market forces and were assumed to be unworkable, as the academic experts I consulted had assured me—and had I been older and wiser, I might have hesitated to pursue the route I took. After only a few weeks' investigation and soundings among the key players, however, I had brushed all cautionary warnings aside and sent the recommendation "upstairs," that the United States should lead in giving the idea a try. With a new administration in place, I argued, the timing was right and with vigorous U.S. leadership there was a chance that it might work, at least for a time. Even if it didn't, a good-faith U.S. effort would earn us a lot of goodwill in Latin America. Sometimes you get what you wish for. In this case, the idea was quickly blessed at the top of State and the White House, with instruction to me to take charge of implementing it.

The "Coffee" Negotiations

For the next two years, my principal occupation became convincing both coffee producers and the major importing countries that a world agreement was in their economic interest, and negotiating an accord.

None of it came quickly or easily. When nations decide to negotiate on trade and finance issues, there are usually initial protestations of good intentions and high-blown rhetoric of common purpose, yet each negotiating party will quickly maneuver to ride the crest just a bit higher than the others—and fear being caught in the trough.

Each nation's negotiating position will reflect its internal politics, and the need to reconcile conflicting domestic interests and compromises can become progressively more difficult. Depending on the political calendar, if an election is in the offing or the domestic situation is unstable, for example, conceding a sensitive position may be well-nigh impossible. Behind the technicalities and dry statistics, there are jobs and livelihoods at stake, and the likelihood that some groups gain while others lose—importers versus local producers, big companies versus small ones, one region against another, business versus consumers, and so forth. Thus, while adjustments in negotiating positions are indispensable, the political courage to make them is too often lacking. Which is why delay, obfuscation, stubbornness, procrastination, and specious last-minute objections are a lot more common than timely mutual accommodation, and why progress in such negotiations is invariably slow and difficult, and the outcome never certain. This is a reality in all high-profile international negotiations, but where economic issues are involved it is especially intense and the coffee agreement talks were no exception.

First, there was the challenge to hammer out an agreed interagency position in Washington on the precise U.S. objectives and negotiating strategies, which brought me face to face with Washington decision making. Bureaucrats are instinctively cautious and resistant to change. Virtually any fundamental reversal of long-established policies stirs up conflicting interests, and reconciling them in a democracy is never easy. Anything new in which the various bureaus, agencies, and departments of government perceive a threat to their power or the interests of their "clients" quickly arouses defensive instincts.

Thus to reach agreement even within the State Department itself required a lengthy and often tortuous clearance process among regional and functional bureaus, in which every phrase, word, or comma in the written instructions could become the subject of protracted bargaining and debate. For the coffee negotiations, the African bureau argued that "their" cocoa producers merited equal attention, and held their clearance hostage to agreement on this point. The Southeast Asian bureau, not to be outdone, made the same claim for the countries in their region that produced tin, lead, zinc, and rubber, and even in my own E Bureau there was resistance and quibbling, reflecting a perennial competition between the guardians of GATT trade rules, which made no provision for commodity agreements, and my own Office of International Resources, where less orthodox views prevailed.

Clearing a U.S. position outside State was just as difficult. The Commerce Department was out to protect domestic coffee roasters and reluctant to approve anything that might restrict their freedom of action. Treasury worried about an adverse impact on the balance of payments, and the Labor Department argued that improved labor standards in producing countries had to be an integral part of U.S. objectives. Meanwhile, the academic members of the president's Council of Economic Advisors went one better and urged reconsideration of the entire policy on grounds of theoretical orthodoxy.

The American Economic Association was scheduled to hold its annual meetings in December, and I had persuaded the organizers to sponsor a special session at which I proposed to present our plans for JFK's new commodity policy, including the willingness to consider commodity agreements in some cases. I was hoping for valuable additional ideas, but my main objective was—naively, as it turns out—to win at least a qualified endorsement of the specific plans for a Coffee Agreement.

When the meeting was called to order, I was pleased to see some of the leading academics in the audience, including some of my teachers from Berkeley and Princeton. I was not prepared, however, for their reaction to my presentation, in which I had described not only the chaos in the world coffee market but also the economic and political impact on U.S. aid programs, on less developed country (LDC) development in general, and on our political objectives in Latin America and elsewhere.

Had I learned nothing from him, one of my erstwhile professors reproached me sorrowfully? Had I forgotten the basic theory of comparative advantage and the facts about the longer-run self-correcting market mechanism of demand and supply? Another professor, one of the most distinguished academics present, who had previously pronounced commodity agreements as impractical, repeated that view and dismissed political considerations as non-persuasive.[145] The development economists objected that commodity agreements merely hampered needed diversification of LDC economies. The international trade specialists cited previous failures to stabilize agricultural product markets, and the economic aid experts objected that the policy amounted to nothing less than an aid program by indirect means.

My protestations that I understood the longer-run implications, but that, all this notwithstanding, the political problem we faced was immediate, and that even limited success and a few years of market stability could be critical for the LDCs and for achieving our political objectives, fell largely on deaf ears. Only a handful of those who had themselves once served in Washington conceded some merit to what we were doing and rose to my defense.

In the end, the doubts of academics and bureaucratic resistance to the contrary, the International Coffee Conference was convened at UN headquarters in New York on July 9, 1962. It ended seven weeks later with an agreement between producing and importing countries "designed to increase the purchasing power of coffee producing nations by maintaining level prices and increasing consumption."

For forty-six days and nights, 350 delegates from seventy-one countries had been locked in nonstop bargaining, and more than once there had been the threat of imminent failure. After several deadlines had been missed, the final deal was struck at the very last moment, at 5:30 A.M. on the morning of August 24, following an all-night session when the last holdouts had finally thrown in the towel and voted their approval.

In the beginning, there had been widespread skepticism. The *New York Times* had cited the coffee traders' view that the idea was "flawless in theory but unenforceable,"[146] and even two days before the final agreement, the *Times*'s Kathleen McLaughlin had still reported "doubts clouding the talks," and a pervasive "air of uncertainty."[147] The *Wall Street Journal* said that it was, in any case, "the worst possible way to deal with the (commodity) problem."[148]

But when success had been achieved, the mood quickly changed. After the deal was struck at the United Nations it was hailed as "the most significant international economic agreement negotiated in recent years," with a beneficial impact on millions of people in many countries.[149] Previous doubters praised it as a "remarkable achievement" and a successful building block in the implementation of JFK's policies and his Alliance for Progress program. One commentator said it was a fine example of "the complex, multi-faceted process of international problem solving."[150] The *Times*, for its part, now saw the agreement as "ushering in a new era of economic cooperation,"[151] and even printed an editorial suggesting the U.S. "go further by calling an international conference to discuss setting up other commodity agreements."[152]

The agreement had been a minor miracle, and most of the media echoed that view. Eventually, the second miracle was that what everyone expected to be a transitional arrangement remained in force for a long time, and worked quite well for a decade or more. It was ratified quickly by most countries, virtually no one failed to sign it, rea-

Left, W. Michael Blumenthal's
mother, Rose-Valerie Markt;
Berlin, 1914

Below, aged thirteen, aboard the SS
Haruna Maru, *en route to Shanghai*

Typical street scene, Shanghai; 1942

Above, interior of a Heim; *Honkou ghetto; Shanghai, c. 1943*

*Below, lining up for "passes" to temporarily leave Honkou
with a Japanese official named Goya, the self-proclaimed "king of the Jews"*

Left, with Stefanie, Blumenthal's older sister; 1946

Below, with former Secretary of State Christian Herter, after appointment as ambassador for Kennedy Round talks; Geneva, 1963

United States Ambassador Blumenthal, outside United Nations headquarters;
Geneva, 1964

Above, Vice President Hubert Humphrey visits Ambassador Blumenthal's delegation; Geneva, 1965

Left, listening to Kennedy Round negotiating speeches at United Nations headquarters

Cigars lit in honor of Kennedy Round success. Left to right: W. Michael Blumenthal;
Ambassador William M. Roth; Dutch ambassador; EEC President Jean Rey; Deputy
Director-General of GATT Finn Olav Gundelach

*Above, briefing President Lyndon Johnson about Kennedy Round at the White House;
1967. With Ambassador Roth; National Security Advisor Walt Rostow; and Deputy
National Security Advisor Francis M. Bator*

*Below, leading American delegation of the National Committee
on U.S.–China Relations, with Zhou Enlai; 1973*

Leading official American delegation to the state funeral of Algerian President Houari Boumediene; Algiers, 1977

Above, with President Jimmy Carter in the Oval Office

Below, with Jimmy Carter and Secretary of State Cyrus Vance, at Heads of State Meeting; Bonn, 1978

Cover of Time, *1978*

$1 bill with signature

Above, with Leonid Brezhnev; 1978

Below, negotiating with Deng Xiaoping; 1979

Above, three generations of Blumenthals: W. Michael Blumenthal; his father Eddy (Ewald), aged 100; his son Michael, aged three; San Francisco, 1989

Below, with German Chancellor Gerhard Schroeder; Berlin, 2003

Jewish Museum Berlin

Above, with German Chancellor Angela Merkel; 2008

Below, with Angela Merkel, viewing an exhibit at the Jewish Museum; 2009

With President Obama at the White House; 2012

sonable market stability was achieved, prices remained moderate, and international organizations chipped in with seasonal financing funds. From the U.S. point of view, the Coffee Agreement achieved the hoped-for political and economic benefits.

The success of the negotiations was also a modest personal triumph, because my name had become closely identified with it. I had been chairman of the preliminary drafting group and for a year had traveled the world to drum up support among the key players. When the actual negotiation got underway, I had led a large American delegation that became the driving force for arbitrating disputes, and for orchestrating political maneuvers at the United Nations, in Washington, and in major capitals.

It had been my first exposure to a high profile international negotiation and my first test as a diplomat. Most of the delegations were headed by senior ministers or officials, among whom I was by far the youngest. It was a thrill to represent my country. My bosses had put their faith in me, and I did not want to disappoint them.

The coffee negotiations also had another important personal effect: they showed me the powerful impact a determined individual in a large bureaucracy can have on the course of events, the major role a single person can occasionally play in shaping outcomes. Time and again I would later see evidence of that, and learn that it requires strong commitment to a cause or idea, a sense of timing, persistence, courage to take risks, and the knack of knowing when to do it. Several times it had seemed that failure was all but certain, and it was then that I had learned something important about myself—that I too could make a critical difference. Here is how the *New York Times* described one such incident:

> A colleague recalls with awe Mr. Blumenthal's tireless efforts to obtain the coffee pact. At a crisis in the negotiations, all of the representatives of the coffee countries were remaining stubbornly in their own separate rooms. Throughout the night and into the small hours of the morning, Mr. Blumenthal dashed from room to room, trying to bring disparate views of the coffee producers together. [153]

Lacking prior experience, I had relied mainly on energy and instinct. Sometimes I had been impatient and anxious for progress with too little tolerance for diplomatic niceties and the long-winded perorations for home consumption that are an inevitable part of most international conferences. Thus I made my share of mistakes and was probably overly hard-charging when a little more patience might have brought the same results. In time I would learn to do better.

Yet when all was said and done, I had been fortunate. I had cut my teeth on a major negotiation, which had done a lot for my self-confidence and established me as a respected member of JFK's international economic team, and as one among the State Department professionals. It had been a great Washington beginning, and soon it would lead to new challenges.

Visits to the Oval Office

The U.S. president has greater powers than any other leader of a Western democracy. Unlike in a parliamentary system, where the functions of government are shared among several individuals, only the American president is head of state, chief of government, commander-in-chief of the armed forces, and leader of his party all rolled in one. The cabinet and senior appointees serve at his pleasure and he can hire and fire them at will. He can sponsor and veto legislation, and determine how existing laws and regulations are administered. He sets the tone for the conduct of foreign relations and can deal directly with other world leaders to project the power and influence of the United States abroad. In sum, though he shares important powers with Congress and the courts, no single individual commands more attention at home and abroad and can dominate the headlines as he can. With good reason, he is often called the most powerful person on earth.

Unlike most Europeans, Americans are not particularly respectful toward public officials, and government service is not, as in other countries, considered a high calling. Yet the institution of the presidency is seen differently. There are always those who oppose a president's policies or dislike him personally, but whether supporters or opponents, most Americans regard their president and the trappings of his office with something close to awe, and when in his presence, they show enormous deference and respect.

I have frequently been surprised how the aura of the Oval Office invariably cows even a president's strongest critics. The top leaders of the American corporate and financial establishment would thunder against Jimmy Carter's policies when they were in my Treasury office and mince few words in criticizing him. "Tell the President directly," I would encourage them, having previously warned Carter to be prepared for strongly held views and plain language. Invariably, however, when ushered into his presence, these powerful men accustomed to speaking their minds would retreat to the mildest hints and suggestions expressed with great deference. "I don't know what you were thinking," Carter would later chide me, "I found those fellows quite reasonable and not nearly as negative as you had feared!"

No modern president's presence, however, was more deeply felt than that of JFK during the 1,000 days of his aborted presidency, including by deputy assistant secretaries rarely summoned into his presence. Thus my occasional meetings with him were always an enormous thrill. The first time it was for an essentially ceremonial visit when the entire U.S. delegation to the inaugural meeting of the Alliance for Progress conference, returning from Uruguay, was brought to the East Room where JFK appeared to congratulate us on our success. Later I was occasionally asked to accompany one of the "principals"—Dean Rusk or George Ball—just in case I had to supply some relevant fact on whatever issue was up for discussion. Each time I would be up late into the night rehearsing every conceivable detail, and approach the great event in a state of nervous tension. As far as I can recall, I was rarely asked to speak on any such occasion, but would remain quietly seated behind the secretary while observing the proceedings from afar.

Yet these were always eagerly awaited occasions, cherished moments appreciated as tangible psychic reward for public service, even if being a silent witness to decision making at the top had its frustrations, as when the president and his senior advisors disposed of matters based on only a sketchy and incomplete understanding of the issues. If it was a subject on which I had worked for weeks, having it thus slip away could be a disillusioning experience.

I well remember one such occasion early in 1962. The issue was sugar legislation, a hot potato with significant domestic and international ramifications over which I had crossed swords for weeks with my counterpart in the Agriculture Department. The United States maintained a domestic sugar price far above world levels, mainly to protect domestic producers, but with some valuable import quotas doled out primarily to Latin American exporters. Such quotas were of critical importance to these countries and with Castro's Cuban quota embargoed, a pending congressional bill had egregiously favored its reallocation to domestic over foreign suppliers. Secretary Rusk had come to press for a presidential veto; Orville Freeman, the Secretary of Agriculture, was there to plead the contrary case.

The day before, a Sunday afternoon, I had been called to Rusk's office to brief a visibly tired and distracted secretary for whom this problem was clearly not a top concern. How much of my argument for a veto he had absorbed was hard to tell. "Alright," he sighed after listening in silence, "I get it. I'm seeing the president in the morning. You better come along, just in case."

The next morning in the cabinet room, the secretaries of state and agriculture took their seats on either side of the president, and we staffers sat behind them. "What's up today?" JFK inquired cheerfully, whereupon Rusk, to my dismay, launched into a highly confused summary of the facts and reasons for a presidential veto—followed by Freeman who, in a booming voice, did no better in arguing Agriculture's contrary case. His "file carrier" and I had contested the issue tenaciously, and to hear the facts mangled at this crucial moment was obviously as painful to him as it was to me. The president then had a perfectly sensible idea: "I'll ask the Senate's whip," he announced, and motioned an assistant to get then-Senator Hubert Humphrey on the phone. This, I knew, would sink our case for good. JFK did not know, and Rusk had forgotten (though Orville Freeman, a fellow Minnesotan certainly had not), that beet sugar is an important product of that state's Red River Valley. Asking a Minnesota senator about vetoing a bill benefiting sugar farmers in his home state was akin to consulting a child about the wisdom of banishing him from a favorite candy store. Humphrey's answer was a foregone conclusion. "Well," said the president after listening to him, still quite cheerful, in ending the conversation, "I think I'll let it go!" Not all White House meetings I witnessed were as disappointing, nor did this one permanently tarnish the thrill of attending them. Yet it taught me that not everything that happens around a president is necessarily well considered and deserving of praise.

My most memorable visit with JFK in the Oval Office was the last one. It was in the early summer of 1963 and remains unforgettable because I would never again see him alive, and because this time he had personally summoned me for a reason that changed my future.

Late in 1962, Congress had handed the president one of the few clear victories of his short administration by approving the Trade Expansion Act (TEA). The TEA was path-breaking legislation granting the President unprecedented powers to cut all U.S. tariffs by a full 50 percent in reciprocal negotiations with other countries. Some tariffs he could actually eliminate entirely, and any deal he made was to be subject only to a final "up or down" congressional vote. Such vast powers had never before been granted to a president, and they had important political significance for building a strong alliance with Western Europe. A ministerial meeting to launch the actual negotiations—henceforth called the Kennedy Round—had just concluded in Geneva at GATT[154] headquarters, and the stage was set for long and arduous haggling with the Europeans and dozens of other countries. Several preliminary talks to prepare the ground for the ministers, for which I had been sent to Geneva, had left no doubt about a rocky road ahead.

The meeting of ministers had not gone well. As a condition for granting the president special powers, Congress had insisted that their implementation be led directly from the White House by a Special Trade Representative (STR) with cabinet rank, for which JFK had persuaded Christian Herter, a Republican former governor and secretary of state, to come out of retirement. Herter, already in his 70's and not in good health, had an excellent reputation but no trade negotiating experience, and his delegation had been large, unwieldy, and torn by internal conflicts. A half dozen assistant secretaries and no fewer than seventeen senior advisors from different departments and agencies had argued amongst themselves, and lobbyists for every conceivable special interest had made life miserable for them. STR was new and untested and the "Governor (the title Herter preferred) had been hard pressed to keep any kind of order. The other countries had been difficult, and the deliberations had almost collapsed in chaos before the actual negotiating could begin. It was clear that something had to be done.

This was the background for the presidential summons, and, for once, I dreaded the prospect of a White House visit because I suspected the purpose. Ball and his staff had concluded that an experienced deputy to Herter was needed to lead the U.S. side in the actual talks, while the Governor would occupy himself primarily with the politics at home. Their choice, to my chagrin, had fallen on me, but I had resolutely resisted them since I desperately wanted to stay in Washington. One of Ball's favorite aphorisms was that in government "nothing 'propinqs' like propinquity," and I had taken this truth to heart. Taking up residence in faraway Switzerland, at the receiving end of instructions from Washington over which I feared I would have little influence, was unappealing. So it was clear that the ploy now was for the president himself to give me the needed push. Yet I was still determined to decline the honor, and for days had rehearsed all possible reasons why there were others—I had a list of names ready—more suitable for the assignment than I.

It proved to be a short visit. Nervous and tense, I was ushered into the Oval Office, where the president was seated in his rocking chair and greeted me pleasantly. First he congratulated me on the coffee talks and thanked me for "helping him." Slowly my resolve began to melt. "Tell me," he then asked, "why do they call it the Kennedy Round?" The reason, I explained, was his successful fight for the TEA, which had made this significant round of trade talks possible, a fact well understood throughout the world. Though he probably knew this, he feigned surprise. "I'm not sure I like having my name attached to it," he mused. "After all, if the negotiations fail I'll get the blame," and then, leaning forward and looking at me directly with his piercing blue eyes: "which is why I want you to go and make sure that doesn't happen." To which I heard myself saying, "Yes, sir, I'll do my best."

And that was how all my excellent reasons for declining the offer were never mentioned and how, soon thereafter, I left the State Department to take up residence in Geneva for the next four years. I hadn't counted on the president's sway in the Oval Office, and on JFK's charm. As with the corporate heavyweights I would later observe, the aura of the environment and the authority of the president of the United States had been impossible to resist.

The Kennedy Round

On July 17, 1963, the Senate Foreign Relations Committee—each Senator using the occasion to press the case for whatever products hailed from his home state—judged me "tough enough" to defend vital U.S. interests, and confirmed me as the president's deputy special representative for trade negotiations, with the rank of ambassador. For a one-time stateless immigrant it was a proud moment.

In those distant days before jet airplanes, diplomats on international assignment still used a highly civilized mode of travel to their overseas posts—they went by ship. Thus, we set sail in August with our three daughters, aged ten, seven, and five, on a leisurely ocean journey to Genoa and thence onward to the place that would be our home for the next four years. Geneva is a medium-sized city, a somewhat provincial Swiss gem on the shores of Lake Léman, but one of the most agreeable places in Europe. Nearby is the lovely Swiss and French countryside of Savoy, the mountains are in plain view, and in winter there is excellent skiing. There are fine restaurants and at four Swiss francs for a dollar, prices were reasonable. With our daughters enrolled in a Swiss school and learning French, and the family installed in a splendiferous ambassadorial residence, complete with cook, butler, and maid, we settled down to a lifestyle to which, Eileen would remind me, "we were neither entitled nor accustomed."

The circumstances for getting started were not particularly auspicious. The Grand Design, of which the Kennedy Round (KR) was to be a part—and especially the hope for European unity—was in some trouble. Some European leaders—Prime Minister Macmillan of Great Britain, Germany's Konrad Adenauer, and de Gaulle of France —were still nineteenth-century men who had difficulty with the American vision of a twentieth-century postwar world. The British had initially kept their distance but eventually declared a willingness to join the Common Market, though not to accept all its terms. De Gaulle, for his part, was suspicious of the U.S.–UK relationship, aspired to Common Market leadership, and suspected British entry of being a U.S. Trojan horse to deny him that role.

The Alliance was thus anything but trouble-free, and only a few months before, de Gaulle had dramatically vetoed the idea of British entry. The media were trumpeting "Atlantic Disarray," and instead of an economically unified Western Europe, there was now the risk of one divided into two competing trade blocs: six countries in the Common Market and seven in the European Free Trade Association (EFTA) arrayed around Britain. Some called it "Europe at Sixes and Sevens."

In February, a high-level policy review in Washington had reached the decision not to confront the French directly over their veto and to push ahead. The Kennedy Round was now seen as an even more important means of providing for some focused momentum, and as a means for Britain's EFTA Seven to reduce the trade discrimination against them outside the external tariff wall of the Six. Perhaps the KR, opined the *New York Times*, could provide the glue necessary "to help overcome the looming Atlantic disarray," a viewpoint supported by the influential opinions of Walter Lippmann in the *Washington Post* and James Reston of the *Times*.[155] Yet the KR faced a bewildering array of institutional and substantive barriers to productive negotiations.

To start, there was the mammoth scope of the undertaking, involving over seventy-five participating countries and, as one paper noted, no fewer than 1,500 individual delegates and observers from every corner of the world.[156] Our delegation alone numbered over sixty officials from various government departments, not counting the steady stream of experts on temporary duty, congressmen, VIP visitors, and assorted lobbyists all clamoring for attention.

One of the biggest barriers to progress was that for the first time, the Six would be negotiating as a unit. The *Times* had flagged this as the "It and They" problem.[157] For their representative—the "It"—to speak with authority, the six member countries—the "They"—first had to agree on his instructions, but their interests and traditions varied widely and reaching a common position in Brussels was glacially slow. The EFTA countries, for their part, lacked political cohesion, and the French did their best to be obstructionist. Their instincts were still protectionist, they had little enthusiasm for real trade liberalization, and they suspected the KR as an American ploy to dominate Europe. Partly the French attitude was also due to ingrained contrariness. De Gaulle, wrote the *Times*, fit the Shakespearean adage that "to be great is to sustain a great quarrel."[158] Meanwhile the Japanese contributed little, while hoping for benefits to their already formidable export engine, and Canada, Australia, and New Zealand, the great agricultural exporters, were insisting on broad farm product liberalization for many products, which even the United States was resisting.

These were just some of the initial problems, and the ministers had even failed to agree on the basic ground rules for the tariff cutting. Would it be "linear"—an equal 50 percent across the board with few exceptions—as the United States had proposed? The Europeans adamantly rejected that and argued that "disparities" in the pattern of tariff rates between the United States and Europe had to be dealt with. The average of all tariffs might be similar, they pointed out, but the United States had a few very high rates which required disproportionate action (though the many very low ones they proposed to ignore). The French had even invented a word for it—*écretement*, or "cutting off heads." *Écretement* wasn't a starter for us, and so the issue remained hopelessly deadlocked. And no one as yet knew how to include the developing countries meaningfully, nor what to do about the myriad of non-tariff barriers restricting world trade, or what rules for cutting agricultural protection would pertain. Finally, there was also the nasty problem of American Selling Price (ASP), a peculiar highly protectionist special arrangement long enjoyed by U.S. producers of benzenoid chemical products. For these, tariffs were assessed not on the value of export prices but on the protected high domestic selling price, thus virtually shutting out the foreign competition. The Six had given firm notice that ASP would have to go and that there could be no deal without it. We, on the other hand, were under severe congressional pressure not to surrender this boondoggle. In the end, this above all else would be the issue that threatened the collapse of the KR until the very last moment.

It took four years to bring the KR to a successful conclusion. Along the way there were plenty of ups and downs, and more than once it looked like collapse was inevitable or that, at best, only token results were possible. Amid these crises, there had been no dearth of criticism and second-guessing, but when we succeeded, the result was hailed as the most successful trade talks ever. Tariffs came down by an average of 33 percent. The intractable ASP and disparity issues were compromised, and even on agriculture and developing country trade there was at least some progress. Politically, European unity was strengthened and the Atlantic partnership reinforced.

When the final deal was hammered out in an all-night session on May 14, 1967, the president whose name the negotiations bore had been dead for over three years. It had taken twice as long as he had expected, but from the moment of his murder, leaving Geneva before the end had ceased to be an option for me. I had taken his Oval Office request to protect his name from a failure as a personal commitment, all the more important to honor because he was gone.

For me it had also been another important learning experience in international negotiation. The right internal organization of a national delegation and its backstopping at home, I found, was critical, but no less so than keeping the team together with a sense of timing for knowing when to compromise and when to stand firm.

My task in the KR encompassed all of that. George Ball later described it as "a formidable assignment [that] required persistence, tough-mindedness and the fortitude to stand up to industry and labor pressures . . . while wrangling with other negotiators who were feeling equal but opposite pressures."[159]

Another important reality was learning that hard work and good ideas are not enough. One needs to know where the power is and engage it personally and directly. Thus I became an inveterate traveler and rarely stayed put in Geneva for long. Every six to eight weeks I would return to Washington to lobby for viable instructions and keep influential members of Congress informed; or to make the rounds to key capital cities, knowing that these were where the decisions behind the instructions to the other negotiators were made.

Finally, there was also the critical fact that a major international effort of this kind usually has to be waged on three fronts. One is the actual negotiation behind closed doors. The others are ensuring full support at home, on the one hand, and managing as best as one can the reports circulating on the outside about what is happening. For the first task, William Matson Roth, Herter's other deputy and the man selected to manage the Washington end of the KR, could not have been a better choice as my Washington counterpart. A sophisticated, meticulous, and highly intelligent Californian newcomer to Washington, he quickly learned the ropes, and we became an effective twosome, with Bill keeping the wolves at bay at home and providing the Geneva delegation with critical support. The Roths, Bill and Joan, have remained close friends to this day.

For the outside job, finally, a good public affairs advisor can be worth his weight in gold, and Harold Kaplan, the man I had selected, proved a particular blessing. Major trade negotiations are especially sensitive. They affect many vital interests, and there is a constant clamor for inside information. Rumors invariably circulate, and "leaking" deliberate half-truths or outright misinformation to undermine or weaken the other side and buttress one's own position is not uncommon. During the many ups and downs of the KR, this extension of the negotiations into the media was always part of the process, with each side maneuvering to present its story in the best possible light. Whose position was the most reasonable? What were truly nonnegotiable demands? Who was dealing in good faith and who perhaps bluffed? Did certain negotiators stand in the way of progress, possibly flying "solo" without backing at home? "Kappy" solved these problems of our posture in the media brilliantly over several years.

Bill Roth spent the last ten days of bargaining in Geneva against the final deadline. Sometimes he would play the "bad guy" and I the conciliator, at other times we would reverse roles, amid alarmist headlines of "Gloom in Geneva" or "Tariff Meeting near Collapse."[160] But when it was all over, and success was at hand, the banner headline on page one of the *New York Times* proclaimed the happy news of "Kennedy Round Success," and President Johnson sent us his personal congratulations. When I received his authorization to sign the final deal (which the Congress ratified quickly) it was one of my proudest moments.

The Importance of Leadership

The sixties were ending and much had happened since John Kennedy campaigned for the Presidency and promised a bright new era of progress. Before three years had passed he was dead from an assassin's bullet, and it was his successor who went on to achieve a historic transformation in American life.

Would the social changes of the Great Society have come under JFK, or did they take the skillful maneuvering of Lyndon Johnson, the accomplished legislative tactician? Would the long-overdue break-through on civil rights have occurred in the sixties without LBJ, and the tireless efforts of Hubert Humphrey, the great liberal from Minnesota, who led the fight in the Senate, and—above all—without the eloquence of Martin Luther King Jr.? We will never know the answers, but these were seminal events that changed U.S. history, and they happened because the right leaders were in the right places at the right time.

In the sixties, the colonial world disappeared for good, dozens of new nations joined the United Nations, and new institutions arose to address their special needs. Yet the demise of colonialism was not without turmoil and pain, as incompetent and venal politicians and dictators took over from the colonial powers and the United States became enmeshed in the former French colony of Vietnam.

In Europe, Jean Monnet's vision of European unification made forward strides, buttressed by decisive American support and an Atlantic partnership which enhanced Western military and economic security and withstood Cold War pressures. And in the sixties, the defeated nations of the war, Germany and Japan, prospered rapidly under effective leadership and supportive U.S. policies.

Some of these historic events I had witnessed from the perspective of an insider close to the decision makers and they left me with many unforgettable memories of the critical role a courageous leader can play. Two, in particular, stand out.

A critical day in the Cuban Missile Crisis was October 22, 1962, which was also the opening day of an Alliance for Progress conference in Mexico City. I was there with a large U.S. delegation led by Douglas Dillon, the secretary of the treasury, an impressive man with an elegant manner, exuding the confidence of a distinguished establishment name. He had always impressed me with his self-assurance and air of being in control at all times. He had, we would learn, been with that small group of presidential advisors, the Executive Committee, or Ex Com, who for days had worked in great secrecy to weigh the alternatives of a U.S. response to the Soviet threat, and he had then joined us in Mexico at the last moment.

I shall never forget the Dillon who called the senior delegation members to the U.S. embassy that night, to brief us on the gravity of the situation and on the president's impending report to the nation. Tense, pale, and obviously exhausted from lack of sleep, he explained that Soviet ships bringing missiles would be challenged on the high seas, and that no one could know the USSR's response. He had brought his wife, and now they sat together holding hands without hiding their nervousness and concern. It is that moment—hearing the president's television warning that "no one can foresee precisely what course (events) will take or what costs or casualties will be incurred," and seeing the face of the man who had helped make the critical decisions clutching his wife's hand—that I cannot forget.

The other indelible memory is of November 22, 1963, when the world heard the news of President Kennedy's assassination. For me, that moment had a special poignancy, because at the very time he died I was on a personal mission for him to Bern, with a letter from him to Hans Schaffner, the future president of Switzerland, which I had been instructed to deliver in person.

The subject—eliminating prohibitive U.S. protection against Swiss watches—today seems a minor matter, but then it was of great importance to the Swiss and a long-standing irritant in U.S.–Swiss relations. The political pressures were fierce in both countries, but finally JFK had decided to act and Schaffner was to be so informed. For JFK it had taken political courage; for the Swiss it would be great news and the president had wanted his decision communicated in the appropriate manner. Schaffner had invited me for dinner, and when I arrived it was he who told me the awful news that the U.S. president whose message I carried was dead.

Whatever the diplomatic protocol, I was unable to hold back the tears. Then I delivered the letter and asked to be excused. John

Kennedy once had written about political courage, and, in a small way, the Swiss had received proof of it on the very day he died.

My years in government had impressed on me the unique position occupied by the United States in world affairs. We loom so large on the world scene that few international developments, whether on questions of security or on economics and finance, do not touch our vital interests. This provides us with opportunities to influence events, but also imposes an obligation of leadership that is not always comfortable or easy. Occasionally we are tempted to sit back hoping that others will take our place, but that rarely works. Unless we take the lead on the major questions, no one else will. Our weight and influence in world affairs is often envied and resented, but our leadership role—however grudgingly and critically—is largely expected. To lead, we must accept the responsibility of our unique position and exercise it with patience and an understanding of our limits. Attempting to go it alone or to impose our will rarely succeeds.

There are broad forces of history and events that lie beyond anyone's control, and there is always historical accident, such as the appearance or departure of a key actor from the world stage at a critical point of time. The assassination of JFK is one such example. Yet sweeping changes and accident are only a framework. They provide the context within which political interaction takes place, and history is made. Politics, I had seen, is the exercise of power, and it is practiced everywhere by men and women with the capacity for both wisdom and fallibility. The right person in the right place at the right time taking initiatives and exercising effective leadership can have a strongly positive impact.

When John F. Kennedy, against substantial odds, had the vision and courage to lead the way for a path-breaking new approach to liberalizing world trade, he made history. When the visionary Jean Monnet provided intellectual leadership for the idea of European unity, he influenced the doubters and inspired disciples like George

Ball, who ensured vital American support. That, too, was the leadership of individuals who made history.

The reverse, of course, was equally true. Had JFK shared Ball's foresight on Vietnam, or LBJ shown greater courage and less stubbornness to reverse course, the story of Vietnam might well have been different. And nowhere was the critical role of leadership by those in power clearer than in the close brush with disaster during the Cuban Missile Crisis. One man in the Kremlin, or at most a very few, made potentially devastating miscalculations that could have led to nuclear war, and if in the White House the advice of the hawks had been taken, the outcome might have been disaster. As I saw so vividly on that night in Mexico City, it was men like Douglas Dillon, thrust into a position of grave responsibility, who helped the U.S. president choose the wiser course.

These are the most important lessons I took with me from my time in the government during the sixties—that it is individuals that count in determining the course of events, not merely at the top, but at lower levels of government as well. I saw it in others, and I learned it about myself.

THE SEVENTIES
A World in Transition

Big Changes

When JFK sent me to Geneva in 1963, he had confidently assured me that it wouldn't be for more than two years, and that I would be welcomed back to a good job when the Kennedy Round talks ended. But that was not how it worked out. The negotiations took twice as long, and when they were over, the president whose name they carried had been dead for more than three years. The New Frontier was history, and a new president was in the White House, dealing with different domestic problems and international challenges from those of 1963. For my part, I would not be coming back to Washington but leaving the government and returning to private life.

In 1961, the State Department had been a dream come true for me, and representing the United States in international negotiations had been deeply satisfying. That I would, not many years later, give all that up for a corporate job would have been unthinkable. In fact, as late as the spring of 1965, I had gladly accepted State's offer to integrate me into the regular ranks of the Foreign Service with the prospect of another ambassadorial post.

Yet when the offer of a major corporate job landed on my Geneva desk in early 1967, I resigned from the Foreign Service and accepted it. A big reason was Vietnam. The United States was deeply mired in that unfortunate conflict in Southeast Asia, and I had long since joined those convinced that it was all a tragic mistake, that U.S. Vietnam policy was folly, and that the chances of achieving our objectives there were remote. I admired President Johnson's domestic accomplishments, but the prospect of defending his Vietnam policy abroad troubled me, and I wondered how I could loyally do the job under these circumstances.

The offer for a senior position in one of America's largest corporations brought matters to a head, just as the Kennedy Round was entering its final phase. The Bendix Corporation, among the seventy largest U.S. companies on the Fortune list, was a Detroit-based manufacturer of high-tech, engineered products for the automotive, electronics, space, and industrial industries, with over 70,000 employees worldwide and annual billion-dollar sales. As a corporate vice president and member of the board of directors, I was to take over their New York offices and run Bendix's extensive international operations. The publicity over my role in the high profile Kennedy Round talks had worked its magic, and the opportunity that the Bendix chairman had sketched for me was at quite another level from the one at Crown Cork. The Bendix job, I realized, would propel me virtually overnight into the upper echelons of the U.S. business establishment. The "push" of my concerns over Vietnam had opened me up to considering the idea; the "pull" of the Bendix offer had done the rest.

On May 16, 1967, the *New York Times* and the world press had reported the successful end of the Geneva talks with banner headline front page stories, and some weeks before I had written confidential letters to President Johnson and Dean Rusk announcing my decision to resign after the negotiations ended. Rusk had replied with a complimentary letter accepting my decision "with deep regret." "In the past six years," he wrote me, "the soundness of your advice and your exceptional negotiating skills have contributed much to foreign policy."

President Johnson sent a congratulatory telegram when the talks ended, and his personal letter arrived a few days later, thanking me for "performing with exceptional skill, energy, intelligence, and devotion." "The enormous benefits of the Kennedy Round," he wrote, "will stand as a continual memorial to your very fine work." Both letters pleased me greatly, but I couldn't help thinking that it was the murdered president who had sent me. The greater personal satisfaction was knowing that "his" negotiations had succeeded, and that we hadn't let him down.

So in late June we sailed for home. Someday, I thought, I would perhaps be back in Washington, though for the time being my government years were over.

We were returning to a very different country. The world was undergoing big changes. So was the United States, and the evidence could be seen everywhere—in how and where people lived, their well-being and their work, and in a new diversity of races and faces. It is part of the American national character to be more individualistic than in many other countries, more flexible in adapting to change, and more pragmatic in adjusting to new circumstances when the need arises or opportunity knocks. There was plenty of that in the seventies.

The U.S. economy was growing, but so were those of other countries. Western Europe was gaining strength, and there was more competition in world trade. Distances had shrunk, and new technologies were changing modern life. Living standards had risen in many places and the world's financial and trading systems had become more intertwined. More and more people were jetting across the world.

Richard Nixon, who became president in January of 1969, had promised a quick end to the war in Vietnam, but the fighting continued for years and cost many more American lives. Protests over urban decay and the slow changes in civil rights were causing disturbances across the nation. U.S. energy self-sufficiency ended, oil imports doubled, and two painful oil crises brought difficult economic times with unprecedented levels of inflation and unemployment. The rust belt struggled, while the sun belt flourished. Old industries stagnated or contracted, while those focused on services and the new technologies grew. Steel production in the United States dropped by 20 percent during the decade, and an explosion in corporate mergers rationalized some industries but also cost jobs and created uncertainties and hardship for many workers.

An important development of the seventies was the changing profile of the U.S. population. The evidence was everywhere—in the streets of the inner cities and in the shopping malls of the suburbs. For one thing, there were many more people. Their numbers had grown steadily in the postwar years, passing the 200 million mark in 1968 and expanding by another 26 million during the seventies. After the war, the baby boomers had fueled a population bulge, but in the seventies it was the first wave of a new type of immigrant that would add another 23 million new Americans by the century's end, with millions more "illegals" crossing the porous southern borders.

The immigrants of the seventies and eighties differed from those of earlier periods, and their impact was unmistakable. In the first postwar years, the numbers had been relatively modest, and most had come from Europe, while those of other parts of the world had been largely excluded. In 1965, however, LBJ had signed legislation that shifted U.S. policy in a new direction. Immigration procedures were liberalized and admissions criteria changed to give preference to political refugees, family relationships, and occupational qualifications. Whereas fewer than 7 million immigrants had been allowed in during the prior three decades, the number now grew from 4.5 million in the single decade of the seventies, to over 7 million in the eighties and 9 million in the nineties.[161] The most important feature of the new legislation, however, was the elimination of the openly racist country of origin quota system.

The effect was dramatic. Henceforth only 10 to 15 percent of new immigrants hailed from Europe, with the vast majority of others natives of Asia, South and Central America, and the Caribbean, plus a sprinkling of Africans. The result was an unmistakably new kaleidoscopic racial and multiethnic mix that enriched the country's dynamism and vitality. Cubans flocked to Florida and revitalized Miami. In New York and other big cities, Americans could patronize the twenty-four-hour convenience stores of industrious Korean shopkeepers; Vietnamese and Thai restaurateurs added to the variety of culinary offerings across the United States; turbaned Sikhs pumped gas in New Jersey; and Latino immigrants from virtually every Western hemisphere country made their presence felt at all levels of economic and community life. By taking entry-level jobs, this abundant source of new labor did much to fuel continued growth and to keep U.S. costs competitive in world trade.

Many immigrants sent their children to schools and colleges where, in the time-honored tradition of America, they quickly moved up the economic ladder. At City College of San Francisco, where I had made my start as an immigrant in the late forties when most of my fellow students had been Caucasians, 60 percent of the student body today are Asians and Hispanics. Less than 7 percent of the U.S. population in the fifties was born outside the United States. Today one in ten Americans is foreign born.[162]

Not only did Americans become more ethnically diverse, they also began to shift the country's center of gravity by moving south and west in large numbers, and their educational qualifications and occupational statuses changed markedly. In the single decade of the seventies, the population of Florida grew by 60 percent, Texas by more than half, and California by 20 percent, while the big Eastern and Midwestern population centers remained static or declined. It was the beginning of a long-term trend, of older manufacturing areas struggling against the new competition from overseas, and the sun belt proving more hospitable to jobs based on new technologies. Eighty percent of Americans were now high school graduates, one in four had gone to college, and vastly greater numbers had become engineers, doctors, and lawyers.

"Americans are the best fed, housed, and educated in the world," LBJ had proudly proclaimed before leaving office, noting that while they accounted for only 6 percent of the world's population, they owned half its wealth, two-thirds of its automobiles, half its radios, and generated half its electric power output.[163]

His Great Society program had achieved some near-miracles. School segregation was declared unconstitutional, the new Medicare was a pioneering healthcare program for older Americans, the most comprehensive housing bill in U.S. history had been enacted into law, the number of Americans officially listed as "poor" was reduced by a third, and the jobless rate had fallen to a fifteen-year low.

LBJ had pursued a deliberate "Guns and Butter" strategy, hoping to deflect disaffection over an increasingly unpopular war. It had worked for a while, but then events took a different turn. The economic good times did not long survive his White House tenure, and the breakthroughs on social and civil rights legislation failed to translate into domestic tranquility. Strong antiwar sentiment overwhelmed the good feelings and led to domestic unrest, including fire-bombing and looting in the inner cities—a time one magazine called "the country's winter of discontent.[164] So LBJ had chosen not to run again, Vice President Humphrey, his Democratic successor, lost the election, and the next three Presidents—Nixon, Ford, and Carter—would preside over a country which was neither peaceful nor content.

The America of the seventies was not a happy place. As the war dragged on, protests and civil unrest dominated the early years of the decade. Two hundred thousand protesters marched on Washington in 1971; similar rallies took place in other cities, and anti-Vietnam agitation kept college campuses in turmoil. Busing controversies and resistance to implementing the new civil rights laws caused violent confrontations in Louisville and various southern cities, while urban decay of the inner cities in the North led to more lawlessness.

The economy also turned sour. By 1973 the nation was descending into one of the sharpest recessions in forty years, and President Ford's State of the Union message in January of 1975 sounded a very different note from LBJ's earlier ebullient boast of national well-being. "Millions of Americans are out of work," Ford wrote, "recession and inflation are eroding the money of millions more . . . the federal deficit and the national debt are both rising . . . we depend on others for essential energy . . ."

The economy would remain under stress throughout the Ford and Carter presidencies and well into the years of Ronald Reagan. Two major "oil shocks," with shortages at the pumps and unprecedented price spikes,[165] were a dramatic reminder of the risks of U.S.

dependence on petroleum imports, while LBJ's Guns and Butter policies led to increasing budget deficits, and sharply higher rates of inflation. The resulting pressure on the dollar raised the cost of vital imports, and a simultaneous slowdown in Europe made matters worse. Thus, in 1976, the United States had its first taste of "stagflation"—inflation between 8 to 10 percent, stagnation in the GDP, and rising levels of unemployment. At the end of the Ford administration, almost 7 percent of the labor force was unemployed, and inflation, having briefly risen to double digits, stood at close to 8 percent.

In the wake of the assassinations of President Kennedy, Martin Luther King Jr., and Robert Kennedy, the resignations of the disgraced Vice President Spiro Agnew and President Nixon, with criminal charges against one and the threat of impeachment against the other, public trust in the government and its leaders sank to a low. As a result, Jimmy Carter, a relatively unknown Southern governor with no Washington experience, had been swept into office in 1976 with the simple promise "I'll never lie to you."

The poor economy had been an important reason for his election, but Jimmy Carter himself would fare no better. A second oil shock in the late seventies was worse than the first, with oil prices reaching levels five times those of 1973. The value of the dollar declined by 50 percent and threatened the stability of the world financial system, and at the end of Carter's administration, the nation was experiencing double-digit inflation and unemployment of over 8 percent, exceeding that of the Ford years.

An energy crisis, double-digit inflation and high unemployment had inexorably eroded his popularity, while policy errors and political missteps did the rest. Four years after gaining the White House, he too would be swept from office and for several more years, the nation would continue to struggle with the problems and challenges of a complex world.

Toward Globalization

The seventies and eighties were transition years from the Cold War world of the twentieth century to the globalism of the twenty-first, the fall of the Iron Curtain being the final and defining event, which came suddenly and when least expected. Yet the signs of a new era of history had begun to accumulate even before.

These were decades with profound new developments, whose implications were poorly understood and unforeseen. The revolution in microelectronics was having a deep impact everywhere, and its astounding advances presaged fundamental changes pointing to an unprecedented globalization of human affairs. Intel's introduction of the microprocessor in 1971 was a momentous event. Over the course of the decade and into the eighties, this single small chip for processing information in a computer, and the exponential increase in its speed and power year after year, began to propel the world on its steep upward path of data storage and communication capabilities, and to revolutionize the way people lived, worked, and related to one another. Medical scientists developed the first fiber-optic endoscope for scanning the entire human body, achieved the first complete synthesis of a human gene, greatly improved organ transplant technology, and made major strides in perfecting superior techniques for heart surgery and the early detection and treatment of cancer.

These exciting advances, however, also brought the first harbingers of the by-products of globalization. The energy crises in the seventies were warning signals of the potential for strain in world energy markets. Thirty years later, this would become a much more significant problem when industrial production in China and India began to grow at rates several times higher than in the rest of the world, and the consumption of oil by these two Asian giants doubled within little more than a decade.[166] Recognition, for the first time, of mounting risks to the environment from so much rapid growth was another key development during the decade.

On the positive side, there was an easing of tensions between the Communist bloc and democracies, major advances in human knowledge, significant economic progress, and early signs of a takeoff toward sustained periods of industrial growth in China and India. All that was to the good. But the other side of the coin was that the emerging globalism created energy shortages that strained the world financial system, and recessions and balance-of-payments crises cascading across borders resulted in damaging swings in international exchange rates.

Nor did the world become a less dangerous place. The Vietnam War cost close to 60,000 American dead, with many more wounded, and as many as a million casualties among the local Vietnamese population. Millions were murdered in Cambodia, while ethnic strife claimed the lives and swelled the number of homeless refugees in Africa by millions more. By the end of the seventies, upwards of 10 million refugees, displaced from their traditional homes, were marking time in refugee camps.

In a critical new development, there were signs inside the Soviet bloc that things were not going well. New technologies were piercing the Iron Curtain, and the desire for independence and a better life in most of the Soviet satellites was becoming difficult to contain. The evidence of Communism's difficulties in keeping up in a high-tech world grew ever stronger. Solzhenitsyn and other intellectuals had begun to publish their works abroad, the literary underground's samizdat writings flourished, Soviet Jews clamored to leave, and the distinguished physicist Andrei Sakharov openly criticized the system. Even Stalin's daughter had fled the country and taken refuge in the West.

On both sides of the East–West divide, rising interest in a rapprochement through détente and nuclear disarmament should have raised questions about long-standing assumptions, but did not because the Cold War had been the dominant reality for a quarter century, and both Western and Communist leaders could think of nothing else. Thus powerful forces on both sides insisted on the continuation of policies assuming that the confrontation would continue indefinitely.

A good example was an article by James Schlesinger which *Fortune* magazine ran as its cover story in February 1976, shortly after he had been dismissed as President Ford's secretary of defense.[167] Titled "The Specter of Soviet Hegemony," Schlesinger ignored a more nuanced reality and painted an alarming picture of a powerful country with satellites firmly in its grip, unabatedly expansionist with a military budget 50 percent greater than that of the United States and of the "grave exposure of Japan, Korea and the Middle East" to an aggressive Soviet adversary.

His views pleading for more U.S. defense spending were particularly stark, but he was by no means alone in such thinking on both sides of the East–West divide, yet much contrary evidence was already on the horizon. Though Communist dictatorships had once loomed as a formidable, monolithic world bloc, and the Soviet sway over its satellites had been absolute, the signs that world communism was increasingly beset by inefficient economies, nationalism, and internal dissension were already many. As a model for export, Communism had clearly lost its luster among neutrals and in the developing world.

George Kennan had been among the first to note the rise of satellite instability as early as in 1968, and observed that "the unity of the Communist world is gone forever." The early apostasy of Yugoslavia and the Soviet–Chinese border clashes, the divergent policies of Romania in the seventies, the activities of the Solidarity movement and the Catholic Church in Poland, and separatist rumblings in Estonia and Soviet Georgia, were among the multiple events proving him correct, and it should have been obvious to Schlesinger and his fellow cold warriors that the Soviets were in no realistic position to undertake serious new expansionist adventures.

Yet the former U.S. secretary of defense and like-minded others were simply unable or unwilling to recognize that Communism was rotting from within. Though the harsh verbal exchanges between East and West continued, the underlying reality was already diverging from standard Cold War assumptions. A joint U.S.-USSR venture into space in 1971 was an early indication of a gradual de facto thaw in East–West relations and of interest to both sides in exploring opportunities for reducing tensions. "Détente" had already entered the vocabulary of the East–West dialogue. The Soviet Union's position in the Strategic Arms Limitation talks (SALT I & II) of later years also showed a heightened desire to ease the prohibitive costs that the arms race was imposing on their domestic economy.

Thus "globalization" was beginning, even if the term itself was not yet in vogue. But these were the years when its major elements were first being felt. The European response was to move to a wider political union with an expanding membership. Elsewhere some of the world's largest nations took note and rushed to catch up. The earlier turmoil in China during the Cultural Revolution was followed in the seventies after Mao's death by big economic and political changes, not the least of which was a rapprochement with the United States, ending a quarter century of estrangement. In 1971, the United States had acquiesced to China replacing Taiwan in the United Nations. A steady flow of informal Sino–U.S. contacts and reciprocal visits followed, culminating in the reestablishment of full diplomatic relations in 1979.

Led by a group of reformers under the veteran Deng Xiaoping, China now emerged from years of isolation, took the first steps to modernize its economy, and embarked on a breakneck pace of development. India also began to awake from its socialist slumber. No one at the time fully realized the enormous significance of these changes, or that they would quickly lead to an entirely new world position for both nations.

In the Middle East, finally, the fall of the Shah and the taking of American hostages in Iran in 1978 to 1979; Islamic fervor in the Asian parts of the Soviet Union; and the Soviet decision to invade Afghanistan were early omens of the rise of a form of religious fundamentalism among Muslims that would, in time, have major implications for the rest of the world.

In the seventies and eighties, I ran two of America's largest corporations, and served in Jimmy Carter's cabinet. Traveling the world as a business executive and government official, I was in a privileged place to observe the unfolding of these events. Occasionally I would play a small role in them myself.

A Corporate Leader

The Bendix Corporation, which I joined in 1967, was a big multinational corporation, a major defense contractor and government supplier doing business with the world's automotive and aerospace industries. Its far-flung international activities, for which I was to be responsible, comprised dozens of subsidiaries across the globe with some 26,000 employees, numerous joint ventures, and hundreds of technology licensing deals.

To have charge of such extensive operations was an entirely new experience for me. Crown Cork had been a one-man show where I hadn't really supervised anyone, and chairing government delegations had been a big job but the negotiators under my charge rarely exceeded a hundred. Now I would be responsible for setting the goals and objectives for sizeable teams of senior line executives and large support staffs, with final say over multiple operations in many countries and accountability for their bottom line.

It was a big new challenge that required a lot of quick study, but it had only been the beginning. Three years later I was promoted to take charge of the company's entire domestic and international operations. Soon thereafter the board elected me chairman and CEO, a job I would hold until Jimmy Carter called me back to Washington in 1977.

My ten years at Bendix in New York and Detroit were as rewarding as any I could have wished for, at a time when globalization was just getting underway and electronics was changing the business world. For corporate leaders taking advantage of the new opportunities there were more exciting possibilities, but also greater complexity and risk. The range of investment and financing choices had broadened, but so had the vulnerability to costly errors in having to weigh unaccustomed political issues alongside traditional business considerations. All this required a new skill set for top managers, one that not all were well suited to handle. As for me, though I was thin on business experience and the related technical skills, the domestic and international sensitizing to politics that my years in government had provided proved beneficial, giving me a broader perspective than that of some of my peers.

There is an extensive literature on what makes for a successful business leader, but the Bendix experience convinced me that the qualities frequently mentioned, such as superior technical knowledge, intelligence, toughness, determination, energy, and a drive to succeed, while useful, are not the sufficient nor the critical ones. Knowing one's own limits, a firm sense of right and wrong, and what some have called "emotional intelligence" are at least as important. Bendix convinced me that personal courage—and an instinct for when and how to use it effectively—is perhaps the single most important quality of all, and that in business as in politics, it is rarely present in abundance. It takes courage to choose among subordinates, to rely on their judgment, and to delegate authority; and courage is essential in recognizing your own deficiencies, in admitting mistakes, and in changing your mind and reversing course.

Emotional intelligence comprises a whole bundle of critical qualities—a healthy self-awareness and the capacity for personal growth, the ability to listen, a comfort with ambiguity, sensitivity, and empathy for the human factor, and superior social skills. Not unimportantly, it also involves recognizing—and discounting—the inevitable flattery from subordinates for what it is, appreciating straightforward advice rather than shooting the messenger of bad tidings and, finally, the ability to inspire others and to respect the limits and the responsibilities of leadership power.[168] Power can, and does, corrupt in obvious and subtle ways, whether in business or in political life.

At Bendix, I learned about leadership by making my own mistakes and by observing the successes and failures of my peers and the impact of those in power on the course of events and on people's lives.

The challenges corporate America was facing in the seventies were the background for the compressed on-the-job training of my early days at Bendix. U.S. industry had dominated the postwar international business scene for years, and with the recovery of overseas markets, direct U.S. foreign investments had exploded from $12 billion in 1950 to an astounding $133 billion by the mid-seventies. American manufacturing facilities in Western Europe had, in fact, been growing so fast that many there worried that the United States had embarked on a deliberate policy to use its superior resources to dominate and enslave them by economic means.[169]

By the late sixties, going overseas, in other words, was definitely "in" for U.S. corporations, and most CEO's were engaged in aggressive international expansion programs, based on the widely-held conviction that this was essential for the success of any ambitious company. A quick drive for maximum growth, buttressed by acquisitions and diversification often into essentially unrelated fields, was an equally fashionable policy pursued by many. Every ambitious CEO wanted to see his company move up on *Fortune*'s list of the 500 biggest corporations, as a kind of personal validation and proof of dynamic management success. As to diversification through acquisitions, if possible into fields subject to divergent business cycles, that was said to be the smartest way to achieve growth while simultaneously smoothing out the inevitable ups and downs of any single industry sector.

In certain circumstances this made good sense. Yet in too many instances, actual results turned out to be less than uniformly positive, with costly disappointments and setbacks. But it took time for that to become apparent. In the business world, fads about new policy ideas and management techniques come and go. They may have a rather short shelf life, but while they last many CEO's find them hard to resist, because many are followers rather than leaders, and more comfortable with emulating others than asking hard questions and swimming against the stream.

My predecessor had rejuvenated the management and accomplished a lot. Yet he too had gone on an aggressive acquisition binge, and along with some successes had come a fair number of unanticipated problems and setbacks. With great faith in the wonders of technology, he had settled on the motto of "Bendix—where technology unlocks the future." The story he was telling investors (Wall Street always likes a "story") was that he was only acquiring businesses where superior Bendix technology could unlock hidden value and make a positive contribution. It sounded great, but in practice it had become the cover for casting a very wide net for businesses far removed from the company's traditional expertise. It even included the purchase of a medium-sized lumber company, whose major asset was 200,000 acres of Western timber lands, the rationale being that its sawmills would benefit from Bendix electronic technology, a nice point in theory, but in the end an illusion in practice.

The result had been steady growth in sales, but uneven and disappointing profits. Yet, focused on growth and technology, he had not been dissuaded from forging further ahead, and it was clear to me that he assumed I would follow the same path at Bendix International. Thus my first problem was to decide whether to do so, or whether a different direction outside the United States might provide less uncertain prospects for the bottom line.

It didn't take long to discover that the relentless pursuit of acquisitions into sometimes unfamiliar fields had been at the root of the profit disappointments and had diverted time and attention from managing the core businesses we knew best. Our lack of intimate knowledge of what had been bought had regularly led to costly setbacks. With this in mind, a new international business plan was developed involving a fundamental reordering of priorities for Bendix's international operations. Henceforth, we decided, managing intensely what we already had and understood would come first, while new businesses would be acquired only as supplements in closely related fields. It wasn't Bendix's domestic strategy, but I guessed that if it led to our greater contribution to corporate profits, it would validate the gamble and be well received.

The international results we soon reported to Detroit from our New York offices turned out even better than I had hoped. International profits grew steadily over the next three years and sales rose by 50 percent. Before long, our concept of a firm multi-year business plan focused first and foremost on the bottom line—a Bendix first—was adopted as a model for domestic operations, and International was crowned as the fastest growing contributor to corporate profits, with new records set year after year.

Nothing succeeds like success. These results had solidified my company standing, and in 1970 I was invited to move to Detroit with the prospect of becoming the corporation's chief executive within twelve to eighteen months.

Three months later we moved from Princeton and settled in Ann Arbor, Michigan. A year later I was handed the corporation's reins.

"People and Profits"

After I took over in Detroit, we changed the Bendix motto to "People and Profits." The idea was to emphasize that good results are linked to people, and that at Bendix the people would always come first.

Corporate mottos are usually platitudes designed more to sound good than to be practical guides to management practice. We, however, tried to live by our motto and to endow it with real meaning. We wanted to try a different, more open style of corporate management, and to prove that it wouldn't harm the bottom line and would lead to good results.

To show that we meant it, I began at the top. We created an office of the chief executive (OCE), in which the top three executives and I instituted a collegial joint decision-making process under which significant aspects of company policies and operations were to be debated, and agreed on by consensus. Nowadays this arrangement has become more common, but in the early seventies it was still rare, and for Bendix it was a definite first. To my great pleasure—and to the surprise of some—the OCE worked smoothly from the start and achieved its intent.

There were other ways, some small and symbolic, by which we introduced a more collegial, open, and less remote management style at the top. For example, I followed a deliberate practice of dropping in on lower level executives in their offices, perhaps to deliver a memo in person, or merely to chat and answer questions and complaints. The door to my office was left demonstrably open to show that the CEO wasn't cut off in his inner sanctum. A telephone "hotline" was installed in my outer office, which any employee could call to ask a question, offer a suggestion, or voice a complaint.

Eventually these new "people policies" drew the attention of *Fortune* magazine, which reported on them in some detail as a successful approach to employee relations and approvingly cited our practice of "working hard and enthusiastically at talking with executives down the line."[170]

Many of these were little steps, but their sum total soon changed the atmosphere throughout the company. For me this had a very special meaning. I hadn't forgotten how often in earlier times I had felt exposed to the whims of those in power, without a chance to be heard, and it pleased me that I was now in a position to do things differently. "I feel strongly about a person having no say because I had a lot of experience with that sort of thing myself," I told the *Detroit Free Press* in what was a deeply felt, personal comment.[171]

In labor–management relations, I was equally determined to try a different, more positive approach. A standoffish and confrontational spirit in dealing with unions was normal in Detroit, but now we set about trying to convince our managers that it would pay not to consider unions the enemy, but to work with them more as partners than opponents. It was a pretty radical idea in the Detroit environment, viewed skeptically by most of my local counterparts including more than a few Bendix managers. On balance, however, it did create a more cooperative and trusting relationship between Bendix and local labor leaders that protected us from many unnecessary and costly controversies. For example, we publicly pledged that we would move or close an operation only as a last resort, and would consult, communicate the reasons, and seek to negotiate the least painful alternative; and that we would execute what had to be done with great care and never move a plant further than necessary, hoping that this would enable our people to commute to the new location and to keep their jobs.

We put this policy to a practical test when we were forced to close a factory in Ann Arbor because it had become hopelessly obsolete. Our internal analysis had shown that the lowest cost alternative was to set up shop far away in a Southern state, which would have meant job losses for virtually the entire Michigan workforce. So we chose instead a middle ground by moving to a less crowded, more favorable Michigan environment, only fifty miles away. The costs would be somewhat higher, yet what we gained in employee and community goodwill and in the grateful response of our experienced, long-time staff, more than offset what we had sacrificed.

And finally, we preached that certain absolute standards of ethical norms were an important part of the new Bendix way. We didn't want to win at any price. We would work hard but not at the cost of sullying our reputation or conscience. "Most of us have a clear view of how to conduct ourselves honestly and fairly in our private lives. As a company we will observe precisely the same standards and do no less," I announced. In time, it was this for which we would receive the most favorable publicity, and was why the media anointed me, with some exaggeration, "the conscience of American industry."

The Bendix years were very important for me. They allowed me to test some long-standing ideas about the responsible exercise of power.

I knew that choosing the right managers was one of my principal responsibilities and that I had to be prudent in my choices. But in practice I hadn't always done it well. More than once I had made the mistake of being overly impressed by the intelligence of a candidate, ignoring the qualities of courage and moral fiber that I knew to be at least as important. And once my mistake had become obvious, I had too often procrastinated in tackling the disagreeable task of correcting it.

I had also learned that to lead is to choose, and that this can be painful and is rarely straightforward and simple. I had seen how my decisions impacted the lives of people far removed from me; that a decision required the willingness to question conventional wisdom and the courage occasionally to opt for the different and unconventional; and that the wished-for outcomes are always hostage to the vagaries of fortuitous timing, or plain good or bad luck.

In the end I had the immense satisfaction of knowing that our more unconventional approach had become a nationally recognized story of success not only in human terms but also in terms of the bottom line. During my six years in Detroit, Bendix revenues doubled from $1.5 billion to over $3 billion in 1976, and per share earnings tripled from $1.92 to $5.82. Dividends were increased three times, we had split our stock, and its value had significantly increased. Each year, we had succeeded in improving our performance, even though the economy had gone through a serious slump and most of our Detroit peers had taken serious hits.

The story of Bendix had not gone unnoticed, and the media had reported it favorably and in detail. The *New York Times* had led its business page with an admiring article headlined "Bendix—A Winner," and I was especially proud of their comment that we had not only become a "favorite of institutional investors," but that "in addition Bendix has become known in the business world as an avant-garde company in terms of employee relations."[172] The leading Detroit paper, meanwhile, had especially emphasized our philosophy of working with and through people: "it's a case of people first and then profits. Above all, people here don't feel forgotten."[173] To top it off, the National Management Association had named me "Management Man of the Year" for what they called "dynamic leadership" and chosen Bendix as one of America's five best-managed corporations.[174]

Public Engagement

Having left Washington, I expected to be merely an interested observer of major domestic and international development. The reality turned out to be quite different, for in parallel with my Bendix duties, I was soon again deeply involved in as wide a range of public issues as I had been during my State Department and White House days. Invitations to join corporate and community boards and to participate in a broad spectrum of business and public activities had come in very quickly, and once I was in the top Bendix job, the efforts to recruit me for various local activities and business, economic, and international organizations had only quickened. Most CEO's are in demand for such extracurricular endeavors, but with my prior government activities and as a Democrat, I was somewhat of a rarity in the corporate world, if only for reasons of "balance." Before long, therefore, juggling the demands of Bendix against involvement in the Detroit business community and other outside activities became quite a problem and handling it responsibly wasn't easy. In fact, when the governor of Michigan persuaded me in 1974 to head a blue-ribbon group to advise him on the state's economic problems, and I had subsequently also gone public with the suggestion for a council to administer a national business ethics code, one Bendix colleague was quoted as sighing to a *New York Times* reporter, "what we don't need around here is for Mike to take on another extracurricular activity."[175]

I turned down far more invitations than I accepted, but some of the organizations I did agree to join were working on significant seventies issues that had special meaning for me. The National Committee on U.S.–China Relations, a group of China specialists and scholars, was one of these and would prove one of the most exciting experiences of the Bendix years. The prospect of a change in the U.S.–China relationship, ending a quarter century of estrangement, was understandably close to my heart and I had avidly followed the Nixon-Kissinger visits to the People's Republic. Their initiative opened the door to the possibility of some nominally private but officially sanctioned contacts, the National Committee had been thrust into the forefront for them, and the invitation to become their board chairman had been too tempting to resist.

Meanwhile, détente was leading to similar U.S.–USSR "private" contacts, where views were exchanged and ways to lower the temperature of the East–West confrontation were explored. The nuclear question, disarmament, military policies, and the possibility for better trade relations were high on the agenda, and on our side the non-official United Nations Association of the United States of America took the lead in these exchanges. For the talks in Moscow, the UNA-USA had enlisted a number of former senior government officials, Sovietologists, and leading executives including, among others, Cyrus Vance, a future secretary of state;

Carl Kaysen, the head of the Princeton Institute for Advanced Study; Marshall Shulman, a Columbia University Soviet specialist; and the CEO's of Exxon and Prudential Insurance. Early in the seventies I chaired several of these UNA-USA missions to Moscow for what would often be frustrating, though highly revealing exchanges with top Soviet officials.

On the domestic front, one of the most gratifying invitations I accepted was to join the Board of Trustees of Princeton University, and I went on to serve on the board for a total of twelve years at a time of big changes for the institution. Prewar Princeton had openly discriminated against blacks and administered an informal quota system limiting the number of Jewish students; admitting women at either the undergraduate or the graduate levels had seemed a faraway idea. There had already been important changes after the war, but the biggest reforms were made under two postwar Princeton presidents, Bob Goheen and Bill Bowen, whose tenure coincided with my board years. It was thrilling to be there when racial discrimination became a thing of the past, and when female Princetonians became a common and welcome sight on the campus. My daughter Ann was a member of one of the first classes graduating women from the university, and her sister Jane followed four years later. That had special meaning for me and made me particularly proud.

My continuing interest in foreign affairs had also led me to the board of the Council on Foreign Relations in New York; to participation in the Trilateral Commission; to U.S.–Japanese exchanges; and to the board of the Rockefeller Foundation, whose work on health and nutrition issues overseas involved field trips to fascinating countries in faraway places.

Without a doubt, however, the most important and memorable of all my non-company activities during these years involved the National Committee on U.S.–China Relations, and my reconnection with the Chinese people just before and just after the country was beginning to emerge from its quarter-century of Communist orthodoxy and self-imposed isolation.

* * *

Back to China

As I sailed down the Huangpu River en route to San Francisco in 1947, I had taken a last look at the receding skyline of Shanghai's waterfront without many regrets. I was a stateless twenty-one-year old with a single sheet of paper from the United Nations in my pocket to identify me. No one cared that I was leaving, and I—to put it mildly—was euphoric to be out of China and determined never to return.

A quarter century had passed when, in the summer of 1973, I came back to the country I had wanted never to see again, but one changed almost beyond recognition and under circumstances I could not have imagined when I left. It would have seemed preposterous in 1947 that one day a red carpet would be laid out to welcome me and that I would be returning for talks with China's top leadership. In fact, it was surprising to be returning at all, yet since then I have been back a dozen times or more, either as the personal representative of the president of the United States, on official government missions, or as a private citizen. Each time I have been received with the same exquisite courtesy and hospitality the Chinese have honed into an art form over 2,000 years and of which they are one of the world's great masters.

In the course of these many visits I have become acquainted with China and the Chinese people as I never did when I lived there, and have grown quite fond of them. I have learned more about the "Middle Kingdom's" ancient culture, and become more aware of the great hardships the Chinese people endured throughout much of the twentieth century, and of the energy and resilience with which they have weathered those storms.

Chinese progress and growing world influence in the latter decades of the last century is not, per se, unique. India and Brazil share that experience to varying degrees. Yet China's story is so different and has so much more potential to impact the world of tomorrow, that it must be considered one of the twentieth century's seminal political developments. China is the most populous country in the world, and no other was as weak, backward, and disunited at mid-century.

China alone was virtually shut off from the West for a quarter century while locked into an especially rigid form of Communist authoritarianism, with major upheavals, policy failures, famines, and great suffering and hardship imposed on its people. No other country, finally, changed course as abruptly, grew as explosively, and advanced as fast and as far as China.

Even the Chinese themselves must be surprised at what they have accomplished, and I often wonder what the late Premier Zhou Enlai would have thought were he alive today. When we met in 1973, I commented to him on the millions of bicycles in the streets (Zhou said there were at least 30 million) and the virtual absence of cars, and speculated that one day perhaps some bicycles might be equipped with little motors. "Never! China is too poor for that," he told me, "and besides, there would be too much pollution, and using their legs is good for our people."

How wrong he was! The juggernaut of Chinese development continues to forge full speed ahead, and thousands of skyscrapers have totally changed the country's urban centers. In 1985, the prewar Park Hotel was still the only tall building in Shanghai. Today there are over 4,000, which is twice as many as in New York City, and additional ones under construction are said to exceed the entire floor space of all currently occupied office buildings in Manhattan.

As youngsters, we crossed the Huangpu River by sampan from Shanghai's Bund to camp in the rice paddies of Pudong. Today, the new Pudong airport disgorges visitors into a vast modern city, where there was once only rural countryside, and then speeds them across bridges and through tunnels into the heart of Shanghai. The world's highest rail line, spanning 1,100 kilometers, has recently been completed in Western Qinghai province, superhighways crisscross the big cities, and while there are few motorized bikes, the streets are choked with far more late model China-made automobiles than bike riders exercising their legs. Only in one respect was Zhou correct: pollution has indeed become one of China's major unresolved problems.

In my lifetime, I have known three utterly different Chinas. The first was the China before 1949 in which I grew up, and only someone who knew it then can fully appreciate how completely it was transformed in the twentieth century's second China, under Mao's Communist rule. The third is the totally new China of today.

In personal terms, it is ironic that the two countries that once gave me the least pleasure and comfort—Germany and China—should, in later years, capture a particularly warm spot in my heart. How this happened with regard to Germany in the nineties I will discuss later. My changed relationship with the Chinese people had its origins in the seventies.

On the late morning of June 3, 1973, I was the leader of a "private" delegation of Americans crossing the border at Lo Wu, near Hong Kong, some twenty-six years after I had left China "forever." A small contingent of officials in identical Mao jackets greeted us, and in carefully rehearsed English wished our National Committee delegation a cordial "Welcome to the People's Republic of China." At Guangzhou's rail station, a short train ride away, a red carpet had been laid out for us, down which we were led to a cortege of ancient cars headed by a Russian-made limousine bearing suspicious resemblance to a vintage model Cadillac. Our destination was the minimal comfort of the Dung Fang Hotel, the only one at the time even remotely fit for official foreign visitors.[176]

We had come as guests of the government, on a visit that would take us to major cities and rural areas for meetings with university scholars, students, factory managers, revolutionary committee members, production brigades, farmers, and assorted officials, and we would also have extended discussions with Foreign Minister Qiao Guanhua and Chinese Premier Zhou Enlai. Our mission was to negotiate the initial cultural and scholarly exchanges between the United States and the People's Republic, which would eventually grow into a steady stream of visitors in both directions. Though ostensibly a private people-people exercise, this new beginning of U.S.–Sino contacts after a quarter century hiatus had in fact been carefully whetted by both governments.

Our delegation from the National Committee on U.S.–China Relations was among the first groups of Americans invited to China, and I shared the excitement of the China specialists among us, for whom this trip was the fulfillment of a lifelong dream.[177] Until then, most American China scholars had never stepped foot in China and for years had been "China Watchers" from afar, reading the Communist press, and interviewing the occasional mainland refugee in Hong Kong or Taiwan. To be experts on a country and culture they couldn't actually visit and see, had been somewhat akin to blindfolded doctors restricted to feeling a patient's skin and gauging his body temperature to make educated guesses about the general state of his health.

Our visit was an opening move in the slow, carefully managed, renewed coming together of China and the United States, haltingly begun with many fits and starts in the early seventies, and culminating nine years later with the reestablishment of full diplomatic relations (in which I would be destined to play an official role).

For many years, there had been intermittent meetings in Poland between ambassadors from the two countries—a total of 134 to be precise—but these had been largely sterile exercises of political posturing and rehashing of conflicting positions. By 1970, however, major new developments had altered the geopolitical equation. The Sino–Soviet relationship was seriously strained, large Russian military forces were massed at the 4,000 mile border with China, and actual fighting had broken out along the Ussuri River. The Chinese had also become concerned that détente in Europe might eventually result in the United States and the Soviet Union ganging up on them. The United States, on the other hand, saw an opportunity to exploit the Sino–Soviet rift and had hopes that a better relationship with China might ease the Vietnam dilemma. Thus both Mao and the United States were now inclined to set ideology aside, and it was these changed geopolitical realities which had proved increasingly persuasive for turning over a new leaf.[178]

* * *

There was a welcome banquet for us in Guangzhou, and the next day we climbed aboard a Soviet-type plane for a nerve-wracking flight to Beijing, our first exposure to the thrills of Chinese air travel in those early days. Seat belts were conspicuous by their absence, passengers roamed the aisles, and luggage was stored in unlikely places, while the stewardess served innumerable cups of tea but showed little concern for elementary rules of passenger safety. After a week of meetings in the capital, we then journeyed north and west into China's interior, then to Hangzhou and Shanghai on the coast, and finally south again before retracing our steps to Hong Kong.

The Guangzhou banquet was the first of many such affairs in the days to come, each carefully stage-managed for entertaining important "foreign friends," and varying in splendor—and number of courses offered—in strict accordance with the hierarchical standing of guests and hosts. Soon we learned what to expect, and to endure these ceremonial occasions. The hospitality was invariably gracious, and the food excellent. With luck, one's neighbor might drop a useful hint or make a revealing private remark. On the other hand, there was also the boredom of lengthy official toasts with predictable, mind-numbing rhetoric reflecting the depressing atmosphere of Maoist China during this latter phase of the Cultural Revolution.

In the streets, the picture was equally mixed. The former villas of the rich had been converted to office use for the massive Communist bureaucracy. Here and there enormous Soviet-style "showpiece" buildings had been erected, and in Shanghai the former, for foreigners only, Race Course grounds had been turned into a People's Park. The thousands of rickshaws with their human cargo pulled along by struggling undernourished coolies, once an integral part of the street scene, had vanished. Nor could a former Old Shanghai Hand fail to note the absence of the once ubiquitous legions of street people—hustlers, pickpockets, beggars, and prostitutes—and to appreciate this surprising feat.

Though not necessarily the methods used to accomplish it. One of the city's so-called Street Committees proudly explained to us how it had been done. Of fifty-eight houses in a single lane on their street, they told us, no fewer than twenty-four had been brothels where 101 girls plied their trade; two others were for gambling, two were opium dens, and five housed families engaged in "superstitious activities." Shortly after the revolution, they said, all these establishments had been closed forthwith. What had happened to the inhabitants, we asked? A few "hooligans," madams and "poisonous weeds" (a favorite Maoism), they explained, had been quickly led off to a public execution, and the girls dispatched to the countryside for lengthy periods of retraining in hard but "honest work," for which all were said to have exhibited much enthusiasm and gratitude to Chairman Mao.

Some of this was evident improvement over the past, but in other respects, time seemed to have stood still. Most houses were little changed from the forties, only more rundown, drab, and indifferently maintained. People lived in the same crowded alleys and lanes, enduring the same minimal comfort and inconveniences. The streets were cleaner and more orderly, but the disappearance of all variety, the evident lack of privacy and spontaneity, and the oppressive general atmosphere of regimentation and uniformity was intensely depressing. Everyone wore the same Mao suits in either grey, black, or dark blue. Lighting was sparse and dim, but the obligatory identical portrait of Mao festooned every wall and public space, along with his monotonously repetitive slogans, calligraphic aphorisms, and platitudinous sayings.

We gradually became inured to the ritualistic recitation of these pearls of wisdom, evidently intended to demonstrate political correctness to us and to one's peers. Enemies and those out of favor were always "poisonous weeds" and "running dogs," and everyone felt obliged, among other things, to "dig tunnels deep," "walk with two feet," "oppose hegemony," "fight imperialism," and "search for truth from facts." Even Zhou, in his meeting with us, had woven some of these phrases into the conversation.

How seriously all this was being taken was not always clear. According to Kissinger's account of his meeting with him, Mao himself had "laughed uproariously" that anyone might be taking seriously the ubiquitous slogans on walls, yet what they symbolized was clearly no laughing matter and served as a constant reminder of the distant Chairman's shadowy presence and control over every aspect of the people's minutely managed lives. Mao, we found, was viewed with a mixture of awe—and angst. On the one hand, there was gratitude that he had ended a century of national humiliation, liberated China from warlordism and foreign domination, and stamped out the excesses of corrupt officials. On the other, there was pervasive fear of running afoul of the harsh system of controls and of failing to support the twists and turns of his policy directives.

The Cultural Revolution, launched ostensibly to rid China of a new bureaucratic elite though in part also as Mao's way to eliminate political competitors, had gotten totally out of control and had caused untold loss of life and great damage. Top government officials, professionals, the educated, teachers, and students, had been forcibly dispatched to the countryside to "learn from the peasants," and universities and high schools had remained closed for years. In what Premier Zhou delicately described to Kissinger as an "excess of revolutionary zeal," competing factions had fought pitched battles over varying interpretations of Mao's wishes, and mindless persecution of the educated classes had set China back for years.

At Beijing's Beita and Tsinghua Universities, we got a taste of the Cultural Revolution's lingering effects. Both institutions had been reopened after 1970, but remained under the control of young cadres who did the talking while the senior professors sat by silently. Committee members Li and Tseng, barely thirty-year old instructors, praised the glories of academics learning from peasants and informed us that education had its limits and that practice was better than theory. How can China be modernized when its universities are closed, we asked? Their answer was that there had been too many "poisonous weeds," and that teaching one's own views was wrong anyway. The elderly American-educated professor at their side listened impassively and spoke up only when asked to by the cadre. "I was severely criticized during the Revolution," he told us bravely, "but in the countryside I learned much."

Chinese bureaucracy has a 2,000-year history, and there was ample evidence that if Mao had really wanted to smash the Communist version, the effort had been a spectacular failure. Bureaucratic control remained more tightly woven than ever, and in Shanghai, we were given a vivid picture of what that meant in China's largest city. The Party Revolutionary Council ruled at the top and handed its directives to each of ten districts, which were in turn divided into several hundred street committees. Each of these was further broken up into dozens of Lane Councils, and these into separate so-called Household Groups charged with assuring ideological purity, making work assignments, authorizing travel, watching over schools, and monitoring every aspect of family life, even personal cleanliness.

On June 15, the day before leaving Beijing, our visibly excited handlers announced that Premier Zhou would receive us at 6 P.M. in the mammoth Great Hall of the People, which Mao had ordered built as a symbol of Communist power on the equally enormous Tiananmen Square across from the Forbidden City. Zhou's evident intent was to signal the importance China attached to the new American relationship. As our motorcade made its way toward Tiananmen, I wondered whether China's long-time premier, second in importance only to Mao himself, would be able to put our astonishing experiences of recent days into some understandable perspective.[179]

In our sessions with countless officials at all levels, we had been struck by their one-dimensional demeanor and the monotony of their revolutionary jargon. Zhou greeted us warmly and made a very different first impression. Dressed in an impeccably tailored Mao suit, he cut a handsome figure and projected an easy air of self-confident authority. He had striking dark eyes, which he fixed on each of us with a smile, and though he spoke in Chinese, he let us know quickly that he understood English well and had been carefully briefed on each delegation member. "Welcome back, Dr. Blumenthal," he told me. "You have lived in our country a long time, and we are glad that you have returned."

Kissinger considers Zhou Enlai one of the most impressive statesmen he has met and has praised his worldly sophistication and charm. Our two-hour meeting with him didn't deal with the lofty matters of state the two had covered, yet he also impressed us quickly as a highly intelligent man who expressed himself with a measure of eloquence that projected friendliness and warmth. But on the more mundane matters we had come to discuss—Sino–U.S. people exchanges, industrial development, trade, and the past and current environment for it—he showed little of the sharp-witted insights Kissinger had found so remarkable. In discussing conditions inside China, he gave no signal that he fully understood—or, at least, was willing to acknowledge—the system's glaring inefficiencies and problems that had held back Chinese development, nor any hint of appreciating the potentials of a less regimented, more pragmatic approach. His message was that China was a poor country with a large population, and that this imposed severe permanent limits, even though Mao's revolution had already worked wonders. Industrial development, he told us, would be steady but slow, and the people had to learn "to walk with two feet." And there was always the problem of pollution, which appeared to be much on his mind as he reminisced about his youth in London "when you couldn't see the sun for days."

His understanding of the advantages of integrating China into the world economy struck me as surprisingly limited, and his expectations for the future of U.S.–China commercial relations no less so. There should be student and technology exchanges, and China had an interest in Boeing airplanes, but "your trade with Taiwan will remain much bigger for the foreseeable future," he said. In view of a serious recent Chinese drought, I asked about China's interest in U.S. grain imports, but Zhou didn't see much potential and dismissingly responded that "we Chinese must rely on our own efforts and solve our own problems, like droughts."

On the broader political issues he was on surer footing, though not particularly subtle in what he wanted us to hear, such as that China was a poor but peaceful country opposed to all hegemonies, whether American or Russian. "You, Dr. Blumenthal," he said in addressing me directly at one point, "you know us well. You know that we must struggle to put at least one bowl of rice into the stomachs of each of our billion people every day," (thus letting slip a hitherto "classified" statistic). "How can we be aggressive?" The long hiatus in Sino–U.S. relations had been largely our doing, he said, and it had been U.S. anti-Communist intransigence that had led to misunderstandings, lost opportunities, and snubs. The refusal of Secretary of State John Foster Dulles to shake his hand in Geneva in 1954 was obviously still on his mind. "He had no reason for it," he complained, and it had taken a long time to repair the damage because "we couldn't talk frankly to you in Poland, since they [the Soviets] were listening to everything we said."

He kept us for over two hours and then sent us off with a familiar bromide we had heard many times before and whose sincerity was open to doubt. "As you travel around our country," he told us in parting, "you'll see how much has been done since liberation and how much more is needed. Your advice is welcome. We want to learn from you."

We left China with mixed feelings. We had seen much that was impressive, but much had also been deeply troubling, and there wasn't one of us who did not breathe a sigh of relief to leave the country's stultifying atmosphere behind. Mao had unified the nation, swept away the vestiges of pre-revolutionary feudalism, killed or co-opted the warlords, introduced civic discipline in cities and on farms, advanced universal education, and made notable improvements in health and hygiene. These were major, even historic feats. Yet they had been accomplished by his putting in place a frighteningly oppressive and profoundly dysfunctional system of government control, leading to major policy failures and, ultimately, to the deadly excesses of the Cultural Revolution, but without achieving a better life for the Chinese people.

Maoism demanded total conformity and obedience, regulated everything, and allowed virtually no individuality or self-expression.

The reclusive, god-like Great Helmsman's "Mao Tse-tung thought" had undergone capricious twists and turns, occasionally bordering on mindlessness, and had been passed down through his strictures and slogans, which everyone was expected to follow blindly. "Learning Truth from Facts" had been a favorite, but that is precisely what Mao had not done. Paradoxically, the system appeared to have imprisoned the leadership no less than the people, condemning everyone to unquestioning acceptance of its costly errors. Mao was a master at using ideology to manipulate the masses and to play off his followers against one another, and punishment could be severe. From the top to the lowest levels, the bureaucracy had learned that obedience, caution, and real or feigned enthusiastic conformity was the only way to preserve one's status and security. Thus we had seen a China caught up in its own rhetoric and marking time, while the people mouthed the slogans and struggled on.

A question we often debated was whether those we had heard dutifully reciting the slogans had really believed them, or had merely gone through the motions. Were they aware that their system didn't work, and how did they feel about their loss of freedom? Surely many must have realized that the Cultural Revolution had been extraordinarily damaging and costly. Did the young cadre at Beita really believe that closing high schools and universities for years, and sending professors and students "to learn from the peasants," had been a good idea? Or had he been intent only on a public demonstration of orthodoxy and loyalty to the regime?

I was among the more skeptical of our group, because I remembered from the years I had lived there, that in China—more than in other cultures—appearance and reality are not always the same thing, and especially not as revealed to outsiders. If one listened carefully to the subtext of some of the comments for their hidden meaning, it had been possible to detect faint hints of this. I no longer remember the name of the elderly Beita professor who sat mute and then told us how justified the criticisms against him had been and how much he had learned from the peasants. I vividly recall, however, that as we were walking to our cars he had suddenly appeared at my side, and murmured in a low voice "thank you for speaking to us frankly. Please greet my old friend, Professor Levy,[180] at Princeton." Then, in a flash, he was gone.

On another occasion a Mao-quoting cadre had praised the spirit of egalitarianism in the PLA, China's military, and cited as proof that officers and soldiers wore identical uniforms without insignia. "But how do the soldiers know who's in charge? Doesn't it lead to confusion in the field?" I had asked. That wasn't a problem, following Mao Tse-tung thought and eliminating class distinctions worked just fine in the military, had been the unconvincing reply. Not quite, apparently. At dinner that night the same cadre had sought me out and with a conspiratorial smile returned to the subject—but well out of earshot of others. "About those PLA uniforms," he laughed a bit nervously, "actually everyone can tell who's an officer. Their uniforms fit better—and their jackets have pockets!"

And finally, there was the matter of the motorized bikes, an idea Zhou Enlai had dismissed out of hand. Later I asked the manager of Shanghai's Forever Bicycle Factory about it, but without mentioning the premier's views. His reaction had been studiously opaque and evasive, yet when the formal session ended he had taken me by the hand and led me to a small shed across the factory yard—filled with a half dozen motorized bikes! "It's our own planning for the future," he explained proudly.

So not all was quite what it seemed in China, even then. Orthodox rhetoric was one thing, but if one listened closely, there were fleeting signs that reality down the line was another. One sensed restlessness below the surface and flashes of individuality and entrepreneurship. That was the Chinese way I remembered from the past, and it gave me hope.

From Zhou Enlai to Deng Xiaoping

As secretary of the treasury, I returned to China several times in the late seventies to negotiate the financial and commercial agreements involved in the resumption of Sino–U.S. diplomatic relations. Mao and Zhou had died in 1976, Hua-Guofeng whom Mao had installed before his death had proved a transitional figure and been pushed aside, and by 1978 Deng Xiaoping was the country's de facto leader.

Mao had barely passed from the scene, but China was undergoing yet another startling metamorphosis. His photograph remained on walls, but his slogans had disappeared, and more and more people were acting as if they had never been there. As to the fiery young revolutionary cadres who had done the talking in 1973, they seemed to have vanished, and asking about them usually elicited only a smile and a shrug.

Deng had firmly renounced the Cultural Revolution and under his leadership China was embarking on a different course with a new model of development called the "socialist market economy." In practice this meant reducing the role of ideology in economic matters, de-emphasis of state ownership, and greater reliance on market forces.

For decades, China had remained detached from the world economy, but now Deng and his followers were opening doors and connecting the country to the international trading system, while pushing domestic development with market-oriented policies. This was a dramatic change from the past, and the people seemed to be taking to it with alacrity. Probably in no other country on Earth, in fact, could so fundamental a reversal of course have been implemented as quickly, reflecting perhaps two unique if somewhat contradictory aspects of Chinese national character: on the one hand, a centuries-old respect for authority and the willingness to bend and accommodate to whatever orders were handed down from heaven, as happened under Mao—and, on the other, an innate streak of individualism and entrepreneurship and the talent for seizing the initiative for commercial opportunity.

This was the new environment in China, as I met with Deng, Hua, and other leading officials for several rounds of talks concerning the resumption of our diplomatic and commercial relations. Usually the sessions took place in the same setting of Tiananmen's Great Hall where I had met Zhou, but though the venue was the same, the atmosphere could not have been more different.

In their backgrounds, there were several similarities between Zhou and Deng. Both were lifelong Communists committed to the Party's monopoly of political power and willing to defend it at all cost (as Deng would later demonstrate when student protesters challenged it at Tiananmen Square). Both had left China as young men for broader experiences and study in Europe, and joined up with Mao after returning home. Both were veterans of the Long March, had endured years of fighting the Japanese and Chang Kai-shek's Nationalist forces, and had been at Mao's side when the Communists seized power.

Yet the differences between them in appearance, manner, and personality were even more important and obvious. The handsome, urbane Zhou was of average height and had the smooth features of a Han Chinese. Deng, who had the more angular, rougher face of West China's Hakka minority, was unusually short, with the squat build of a sturdy fireplug. Zhou's speech was polished, but he often spoke with a certain elliptical indirectness that could leave the listener wondering about the full meaning of his words. The undersized Deng's manner was equally self-assured, but exuded a palpable aura of determination and personal strength in a much more direct way, coupled with an unambiguous straightforwardness Zhou lacked.

Both had been part of the top leadership under Mao for many years, but differed greatly in character. Zhou had always been Mao's loyal lieutenant, one of the few of the old guard to have survived all internal rivalries, purges, and even Mao's chicaneries against him personally. Some claim that behind the scenes he had tried to ameliorate the effects of Mao's worst excesses, but if so, he lacked the strength to accomplish a great deal, and it had never been done at risk to his own position. Others said that behind the polish and urbanity, his dominant character trait was a finely honed instinct of self-preservation and that, when needed, he was willing "to cut your throat for it."[181]

Unlike Zhou, Deng had demonstrated the personal strength and courage to fight for his convictions by opposing Mao on more than one occasion. In particular, he had consistently argued for more pragmatism on economic matters, for which he had twice paid a heavy price by being purged as a "capital-roader"—a pejorative label which in Mao's day could be fatal. Stripped of his position during the Cultural Revolution, he and his family had been banished and suffered greatly, though Deng had continued to stand firm and barely escaped with his life. His son was beaten so severely that he remained confined to a wheelchair for the rest of his life.

My most memorable meeting with Deng came during a much publicized nine-day visit to China in February 1979, at a historic moment in Sino–U.S. relations. The United States and China had agreed to the simultaneous opening of their embassies on March 1, and President Carter had sent me to Beijing to represent him at the ceremonies for this milestone event. Several other outstanding issues remained to be settled, including final agreement on Chinese compensation for the loss of U.S. property and assets seized by the Communists in 1949, and framework agreements for the normalization of future trade and commercial relations.

The planning and preparations for my visit had been under way in Washington and Beijing for weeks, and a large delegation was to accompany me. Public interest in the trip was unusually high and the embassy opening and economic issues to be discussed were so newsworthy that an impressive complement of some twenty journalists was on board our special plane when it touched down at Beijing airport on February 24.

My impending trip to China was now front-page news in all the leading media, and would unavoidably unfold under the changed circumstances of China's recent invasion of Vietnam, which the U.S. had roundly condemned for "greatly complicating the Blumenthal mission," as the *Wall Street Journal*'s Richard Levine, one of the traveling journalists, put it in his first story from Beijing.[182] Levine was a fine journalist, and had hit the nail on the head. A further added "complication" was that I had secretly decided weeks earlier to deliver the banquet toast in Chinese, but had carefully kept this news nugget to myself. The problem, however, was that even when I lived in China, my speaking ability had been limited to a modest version of "street Chinese" in the dialect of Shanghai, which is practically a foreign language compared to the proper Chinese of Beijing. Getting me ready for a toast delivered in Mandarin Chinese had thus required virtually learning the toast—a mini-speech really—by heart, and the efforts of a coach with the patience of Job to tutor me over the course of three weeks until she had finally pronounced my Beijing dialect as "understandable." Now the version I had memorized had been expanded to include tough talk on the Vietnam matter, and to retool myself for that in a few days was out of the question.

For a while I had considered scrapping my linguistic excursion, before deciding on a better idea: delivering the opening and final parts as planned in my carefully rehearsed Chinese, and pausing to issue those official U.S. government's words of warning in stern English:

> Our bilateral relations will only flourish in a world of peace and stability. Respect for the independence and territorial integrity of all nations and reliance on peaceful means to resolve disputes are fundamental principles of international conduct. Any erosion of these principles harms all nations. Even limited invasions risk wider wars.

The Chinese had initially been stunned to hear me speak their own language, but then responded with sustained applause. "Blumenthal captivated his hosts," the *L.A. Times* reported, adding that they had "'faintly' (sic) praised the Chinese as 'understandable,' with a slight Shanghai accent."[183] My tutor had evidently done her job well!

As to the official U.S. rebuke on the Vietnam invasion, delivered in English, the message had been received and acknowledged with polite silence. As far as they were concerned the disagreement wouldn't affect the embassy opening and our economic negotiations, the Chinese told the press. This, of course, was what we had wanted as well, and thus my fractured linguistic acrobatics had evidently helped to create the right climate for what would follow.

I met with Deng at 4 P.M. the next afternoon in the large Southern Chamber of the Great Hall for a two-hour-long review of the future for Sino–U.S. economic relations and the political environment for it.

It was a remarkable meeting. There was, for one thing, a minimum of the usual preliminary chitchat and exchange of polite nothings, and no evidence that Deng felt it necessary to package his economic views in the kind of Maoist-Marxist ideological language I had been accustomed to hearing from others. China's de facto leader had clear views he was willing to state plainly, he knew what he wanted, and he had come to do business.

Deng quickly proceeded to lay out his views of developing China's domestic economy pragmatically, by relying less on controls and more on private initiatives, showing clearly that he understood the immediate steps needed and their longer-run implications. All this he discussed in the kind of straightforward manner that had hitherto been a rarity in China. He said that to be successful China had to become connected to the world economy, and that normalized Chinese-American commercial ties were a part of that. As to the matters I had come to discuss—settlement of U.S. claims, a commercial agreement, and setting up a joint U.S.–China economic council—he said unambiguously that China was ready to act quickly and assured me that he expected my trip to be successful. "You have Western competitors with whom we want to trade, and we will give away nothing. But our side is willing to make a deal," he told me.

Deng had also shown that he was a canny politician who understood the importance of the Western press and public opinion. He was obviously aware that as a first item of business I would deliver President Carter's message urging an immediate withdrawal of Chinese troops from Vietnam, and that this would be the lead in the reports on our meeting filed by the throng of U.S. journalists waiting outside. I had to admire the effective, if unconventional way he handled the matter with a simple expedient. Discarding normal protocol—an unusual step for a Chinese leader—he had, I was surprised to discover, arrived at Tiananmen a quarter hour ahead of me, and gathered the American journalists around him for a little impromptu "briefing," with arguments sure to appeal to Americans. Vietnam was the "Cuba of the

Orient," he told them. Castro's Cuba and the one of the Orient were aggressive, and both were backed by the Soviets. Vietnam's incursion into Cambodia had required "teaching them a lesson," but not to worry, China didn't want "an inch of Vietnam's territory." As far as China was concerned, none of this should interfere with solving the economic issues to be discussed during my visit.

His skillful ploy had worked well. As he had expected, his comments led the stories filed for that day and had, as hoped, lessened the effect of the Carter message even before I delivered it, while creating a positive tone for the mood and prospects for the rest of my mission.

As we settled down to talk, he listened politely to Carter's message, and then made much the same arguments, making light of the "temporary problem" in Vietnam and stressing his hope for good progress during my stay in Beijing.

On the specifics, I was hearing the kind of straight talk that had been largely absent in Zhou's cautious and limited views on economic matters. No doubt, Zhou had been less free to talk plainly while Mao was still alive, yet I hadn't hitherto heard the same clarity from Deng's officials either, and his mastery of the specifics was equally impressive. China, he said, "looked with favor" on substantially expanding its world trade, "eagerly looked forward" to greater Sino–U.S. commerce, and wanted to buy agricultural goods and equipment to modernize its own agricultural sector. To pay for it, there were Chinese mineral and raw material resources to sell, and also prudent borrowings; there was even an interest in eventually joining the IMF and World Bank. As to my meetings in Beijing, he thought the U.S. claims issue could be settled quickly; there could be agreement on setting up a U.S.–China economic council, and at least substantial progress could be made on working out the framework for a Sino–U.S. commercial agreement.

It had been a remarkable performance, and I was able to report to Washington that Deng was obviously sure of himself and in full charge. In less than two hours, Deng had effectively laid down the markers for the success of my mission—which was precisely what happened in the coming days. We had haggled for months over the Chinese payments to settle outstanding U.S. claims, but two days after my meeting with Deng, our last offer had been accepted. The U.S.–China economic council, to be chaired by Vice Chairman Yu and me, was also agreed on, as was the framework for a bilateral commercial agreement.

My mission had been more successful than we could ever have hoped, which was good news in Washington. But it had also been a memorable journey on a very personal level. Before leaving China, the delegation had stopped off briefly in Shanghai, where I led my colleagues and the press on a nostalgic walking tour of the old Shanghai of my youth. My proudest moment was to personally raise the Stars and Stripes over the newly reopened American embassy. The poignancy of the extraordinary way in which my life—and my relationship with China—had come full circle was not lost on me. I had come back to represent the president of the United States in presiding over the U.S. embassy's reopening and to play a part in the establishment of a new relationship between China and my adopted home.

In politics, as in business, effective leadership has at least three critical components—a clear vision, the talent to enunciate it convincingly, and the courage and skill to shape the conditions and seize the opportunity of implementing it at the right moment. Deng Xiaoping was such a leader, perhaps one of the most important of the second half of the twentieth century, and one who had as great an impact on the world of today than anyone I can think of.

Like Mao and the other Communist revolutionaries, he grew up believing in orthodox Marxism based on central planning, collectivized agriculture, and total government control of every aspect of economic life. Yet he alone had the vision to understand the implications of a changing world and of the failure of China to keep up with an unfolding globalization. Deng had the insights, character, and courage to see what changes were needed in China, and the political strength and astuteness to carry them out once he had the power to do so. Some of what happened in China under his leadership may have been inevitable—sooner or later. Yet the speed and height of China's rise as an important economic power was not. That was not the result of happenstance or random events but of leadership, and it surely wouldn't have happened had Mao and Zhou remained in charge. Hitler and Stalin, the two great dictators, and Roosevelt and Churchill who rallied the West against them, were towering figures who had a great impact on the history of the twentieth century, for better or for worse. Deng Xiaoping, who made China a major economic power at the century's end, must legitimately be added to the list.

When Deng came to power, China was a poor and backward country, isolated from the world and with an economy held back by a vast state bureaucracy, backward agriculture, an obsolete industrial plant, and dysfunctional central planning. Deng reversed course, decollectivized agriculture, promoted the private sector, substituted markets for planning, and opened China's doors to the outside world. The results far surpassed all expectations, probably including even his own. China's GDP has increased more than ten-fold, and continues to grow by 8 to 10 percent a year. In terms of purchasing power parity, though not per capita, China's economy is today the second largest in the world, and second only to that of the United States. When I negotiated the first trade agreement with China in 1979, combined U.S.–Sino trade amounted to $1 billion. Today it is more than 200 times as large, and China's trade surplus with the United States alone exceeds $100 billion each year. Agricultural productivity is up, and based on its abundant supply of labor, China's export-driven manufacturing sector is booming. Walmart alone bought some $18 billion worth of Chinese goods in 2005, making it arguably China's seventh largest trading partner, ahead of Australia, Canada, and Russia.[184] China's major cities have been modernized and are virtually unrecognizable when compared to what they were in 1979, stores are well-stocked with an abundance of consumer goods, and a growing middle class enjoys a rising standard of living far beyond anything previously known.

But what of the future? Can China continue its rapid growth? Can that growth be maintained indefinitely, even as political freedom remains severely restricted? How will China use its growing power internationally? Success has brought major new challenges at home and abroad that even Deng could not have anticipated. The question is how successful China's current and future leaders will be in managing the wide range of complex problems they must face in coming years.

There are over a billion people in China, and the population is aging rapidly. Growth has been quite uneven, and the gap between rich and poor has widened dangerously. While the large cities have been booming, at least two-thirds or more of the Chinese people still live in varying degrees of rural poverty, millions subsist on as little as $1 a day, and up to 150 million have left the countryside for a marginal existence in and around urban centers.

The kind of endemic corruption in the China I once knew is back, and the more than 80,000 public protests the authorities have acknowledged to have occurred in the single year of 2005 are evidence that the rural poor, pensioners, the unemployed, and those left behind by urban expansion are resentful of the absence of reliable legal restraints on venal officials and of those who flaunt their new wealth. The establishment of a comprehensive legal structure that is fair and universally enforced remains one of China's great domestic challenges. Decades of Communist mismanagement have yet to be fully overcome, and the more sustained the rapid growth, the more problematic the growing bottlenecks of an inadequate infrastructure, rising levels of pollution, and the survival of the remaining highly inefficient state enterprises alongside a free-wheeling market economy.

China's growing economy and political influence have substantially changed world geopolitics. The country is a major exporter and a voracious consumer of energy and critical raw materials, which puts substantial pressure on the world economy. Prudent management of the domestic economy will thus also require the maintenance of open world markets for its products, and this, in turn, raises the questions of how China's trade and foreign exchange policies will evolve and how the inevitable vicissitudes in their respective markets will affect them. The challenge is whether they will manage wisely, and as a responsible participant in the international system, with sufficient transparency and a willingness to share international burdens. The alternative, of a perennially undervalued currency, protectionist policies, lack of attention to the international impact of serious environmental pollution, and a failure to curb the counterfeiting of branded products and violation of intellectual property rights, would surely run the risk of adverse reactions abroad. How China will handle its large military forces will also be closely watched.

Thus a realistic view of China today should mix caution with admiration, which many eager foreign businessmen and China enthusiasts, who see only the dazzling developments of recent years, would do well to bear in mind.

THE SEVENTIES II
The Carter Years

A Problematic Presidency

In his memoirs, Jimmy Carter reminisced that when he was inaugurated the thirty-ninth president of the United States on January 20, 1977, it was "a perfect day when everything seemed right." All had fallen into place for him. His popularity had risen considerably after his narrow election victory, and for the moment even the perennially fickle media were friendly and supportive. His choice of a cabinet, including many members with substantial Washington experience, had been well-received. His White House staff was to consist mainly of Georgians and young campaign aides who were not well-known in the capital, but that was hardly an uncommon practice for incoming presidents. John Kennedy, after all, had had his "Irish Mafia," and Lyndon Johnson his Texans.

As a candidate Carter had laid out an exceedingly large and ambitious agenda of action, and now he was eager to get started on implementing the many promises he had made during the campaign. The country appeared to be in his corner and the prospects for his presidency looked bright. "In Washington a new spirit seemed to be a-borning," *Newsweek* reported.[185]

A peanut farmer and one-term governor of Georgia without national political experience, Carter had been a surprise winner in the quadrennial presidential sweepstakes. No one had given him much of a chance, and a year before the election he had rarely figured on the lists of serious White House prospects. Yet by traveling around the country for several years, working tirelessly at the grass roots, and shrewdly assessing the national mood in the wake of Vietnam and Watergate, he had made a virtue of his lack of Washington experience and sold himself as an outsider and proven political manager intent on restoring honesty and integrity to the Oval Office. These had been the principal themes of his campaign, and they had worked.[186] As his speechwriter Rick Hertzberg put it, "The fact that he was unknown was part of his appeal. And he brought simple verities to the campaign trail; a promise not to lie to the American people, a promise to be good, a promise to love."

With dogged determination and relentless effort, sustained by unshakable confidence in himself, he had often bypassed party leaders with direct appeals to the people and, to the surprise of the pundits, outsmarted his competition, captured the nomination, and gone on to beat the incumbent President Ford in the fall election. Careful cultivation of an image of an honest, morally strong outsider—a new political leader more in touch with average people than with the traditional Washington establishment—had resonated well among the voters. Even so, the election had been a cliffhanger. The shift of a handful of votes in just two states would have changed the outcome, and hours after the polls closed the results had still hung in the balance. But in the end Carter had prevailed. Now, as he stood atop the Capitol steps, he had achieved his great ambition and was ready to move into the White House and go to work.

Jimmy Carter had not been my preferred candidate for the nomination. After he had pulled it off, however, he invited me to join a small group of advisors to brief him on economic policy issues at his mother's Pond House, a modest cottage near the family home in the little village of Plains, Georgia. For me, these excursions into an unfamiliar Deep South rural environment were a fascinating new experience. I quickly concluded that Carter was a formidable man, and seeing him in action on these occasions, a yellow pad on his lap, asking penetrating questions and taking copious notes, had given me a healthy respect for his impressive intellect, seriousness of purpose, and capacity for hard work.

He was unlike any other politician I had ever met. Though he smiled readily, he was clearly no backslapper exuding that easy air of familiarity common to many politicians. There was nothing particularly special about his physical appearance or demeanor comparable to Kennedy or Johnson, the two presidents I had worked for in the sixties. Carter had neither the physical presence of Johnson nor the charm of Kennedy. Though cordial and friendly, he seemed inwardly tense and tightly controlled and came across as somewhat shy, reserved, and on his guard. Yet it was his remarkable seriousness of purpose and outward air of even-tempered equanimity under pressure that impressed me. What he did reflect, above all, was firm confidence in himself and the ability to maintain control at all times. I thought it was evidence of an inner serenity sure to serve him well in the Oval Office.

I realized that Carter was very different from the two Oval Office occupants I had known. For one thing, he would be the country's first president from the Deep South, the first born-again Christian, and the first with the background of a small businessman, rather than having been a lawyer or life-long politician. A Naval Academy graduate, he would also be the first president too young to have seen active duty in the Second World War, but his training as an engineer working on nuclear submarines under Admiral Rickover seemed to qualify him well for leading the country in the emerging high-tech world of the late seventies.

After the travails of Vietnam and Watergate, three political assassinations, the resignation of a vice president accused of criminal wrongdoing, and the disgrace of Richard Nixon, Carter's sincerity, moral strength, solid values, and the promise to the voters that "I'll never lie to you" had struck me as just the right prescription for the times. Two things in particular gave me hope. The first was that, though very ambitious, he seemed a thoroughly decent and honest man unlikely to abuse the powers of his office. The other was that his studied cultivation of the image of simplicity and moral strength, with carefully calculated symbolic gestures—like carrying his own bag and staying in ordinary Americans' homes—gave promise of the requisite skills and right instincts for generating voter support for his programs.

Inauguration day had been hellishly cold, and though there was brilliant sunshine, the solar heating Carter had ordered installed for the VIP reviewing stands in front of the White House—a symbolic gesture to underline the nation's energy problems—was not exactly a roaring success. I was there as Carter's designated secretary of the treasury, and former Vice President Hubert Humphrey, gaunt from battling cancer, and his wife Muriel stood next to me when the new president, hand in hand with his wife Rosalynn and daughter Amy, walked past us with big smiles and cheerful waves to the viewers. Extremely uncomfortable in the bitter cold, we nevertheless were upbeat. Even the much reduced Humphrey was in good spirits, and we agreed that there was justification for optimism and hope.

I had first met Hubert during the Kennedy Round, well before he became vice president, when we had developed something of a friendship. As a senator, I considered him one of the most likeable and interesting members of Congress. Elected politicians are not always the most loveable people, focused primarily on themselves and, at best, "fair weather friends." Perhaps it goes with their job, but when they sense political risk to their position, past protestations of friendship and support can be quickly forgotten. Raking you over the coals in public while assuring you of their support in private is not uncommon. "It's only politics, Mike," Connecticut Senator Abe Ribicoff once consoled me when I remonstrated with him that excoriating our Kennedy Round delegation on the Senate floor didn't square with the compliments he had paid our work while visiting Geneva.

Hubert was not like that. He could be counted on in public if we agreed in private. As a Minnesotan, he had a particularly keen interest in agricultural trade and had made a number of trips to visit me in Geneva to check up on the negotiations, where he had been especially nice to our three young daughters, and it was during these visits that we had first grown close.

Hubert and I often traveled the European circuit together, where he awed me as a tireless worker, until late into the night. But though an indefatigable advocate of U.S. interests abroad, he was also a true champion of the little people at home and took genuine pleasure in advancing the lot of minorities and the disadvantaged.

A Very Short Honeymoon

A day after the inauguration, on January 21, I stood in the East Room of the White House with other members of Carter's new cabinet as the Chief Justice swore us in en masse. Jimmy and Rosalynn Carter smiled proudly, and our families and friends watched from the sidelines.

Thus all the stars seemed to be aligned right as the new president settled in at the Oval Office, and his administration got underway.

Most presidents can expect to enjoy the warm glow of favorable ratings during their initial "honeymoon period." Their first months in office are often the most productive of their presidency, a time when their legislative proposals have the best chance of success. For Kennedy and Johnson the honeymoon had lasted through their entire first years. In the initial Gallup Poll taken after the inauguration, 75 percent of those surveyed had given Carter a favorable rating, so there was reason to expect that the new President would fare equally well.

Reality, however, was different. Four years later Carter was decisively swept from office, and to this day he is considered one of the less successful presidents of the twentieth century. Along with some painful setbacks, he did achieve several significant successes in foreign policy, but it is in domestic affairs where he had major difficulties and suffered his biggest defeats. Only a modest portion of his program was implemented, and many of his major legislative initiatives either failed outright, or could be enacted only in a much reduced and watered down form.

His political honeymoon was exceedingly short,[187] and well before the end of the first year, his administration was sputtering and in trouble with the Congress. His fall from grace in the public mind came quickly, and once it began it could not be reversed even in the face of periodic good news developments. Somehow, nothing Carter could do during his four years as chief executive succeeded in reversing the public perception of him as an inept president.

From a high of 75 percent shortly after he took office, successive Gallup Polls recorded a steady drop in his job approval ratings. By year-end, a scant 50 percent of those surveyed still approved of his performance, and by April of 1978, only 40 percent still thought he was doing a good job. In the summer of the following year, Gallup reported that only a miserable 26 percent still held a favorable view of Carter's performance. Even Bill Clinton during his impeachment trial would not do as poorly, and only Truman—briefly, and Nixon during Watergate—had done worse. During Carter's losing bid for re-election in 1980, when he was pulling out all the stops in a last-ditch effort to reverse his fortunes, just one in three of those polled by Gallup gave his performance a favorable rating. With his decisive defeat by Ronald Reagan in November, he became one of only two postwar presidents who, up to then, had failed to be reelected.

Most Americans who remember the Carter years, and most historians, still consider him a failed president. In 1999, a cross-section of scholars ranked him thirteenth of the fifteen twentieth-century presidents for leadership;[188] and in an average of ten separate such surveys taken since 1982, he is tied with Gerald Ford as the worst in this century, and a mediocre twenty-seventh out of forty-three presidents in all of U.S. history.

How could so much that looked so hopeful at the start turn sour so quickly? Was the failure of the Carter presidency inevitable, and no fault of his own? Was it the result of bad luck, or, as many contemporary observers and historians argue, does the explanation rest largely with Carter himself? The answer is that both of these factors contributed critically to his problems, and working closely with him for more than two and a half years, I saw plenty of evidence of that. Carter certainly had his share of bad luck, but as a political leader in the Oval Office he was also—much too often—his own worst enemy. More than anything else, it is this that doomed his presidency.

Adverse circumstances did conspire against him. He had to deal with an inherently intractable environment, the worst postwar energy crisis, exploding gas prices, unprecedented inflation, and revolution in Iran—none of which was foreseen and all of which were beyond his control. Furthermore, big changes in the domestic economy unfavorably impacted the opportunities for implementing his many major new initiatives. In the fifties and sixties the country had experienced sustained periods of growth, rising living standards, and full employment. This had allowed Lyndon Johnson to finance many new Great Society entitlements, and any number of special interest groups had become accustomed to a growing share of this largesse. In the Carter years, however, productivity had dramatically slowed and government resources were much more limited. Real per capita income between 1977 and 1984 was actually declining, unemployment was rising, and Carter's problem was how to tighten the belt, which did not endear him to the public. A cost cutter and penny pincher, after all, is rarely as popular as a generous giver.

The Carter years also coincided with a moment in U.S. history when the political landscape had greatly changed. Against the background of a decade of cynicism and distrust in government following Watergate and Vietnam, and with the breakdown in the congressional seniority system following some post-Watergate reform, he was confronted with a less dependable, fractious Congress, in spite of nominal Democratic majorities. Given his ambitious program for reforms, getting anything done had become much harder.

As a candidate, he had benefited from distrust in government and the weakened traditional control of the parties and the congressional leadership, and was swept into office as the outsider promising to clean up the mess and restore confidence in government. But, as he soon found, it also made governing a lot more difficult, though he was not the first president to discover the limits of presidential power along with its possibilities. A long time ago, Harry Truman had complained that he often sat in the Oval Office and gave orders but nothing was done, and John Kennedy had similarly noted ruefully that "the powers of the Presidency are often described. Its limits should occasionally be remembered."[189] Carter, at a difficult moment in the twentieth century, would make the similar discovery that great power also has great limits.

Yet bad luck and a difficult economic and political environment are only part of the story. It is true that Jimmy Carter drew a difficult hand, but it is equally true that he often played it badly, and that some of the more spectacular disasters of his administration were of his own making—the consequence of self-inflicted wounds, of decisions taken or not taken, that a more skillful Oval Office occupant might have handled differently. In close proximity to him, I eventually realized that the root of his problems was that by background, character, and experience, he was not ideally suited for presidential leadership. Specifically, his impressive cognitive powers were not matched by an equally high level of emotional intelligence[190] and political fingertip feeling—two character traits that are a sine qua non for mastering the enormous challenges of the presidency.

To be an effective leader, a president must be clear about his priorities, husband his time, and guard against getting lost in details best left to others. Above all, he must know his limits, which presumes the capacity to select strong and experienced advisors, to trust them and be willing to delegate responsibility to them matched with adequate authority to act on his behalf. It also requires the strength and flexibility of mind to recognize error and to compromise and change course when things don't work out. For this, in turn, it helps greatly to have a reasonable sense of organization and an innate feel for people and what makes them "tick." Finally, a successful presidential leader must also be an effective communicator of his basic goals and ideas—"the vision thing," as the first President Bush once called it.

Jimmy Carter unfortunately had problems in many of these areas. Smart, decent, hard-working, and honorable, he has a first-class, though rigid, mind, and it gradually became evident to those of us who regularly interacted with him that there were elements of his temperament that got in the way of his effectiveness. Things he considered his greatest strengths—his unshakable confidence in himself, his mastery of detail, and a management formula that he believed worked for him as Governor of Georgia—were also the sources of his blind spots and damaging errors in the Oval Office.

He had come to Washington as an outsider, and had not hesitated to run against the leaders of his own party. Yet once in office, he failed to realize that he was now on their turf and needed their help. Among his predecessors, Truman, Kennedy, Johnson, Nixon, and Ford had all served in Congress. Eisenhower had not held elective office, but he had been in and around Washington for many years. Jimmy Carter did not know either Washington or Congress, which was a problem but need not have been a critical one. Bill Clinton and George W. Bush faced the same challenge but dealt with it by surrounding themselves with experienced Washington hands; Clinton additionally had a finely-tuned political antenna and learned quickly.

Jimmy Carter did not. His management experience as governor of Georgia had been one of the principal selling points of his successful presidential campaign. Yet, in Washington this proved one of his greater weaknesses, for in organizing the White House staff and managing his relations with Congress, he made two critical mistakes. One was to resist appointing a chief of staff until well into the third year of his presidency. With supreme self-confidence, he attempted to make too many decisions himself, and chose instead a "hub and spokes" approach for his White House organization. He would be at the center—the hub—and his assistants were to be the spokes with equal and unfettered access to him. The result, more often than not, was mixed signals, delays, stumbles, and confusion.

A second mistake compounded the problem. Most presidents bring a few trusted associates and friends into their inner circle, men and women on whose complete loyalty they can rely. Most realize, however, that they also need staff with the special knowledge and experience they lack and who know how the system works. Coming from outside Washington, this was an especially important requirement for Carter. Nevertheless, most of his key White House aides were inexperienced Georgians as innocent of Washington's ways as he. Some eventually caught on, but others did not. From the beginning, it was this—an inadequate White House organization and staffing—which was at the core of many avoidable errors which hurt him badly.

I was Jimmy Carter's first secretary of the treasury, and served him to the best of my ability for over two and a half years. In July of 1979, at a low point in his fortunes, he reshuffled his cabinet, and I was one of several members whose resignation he chose to accept. Simply put, he fired me. By then, sadder but wiser, I was more than ready to go.

I bear him no grudge. From the beginning, I respected him as a well-meaning and honest man. I was proud to be in his administration, I cheered his successes, and I shared in the pain of his setbacks. He always treated me with unfailing courtesy and respect, and to the best of my recollection no harsh or angry word ever crossed his lips in our many personal meetings. In his written memos he could sometimes be curt and impatient, and in my personal files there are two or three petulant and scolding notes, but they were rare exceptions to the greater number of complimentary ones.

I agreed with most of his policy goals. I applauded him as a peacemaker in the Middle East, for his successful Panama Canal fight, the Tokyo Round Trade agreement, his China policy, his courageous stand on human rights, and his principled efforts on behalf of the less privileged in American society and around the world.

I also believe it is wrong to dwell only on his failures without recognizing his notable successes. He deserves credit, for example, for achieving important civil service reforms, with long overdue advances in a difficult area that no other president had tackled before him or has since. Though it was a far cry from his ambitious proposals, he did finally achieve the enactment of limited energy legislation to reform the domestic market and to promote more efficient energy use. Thirty years later, none of his successors had done more. The same also applies to the modest tax reform package that was enacted, a much needed increase in the minimum wage, and the sweeping deregulation of the airline industry, which brought substantial savings to the consumer. Carter was also a committed environmentalist, and his Superfund to clean up toxic waste, as well as a landmark Alaska Lands Act to protect pristine land for hunting, fishing, and limited lumbering in a 150 million acre area (greater than California) are particularly noteworthy achievements in the light of what has happened—or not happened—on environmental matters since.

Carter's presidency, finally, was free of any international crisis for which he bears responsibility. The United States remained at peace, he did not enmesh the country in war, and the international reputation of the United States as a beacon of freedom, democracy, and the rule of law remained intact. From the perspective of what has happened since, these too are important achievements on the positive side of the Carter record.

As I shared in his triumphs and defeats, my years with Carter were often the most difficult and frustrating of my professional career, but at other times also the most gratifying. Like him, I made my share of mistakes, and there are things I would do differently were I to do them again. To be privy to the enormous pressures and difficult choices a president faces day after day taught me more about what it means to lead in high places than any corporate job ever could have. I saw that history is indeed made by people, but that they too are hostage to events over which they have no control: to accident, personalities, and to their own character weaknesses and strengths.

The experience of the Carter presidency is instructive in many ways, and I cannot do full justice to it in a single chapter, any more than to my role in it. What I can do is tell the behind-the-scenes story of a few events to illustrate what happened at some critical moments, and explore how these contributed to defining Jimmy Carter's presidential years.

Into the Carter Cabinet

I first met Jimmy Carter at a luncheon in the elegant third-floor private dining room of the 21 Club in New York City, a week after he had won the Democratic nomination. The "21" was (and is) the prototype of a luxury watering hole for the expense account crowd in Manhattan. Only a few months later I would argue before the Congress on Carter's behalf that it is wrong for business luncheons at such establishments—the "two-martini lunch," he called it—to qualify as a tax-deductible business expense. It has occurred to me that it is an ironic twist of fate that this, of all places, should have been the venue for our first face-to-face encounter.

The day was July 22, 1976, and I was among several dozen corporate executives invited by Henry Ford II and some of his friends to lunch with the recently anointed Democratic nominee. The attendees were overwhelmingly of a staunchly conservative Republican persuasion, but they were eager to look Carter over, and he in turn had come to assuage their worst apprehensions about him. As I recall it, he shook hands, smiled a lot, talked briefly, broke no new ground, but tried manfully to reassure this select gathering of America's corporate leaders that—populist campaign rhetoric aside—he was not anti-business and would do nothing rash or harmful on jobs, taxes, or the treatment of multinational corporations.

It is doubtful that many votes were changed that day, but as one of the few Democrats present, I was pleased that Carter had come across as moderate and reasonable, and that rather more of the attendees left favorably impressed than I had expected. I had shaken Carter's hand briefly and asked an easy question to which he had given a soothing predictable reply, but for him I was undoubtedly only one of the many faces in the crowd that day.[191] Neither of us could have known that this was, in fact, the beginning of a close and intense three-year relationship.

A few weeks later, on August 18, I was surprised to find myself sitting on a metal folding chair near the Democrats' standard bearer in his mother's Pond House among the pine trees of southern Georgia. President Ford was battling Ronald Reagan for the Republican nomination in Kansas City, and Carter was using the week when media attention had shifted westward for briefing sessions on domestic affairs, energy, and the economy. I have no idea how I came to be on the roster of the fifteen or so invited economic policy mavens, many of them the usual suspects from prior Democratic administrations, but I do recall that I was pleased to be there and to observe him in action.

He was taking time out to consider his position on key economic questions, the consensus being that these would figure importantly in the upcoming campaign. The news was not very good, and the principal focus was on ways to stimulate the domestic economy and on U.S. trade and financial policy options. The recovery from the sharp recession of 1975 appeared to have stalled and the economy showed signs of slipping into stagflation. GNP growth had slowed, productivity was down, consumer debt up, and joblessness stood at 7.8 percent, the highest level since January. At the same time, the wholesale price index had increased 6.6 percent over the prior year, a development that the Ford administration's spokesman had termed "worrisome." Growth in Europe was sluggish, there was upward pressure on oil prices, the Tokyo Round of international trade talks wasn't making enough progress, and the question was how to improve economic policy coordination and cooperation among the major powers.

Carter was deeply involved in the politics of the campaign, and I had expected him to be interested primarily in economic proposals that would "play well in Peoria." It struck me as remarkable, therefore, that he was as eager to probe and understand the underlying facts and figures of the issues, as he was to consider the public appeal of the policies he might advocate, and that he conducted our meeting a lot more like a graduate seminar than a political strategy session. He was informally dressed in a plaid shirt and jeans, but his approach was highly focused and anything but casual. Asking confident and penetrating questions, he probed for details, took copious notes, and kept us on our toes for a full four hours with little small talk and no interruptions. I considered it quite a performance. As I reflected on the day's events on the Bendix plane back to Michigan, my main sense from this first extended encounter with Jimmy Carter was that he was an unusual politician with an inquiring, superior mind, and that if he became president the country would be in good hands.

Carter's double-digit lead in the polls in August had dissolved into a virtual standoff with Ford by the time of the election, and his victory had been uncomfortably close. His surprise success in the primaries had fostered the public impression of him as a canny politician backed by an effectively organized, well-functioning elections staff. Several gaffes and stumbles in the contest with Ford, however, had tarnished that image, and party insiders grumbled that confusion and mismanagement inside the Carter camp had come perilously close to costing the Democrats the election. When the same complaints were heard again during his early months in office, it would be said—with hindsight—that the missteps of the campaign had in fact been the first omen of the problems of the Carter White House.

For me, there had been no further contacts with the campaign until late November, when a phone call from a Carter staffer suddenly summoned me back for another briefing session at the Pond House. This time, however, the meeting unfolded under very different circumstances than it had in August. Carter was now the president-elect, he was about to name his cabinet, and there was intense public interest in his every move. Veterans from previous Democratic administrations and legions of ambitious campaign workers were openly maneuvering for jobs in his administration, the air was rife with rumors on who was in or out, and the media were filled with allegedly "inside" stories about names high on the Carter cabinet list.

Thus news of the impending meeting with Carter immediately generated widespread speculation that this time the group invited to consult with him, which included several CEOs and senior Wall Street types, was actually the short list of candidates for his economic cabinet. *Time* published a "Talent File" and anointed me a top contender for Treasury or Defense, and others speculated that I was exactly what Carter was looking for—a Democrat, liberal on social issues but conservative on economic questions.

I had a satisfying and lucrative job at Bendix with plenty of challenges. Until the election, abandoning it for a senior assignment in Washington had seemed an unlikely possibility, and I had given little thought to this. As the news stories multiplied, however, and the phone rang off the hook with friends and colleagues fishing for information and offering encouragement and advice, it didn't take long for the spark of ambition to ignite. At the end of the Kennedy Round I had told myself that someday there would be another opportunity for public service, and the lure of it was still there. I thought that a cabinet post was probably a dream, though a very appealing one, but if it came to pass, it could be an incredible opportunity that might never come again. Suddenly I wanted to be asked and began to hope that I would be.

At our meeting on December 1, the issues covered were little changed from those in August, except that this time the spotlight was on Carter's actual legislative proposals. The consensus of the group was that some kind of Carter economic stimulus package was called for. I was about to start for home when Carter pulled me aside and raised the question I had hoped for: "Will you come and help me—on a permanent basis?" he asked. Just in case, I had carefully rehearsed a cautiously positive reply, emphasizing my Bendix responsibilities and wondering what he had in mind. "I'll call you," Carter promised, and with his trademark smile wished me a safe journey home.

He telephoned the very next day, warmed my heart by wanting to know which cabinet post would suit me best, and after a brief conversation, asked me to meet him in Atlanta the following week. It was there, during a brief private meeting, that he first told me that I was a serious prospect to be his secretary of the treasury.

I had only half believed the press stories, and Carter's confirmation of them stunned me. The Treasury is one of the oldest of the government departments and the secretary is second in cabinet seniority only to secretary of state. He supervises 125,000 employees,[192] and by tradition is first on the president's economic team, the manager of the country's fiscal affairs, and the senior U.S. official on international financial matters. His reach and range of responsibilities is substantial, and to be seriously in the running for so senior an appointment on Carter's team was overwhelming.

Carter had let it be known that he was committed to an especially deliberate and thorough selection process for his cabinet and sub-cabinet posts, and that Vice President elect Mondale and he would carefully interview the top contenders to make the final choices. Perhaps I was an exception—though I doubt it—but in my case at least, the reality of this, my only "job interview," unfolded quite differently. I kept detailed notes of it, and in the light of subsequent events, they are rather revealing.

In its entirety, our discussion that day lasted a total of forty minutes, barely half of it with the two of us alone engaged in rather casual conversation. He had met me only twice before, both times as part of a larger group. Undoubtedly he had a pretty detailed dossier about me at his disposal, assembled from public records and supplemented by the results of a standard FBI background investigation and soundings with former colleagues. Yet I probably knew more about him at that moment than he did about me and this would have been his first chance to really get to know me, and probe my substantive views. Yet in our few minutes together he neither dug deeply, discussed what he expected from his treasury secretary, nor inquired about my views of the issues. He merely asked whether there were any skeletons in my closet about which he should know, and when I reassured him that I was "clean," he invited me to sketch my background for him—from immigrant to CEO—interrupting me occasionally with a question or comment. Little else of substance was said. After twenty minutes, Vice President elect Mondale and Hamilton Jordan, Carter's principal assistant, joined us, and the very general conversation continued for a short time longer.

Walter "Fritz" Mondale was another Minnesota Senator with whom I had a long-standing friendly relationship going back to the time I had helped him raise money for one of his election campaigns. Fritz and I saw eye to eye on most issues, and the choice of him as Carter's vice president had been welcome news. He was easy to get to know and work with, and I had always felt close to him, which, I had reason to believe, was reciprocated on his side. In the subsequent difficult Carter years, he remained a reliable friend inside the White House, one of the few senior people around Carter on whom I could count for understanding and sound advice.

Mondale had been the only one—briefly—to delve into anything of substance, asking me about the trade-off between inflation and jobs, and how Bendix handled the Arab boycott against Jews. Then Carter wanted to know why big business was so lukewarm toward him (because you're a Democrat, I told him). That was it. Before much more time had passed, Carter and Mondale, who were under great time pressure, excused themselves and left.

The meeting thus was significant primarily for what was *not* discussed that day. The question of how Carter expected economic policymaking in his administration to function, or what role he saw in it for his treasury secretary, was never mentioned. Yet it should have been. Nor was there any further discussion of his economic program and my views of it. He did not explore whether we saw eye-to-eye on these matters, nor did I raise such issues or ask how he expected me to do the job, or how he saw his relationship to his staff. It would have been better if we had taken the time to explore these critical questions in some depth, but we did not. Perhaps it wouldn't have mattered, but in the light of what happened later, it was a serious omission for which I am as much to blame as he.

At 1:34 P.M. on the following Monday, December 13, Carter

telephoned again. "I have decided to appoint you my secretary of the treasury. I am proud of you," he told me. "Thank you, I'll be honored to serve and to do the very best job I can," I replied. The following day I was back in Atlanta and stood next to the future president as he announced that he had chosen me as the sixty-fourth secretary of the treasury of the United States.

Getting Started

By Christmas, the Cabinet was largely in place, and between December 27 and 29 Carter assembled his cabinet appointees and staff for a get-acquainted and planning session at The Cloisters, an elegant resort on Sea Island, off the Georgia coast.

It was the first opportunity for many of us to see the president-elect in action and to get a clearer picture of what he had in mind for his administration. The mood was upbeat, and everyone looked forward to exhilarating times. Though sometimes puzzled by what we heard, no one was willing to raise doubts and spoil the fun in the face of so much positive energy.

The quietly ebullient president-elect set the tone with surprising informality but enormous self-assurance about his intentions and the certainty of rapid progress. A front-page *New York Times* photograph showed him casually dressed in sweater and slacks on a couch, with Mondale and some of us similarly attired relaxing around him.[193] Ham Jordan, the architect of Carter's campaign, appeared nonchalantly sporting a pair of old pants and working boots. Rosalynn Carter attended as well, and once or twice struck a startling pose seated on the floor directly in front of her husband, holding hands with him while listening to the proceedings.

The men and women Carter had called together comprised two distinct groups with very different backgrounds. On one side were the Georgians, including Rosalynn; Atlanta lawyer Charles Kirbo, Carter's political confidant; and a contingent of aides slated for his White House staff who had served him in Atlanta or played key roles in the campaign. Among the latter, Ham Jordan and his spokesman, Jody Powell, were the most senior. Virtually all were still in their twenties or early thirties, with little or no prior federal government experience.

What distinguished the Georgians from the rest of us—Carter's cabinet choices—was not only their Southern accents, but also their long association with him and each other, and the bond of successful battles fought together on behalf of their leader. Virtually none appeared to hold strong substantive views on the issues beyond an unquestioning commitment to their boss and to the themes and symbols of his candidacy.

During the campaign, Carter had promised a cabinet of fresh faces. Many he had chosen hardly fit that description, however, the senior posts having gone largely to familiar Washington hands with experience under previous Democratic presidents—among others, Cyrus Vance for State, Harold Brown for Defense, Jim Schlesinger for Energy, and Joe Califano for HEW. There were two notable exceptions. One was Griffin Bell, a former federal judge, prominent Atlanta lawyer, and long-time Carter supporter, who was to be his attorney general; the other was Carter's close friend Bert Lance, slated for OMB.

Well over six feet, and of ample girth, Thomas Bertram Lance stood out as a large man with a large presence, and it was understood that he would play an important role in Carter's administration. He and the future president were born-again Christians (a book of religious poems authored by Bert's wife, LaBelle, awaited each of us in our rooms) and obviously very close. Whereas the others treated Carter with respectful deference, Lance related to him more on an equal basis, and their bond of friendship and trust, with occasional good-natured joking in both directions, was apparent.

Lance was a cheerful extrovert, always good for an apt story or southern aphorism, and was as outgoing and expansive as Carter was reserved and tightly controlled. Whereas the future president took evident pride in his factual mastery of the issues, Bert cheerfully admitted to ignorance of the substance of his impending OMB responsibilities, with frequent flattering reminders to Charlie Schultze, the head of

OMB under Lyndon Johnson and the incoming chairman of the Council of Economic Advisors, and to me that he intended to defer to our superior wisdom. Whereas Carter lived modestly in Plains, Georgia, Bert resided in an enormous, unapologetically ostentatious mansion in Atlanta, where he threw an elaborate dinner party for Schultze and me a few days later.

Carter had emphasized a deliberate management style and careful planning. Reflecting this theme, we were handed an impressive flowchart of initiatives for the first several months, and a twenty-nine-page "Suggested Carter Administration Agenda" that served as the basis for our discussion.

Both were formidable documents: very ambitious, with lots of action and tight deadlines, but with puzzlingly little regard to the realities of the congressional calendar. The suggested program, which closely tracked the positions and promises of Carter's run for office, was described as an action blueprint "to convey a clear impression that the President and his Cabinet will provide leadership . . . to carry out the President' campaign commitments,[194] . . . to build upon successful themes established in the campaign . . . of the President as unifier and healer, a leader close to the people, an outsider who will shake things up, who will make the federal bureaucracy work efficiently and without waste, and who is energetic and effective to solve national problems such as recession, inflation, energy and international problems such as arms control."[195]

As campaign image creators, these themes had worked well. Translated into a plethora of specific initiatives to be implemented over the span of a few months, they struck me as overambitious and a bit presumptuous. Yet Carter obviously believed in them, even if no president had ever been able to reform the institutions of government fundamentally, to make the bureaucracy work without waste, or to "solve" such perennially complex problems as recession, inflation, energy, and arms control. Setbacks or failure were not to be an option, we were told.

The agenda led to spirited debate on details, but not on its basic thrust. The climate of the discussions was not conducive to that, as we were just getting to know each other and inevitably engaged in a mutual feeling out process with everyone on their best behavior. The Carterites accepted it all without reservation, and the rest of us were anxious to show our loyalty and commitment to Carter and his ideas. So no one was willing to rock the boat and question the realism of the underlying assumptions. With hindsight, it was a mistake that no one did.

The result was agreement on a veritable flood of executive actions and legislative proposals crammed into the administration's first few months. Priority One was a multifaceted economic stimulus tax and spending package to be sent up to Congress in the first week and confidently assumed to be on the president's desk for signature by the end of March. Within thirty days the new Carter budget was to be submitted, as well as a whole host of "reform" bills: budget reform, election reform by March 20, and regulatory reform a week later. Within ninety days, Carter expected to make good on his promise to send Congress a comprehensive energy program. Lesser initiatives on farm, veterans, and seniors issues were also planned. Califano was instructed to have comprehensive welfare reform proposals ready by May, and I was tasked with preparing the draft of a big tax reform bill for submission to Congress in the fall. Vance was to commence negotiation of a new SALT agreement with the Soviets, for which a satisfactory conclusion was contemplated for about the same time. All this Carter intended to supervise, even as he would be busy addressing the United Nations, meeting numerous heads of state, attending a London economic summit, traveling the country, and holding press conferences and fireside chats along with weekly cabinet meetings, and more.

Much of this involved highly complex and controversial issues that had long defied resolution and on which powerful special interest groups were dug in on all sides. It also required consideration and approval by a fair number of separate committees of the Congress and carefully coordinated prior consultation with the leadership. To

move forward on all these fronts at once and expect a favorable outcome, was a tall order indeed.

Taken as a whole, there were three features of this program that
defined the Carter style: great ambition to do a lot quickly, unquestioning confidence of success, and a fondness for setting tight and
arbitrary deadlines for action. The president-elect evidently believed
that this was the best way to make it all happen. If he had any expectation of having to pull back, there was no sign of it.

During the campaign, Carter had stressed a new presidential
management style to make the machinery of government more efficient and more responsive to the people. Now he spelled out what
he had in mind. He would organize his staff differently than other
presidents had, and reduce it by a third. He would dispense with a
chief of staff, deploy the "hub and spokes" approach and make the
important final decisions himself. There would also be true "cabinet
government." The cabinet members were to be the sole policy advisors, and no one on his staff would be allowed to come between them
and him. "There will never be an instance while I am president," as
he put it after we were sworn in, "when the members of the White
House staff dominate or act in a superior position to the members
of the cabinet."[196]

It sounded too good to be true, but I wasn't quite sure how it
would work in practice. After all, unlike a parliamentary democracy
where the cabinet is drawn from, and responsible to, the legislature
where each one has his own political standing, the U.S. cabinet is
appointed by the president, and serves entirely at his pleasure. Previous cabinets had rarely met more than once a month, and most presidents had considered these meetings largely a waste of time. Carter,
however, told us he would convene us weekly—every Monday at 9
A.M.—and that he planned a full two hours for discussion of all major
issues, with everyone expected to give their views.

He also wanted us to administer our departments independently
and free from White House interference, which sounded great but was
another decisive break with past practice. The White House had usu-

ally exercised strong influence on appointments to sub-cabinet posts down to the level of assistant secretaries and their deputies, partly to reward political supporters and partly to ensure control over departmental operations. Carter now said that he would essentially cede the choice of our subordinates to us, subject only to final approval for a few of the top jobs. He also assured us ready access to him, and encouraged us to send him frequent decision memos, which he promised to return quickly, with comments in the margins.

Presidents have an enormous range of public responsibilities beyond policy formulation and cabinet interaction. They give speeches, take trips, meet foreign dignitaries and civic leaders, and jump in to put out fires. Some past cabinet members had only rare contact with the president—Nixon's secretary of the interior once complained that in eighteen months he had seen the boss exactly twice. Yet Carter promised us unfettered access and memos usually returned "in twenty-four hours." Was that possible? While he and I were chatting after one of the meetings, I couldn't resist voicing my pleasure at the prospect of so much personal interaction, but also some gentle doubts. "You know," I told him, "you may find yourself up to your eyeballs in memos. Do you think it will work?" Carter, however, was unconcerned. "Oh, don't worry, Mike," he told me, "I am always at my desk before 7 A.M. Besides, I like to read."

Thus a supremely confident Jimmy Carter laid down his ambitious plans and sent us off to organize our departments. But the two days at Sea Island had left me with plenty to think about. Other presidents, before and after him, have run for office promising to tackle long-standing, difficult problems. In none of this had Carter been unique. Nor was he alone in having made lots of campaign promises. Stuart Eizenstat, an able young lawyer who stood out among the Georgians as virtually the only one with prior Washington experience and knowledge of the issues, had compiled all of them—Stu's "Promises Book,"—listing 600 separate pledges and running to 100 pages. What was different about Carter was the confidence that he could redeem most of these pledges and that he would quickly do so.

Did he fully appreciate what awaited him, or was he in for unpleasant surprises? I could not help wondering, but then I put these thoughts out of my mind. The die was cast, he had almost made a believer of me, and I was rooting for him and determined to do my part. Later I would remember that it had been during these first two days, even before the new administration was installed, that the seeds of future trouble had been sewn, and when the shape of the problems Carter would encounter were first apparent.

First Setbacks and Disarray

"Enraged congressmen, unforeseen foulups, a shortage of qualified help, touchy foreign leaders—they are all bogging down Carter's attempt at a fast start. Lesson: power politics in Washington is a different ballgame."[197]

This is how *U.S. News & World Report* summed up the record of the first hundred days. In June, *Fortune* said Carter's management style, lack of precision, and pushing forward with too many contradictory policies had stamped his administration as inept.[198] *Business Week* complained that "the bad start" had turned the economy off track, and by the late summer the stock market was down 20 percent from year-end levels. Liberals were grumbling, conservatives were gloating, and Congress was restive.

There was no getting around it: midway through its first year in office, the Carter administration was in disarray. Setbacks in the Congress, unexpected problems, and the bad press had plainly rattled the president, who looked tired and harassed. The more he assured us in cabinet meetings, as he frequently did, that he was "perfectly at ease" (a favorite expression), the more I suspected that the opposite was probably true. To our collective frustration, the image of an accident-prone and inept administration was taking hold.

We had come out of the starting box in a whirlwind of activity. An economic stimulus program had been announced within a week. His energy proposals were unveiled in ninety days, a Carter budget and proposals for budget reform and government reorganization had been submitted, and for good measure Carter had announced his intention to veto nineteen water projects which he considered "pork." Work on major welfare and tax reform bills was also in the works. Cy Vance had been dispatched to Moscow to explore a deal on SALT, and the president had held news conferences and fireside chats, declared the fight for his energy program "the moral equivalent of war," pronounced himself on human rights, and a lot more.

The overall results had been mixed. The stimulus program had been received with less than wild enthusiasm in the Congress. The idea of a tax rebate—one of its centerpieces—had been abandoned because of opposition in the Senate and a stronger than expected economy, but the rest of it had then been enacted. In April, Congress had given the president the reorganization powers he wanted (an important victory), and cleared a jobs bill.

The problem was, however, that some of these successes had been achieved at the cost of considerable congressional frustration over an overload of initiatives, too many dropped balls, grumbling about the White House staff, mixed signals and inconsistent pronouncements, and much puzzlement and anger over his water projects stance. One Democratic leader later grumbled that Carter "let fly enough balloons over Capitol Hill to make one wonder whether he was deliberately trying to make this place look like a circus."[199]

Some setbacks had been due to circumstances beyond Carter's control, and a Congress more fractious and assertive than anyone had expected. In major part, however, the problems were the predictable consequences of the president's approach to government. Specifically, surrounding himself with inexperienced staff had gotten him into trouble because of slights and mishandling of powerful members of Congress, unanswered phone calls, and frayed relations with important constituent groups. The absence of a strong chief of staff wise to Washington's ways, the lack of clear lines of responsibility and authority, too many advisors providing conflicting reports, and the many important decisions Carter had reserved for himself had led to delays, confusion, inconsistencies, and much internal dissension. Finally, the sheer mass of complex and controversial initial proposals without enough congressional consultation, had overloaded and irritated its committees. Carter's habit of deciding issues without sufficient prioritizing, without noting their interrelationships, and without a clear general framework, had led to contradictions and blurred the overall thrust of his goals.

The deficiencies of staffing and the approach to organization had been particularly damaging. During the campaign, Carter had promised to cut the White House staff by one-third and when he had followed through on that, the public relations impact was positive, but the understaffing of paper flow management and liaison with the outside was causing big problems. In truth, more rather than less staff would have been better.

His inexperienced senior staff from Georgia was clearly overmatched. Bob Lipshutz, his general counsel—an important job—had never served in Washington and was simply out of his depth in this sensitive position, and Frank Moore, in charge of critical congressional relations, proved another egregious problem for him.

Tales of Frank's missed meetings, unreturned phone calls from key committee chairmen and slights to their egos were soon legion around town and I would regularly get an earful of them. "I can't get through to him," the frustrated Ways and Means Chairman Al Ullman would complain to me. Others like Dan Rostenkowski, a strong voice on that committee whose goodwill Carter badly needed, were less inhibited. "What the hell is going on there?" he would growl at me adding a few choice expletives. "These guys are amateurs."

His much touted "Cabinet Government," implying serious cabinet deliberations, also proved illusory. At a June meeting, for example, we were regaled by the interior secretary's announcement of a California trip, the health and human services secretary's boast to be the first Democratic secretary invited to address an American Medical Association convention, the commerce secretary's discourse on porpoises caught in tuna fishermen nets, and the secretary of transportation's alerting the president to the need to discuss seat belts with him. Even the president's own interventions rarely dealt with serious policy questions and were more in the nature of pep talks laced with occasional compliments of various secretaries. In the U.S. system of government, cabinet deliberations simply do not mean much, and Carter's efforts to change that just didn't work.

The mostly meaningless cabinet meetings were merely a waste of time, but muting the White House's traditional strong voice on senior departmental appointments—another move Carter had been proud of—had unintended consequences that were more serious. Without a role in the selection process, the staff tended to consider many departmental executives "the secretary's people," and to suspect them of pursuing his rather than the president's interests. Thus as inevitable disagreements over policy arose, they would be misconstrued as evidence of disloyalty, and the resulting backbiting and leaks to the press exacerbated the administration's image of internal dissension.

While Zbigniew "Zbig" Brzezinski, the president's national security advisor, a smart and canny bureaucratic operator, played a strong and influential coordinating role on international matters, it was a major problem that no one on the staff had been appointed to fulfill an analogous function on economic matters. Formally, I had been tasked to chair the Cabinet Economic Policy Group (EPG), and the hardworking Stu Eizenstat had the title of domestic policy advisor. In reality, however, Carter's penchant for delving into lots of detail and insisting on making too many decisions himself often led to mix-ups and conflicting policy pronouncements.

Many of his stated positions—for example, balancing the budget, curbing spending, and fighting inflation—were in conflict with his ambitions for energy and welfare reform, all of which cost money. Yet he wanted it all, and as he considered each issue separately, the connections were often lost on him. The birth of his energy program—in ninety days—was a good case in point. Its tax and spending elements were bound to have a significant impact on the economy and should have been carefully considered. Yet the president's decision to work out the program directly with his energy secretary and to exclude others caused much confusion.

Until early April, Charlie Schultze, his chief economist, and I had been kept totally in the dark and knew little beyond rumors about proposals for special gas taxes, higher oil and gas prices, and tighter fuel efficiency standards for industry. The aim was to promote efficiency and reduce consumption, but there were two big problems. For one, these measures hatched in secrecy were so far-reaching, complex, and controversial as to be totally unacceptable to the Congress. For another, there were major macroeconomic implications running directly counter to the administration's fundamental economic policy goals.

Charlie and I were sufficiently concerned to decide—albeit reluctantly—that the drastic action of confronting Carter with some very blunt talk was called for. The first step was a joint phone call to the president, noting that we had been left uninformed and insisting on being let in on the details of the plan. Its wider impact, I told the president, could have major consequences and be highly counterproductive to his interests. Carter was clearly irritated and taken aback. "Well," he responded with petulant sarcasm, "I thought Charlie and you knew everything. But if you both feel that way, it must be so."

Undeterred, we followed up on April 5 with a blunt jointly signed memorandum that minced no words in its opening paragraph:

> The energy program, as we presently understand it, will be very far-reaching with major impacts on the economy as a whole, on individual industrial sectors, and on our international relations. It is important that the implications of these effects be understood by us with sufficient clarity to allow us to make the best possible choices. We don't think they now are.

It is likely that the President had not been aware of these considerations. At any rate, our memo clearly shocked him into action, and he ordered Jim Schlesinger, the energy secretary, to give us a detailed briefing—two weeks before the scheduled announcement. At the last moment, we were therefore able to do some limited damage control, eliminating some proposals and rewriting others. When announced on April 20, the program had predictably rough sledding in the Congress and, eventually, only a pale version of it could be enacted. It would have been difficult to pass under the best of circumstances, but had it been considered more carefully from the start with closer congressional consultation, at least some of the negative reception, and the conflicts with other critical parts of Carter's economic program, might well have been avoided.

Without a chief of staff or full trust in strong, experienced advisors to help him manage economic policy and domestic affairs, Carter worked harder and harder, read reams of material (eventually his wife Rosalynn and he took a speed-reading course), and struggled to cope with a mountain of memos on which he would make his marginal comments and decisions. His heart was in the right place, but that slips and errors occurred too often under these circumstances is hardly surprising.

Sometimes his penchant for spending time on detail boggled the mind. Once, a short decision memo concerning the perennial question of building an Alaska pipeline and summarizing the findings of a technical task force report of well over a hundred pages had been placed on his desk. The lengthy report had been attached to the much briefer action memo for his attention, but when it was returned an astonished treasury assistant secretary, idly leafing through it, was stunned to find marginal notations in the president's handwriting not merely on the summary, but on the big report itself—including the president's views on the diameter of the pipe to be used: Jimmy Carter had read the entire document! Even with his speed-reading skills it must have been quite a challenge.

On another occasion, presenting him Treasury's recommendations for his tax reform program, I was no less astonished at the technical details in which he insisted on immersing himself. The U.S. tax system is highly complex, and beyond the IRS and Treasury's tax policy staff, only a limited number of tax experts have fully mastered it. Carter, however, spent many hours trying to get as full an understanding of it as possible. In the May 18 meeting, he reminded me and the Treasury staff that a relatively obscure provision—a special tax benefit to coal miners—was not on our list of proposed eliminations. "There is little revenue involved in this, and Congress will never do it. It's part of the Holy Grail up there," Assistant Secretary Larry Woodworth, an acknowledged expert, explained. Larry had spent years as the staff director of the Congress' Joint Committee of Taxation, but Carter would have none of it. "Put it back in," he ordered sternly.[200] Predictably, I was laughed at when arguing passionately for its elimination before the Congress.

The Lance Affair

Carter's first six months had been rocky, yet some of this was still being ascribed to the teething troubles of a new administration, and there was plenty of scope to erase the early image of missteps and stumbles. Unfortunately, his handling of the problems concerning his good friend Bert Lance in the summer of 1977 further deepened public misgivings about Carter as a political leader. Eventually this, as much as anything, would become a critical factor in solidifying the negative public image from which he never fully recovered.

The "Lance Affair" was the biggest political story of Jimmy Carter's first year in office, and it rocked the Carter administration to its foundations. As major Washington scandals go, the substance of the crisis—revelations about Lance's tangled personal finances and alleged violations of banking and campaign finance laws—though embarrassing, was not particularly earthshaking. The President was never accused of personal wrongdoing, and none of the charges against Lance had to do with his conduct as director of OMB. The real damage, therefore, came not from the charges themselves, but rather from how Carter handled them.

That the unflattering and damaging stories about the President's close friend had explosive potential and required prompt and astute handling was clear from the beginning. Lance, after all, was no ordinary director of OMB, but the president's closest confidante and the man Carter had chosen to balance the federal budget in four years and to implement his promise to boost government efficiency. In an administration that had stressed the highest standards of moral probity and sound management, merely the undisputed facts about Lance's messy personal finances and record as a banker—regardless of whether they were outside the law or only evidence of exuberant risk-taking and plain sloppiness—were sure to raise questions about his suitability as OMB director.

Had Carter recognized the explosive potential of the Lance story and moved quickly to contain it, the damage to his administration and to himself might well have been limited. Indeed, deft handling might even have enhanced his reputation as a leader. Unfortunately, it was an opportunity he missed. Well after the handwriting was on the wall, Carter surprised the country by continuing to defend and praise his friend openly and, at a particularly inopportune moment, to announce publicly that nothing he had heard greatly troubled him; indeed, that he was "proud" of Lance.

The result was that the focus of the affair shifted—unnecessarily, as we shall see—from Lance to the president himself, with questions about his leadership and judgment, his political tin ear, and even about the solidity of his ethical standards when they involved close friends. The consequences for Carter's image were serious.

The principal charges against Lance involved his activities at two Georgia banks, one family-owned and the other led by him as chief executive. The investigation fell under the purview of the Controller of the Currency (OCC), a Treasury agency, thus putting me squarely in the middle of the affair. I realized at once that I faced a major problem, potentially the most difficult one yet as secretary of the treasury. Though the OCC acts largely independently through a professional career staff of examiners, I knew that I would invariably be identified with whatever its reports revealed, and that being associated even indirectly with investigating charges of malfeasance against a cabinet colleague and the president's close friend was bound to be a sensitive and unpleasant task.

From the start, my instruction to John Heimann, the comptroller, was to proceed as fairly as possible and to conduct the investigation as he would any other. Any suspicion of special handling or cover-up would have made a bad situation infinitely worse for the president and all concerned, and when I reported my marching orders to Carter in a private meeting on July 15, he immediately agreed that this was how he wanted me to proceed. Carter, however, felt extraordinarily close to Bert Lance, so in subsequent weeks for me to be repeatedly in the position of bringing him bad news about his friend was always difficult. It was obvious that the president was greatly troubled by the affair, but he seemed to appreciate my position and, much to his credit, he never complained.

Not so Lance's friends on the White House staff, who suspected me of overzealousness, deliberate press leaks, and scheming to harm Lance. Henceforth, anonymous criticism of my work at the Treasury and rumors about my poor standing in the administration, usually attributed to unnamed "senior sources," regularly appeared in the press—until Carter finally put a stop to them.

The office of the Comptroller of the Currency is a Washington backwater rarely in the news. Its main job is to regulate the nation's several thousand banks with national charters, and though it is formally under the Treasury, the secretary rarely lays eyes on the comptroller. What contacts there are, usually are delegated to his deputy or one of the assistant secretaries. Ironically, after routine approval by the White House, Heimann's appointment had become effective just days before the Lance Affair exploded. Thus, virtually overnight—much to his discomfort—Heimann had found himself centrally embroiled in a national story with lots of political dynamite.

At the time of Lance's Senate confirmation in January, and during his failed campaign for Georgia governor, there had been occasional rumors about past problems with family bank overdrafts, including references to the sudden closing of an investigation by the local U.S. attorney, but no one had paid much attention and the Senate committee chaired by Senator Abe Ribicoff had easily confirmed him. The stories had never entirely stopped; a few weeks later the *Village Voice* had run one entitled "Cracker Credit," but it too had been ignored.[201] A more detailed one in *Time* magazine in May, however, had developed more traction.[202] It reported that Lance was "knee-deep in debt," and that because of large write-offs at the National Bank of Georgia (NBG) after his departure, the stock had substantially declined in value, possibly making it difficult for Lance to meet his obligation to dispose of his holdings, as required by conflict-of-interest rules.[203] *Time*'s predictions soon proved correct. Bert had in fact appealed to the president for help, and on July 11 Carter sent a letter to the Ribicoff Committee citing undue financial hardship and requesting an extension of the December 31 deadline by which Lance was to sell his stock.

Predictably, the media had pounced on the story, and all kinds of rumors about the Lance record in Georgia, with hints of various illegalities, appeared in the press. The most inflammatory charges came from *New York Times* columnist William Safire,[204] no friend of the administration and out to stoke the fires with all kinds of accusations. Much was questionable and exaggerated, but his twice-weekly column appeared in a hundred newspapers nationally, and its impact was serious. Amongst other things, Safire claimed Lance had "used his public job to line his pocket," taken out "sweetheart loans," used political influence to channel teamster funds to the NBG, and sent a Tennessee banker friend to see me without informing me that he owed his bank $443,000.[205] According to Safire, there had also been a suspicious quashing of a U.S. attorney's investigation of Lance's record, a day before Carter nominated him.

A visibly nervous John Heimann, only days on the job, now

asked to see Deputy Treasury Secretary Carswell and me at the Treasury to report that he was under great pressure to investigate these charges, all the more so since there was also the suspicion that prior OCC examiners had glossed over Bert's banking problems. If true, Heimann worried, this would raise damaging questions about the integrity of the office he had just taken over. Carswell and I heard him out, recognized the problem he faced, and agreed that he had to proceed, with instructions to do so with great objectivity and care to avoid the appearance of either a cover-up or a witch hunt. It is this that I had reported to the president in our private meeting on July 15.

Meanwhile, the pace of daily Lance stories accelerated and swept through the media. An embarrassed Ribicoff Committee worried that it had approved Lance too quickly, and at least two other committees of Congress also started digging, all of which was further grist for the rumor mill. Some of the reports were accurate, others had only a grain of truth, and some were pure speculation, but none of that mattered any longer; the Lance story had quickly taken on a life of its own. Lance's Georgia record was being minutely dissected in public, together with stories about his Chicago and New York loans, allegedly obtained by dubious means.

It was, in other words, a typical Washington scandal story—the public followed it avidly, and, to the great discomfiture of Carter and his staff, no one could stop it. Neither the president nor his assistants had ever been through anything like it before. Strongly committed to Lance's cause, Ham and Jody in particular resented some of the more mean-spirited stories about their friend. Lacking sufficient experience to understand the inevitability of leaks given the many investigators on the case, they assumed that much of it was a deliberate plot, probably by Treasury, to destroy Lance. Their energies should have been focused on damage control and on containing the risks to the president. Instead, they let it be known that it was a Treasury vendetta against a blameless man and that the unfavorable information coming to light about him was nothing more than a deliberate effort by Heimann and me to harm him. The atmosphere between Treasury and the White House staff became tense and poisonous.

The president actually was a lot more cautious, though he too did not fully understand the dynamics of the capital's rumor mill. "Can't the comptroller stop all those leaks?" he asked me plaintively at one of our meetings. When I reminded him that dozens of investigators from multiple agencies and the Congress were involved, and that the source of leaks was impossible to know or stop, he professed to understand and nodded sadly. Ham and Jody obviously continued to feel otherwise and the unfavorable "anonymous" stories about me continued.

About five weeks later, Heimann finally issued part one of his meticulously detailed OCC report. A formidable three-volume, 395-page document weighing some seven and a half pounds, it did not make for pleasant reading. The most positive news in it was that, contrary to the more lurid speculation, the comptroller had found no proof of illegality in any of the matters he had examined. There were, however, any number of embarrassing details sure to cause trouble. For example, the report noted that the findings "raised unresolved questions about what constitutes acceptable banking practice," and accused both banks under Lance of unsafe and unsound banking operations and permitting massive overdrafts on the personal accounts of its officers. Many unresolved questions remained which were to be the subject of a second report still in the works.

The White House had hoped for an exoneration, but though the "no illegalities" conclusion was duly noted, the public reaction to the report proved a PR disaster, and criticism of Lance's record increased. *Time*'s conclusion that "his parlous financial finances make him an unconvincing spokesman for Carter's philosophy of tightfisted national spending"[206] was typical, and the chorus of those opining that there was no way the President could keep him at OMB grew louder.

From the beginning, Carswell and I had detected a puzzling air of White House unreality about the crisis and a failure, born of hope and the determination to save Lance at all costs, to appreciate the seriousness of the OCC's findings and the need for prompt action. Bob Lipshutz, Carter's General Counsel, should have played a particularly important role, yet he struck us as slow and in over his head, a worry I expressed in my notes after our final briefing of Carter on August 12:

> Lipshutz in all this shows his weaknesses . . . always two steps behind Carswell. President should be better served.[207]

Hoping for maximum realism, Carswell and I had done our best to keep the President fully apprised about the likely nature of OCC's findings, stressing that even if no criminal conduct turned up, appearances of all else would be bad, and that the revelation of more troubling findings in part two of Heimann's report remained a possibility. My records indicate four separate briefings in the Oval Office, the first on July 23, and subsequent ones on August 2, 11, and 12. Lipshutz was usually present, and separately Carswell had numerous phone conversations with Ham and him to provide further details. At the August 12 meeting, with the OCC Report imminent, we tried especially hard to urge caution. "The good news is that there is no finding that Bert has broken the law," I began my briefing for Carter that day. "Good, good," he said, smiling broadly. "But all else will sound terrible, Mr. President," I cautioned, not relishing being once again the messenger of bad tidings. Appearances would be grim, and great restraint was necessary, I warned, since many open questions remained.

We left satisfied that we had done all we could and that the president and his advisors had been duly warned, hoping but unsure that we had gotten through. Yet even we were unprepared for the colossal lapse of political judgment with which Carter would turn the embarrassment of Lance into a full blown disaster for himself. Instead of a measured hopeful response noting Lance's clearance of criminal wrongdoing, the president chose instead to ignore all the negatives and declare the OCC report an unqualified endorsement of his embattled OMB chief. His "faith in the character and competence of Bert Lance has been reconfirmed," he announced in a hastily-convened press conference. Lance's services to this country can and should continue. And then, turning to him: "Bert, I'm proud of you."

The OCC report had raised grave questions about Bert's record, and about whether seeking personal loans from banks with which his own bank had corresponding relationships was acceptable, even if not strictly illegal. It had criticized his massive overdrafts and noted numerous violations during his political campaign. A second OCC report was due, the SEC was not satisfied, and several committees of Congress were investigating. Even the American Bankers Association had felt it necessary to state publicly that Lance's banking practices were anything but par for the course. All of that Carter had now brushed aside, in the vain hope that boldly declaring victory would save Lance and put an end to the story.

Wishful thinking had blinded the political judgment of the president and his advisors. There was no chance that Heimann's first report would close the books on the affair: "President Carter leapt upon the report . . . as the cartoon character stranded in the desert leaps for a bucket of water only to discover it is a mirage," the *Baltimore Sun* editorialized. "We find less (in the Report) to justify President Carter's remark, 'Bert, I'm proud of you,'" concluded the *Wall Street Journal*.[208] Such statements reflected the now virtually unanimous view that Lance should never have been appointed and had to go, and that the president's inexplicable response raised questions about his political judgment and the competence of his staff.

On September 7, Heimann issued his second report, again clearing the embattled OMB chief of illegalities but suggesting further improprieties. That Lance would have to leave Washington was now a certainty. Senator Ribicoff called at the White House and let it be known that he had urged Lance's resignation, and a few days later the Senate Majority Leader Robert Byrd did likewise.

Even the White House now realized that Lance couldn't be saved. Only one final act remained, and on September 15, Lance appeared before the Ribicoff Committee and with Clark Clifford, the seasoned Washington troubleshooter and wise man, at his side testified ably to defend himself. It was an opportunity he had demanded and Carter had insisted on—to let him go honorably. By all accounts, Lance acquitted himself well, but it was too late.

On September 21, two months after the crisis had exploded, the president stood beside his good friend and, his eyes brimming with tears, accepted his resignation "with the greatest regret and sorrow." Finally, the crisis was over and Carter could turn back to the business at hand.[209]

For Jimmy Carter, the Lance Affair was a disaster. He had been late to grasp the dangers of the crisis and had failed to act promptly to insulate himself from its potential damage. By his unequivocal defense of his friend's less than stellar record, he had turned the spotlight on himself in ways that "didn't reflect favorably on his sense of political reality."[210] Above all, he had put into question what had been his greatest asset: his reputation as a champion of ethical purity.

"What it tells us about Jimmy Carter, the President, . . . provides a different insight that even his supporters must find disappointing and disturbing," one paper concluded.[211] It showed, commented another, that Jimmy Carter's leadership was in trouble, that the White House didn't function well, and fortified the impression that no one was really in charge: "Every President has to blend his special strengths into a formula for leadership . . . Jimmy Carter hasn't yet produced that special sense of authority other Presidents had, each in different ways."[212]

At Sea Island I had wondered about some of what I had heard, and six months into a fairly close working relationship with Carter, I still found it difficult to read him or to understand his motivations. The Lance affair had only deepened the confusion. What had caused him to ignore all the warning signs? If it had been because of his basic decency and loyalty to a close friend and distress at seeing him depart Washington under a cloud, these had been admirable tendencies, though a considerable cost to him personally and to his image as a leader. Or had he merely been poorly advised by his young and inexperienced staff? Did he know that the inadequacies of his general counsel had cost him dearly, or that his ineffective congressional relations advisors had exacerbated the tensions over Lance with the Congress?

In my dealings with him, there had always been a shyness, a certain wariness, an evident unwillingness to confront, criticize, trust, or explain, and a disconcerting tendency to play things close to the vest. It had made communication with him difficult, and in the Lance affair—for reasons none of us fully understood—it had been no different. All presidents do it to some extent, perhaps as a necessary form of self-defense and as a way to keep their powder dry. Carter, I thought, seemed to display that tendency to excess. Secretary of State Cy Vance was a personal friend, and once I mentioned to him that in my personal relationship with the president, I had found him curiously unwilling to open up, and to have it out. Did it mean that there was a personality conflict between us, that perhaps we just "didn't click," I wondered? "Forget it," Cy had told me. "You are not alone, we all have that problem."

The Economy in Crisis

When James Callaghan, the British prime minister, called at the White House on March 23, 1978, the top issue on his mind was the deteriorating U.S. energy and inflation situation and its impact on the world financial system. The news was bad, the immediate prospects gloomy, and, like many European leaders, Callaghan was uncertain about the thrust of the U.S. administration's policies and worried about the rumors of conflict and confusion in Washington. Another G7 summit meeting was slated for Bonn in the summer, and Callaghan had come to test Carter's intentions and to gauge the prospects for significant U.S. action on energy and inflation as a basis for a successful summit.

Since mid 1977, the U.S. economic situation had steadily grown more precarious. Record oil imports had quadrupled the U.S. payments deficit in one year, Carter's energy legislation was stalled in Congress, and inflation was near 8 percent and rising. The dollar had already lost over 15 percent of its value against major currencies, and had put the sluggishly growing European and Japanese economies at risk from the adverse impact on their exports. One worry was that nervous exchange markets could spin out of control and precipitate a real financial crisis, but there was transatlantic disagreement about who had the main responsibility for taking corrective action. The United States wanted Europe and Japan to stimulate their economies as one way to stabilize exchange markets by taking pressure off the U.S. currency, but the Europeans strongly resisted that and pointed the finger right back at the United States. German Chancellor Helmut Schmidt had been particularly blunt (Germans being, for historical reasons, the most allergic to the risks of domestic inflation) in arguing that it was first and foremost America that had to do the heavy lifting and suffer the pain of significant domestic belt-tightening and strong measures to cut down on energy consumption.

The president had asked me to join him for the Callaghan meeting that morning, and with typical British understatement, following the usual persiflage of mutual assurances of friendship and good feelings, the prime minister had opened the discussion with an expression of "some concern" about U.S. inflation, the falling dollar, and the international situation in general. Did the president agree this was a real problem, he inquired gently? "I do, I do. Mike is worrying me to death about it," Carter responded with some passion, and then turned to me to lay out the U.S. view.

The previous fall I had begun to warn him that rising domestic inflation was far more serious than the official predictions, that the related deterioration in the balance of payments/dollar weakness was developing into our potentially most dangerous challenge, and that even in the face of contrary domestic political pressures, the situation required a decisive shift of our policy priorities from reforms and spending to inflation fighting and crisis prevention.[213] So I was secretly pleased. His comment, and inviting me to answer the prime minister, were the first tangible, if implicit, evidence that my increasingly more urgent pleas for action might actually have had an impact.

Though Callaghan hadn't said so, he was probably well aware that there was substantial disagreement among Carter's senior advisors over the meaning of the economic indicators, and the appropriate response. What, however, he probably could not have fully appreciated was that the failure to agree on clear policies had at least as much to do with the deficient organization of Carter's motley assortment of advisors and the president's style of decision making, as with the substance of the underlying issues themselves.

The president, however, knew—or should have known—the problem. Just two days earlier, on March 21, I had seen to it that no fewer than three separate memoranda on the subject had landed on his desk. In two of them I had, as chairman of the Cabinet Economic Policy Group (EPG), clearly spelled out the different views among his advisors and presented him with alternative programs of action.[214] The third, a bluntly worded private one, had been yet another urgent plea to him to make a clear decision, and to come down on the side of giving highest priority to fighting inflation and shoring up the dollar:

> You requested a decision memorandum . . . It reflects basic disagreement among your advisors on the most critical point at issue . . . I am deeply concerned . . . The dollar situation is very dangerous and inflation is now the key domestic issue, a view shared by Miller (Fed), Schultze (CEA), Vance (State) and Kreps (Commerce) . . . The contrary view held by your domestic advisors, is that inflation and the dollar are not the highest priority; that other commitments (urban programs, agriculture, transportation, federal pay, etc.) are equally vital . . . they counsel that you delay, consult, review, and hedge your stand on virtually every important element of a program to shore up the dollar and fight inflation . . . The problem, however, is not one of choosing inflation over unemployment, because (in my view) the former

will inexorably lead to the latter . . . If you do not get out in front, Fed action on monetary market policy and further disturbances in the dollar will force your hand. Action now to stem energy imports, to fight inflation, and to shore up the dollar are the key to everything else you want to do. I urge that you point us clearly in that direction . . .[215]

The problem had been that, with conflicting advice pouring in on him, Carter had always listened attentively to my warnings and rarely disagreed, yet never seen fit to follow up with a clear decision and unambiguous stance, opting instead for public exhortations and essentially symbolic acts that did little and fooled no one. I don't know whether the British prime minister left Washington reassured or still concerned, as the *Wall Street Journal*'s astute Richard Levine had pointed out months earlier, that Carter would "continue to waver between emphasizing the fight against unemployment and the fight against inflation."[216]

In this instance at least, perhaps energized by the Callaghan meeting and my urgent memoranda, Carter did respond promptly. Yet his decision again remained hedged. A few days later, he issued a statement declaring inflation as the nation's top economic problem, but the rhetoric was still not matched by tough action. A number of the least controversial Economic Policy Group's recommendations were approved, but those with teeth were not. He had qualified a recommended public commitment to a significant budget deficit reduction by adding "if the opportunity arises," and postponed an announcement limiting federal pay increases "pending more consultation." The settlement of a coal miners' strike with a clearly inflationary three-year, 38 percent wage hike elicited only a mild expression of disapproval, while the idea of a potentially powerful anti-inflation TIP (tax-incentive) plan was rejected in favor of a largely ineffective voluntary wage-price deceleration program.

Thus at a crucial moment in the spring of 1978, the president continued to temporize, the policy apparatus sputtered, his advisors remained divided, and the external appearance of uncertainty and disarray persisted.

Throughout much of the rest of the year and into 1979, the economic situation deteriorated further. Oil imports jumped from 32 billion barrels in 1978 to 46 billion in 1979, and domestic inflation, which had averaged 7.6 percent in 1978, reached 11.3 percent the following year (soaring briefly to 13.5 percent in 1980). The result was a terrible case of U.S. stagflation during the latter part of Carter's time in office: real GNP growth slowed to 3.2 percent in 1979, and turned slightly negative in 1980, the dollar dropped another 10 percent against major currencies, and at the end of 1978 a threatening full-blown international currency crisis was barely averted—ironically only by our taking even stronger belt-tightening measures than we had advocated six months before.

As rising inflation coupled with slow growth and renewed pressure on the dollar in 1978 was shaping up as an increasing economic crisis, the situation was generating lots of negative media reports of an inconsistent response by the administration and evidence of disarray among Carter's advisors. The White House mood was nervous and gloomy, and the president's approval rating reached new lows.

In the intervening months I had spoken and written to Carter countless times about two critically needed changes in the administration's economic policies. One was that the inflation-dollar problem was so serious that his response could no longer be half-hearted—that he needed to be seen as fully committed to fighting inflation as his highest priority and to back up his statements with a program that had real teeth, leaving no doubt about his intentions. The second was to bring more discipline into the administration's process of economic decision making by appointing an economic coordinator on his staff and anointing him, or him together with the EPG's chairman, as his chosen instrument for sorting out policy options and presenting them to him in a manageable form. He would then have to trust them to execute his decisions in a coherent manner.

Yet Carter's habit of making ad hoc decisions outside a clear framework, leaning one way or another in response to conflicting advice, had continued and remained at the heart of the inconsistencies in his economic policies. Finally, in May of 1979, very late in the game, with the situation more serious than ever, I thought that perhaps the time was ripe for one last real attempt to get him to act.

The memorandum I sent him on May 8, 1979, once more laying out the problem and outlining the specific changes needed, was as direct as anything I had ever said or written to the boss:

> We have obviously had great difficulties in formulating, selling, and effectively following up on our economic policies. Decisions come late and are leak-ridden; they too frequently are inconsistent with each other or reflect no defined set of priorities; and they too often receive divergent explanations by Administration officials.
>
> A key reason for all this is that the Administration's economic decision-making procedures lack discipline and consistency.
>
> No one is in charge of a process mandated by you as the exclusive instrument for seeing to it that economic policy is made, executed and presented in an efficient and coherent manner. Accordingly, there is no vehicle for you to approve priorities, and provide overall guidance and control, without wasting your time on details and minor matters.
>
> This has led to a confusing fragmentation of economic policy—frustrating to *everyone* involved. It has also led at times to inadequate economic staff work—for the DPS and NSC staffs have chiefly political or programmatic concerns and have little economic expertise or perspective.[217]

This time it seemed that my rattling of the cage might have worked. A week later, Carter sent us a handwritten note, approving the changes "based generally on Mike's memo."[218] On June 1, a press release along the same lines was issued,[219] yet once again he had neither designated a White House economic coordinator, nor spoken clearly about the primacy of the anti-inflation fight. Still, I was slightly encouraged. Perhaps, I thought, there was still hope at this late moment for an effective new approach.

My Resignation

I was wrong—it was already too late.

By mid-1979, the economy had further heated up and was threatening to spin out of control. OPEC was raising prices—42 percent in the first six months—and soaring energy and housing costs had pushed domestic inflation to 13 percent, the highest level in thirty years. Decontrol of domestic oil—a cornerstone of the president's energy program—had raised energy prices but hadn't dampened business and consumer spending as the prognosticators had expected. A vicious cycle of heightened inflationary expectations had instead led to accelerated spending by business and consumers trying to stay ahead of the game. The price of gold was up to $300 an ounce (it would more than double a year later), and with real GNP declining, the administration had been forced to admit that a recession was now a virtual certainty.

At the end of June, after a difficult summit meeting in Tokyo, including a particularly emotional confrontation with Helmut Schmidt —always a thorn in his side—over their exchange of correspondence on nuclear forces in Europe (the TNF issue),[220] Carter was aboard Air Force One returning to a sullen country. Teachers were striking, gasoline was in short supply, and in parts of the country long lines of irritated drivers crowded the pumps. Gas prices were up by over 50 percent in six months and inflation remained in the double digits. In Tokyo, Carter had been strongly pressed for decisive action to curb the voracious U.S. demand for energy by the other leaders, and a national address on the energy issue (his fifth) was in the works, though precisely when, and what specific new measures he would announce, was still being debated by his advisors.

I was with Carter on Air Force One flying home, but the news reaching me from Washington where drafts of the speech were supposed to be readied for him was anything but encouraging. His advisors remained locked in a tense struggle over key elements of the new program, there were leaks to the press, and no one was in charge to bring order into the process.

Before touching down at Andrews Air Force Base, I had sat with the president in his private compartment reviewing the situation and discussing his options. Carter looked tired and more dispirited than I ever remembered seeing him, a far cry from the confident and optimistic achiever of earlier days. He was clearly worried and uncertain about his next move, and I had done my best to convince him that there was still time to have an impact, and that this was the right moment—perhaps his last chance—to seize the initiative with a positive bold scenario.

My main point was that there was opportunity in the crisis and that he should seize it. He should hit the ground running, mince no words about the difficulties confronting the nation, much of which he could blame on OPEC, and announce a dramatic response: a really tough energy-saving and anti-inflation program, calling on all Americans to close ranks behind him to meet a major challenge at a moment of national emergency. If done right, it might change the prevailing national mood of pessimism. There was political risk in asking for sacrifices, to be sure, but the risks of doing less were even greater, and for him there was a unique opportunity to demonstrate the kind of strong and determined presidential leadership Americans admired. The people, I said, were ready for it.

I had laid out a list of the specific moves he should consider— among them a dramatic billion-dollar synthetic fuels program, standby authority for gasoline rationing, easing or eliminating the red tape of gasoline allocation and price controls, a crash program of export promotion, a list of productivity-enhancing measures, and a tough austerity program with a renewed commitment to working toward budget balance, the impact of which on lower income groups would bed offset by proceeds from a windfall profit tax. Announcing the establishment of a small group of trusted advisors inside the White House to manage the process would give assurance to the outside that he meant business and was organized to follow through.

According to my diary notes: "we discussed the list and he seemed to like it. He asked me to give him a cleaned up version in

Washington, and mentioned that his speech was set for the evening of July 5th. I said that was great."

Air Force One was about to land, and that's how we parted. It was, as it turned out, the last time—but one—when the two of us would talk alone.

Jimmy Carter never gave that speech. Back in the capital, he had started things off with a large assembly of his advisors in the Cabinet Room, primarily as a "photo op" to underline the importance of his forthcoming speech, which the public now awaited anxiously. This had been followed by nonstop sessions of the working group, some in the president's presence, where I was disconcerted to note that the familiar arguments over the primacy of energy and inflation-fighting versus stimulating growth and counteracting unemployment had not abated. Even the date of the speech remained controversial, with Carter's political advisors finally winning the argument that he needed to speak out at once.

I had given Carter my list from Air Force One and by mid-week something like a near-final version had emerged and been shipped to him at his Camp David retreat. The thrust of my advice had been that he needed to do something dramatic, and apparently he had taken at least this element of my recommendations to heart—though not as I had intended. For what now ensued—little more than twenty-four hours before his scheduled address to the nation—would be one of the more astounding events of any recent presidency. Two hours after the draft had reached him, Carter reversed course and stunned his advisors and the public by abruptly canceling the much advertised speech while resisting all explanations for the decision.

The news hit like a bombshell. The story was that Carter had held a teleconference with the vice president, along with Ham Jordan, his principal assistant, and Gerald Rafshoon, his media advisor, simply called the whole thing off—and gone fishing. Nothing further could be learned.

None of us knew what was going on. The media reported that

for a day "the capital wallowed in mystery," and that the reaction of senior officials was "a mixture of consternation, dismay, resentment and laughter beyond tears." The universal view, according to these reports, was that the unexplained sudden cancellation had caused Carter further political damage and added to the administration's image of confusion and incompetence.[221] The air of mystery was reinforced a day later by an elliptical White House statement that nothing was known about the president's return to Washington, but that he was now "assessing broader domestic issues" and had asked Pat Caddell, his pollster, and Gerald Rafshoon, his media advisor, to join him and would consult with eight governors and other national leaders.

The unusual silence of the White House press office hadn't been helpful. What worried me particularly were the almost immediate negative international repercussions, with the dollar again taking a beating in foreign exchange markets. After being told that Carter was unavailable (the operator said he was taking a walk and couldn't be contacted), it had taken my insistence in the strongest terms to reach him some hours later and to clear a reassuring statement that "he intends to propose strong measures to restrain the U.S. demand for imported oil," which had precariously quieted things down.

Over the ensuing days, a steady stream of visitors—politicians, business leaders, academics, and assorted elder statesmen—had been ferried up to the presidential retreat at Camp David to offer their advice while, in the absence of an official explanation, leaks and rumors abounded about what was going on. The president was concerned about how to exert leadership in an era of cynicism, some visitors revealed. Others reported that he was unhappy with his Cabinet and staff and intended to make major changes. Here and there, the stories noted that the secretaries of energy; health, education and welfare; and the treasury, amongst others, were the primary candidates to go.

The public reaction to Carter's sudden cancellation of the much advertised speech proved uniformly negative, much as he had apparently been warned that it would be. Later the president himself recalled that a distraught Vice President Mondale had argued strenuously against it, a warning he had chosen to ignore.[222] An experienced Washington hand, the vice president obviously had a more realistic sense of the likely political downside, and Carter should have listened to him. Tom Wicker's comments in the *New York Times* that "Carter has reached the low point not only of his administration but perhaps of the postwar Presidency" and that "the cancellation was the worst PR blunder since Nixon's "Saturday Night Massacre'" were not atypical. The *Boston Globe* pronounced Carter "a disaster as a leader on energy," and Bill Safire, never an administration friend, gleefully devoted his column to "Carter's 4th of July Panic,"[223]

A *NYT/CBS* poll the following week reported bad news: Carter's approval rating had sunk to 26 percent. More than half of Democratic voters favored Senator Kennedy as their party's standard bearer in 1980 against only 16 percent for Carter. Reagan would beat him in a general election, and, most surprising of all, even the South—Carter's strongest bastion—was no longer behind him. In political and public relations terms, the speech cancellation and the week's spectacle of presidential consultations at Camp David was shaping up as a real disaster.

On July 11, Carter finally ended his Camp David retreat.

He had consulted with no fewer than 130 visitors; on the last day alone, forty had been helicoptered in and out in two shifts. No one knew precisely what he planned to say on energy, inflation, or anything else. Some reports were that he had been told bluntly he was being poorly served by his staff, and that big staff and cabinet changes were in the works.

Everything was now riding on the speech he was about to give, with as many as 80 million Americans expected to hear him. He had taken a big gamble, and no other speech of his presidency promised to be as important as this one. Given on July 15, a Sunday evening, the long-awaited speech was perhaps one of the strongest of his presidency but also one of the most unusual. The six-point energy program he announced was a good step forward, but though there was rousing rhetoric, nothing he called for was truly revolutionary and none of it required other than modest sacrifices from the public. To a degree, he had still hedged his political bets.

Most of his thirty-three-minute address hadn't been about energy at all, and historians remember it today as his "Malaise"—or more accurately—"Crisis of Confidence" speech (the word *malaise* was never mentioned). The more remarkable part of what he had to say dealt not with energy or inflation, but with his self-criticism as a leader and his promise to do better, and with a national "crisis of confidence." There was, he said, a "moral and spiritual crisis sapping the nation's faith in the future," with public pessimism and selfishness and "a loss of unity of purpose threatening to destroy the social and political fabric of America."[224] As proof, he had cited recent polls indicating that, for the first time, the majority of Americans believed that the next five years would be worse than the last five.

The reception to the speech was mixed. Democrats approved, and some were openly enthusiastic; Republicans, arguing that the crisis was largely of the president's own making, were predictably less so. From Carter's viewpoint, the best news was that opinion polls taken immediately afterward showed that the broader public had liked it, and that his approval rating had moved back into the low 30s.

My own reaction had been mixed as well. This time he had spoken with confidence and sounded strong and presidential, and I had liked his energy program, though I had hoped he would go even further. On his diagnosis of America's mood I had considerably more doubt, and the notion that America's sour mood implied a deeply-rooted fault line in the national psyche struck me as questionable. With rampant inflation, gas lines, and the threat of rising unemployment, pessimism about the future was hardly surprising and not necessarily a permanent phenomenon.

Sometime later Bill Roth, my friend and erstwhile Kennedy Round colleague, told me an interesting story. In his race for the Democratic nomination for California governor in 1975 (he came in fourth in a field of eight), he had employed Pat Caddell, who became president Carter's pollster, for a similar assignment. At the time, Caddell had reported precisely the same finding to Roth—that Americans "felt the future looked bleaker than the past." Carter's citation apparently had its origin in Caddell's rediscovery of this interesting fact "for the first time," four years later. Which proved something I had long suspected: pollsters are not immune to allowing their own prejudices and pet ideas to color their interpretation of poll results.

When admitting the administration's failures in his speech, the president had fleetingly referred to a lack of loyalty and discipline in his cabinet, which I had taken as confirmation that changes were in the offing. From Carter's perspective—to dramatize a new approach—I thought this neither surprising nor wrong. It's what presidents do at times like these. As for myself, I was ready to call it quits. Some months earlier I had independently concluded that my usefulness to the president was at an end and that I should leave. Our relationship had always been proper, even cordial. But the economy was in trouble, the internal-policy apparatus didn't work, and, given the circumstances, there wasn't much chance that this would change. Yet heretofore I had always hesitated to take the last step—partly out of loyalty to Carter and from the fear that to walk out while he was in trouble, eighteen months before his reelection campaign, was dishonorable and could be misinterpreted; and, frankly, partly because of personal pride. To resign was to confirm failure, an act to which I was unaccustomed.

The events at Camp David, as far as I was concerned, had been the final straw and steeled my resolve to go even if Carter wanted me to stay. Unable to speak to him personally, I had asked Cy Vance and Stu Eizenstat, who had each been called to Camp David, to alert Carter to my decision. Both promised to do so, even though they had also tried to persuade me to stay. Stu, I would learn later, had argued strongly to Carter that to allow me go was a mistake.

Following his speech, the president had called a cabinet meeting for the morning of Tuesday, July 17—principals only. When the president entered the Cabinet Room from the Oval Office at 10:30 that morning, the only non-cabinet member present was Ham Jordan, formally dressed for the occasion in a blue suit with tie. Something special was clearly in the works. The mood around the table was serious and solemn. No one knew what the president planned to do but he had, after all, let it be known publicly that he considered some of us disloyal. There was none of the usual lighthearted banter that often preceded cabinet meetings and as we sat in silence, Carter launched at once into a lengthy explanation of his absence.

He had divorced himself from contact with the cabinet, he said, to review the status of his administration and ponder needed changes. He had concluded that a new beginning had to be made, a "change of life," and that this would involve changes in his cabinet and staff. Looking at no one in particular and quite obviously ill at ease, he spoke of unspecified cabinet disloyalty with some of us not following the administration line, adding quickly that the staff also needed tightening. On this he planned to be ruthless: at least eight or ten staff would be fired, "whether from Georgia or not."

Then, launching into effusive praise of Ham, he announced that he was appointing him chief of staff to improve the functioning of the executive office. And finally, ending his twenty-five-minute monologue, came this bombshell: he wanted each of us to submit our resignation—in writing—and he would inform us in due course which he chose to accept. Then he asked for comments.

A moment of stunned silence followed. There was evident embarrassment around the table, not so much about what Carter had decided to do, as about the way he had justified it and proposed to proceed. Appointment of a chief of staff was certainly long overdue. Appointing Ham, however, was surprising and quite a gamble if Carter meant to bring order into the executive office's disarray. Ham was smart and enjoyed Carter's total trust, yet everyone knew—and Ham had often said so himself—that his talents lay in political strategy and not in orderly management. His monumental lack of discipline and disorganization in fact were legendary. Entrusting him to bring order into the White House policy-making process seemed a long shot.

That Carter had justified the cabinet changes on the basis of alleged disloyalties was equally puzzling. Except for a brief sharp exchange over some pronouncements by Andy Young, his UN ambassador, which Carter had quickly shut off, it had remained a charge left unexplained an uncomfortably dangling. I certainly had never heard anything like this from him directly and had no idea what specific instances he had in mind.

Of everything we had heard, however, his request for the formal resignation of the entire cabinet, en masse, was the most peculiar. When this news got out, it was certain to be misunderstood by the public. The effect, particularly abroad, could be especially damaging. Why a mass resignation when only a few were on his list? The reality was that he needed no such resignations at all, neither orally nor in writing. Did he not know that all of us served at his pleasure and could be asked to resign at any time?

Cy Vance was the first to speak up, assuring the president of the entire cabinet's fealty and pledging our full support. However, mass resignation, he urged, was unnecessary and not a good idea; individual resignations by those of his choosing was all that was needed. Whereupon gradually our silence and consternation gave way to a mixed chorus from around the table echoing similar sentiments. In different words, everyone pledged their loyalty and support, and a few hardy souls commented that an honest expression of divergent viewpoints in internal deliberations was healthy, and not evidence of disloyalty.

At this point the president excused himself, while Ham stayed behind to hand out questionnaires for our evaluations of the effectiveness of each of our own staffs. "And on this happy note," according to my diary, "we all left."

Two days later, at 1:30 P.M. on Thursday, July 19, I walked into the Oval Office for my last meeting with Jimmy Carter.

Later it struck me that in one important respect this meeting, formalizing my departure, was not dissimilar from the one in 1976 at which he had offered me the Treasury post. On both occasions our conversation was quite pleasant, yet devoid of the substance the occasion demanded. Then there had been no discussion of what he expected of me or the nature of our relationship. Now almost nothing was said about the reasons I was leaving and why we both agreed that the time had come to part company.

Greeting me cordially, an awkwardly smiling Carter had beckoned me into his inner office hideaway and, once I was seated on his couch, burst out without preliminaries, as if anxious to get the matter out of the way, that he accepted my resignation. In his memoirs, he confessed that he dreaded making the cabinet changes,[225] and I knew him well enough to see from his body language and his forced smiles that this was so. He was clearly intensely uncomfortable, but once I had responded that I agreed, that my offer to resign had not been pro forma and that I had independently resolved to go, he was visibly relieved, and the rest of our twenty-five-minute session was remarkably harmonious and relaxed.[226] Not a harsh word was uttered, there was nothing about "disloyalties," and no other unpleasantness was mentioned.

Even today—some thirty years later—my notes on our last meeting make wondrous reading given the circumstances. Only nice things were said and so many compliments were exchanged that an eavesdropper might have had difficulty understanding that we were saying our goodbyes. The president launched into a ten-minute accolade praising me as an excellent secretary who had done an outstanding job, expressed admiration for my character and the strength of my convictions, and complimented my policy judgments and advice to him as generally proper and correct. Amazingly, the reason he gave for letting me go, he said, was not policy differences or disagreements between us but rather some (unspecified) "friction with some of my staff." Some—only some—he had added hurriedly. Others, including those working on economic matters with me had actually urged him strongly not to let me go. So he had long hesitated and made his decision "in spite of their pleadings." "If Bill Miller"—the Federal Reserve Chairman whom Carter had asked to follow me as treasury secretary—"had turned me down," he concluded, "I would have asked you to stay." It was, to say the least, an astonishing statement.

Yet, I was greatly relieved. My main concern had been to leave a job I had found increasingly impossible to carry out. A harmonious departure suited me fine.

Thus we chatted amiably for a few minutes more. Carter said—as he often had—that he was "proud" of me and wished me luck for the future. I thanked him for the honor of having been allowed to serve, we touched briefly on the tough economic policy issues he faced, I urged him to trust my successor and give him his full support, and then I asked to be excused. "Can I count on your future advice?" Carter asked me in parting. "Will you be sure to come and see me when you're in town?" "Anytime, Mr. President," I replied as we shook hands for the last time, knowing full well that these were platitudes. "I'll come whenever you call."

Jimmy Carter hated the unpleasantness of personal confrontation and avoided such controversies at the cost of leaving much unsaid. Our last meeting, like many others, had been no exception. Both of us understood that even that final encounter had merely been polite, that our parting words had avoided the real issues. For me, and for others, it had often been that way from the beginning.

Now it was over. My service as the sixty-fourth secretary of the treasury had ended.

Looking Back

Jimmy Carter was an unlucky president. He had reaped the bitter fruits of past domestic policy errors, and had been the victim of adverse international developments beyond his control. His last year in office would be no different. In 1980, oil prices doubled and the economy worsened. In January, the Consumer Price Index (CPI) was rising at an annual rate of 18.2 percent and wholesale prices were up even more. In April, unemployment topped 7 percent, with over 7 million Americans jobless; by early summer another million had lost their jobs. The stock market was down and at $850 an ounce, the price of gold had reached dizzying heights.

Internationally, the Iranian hostage crisis added to the president's woes. At moments such as these, the public might have been expected to rally behind the president, yet as his dramatic rescue effort foundered in the Iranian desert, it had merely added to the public dismay over the seemingly helpless Carter. Worse yet, when Cy Vance, who had strongly opposed the raid, resigned, the administration's entire foreign policy had been put into question.

In the spring, as he began to gear up his reelection campaign, there was more bad news when Senator Ted Kennedy attempted to deny him the renomination and defeated him in the New York and Connecticut primaries, and in five of eight primary elections on Super Tuesday. The polls indicated that Ronald Reagan, his likely Republican opponent, was leading him nationally by twenty-eight points.

The news had improved somewhat in the fall. In August, Kennedy had thrown in the towel, the Democratic convention had renominated Carter, and inside his camp hope had risen that the president might yet snatch victory from defeat. But in the end, it all proved too late. Carter remained unlucky to the end, when a last-minute deal to free the hostages in Iran failed. Had it happened before the election rather than after, it surely would have swung some votes. Finally, Ronald Reagan, who had himself stumbled in the closing weeks of the campaign, had bested him in their last debate just days before the election by asking voters a potent question: "Are you better off than you were four years ago?"

That had sealed Jimmy Carter's fate. On November 4, the incumbent president who four years earlier had entered the White House so full of hope and confidence, lost his bid for reelection by a humiliating 10 million votes, and the electoral vote count had been even more decisive.

* * *

The U.S. presidency is unique. It is the most complex leadership job in the world, and there is no real preparation for it. Only the American president is at once head of state, chief executive of the government, and commander-in-chief of the most powerful nation on earth. To call the American president the leader of the free world may be somewhat overblown, but at least he is unquestionably its most important and influential voice.

To be successful as president, luck and fortuitous timing are always a factor, though not the only critical ones. Contrary to popular belief and the assertion of many candidates, even prior experience—whether as governor, legislator, mayor, or business executive outside Washington—isn't the key to success, and neither is management skill. Few politicians are natural-born managers, and many of our most successful presidents haven't been especially known for their superior management talents. Besides, the Oval Office incumbent doesn't really manage or run anything in the normal sense of the term, nor is running a business relevant experience for this unique job.

From my observation in close proximity to the White House, I have concluded that what matters most is neither prior experience nor management skills, but the right presidential personality, by which I mean his temperament—the sum total of the personal qualities a president brings to the job, the most important of which are inborn, cannot be learned, and are hard to predict in candidates for the office. The public cannot know them when casting their votes, and even the winning candidate, however self-confident he may be, cannot fully appreciate what awaits him.

To succeed in the presidency, the proof of the pudding is always in the eating, for which Harry Truman is perhaps the best case in point among modern White House occupants. When he was unexpectedly thrust into the job, most people considered him only modestly suited to the task. During his brief tenure as vice president no one had bothered to keep him informed about the critical issues of the day, and in his ten years in the Senate, his legislative achievements had not been especially noteworthy. Yet once in the White House, Truman rose to the occasion more ably than anyone thought possible. History ranks him today as one of the strongest and most effective presidents because he had the temperament of a leader.

He was tough, courageous, and—most important—realistic about both the uses and the limitations of his power. No great orator, he was nevertheless a folksy public speaker, effective in projecting a combination of simplicity and strength that impressed his audiences and left no doubt about his intentions. Internationally he had a clear eye for the military and economic components of rebuilding Europe and for organizing the Western alliance in the Cold War and, above all, the wisdom to choose proven advisors like Eisenhower, Marshall, and Acheson. In sum, to everyone's surprise, Harry Truman proved to be a strong presidential leader because, where it counted most, he had the right innate qualities and personality for the job.

A president is powerful only if he knows how to persuade and build consensus. He must know how to propose and advocate without overreaching, and he must understand his own limits and the people he needs to persuade. He must have a feel for when and how far to move ahead, and know when quiet negotiation in private is required and when to go public and use the "bully pulpit," for which some rhetorical skills and a talent for a degree of mystery and drama are important.

A winning presidential personality encompasses many things. Its essence, I believe, is an intuitive sense of power, writ large—by which I mean a feel for how things work; who and what is important; how to keep one's priorities straight; how to maneuver through the thicket of conflicting positions, interests, personal ambitions, and egos; and how to reach out and bring even some of his enemies to his side to achieve a desired result.

Inside the White House, the president lives in a kind of cocoon, and it takes a particular temperament not to become imprisoned by it. Knowing how to retain a sense of balance and realism in this isolated environment isn't easy. It requires the ability to distinguish fact from flattery, to build bridges to the outside world and the press, to have an ear for the national mood, and to be able and willing to digest divergent advice. For that it helps enormously to be a good "people person," to have an innate understanding of the people he deals with and to be skillful in interacting with them. Knowing how to choose, trust and rely on the right ones is critical.

A talent for framing the larger issues and defining concepts of his administration in understandable ways for a national and international audience is another important requirement, because the presidency involves both style and substance. Presidents have usually succeeded best when they have built on the inherent stature of the office by investing it with their individual brand of respect and charisma. To establish an image of competence, authority, and personal strength, and to impress and inspire are important parts of effective Oval Office leadership.

Few presidents considered successful by historians have been equally well-endowed with all of these personal attributes and skills. Teddy Roosevelt advanced his agenda with an image of fearless personal daring, his stewardship of America's natural resources, and by successfully projecting American power and energy toward the outside world. Woodrow Wilson galvanized the nation and the world with his vision of American leadership in establishing an international rule of law. Franklin Roosevelt had almost magical charisma, was second to none in knowing how to "get his ducks in a row," and stood out as a masterful public communicator. Dwight Eisenhower conveyed the aura of trusted hero and reassured the public with an instinct for orderly procedures learned over a lifetime in the military.

John Kennedy's administration was hardly a model of orderliness. But in his short time in the White House, he managed to inspire a whole generation with his oratorical elegance and wit. Ronald Reagan, on the other hand, was not as intellectually powerful nor as much of a hands-on president, but he knew how to delegate, had a few simple priorities that he pursued tenaciously, and could draw on his actor's knack as a public speaker. Bill Clinton, finally, didn't inspire personal trust in the mode of an Eisenhower, yet his innate capacity for radiating empathy with diverse groups of voters, his grasp of the essence of key issues, and his undeniably masterful political touch fit almost any audience or challenge.

The current Oval Office occupant, Barack Obama, though without long years of political experience, appears to be blessed with a larger number of requisite skills for a successful presidency than most. An inordinately skilled communicator, he exudes confidence and charisma. More than was true for most of his predecessors, his organizational instincts appear to be superior, and he has reflected this in the choice of his cabinet and experienced staff. As a former legislator, he has demonstrated a clear sense of the importance of good congressional relations and of reaching out to a wide variety of competing interests and constituencies. Perhaps as important as anything, he appears to be comfortable enough to surround himself with strong personalities and reflects an inner serenity of purpose in dealing with them.

Jimmy Carter is a good man with many admirable qualities and a superior intellect. As president, he had some noteworthy accomplishments, worked incredibly hard, and was diligent to a fault. Unfortunately, it was not enough, because Carter lacked the right combination of critical character traits essential for success in the Oval Office.

The principal themes of his election campaign (along with truthfulness) had been management competence and distance from Washington. But governing is different than running for office, and, ironically, it was precisely in these areas that he would make his biggest mistakes and suffer his greatest setbacks. Choosing a particularly ambitious agenda, and attempting to implement it without sufficiently understanding the political reality of his dependence on congressional leaders with different priorities, led to costly errors. Poor choices in the selection, organization and management of his White House staff caused him unneeded trouble in handling the inevitable crises any president faces. Reluctance to delegate lesser decisions to others and his proclivity to lose himself in details and to make too many decisions himself ultimately reinforced the image of confusion and contradiction that bedeviled him in office.

Carter thus was often his own worst enemy and lacked a realistic appreciation of his own limitations in his role as president. He was proud of his accomplishments as governor, but it took him a long time to understand that Atlanta and Washington are worlds apart, and that how he had operated in the state house was a formula for failure in the White House. As governor, yielding to his penchant for delving into the details of many issues may have worked, but as president it diverted him from a clear focus on those few critical decisions the chief executive must preserve for himself, and by which his administration will ultimately be defined and judged.

Time is a president's scarcest resource, but by insisting on involvement in the kinds of details he had apparently handled in Atlanta, and which in the White House are best left to others, Carter used his time badly. The evident pleasure it gave him to master such details, appears to have satisfied a deeply-ingrained psychological need. "Send me lots of memos," he had urged us at Sea Island, while brushing aside my gentle warning that the enormous responsibilities awaiting him were sure to put severe limits on his time and capacity to absorb them. In fact, shortly after taking office, he still confided to his diary how much he "enjoyed studying the paperwork."[227] As revealed in his later published *White House Diary*, he would note with satisfaction the time spent—not on the politics—but "the causes of abortion,"[228] or "the background of health legislation,"[229] and how much pleasure he derived from doing his own speech writing.[230] Opining on the correct diameter of Alaska pipe, becoming preoccupied with gas bubbles in nuclear reactor design, or focusing on the merits of relatively minor provisions of the tax code were all evidence of his innate need "to know as much as possible about the issues I must decide."[231] Even when telling himself to ease off—as his diary shows he occasionally did—it appears to have been inordinately difficult for him to do so.

Carter was often too sure of himself, and the understanding he thought he had gained from in-depth study of issues frequently hurt him more than it helped. Convinced of his deeper knowledge and the correctness of his goals, he was more inclined to explain and insist than to compromise and bend when the politics demanded it. When he thought he was right, taking half a loaf was difficult for him. Surprisingly for someone who had reached the highest office, he was not very good at the political nitty-gritty, more analyst than politician, more focused on the substance of issues than skilled at dealing with congressional leaders on whom he depended to translate his initiatives into law.

Nor was he a very successful "people person." Though unfailingly courteous, he was by temperament somewhat of an authoritarian, most at ease with those he could direct and who agreed with him. It is this, I believe, that caused him to rely on and cling to a predominantly young staff largely inexperienced in Washington's ways. He valued their unquestioning acceptance of what he wanted above all else. That, I think, is the main reason why he retained a pliant but weak congressional-relations and legal staff long after there was evidence of its deficiencies. Had he been more astute and realistic in this regard, the disaster of the Lance affair might well have been avoided and the functioning of the executive office substantially improved.

Convinced of their complete fealty and the correctness of his deeply-held beliefs, he depended on them, which appears to have insulated him from the realities of his situation more than we realized at the time. In his *Diary* there is plentiful evidence of his isolation regarding, among other matters, a realistic sense of his declining popularity, his standing with key members of Congress, and the relations among his cabinet members and with his staff.

Carter, finally, also lacked the charisma of some of his predecessors and was not a talented communicator. He neither trusted nor liked the media, considered interviews with key publications like *Newsweek* "a complete waste of time,"[232] and balked at attending the White House Correspondents Dinner,[233] something all presidents do. Serious, earnest, and fixated on details, he lacked the light touch and a helpful sense of humor. When he gave speeches, his timing tended to be a bit off, his delivery was flat, and sometimes he paused and smiled at the wrong moments. Jim Fallows, his speechwriter, called his elocution "passionless;" the influential political observer I. F. Stone thought "there was no music there." His advisors occasionally suggested that a speech coach might improve his performance, but Carter was said to have stubbornly resisted it.

He believed too many things all at once and never succeeded in convincing the public that he had worked out the deeply internalized conflict between his liberal desire to help America's working people and the less advantaged on the one hand, and his innate conservative instincts of frugality and balanced budgets, on the other. It was a part of his nature that he expected to achieve it all, promised too much, and raised expectations that could not be met. The appearance of contradictions and confusion was a direct consequence, and in the end it was this that contributed to history's judgment of Carter as president.

When friends want to know about my time with Carter, they often ask whether I enjoyed it. That, I usually tell them, is not the right question: the more relevant one is whether I think it was worth it, to which the answer is unequivocally affirmative.

Fritz Stern, a great historian, has made the point that involvement in contemporary events can provide useful perspectives for an understanding of history.[234] My lifelong interest in public affairs was motivated by similar considerations, and the experience of my two excursions to Washington and having an active role in government affairs bears it out. The Treasury years, in particular, gave me a unique perspective on people and events at the top of government, and were a particularly important learning experience, in part because setbacks during difficult moments are at least as instructive as successes during good times.

An inside view of decision making at the centers of power in Washington and other world capitals taught me above all that in history very little is preordained. Observing the president of the United States at work showed me that in the interplay of many outcome-determining factors it is the personalities and temperaments of those who hold power that are the most important.

The Carter experience also taught me that fundamental change—Jimmy Carter would have called it "comprehensive"—is difficult to achieve in government, and exceedingly rare. In spite of the sweeping promises of most candidates for high office, voters would do well to remember that, except in rare instances, only incremental and gradual progress on major public policy issues is usually in the cards.

On most Thursdays at noon, the president had a standing luncheon appointment with his top economic team. These sessions taught me one other critical lesson: the information available for presidential decision making is not always dependable, and his power to affect the course of events is often more limited than is believed.

The first order of business usually involved Charlie Schultze, the CEA Chairman, laying out the latest statistics, forecasts, and computer runs—a likely tenth of a percent change here, or two-tenths there—in those days, mostly in the wrong direction. When invited to comment, I would often remind the president that these forecasts were only as good as the models simulating the past on which they were based, and that they might or might not be totally relevant in the special circumstance we faced. My point was that we needed to guard against the illusion of spurious accuracy, which could lead us astray. Sometimes I would then cite "anecdotal evidence," gleaned from the Treasury's Wall Street and international sources, suggesting a different (and usually more dire) future scenario. Carter always listened attentively, yet I was pretty certain that given his engineer's fondness for "precise" numbers, Charlie Schultze's statistics meant more to him than my qualifying "war stories" intuition.

The point is not that I was smarter, but that the facts and statistics on which a president's advisors base their recommendations for economic policy decisions are not always as certain and determining as they seem. Their advice almost always needs to be seen as the informed guesswork, hunches, and personal prejudices they reflect, especially in extraordinary times. It was Jimmy Carter's misfortune that his time in the Oval Office occurred at such a moment.

THE EIGHTIES
Globalism

Technological Change

More often than not, historical accident determines who has political power at critical moments and makes those key decisions that determine the course of events. Who the leaders are, and how wisely they govern and choose their advisors, depends on their character, temperament, and leadership qualities. Which is why even seminal historical developments are rarely preordained and hard to predict. The late historian Arthur Schlesinger Jr. called this "the inscrutability of history."

There is, however, one critical exception to those with their hands on the levers of power taking a central role in shaping history, and it occurs when human affairs are powerfully affected by exogenous events that have nothing to do with political decision makers and are quite beyond their control. The prime example with lasting historic consequence of this sort of development is revolutionary technological change. The pace of scientific discovery and technological innovation has its own rhythms. Major breakthroughs just happen, and when they do, they can change history in ways as dramatic as any decision by political leaders. The 1980s were such a time.

James Watt's eighteenth-century invention of the steam engine and subsequent advances in manufacturing led to the Industrial Revolution, which rendered obsolete traditional societies based on agrarian and handicraft economies, opened an entirely new era of human history, and brought on changes with far-reaching political and social consequences for Western societies. New wealth was created, living standards rose, and the conditions of life improved for many, though the revolution also caused new problems and ushered in a period of transition fraught with uncertainty and instability. International power relationships shifted, and Britain emerged as the most powerful nation on earth.

Some two hundred years later, the revolution in electronic technology during the closing decades of the twentieth century was a similar exogenous event beyond the control of politicians. In its deep and permanent impact on human history, it dwarfed even the significance of the two world wars and Hitler's devastating brief rule. It too ushered in a period when path-breaking new knowledge resulted in both enormous advances in our lives, but also troubled times and unsettling instabilities and upheavals.

The globalization of human affairs is the direct result of revolutionary developments in microelectronics that spawned a sea change in how we think, produce, and trade, and how knowledge is generated, disseminated, and used. Microelectronics effectively ended the industrial era and propelled the world toward today's Information Age, permanently making obsolete whole industries and creating entirely new ones virtually overnight. Leaving no corner of the globe untouched, reordering the world economy and reshuffling the entire geopolitical order, it caused a revolution in human affairs that can justifiably be called "the mother" of history-shaping exogenous happenings.

Its origins go back to the years following the Second World War, when a series of interconnected inventions and new technologies—transistors, printed circuit boards, modems and silicon wafers—gave birth to the modern electronic computer. But the true quantum jump in technological change only occurred in the late seventies and eighties with the introduction of the microprocessor—the "computer on a chip," which can perform billions of calculations per second and transmit information to any place in the world with the speed of light. This is the device at the heart of our networked world of today.

During the eighties I led one of the world's major information systems companies at the cutting edge of these developments, and as CEO of the Burroughs Corporation (later Unisys), I became closely involved in many of these dramatic events. Traveling the world as globalization was spreading brought me into contact with political and business leaders in the major countries of Europe, the Soviet Union, the Middle East, and Asia, and made me a witness to the many ways in which they coped with the avalanche of breathtaking changes.

The globalizing effects of perhaps the greatest technological revolution in history weren't at first appreciated, but by the end of the eighties most people had grasped their full implications. I recall the moment, far away in China's interior, when my own eyes were first opened to what was happening.

In 1981, on a business trip to China, I had stopped off in Hefei, the capital city of Anhui Province. With some 65 million inhabitants, Anhui is large—about the size of France—but one of the poorer interior provinces and infrequently visited by tourists. I was there at the invitation of Zhang Jingfu, China's former minister of finance and my principal interlocutor in Treasury days. Subsequently promoted to provincial party secretary, he was then Anhui's undisputed boss.

The invitation to be his guest in Hefei had been a gesture of friendship, which I had gladly accepted. Following an elaborate welcoming banquet, Zhang, ever the good host, had inquired after my wishes. Perhaps, he thought, I might like to tour the city or see some new factories. When I instead suggested a trip into the surrounding countryside, he readily agreed and in the morning we set out in his limousine, accompanied by a mini-caravan of officials and guards. Three years had passed since the beginning of Deng's reforms and I was seeing the first evidence of big changes in Beijing and the coastal areas. Now I was curious about any signs of change in the more distant countryside where the bulk of the Chinese population lived (and, thirty years later, still does).

On the surface it seemed that nothing much had changed. The fields looked exactly as I remembered them from the old days—rice paddies intersected by muddy footpaths as far as the eye could see, and straw-hatted men, women, and children bent over their back-breaking work, ankle-deep in paddy water. Here and there a buffalo lashed to a waterwheel was trudging around in circles—a time-honored irrigation technique—but no other labor-saving machinery of any kind was in sight. The landscape was dotted with the traditional simple mud and bamboo farm houses next to small enclosures that held the occasional pig wallowing in the dirt and a few chickens and ducks pecking at the ground. For an old "China hand" it had a familiar feel to it, and was as far from modernity as much of China's vast countryside had always been.

An elderly man puffing on a long-stemmed pipe was squatting on the ground in front of a house visible from the road, and when I suggested we make our way over to talk to him, Zhang had agreed, though without much enthusiasm. The Chinese like planning things out for important visitors to avoid embarrassing surprises. This clearly hadn't been programmed, but since there was no gracious way to refuse me, he led the way up the foot path to the old man's home.

After admiring a small boy, a grandson whom the old man was guarding, and exchanging opening pleasantries, I asked how life was treating him these days. The answer: "good, better than a few years ago," visibly pleased the smiling Zhang. In the China of my youth, most country folk were illiterate and lived a pretty restricted life, their knowledge of the outside world largely limited by the distance they could walk or pedal to the nearest village or market town. The area had been electrified, which denoted some progress, and to probe a little further I asked whether he had a radio, which I thought might be a small indicator of progress. The old man brightened up visibly, and suggested that I do him the honor of coming into the house to see for myself.

The single room had a familiar look to it. The furnishings were sparse and basic: a table, a few chairs, a coal stove for cooking, and two simple wooden platforms with blankets and quilts for sleeping.

THE EIGHTIES | 337

A calendar, some calligraphy posters, and a Mao photograph adorned the walls. That was about it, except for an elaborately embroidered curtain draped over one wall. "No radio!" our host announced dramatically as he pulled the cover aside, revealing—a television set!

He had obviously wanted to surprise me, and TV in these surroundings had certainly been the last thing I expected. "Does it work well?" I asked, which produced the real shocker. For, as he turned it on with a flourish, there appeared—just at that moment—the familiar face of none other than ABC White House correspondent Sam Donaldson firing questions at the U.S. president as he boarded his helicopter—dubbed into Chinese!

Standing in that little one-room Chinese farmhouse thousands of miles away from Washington, and watching our host exposed to a U.S. news report, was an eye-opening moment I have never forgotten. This was 1981. In the United States, personal computers were just making an appearance. Only three years earlier, China had still been largely shut off from the outside world, and an illiterate Anhui farmer was unlikely even to have seen a photograph of the world beyond China's borders or, for that matter, of much outside his immediate orbit. The world, I realized, was changing and would never again be the same!

The rapid evolution of microelectronics made the eighties perhaps the historically most important decade of the century. The new technology proved an important factor in the demise of the tottering Soviet Empire, ended the Cold War, and reordered the world's geopolitical map. Beginning in the eighties, it became the basis for the astonishingly quick rise of China as a major economic factor in world affairs, with India soon to follow. The rapid spread of AIDS across the world, and the subsequent breakthroughs in containing and treating that scourge would similarly have been unlikely in the absence of the impact of the new technology on travel and communication on the one hand, and on revolutionary advances in medical science on the other.

The eighties were the time when the effects of this, the twentieth century's great triumph in human inventiveness and ingenuity, first became apparent, yet they were also troubled years when new violence threatened world peace. The transition to the Information Age produced uncertainties and upheavals worldwide. The Soviet Union became embroiled in a losing war in Afghanistan, and there were the first stirrings of Muslim fundamentalism and the threat of terrorism, with repercussions that remain a major source of instability to this day.

The Mighty Microchip

The foundation for the microchip revolution had been laid at the dawn of the computer age a half century before.

Man's efforts to devise mechanical computing machines are at least 300 years old, but electronic computing was born only in the Second World War, the result of a top secret, eighteen-month, round-the-clock effort at the University of Pennsylvania to utilize electronic technology for calculating trajectory tables for artillery shells. What emerged was a monster machine the scientists dubbed Electronic Numerical Integrator and Computer, best remembered by its acronym ENIAC—a 60,000-pound colossus that occupied the floor space of a medium-sized house and required a team of six operators to keep it running. For the switching of electronic signals, a task performed today by a "chip" no larger than a small fingernail, the ENIAC utilized no fewer than 18,000 vacuum tubes, generating so much heat that a prodigious system of ventilation had to be devised to cool them. Though probably apocryphal, the story is told that its 100,000-watt power requirements were so great that the lights of the entire city of Philadelphia dimmed every time ENIAC was switched on.

The early consensus was that the use of this exotic invention would remain largely confined to scientific purposes only. No one remotely suspected that the ENIAC, or its postwar improved version, UNIVAC, marked the dawn of a new age, and that within little more than a generation computers would become an indispensable tool in factories and offices around the world; be embedded in the most advanced devices in laboratories and hospitals and the most mundane ones in the home; monitor our automobiles and guide us to the moon—or that schoolchildren barely six years old would be taught to use them to learn and to play.

The computer age can be said to have begun in earnest in the early sixties, when IBM abandoned electromechanical tabulating technology and brought its first transistorized (solid state) computer to the marketplace. Transistors replacing the cumbersome vacuum tubes were the first major breakthrough, but over the next years several parallel technological improvements followed, among them printed circuit boards and Bell Labs' development of the modem, a device to carry digital data over phone lines that revolutionized computer communication and allowed terminals to be placed anywhere. Probably the most critical step forward was the development of the semiconductor—combining multiple transistors on a single silicon wafer "chip" by means of photolithography—which, among other things, eliminated the unwieldy cabling in earlier machines.

It was at the beginning of the seventies, however, that the next giant leap forward occurred with the introduction of microprocessors, the heart and soul of all modern computers to this day. Building on the advances of previous years, chip manufacturers had perfected the technique of doubling the number of transistors on a single chip every eighteen months, thereby greatly boosting the capabilities and speed of the circuits embedded in them and building in enough memory and logic to enable the tiny chip to do all the processing of a full-sized computer.

The rapidity of improvements in chip performance in the seventies was mind-boggling. Intel's first microprocessor. introduced in 1971, and consisting of 2,300 transistors capable of executing forty-five instructions per second, had been greeted as a near-sensation. Less than ten years later, the number of transistors embedded in a single chip had risen to 134,000, and by the end of the eighties to well over a million. A few years later, Intel's Pentium microprocessor had no fewer than 5.5 million transistors crammed on it, as part of an unending expansion of capabilities that still continues. Today chips can store a vastly greater amount of memory, process billions of instructions in fractions of a second, and communicate them to anywhere in the world with the speed of light.

It was these constant path-breaking technological improvements that were the key to the rapid expansion of the computer industry in the seventies and beyond. Just as I was learning about the computer business at Burroughs, the confluence of ever more powerful and versatile microprocessors and major software improvements led to the introduction of the personal computer (PC), and the advent of the "networked" world as we know it today. PCs that equaled or exceeded the performance of earlier big mainframe systems became affordable in every office, home and schoolroom, and the simultaneous appearance of a standard, easy-to-use operating system greatly expanded their usability and appeal to vast numbers of ordinary users. Invented by Bill Gates and his partner Paul Allen, the operating system generated a flood of new applications for every conceivable purpose and allowed all PCs to be compatible and connected to one another. It also made Gates's company, Microsoft, one of the fastest growing companies, and Gates one of the richest men in the world.

PCs changed everything, and the microchip became a ubiquitous device embedded in "smart" cards—in retailing, e-commerce, and video games. It also brought on the everyday use of cell phones throughout the world and spawned a revolution in navigational technology, medical diagnostics, and myriads of other things. Most importantly, PCs and microprocessors became the key to the development of the Internet and today's World Wide Web.

New Corporate Challenges

The phone call from Detroit inviting me to audition for Burroughs was a big surprise. Relaxing in Hawaii after leaving the Treasury, I had no clear idea what I wanted to do next. Through accident more than design, my professional life had evolved in roughly equal ten-year stints in the three quite different arenas of academia, industry, and government. Accumulating worldly riches had never been my primary ambition, and twice I had willingly foregone a generous corporate income and its perks for the humble remuneration of public service. What had mainly driven me had been the memory of the refugee years with their fears and frustrations—the sense of being powerless to control and shape my own life, to desire to prove myself and to be recognized for it. For me, like others, these early experiences had marked me with a lifelong "refugee mentality" fueling my ambitions. What I wanted above all was what I had once missed so deeply: to be able to control my own destiny and to gain the status and recognition that results from being in charge and making a difference. My greatest satisfaction had come from having the power to build things, to set goals and lead big groups of people. Weighing my options for the future, I realized that this was still important to me.

There were opportunities to turn in many directions. I had already heard from corporate headhunters, and the nation's leading impresario of the VIP lecture circuit was eager to book me on a national speaking tour with promises of handsome honoraria. Several publishers had offered advances for a book on the Carter administration; there had been feelers about corporate board appointments and inquiries about my interest in academic administration. All this I had filed away, but now that Burroughs was pressing for a quick reaction, a choice had to be made.

Giving speeches would be a temporary diversion at most, and writing a "tell-all" book on Carter I rejected as dishonorable. What I did best was managing and running things, and in that regard academic administration had its appeals but also its drawbacks. I had seen at Princeton that the petty jealousies of campus politics can be nastier than the maneuverings of corporate executives, and that there is more than a grain of truth to the facetious explanation that it's because "the stakes are so low." Nor was academic administration particularly well-paid in those days, which was frankly also a more than negligible factor.

I had accumulated a modest financial cushion at Bendix, but three years on the government payroll had made a substantial dent in it. While at the Treasury we had maintained homes in Washington and Ann Arbor and put our three daughters through college, but two were still doing graduate work, and Jane, our youngest, was thinking about medical school, which meant at least six more years of considerable expense. And it was also time to think about our retirement finances, since my checkered career hadn't kept me in any job long enough to accumulate meaningful pension rights.

The single most important decision, however, was not about my work but my marriage, which had been in disarray for some time. Eileen and I had been together for twenty-eight years, which is quite a long time. We had fallen in love when barely out of our teens, raised three great daughters, and for much of that time lived comfortably in a relationship free of serious disagreements. She had supported me loyally along the way, and I had reciprocated in backing her in her own professional interests, leading to a doctorate in educational psychology.

In some ways, it was a familiar story. In our fifties we were no longer the same as we had been at twenty, and gradually a lot was no longer being said between us. A typical midlife crisis perhaps, and much of it probably my fault, but I was feeling the void more and more, and I think she did too. In Washington we had lived apart on and off, which hadn't solved anything. Our grown daughters were out of the house, but there was still a strong bond between us, and the idea of a failed marriage depressed me.

Some weeks and several visits to Detroit later, Eileen and I made two fateful decisions. One was that I would accept the Burroughs offer. The other was that we would return together to Ann Arbor and give mending our marriage another try. In this, sadly, we failed. After shared memories and many years together, no breakup is free of pain, guilt, and regrets. Ours, at least, was devoid of mean-spiritedness and rancor, for which I will always be grateful.

In time, each of us moved on, the wounds healed and good things happened. Eileen's post-divorce life has been extraordinary. In the eighties she served with distinction in Nepal and Romania as one of the Peace Corps' oldest volunteers, for which she received well-deserved national recognition. Recently she has been deeply involved in development work in Africa and Central America. And, with the births of our eight grandchildren, she has been as devoted a grandmother as she has been a mother. We are still fond of each other and remain friends.

My own personal life evolved no less positively, though in a rather different way. In 1983, I fell in love with and married a remarkable young Californian. Our son, Michael Edward, was born three years later. Barbara and I have been married thirty years now, and, though a generation apart, we were soul mates from the start and raising a son added a special dimension to our lives. Beginning a new family wasn't an easy decision, so the pleasures of our threesome over these many years have made our successful union all the sweeter.

Bright, personable, levelheaded, and beautiful, trained as a computer scientist with a doctorate in business management, Barbara has been a wonderful companion and mother, while building her successful career as university teacher and management consultant. In the course of my life there have been some setbacks, but a lot more lucky and unexpectedly good things have happened as well. Barbara and Michael, and his three half-sisters, Ann, Jill, and Jane, have been the greatest gifts of all.

Eileen and I returned to Michigan at the end of 1979 and I joined Burroughs, a computer manufacturer and information services company. It has occurred to me that the two Michigan companies I worked for—one in the late sixties and the other in the eighties—are excellent paradigms for the technological upheavals of those decades.

In some ways the companies were rather similar. Roughly equal in size, both Bendix and Burroughs were Detroit-based with deep roots in the community. Executives of both companies were part of the local business establishment and sat side by side on the key community boards and committees. Their headquarters were less than five miles apart, and attesting perhaps to the insularity of Detroit, four Bendix directors also served on the Burroughs board.

The differences, however, were greater than the similarities. Bendix was a typical large industrial company, and had symbolized the pre-eminence of U.S. manufacturing multinationals from the fifties to the seventies. "Motown" was at the center of the Midwestern belt of U.S. industrial manufacturing stretching from Wisconsin to Ohio, and the top executives of Bendix's key customers—Ford, GM and Chrysler—were among the country's best known and most respected business leaders. It was no accident that it had been Henry Ford II who in 1976 had assembled the nation's leading CEOs and presided over the proceedings at the 21 Club in New York where I had first met Jimmy Carter.

When I joined Burroughs over a decade later, the situation had fundamentally changed. U.S. industrial manufacturers like Bendix remained in traditional businesses that were growing slowly—some production was being shifted overseas, profit margins were tight, and foreign competition was making inroads into their traditional markets. Detroit was feeling the effects, and the signs were hard to miss. The city's infrastructure was crumbling, abandoned factory buildings stood empty, industrial jobs were scarce and unemployment high. Those Detroiters who could afford it had fled to the suburbs or left Michigan altogether, and the population was shrinking.

The reality was that by 1980, high-tech electronics had replaced manufacturing and "metal-bending" as the most dynamic and profitable sector of the economy. California's Silicon Valley and similar high-tech enclaves in Arizona and Texas were booming, and the center of gravity was shifting from the "rust belt" to the "sun belt." While automakers and industrial companies like Bendix were downsizing and cutting employment, it was companies like Burroughs, a computer and information systems provider, who were the rising stars. By the end of the eighties, many of the industrial giants who had led the Fortune 500 list in the sixties—steel companies, rubber manufacturers, and metal fabricators—had disappeared from the top and been replaced by electronic powerhouses like Xerox, Hewlett-Packard, and others. IBM, the world's largest computer company, was firmly established among the half dozen of America's biggest and most profitable corporations. Tom Watson, its boss, and Andy Grove, the guiding spirit of Intel, where the ever-more powerful semiconductors that fueled the electronic revolution were being developed, had displaced Henry Ford as America's most admired CEO's.

As world-wide shipments of computer systems more than tripled or quadrupled in the seventies, Burroughs had also expanded rapidly. The history of the company went back to the early years of the century. Once a manufacturer of electromechanical calculators and accounting machines, Burroughs had successfully made the transition into electronics and gradually transformed itself into a computer company marketing its brand of mainframe systems across the world.

Many companies—giants like GE and RCA—had tried to do the same but found IBM's competitive advantage too formidable and abandoned the field. That Burroughs had succeeded was largely due to long-time CEO Ray Macdonald, a man with the right instincts and background to make the risky technical bets that had successfully converted a medium-sized enterprise into a multi-billion dollar multinational corporation. By 1980, Burroughs was among the largest U.S. computer companies and one of the seventy-five top corporations in the country.

I knew Ray from Bendix days and had admired his work, though his was a familiar story: as he aged, and as the company became very large, it outgrew him and he became a victim of his own success. Managing a multi-billion dollar, far-flung enterprise requires different skills than building a much smaller one. CEOs tend to repeat themselves, and what once worked well no longer met the company's critical needs in a changing marketplace. Ray had run into the same problem. A martinet who tolerated no disagreement and preferred to make all decisions himself, he had eventually lost control over the company's increasingly more complex operations and made costly mistakes in the fast-moving computer field.

Most of all, when he retired there was no one ready to take his place because he had left behind relatively weak management more accustomed to following his orders than to leading. Problems accumulated, growth threatened to stall, and the concerned board cast around on the outside for someone to take the helm just as the news broke that I had left the Treasury. Somehow they had concluded that I might be the solution to their problem and offered me the job.

My immersion into the computer world at a particularly fateful time opened up another exciting new chapter in my life. I was back doing what I liked best—managing a big organization in need of change—and, unexpectedly soon after my departure from the inner circles of Washington, I was in another industrial leadership position. Having fought a losing economic policy battle inside the administration and been fired by an unpopular president hadn't hurt a bit—it had actually enhanced my standing within the business and financial community. One indicator was the large number of offers to join the boards of major corporations and financial institutions, from which I ultimately chose those of Equitable Life Assurance Company and the Chemical Bank, Pillsbury and Tenneco corporations. The Business Council and Roundtable, the nation's two top corporate leadership groups, inducted me as a member; Princeton reinstated me as trustee; and the Council on Foreign Relations in New York elected me to their board, which allowed me to continue pursuing my interest in international affairs. At various times during the decade I also became involved in several bilateral business groups, among them those of U.S.–Japanese and U.S.–Brazilian businessmen. As chairman of a group of private U.S. defense experts, Sovietologists, and corporate executives I led several delegations to Moscow for discussion of Cold War issues with Soviet officials. In short, even as I became an insider in the exploding world of electronics, I also found myself in a central place for witnessing the effects of the ongoing technological revolution on world events.

My first challenge, however, was at Burroughs. The company needed new ideas, a sharper focus, and a faster reaction to the rapidly changing market for its products. Key decisions had to be made about product strategies, R&D budgets, marketing; field support programs, and new management blood. Within the first year, we recruited several new senior executives, made decisions about new products, refocused R&D spending, revamped field operations, and launched cost savings programs, supplemented by key acquisitions to strengthen our product offerings and operational capabilities. The most pivotal move, however, was the 1986 merger of Burroughs with Sperry Corporation, one of our mainframe competitors. With the resulting newly named Unisys Corporation, a major step was taken to double our size and add critical mass in a fiercely competitive marketplace, while significantly reducing the new Unisys's cost base.

Purely in terms of the financial results, these moves proved quite positive for much of the eighties. Annual revenues had doubled by the mid-eighties, and by the end of the decade doubled again to a respectable $10 billion. Profits, which in 1980 had been an anemic $134 million, reached a peak of almost one billion toward the end of the decade, and in the company's best year, per share profits had virtually tripled from 1980 levels.

Still, the numbers do not tell the entire story. With the rapid pace of technological change, most large computer companies, including IBM, remained for too long intent on developing ever more powerful mainframes, without appreciating the potential of a networked world of personal computers. Unisys fell into the same trap, and all such companies had to go through a difficult process of adjustment to come to terms with PCs. Many actually failed and disappeared. Unisys survived the shakeout (though it is a very different and much smaller company today)—which indicates that perhaps we made more right decisions than wrong ones. That is something that not all computer companies who prospered until the eighties can say.

Turbulent Times

The rapid spread of microchip technology during the eighties created the basis for significant advances in living standards and greater political freedom for millions, but the beginning was unusually turbulent. In the early years nothing seemed to be going well.

Early on, three sensational attempts on the lives of world leaders, one of them fatal, shocked the world. President Reagan was seriously wounded in Washington, as was Pope John Paul II in Rome. In Cairo,

Egypt's Anwar Sadat died under assassins' bullets while watching a military parade.

In the United Kingdom, Jim Callaghan's Labor Government had lost power in 1979, a year before Jimmy Carter was swept from office. In France the next year, Giscard's center-right administration was turned out by the voters, and soon thereafter Helmut Schmidt's Social Democrats were ousted in Germany. Some noted that the malaise that Jimmy Carter had diagnosed for the U.S. seemed to have spread to the rest of the world.[235]

The situation in the Middle East had also become highly complex. Revolution in Iran, the assassination of Sadat, the Soviet invasion of Afghanistan, and the Iran–Iraq war pitting Sunni against Shia was stirring Muslim fundamentalism and threatened to destabilize the entire region. The Arab–Israeli peace process remained at an impasse. At the same time, OPEC price policies were having a significant negative impact on virtually all Western economies.

With Carter's successor, Ronald Reagan, installed in the White House, the U.S. economy continued to be battered by high oil prices and stagflation. Unemployment in 1981 was at 7.8 percent and interest rates were in the double digits; a year later real rates (after inflation) were still at a historic high. The public was unhappy, and the pundits were saying that, with productivity low and U.S. factories being outdone by Japan, America had lost its postwar industrial leadership edge. While Detroit struggled, Japanese and other foreign car imports were up by 20 percent. Nor were general domestic affairs in the best of shape. Race riots wracked Miami, and U.S. prisons were overflowing. Murders were at a historic high and Beatles star John Lennon's killing outside his apartment building in New York shocked the nation. Over the previous ten years, the number of murder victims in the United States was almost five times as high as the number of U.S. soldiers killed in Vietnam.[236]

Economic growth in Europe was also sluggish. As the OPEC cartel, strengthened by a belligerent Iran, pushed up the world price of oil, the resulting currency dislocations and the falling dollar were harming European exports and putting the international system under pressure. Yet, amid much finger-pointing, a consensus for coordinated action was lacking. Protectionist sentiment grew on both sides of the Atlantic, Americans and Europeans squabbled over imported steel, and Japan was under pressure to restrict its burgeoning car exports.

The West's problems paled, however, compared to those faced by the Soviet Union and its satellites. In Eastern Europe economic growth had slowed even more markedly than in the West. Productivity was low, pollution horrific, and living standards stagnant or declining. With inadequate domestic capital formation, Eastern Europe's hard currency indebtedness to the West had soared.

In the Soviet Union, the strains of the Afghan war and of an inflated defense budget and heavy subsidies for inefficient industries were severe. The major problem was that, while in the Western free market economies the difficult process of restructuring to adjust to high energy costs and to take advantage of new technologies got under way, the centralized command economies of the East were falling further behind. The reason was simple: a key prerequisite was flexibility and access to the free flow of information lacking under Communism. The thought was not lost on the people behind the Iron Curtain, and gradually the signs of political restlessness in the USSR and its client states multiplied.

Yet with Ronald Reagan in the White House, the Cold War showed no signs of abating. The consensus was that the Soviet threat was as real as ever, and as late as in April 1984, a Pentagon study asserted that a very large armament imbalance in favor of a Soviet Union bent on world domination remained a fact of life. Cold War rhetoric was heating up, Reagan spoke of an "evil empire,"[237] raising the specter of Soviet military power, and the outlook for détente seemed dim. In the Soviet Union there was serious worry about a U.S. nuclear attack.

In a lead article in *Foreign Affairs* in the spring of 1981, George Ball, surveying the international landscape and lamenting this state of affairs, reflected the sour mood of the U.S. foreign policy establishment. After four years of the ineffectual Carter and with little confidence in his successor, George noted with dismay that America's friends were questioning America's capacity for leadership or, for that matter, for managing its own affairs. "At a time when the Soviet Union was systematically extending its military reach," he wrote, the United States "was falling into apathy and incompetence . . . No longer did we display the mastery of events that had given confidence in our economic and political leadership." As Ball saw it, "the most notable development of the period was the decline of America's standing with its friends and allies—and, indeed, with other non-Communist nations."[238] For the usually positive-minded and level-headed Ball, these were unusually atrabilious statements, uncharacteristic for someone whose mantra had always been that "optimism is the only serviceable hypothesis for the practical man."

George was of the generation of Americans who had come of age when the Allies defeated Nazi Germany and Imperial Japan and America emerged from the war as the strongest and most prosperous nation on earth. This generation firmly believed in the framework of international institutions created after the war, and many of them had played a big role in fashioning the Atlantic alliance. As a close friend and ally of Jean Monnet, "the father of Europe," George had steadfastly argued for U.S. support of European economic unity, often in the face of vociferous domestic opposition. With a clear sense of the U.S. interests that mattered most, he had eventually prevailed by stressing the larger longterm benefits to U.S. prosperity, and the security from the Western trading system that would flow from economically integrated and more viable Common Market economies. The reduction of trade barriers in the Kennedy Round of the sixties, in which the United States had led the way, had been an expression of what in the end had turned out to be a highly successful U.S. policy initiative, in which he had played a major part and of which he was justifiably proud.

In the adult experience of his generation, in war and in peace, Europe had always been the main focus, and since 1945 containing an aggressive Soviet Union had been the central preoccupation of U.S. foreign policy. "If we don't lead, nobody else will," I had often heard it said in Washington. It evidently pained and puzzled George that suddenly the members of the Alliance were quarreling among themselves and that U.S. leadership was faltering and being questioned—for which he put much of the blame on Washington's sins of omission and commission over recent years.

In part he was correct, yet with the benefit of historical experience, even the usually farsighted Ball was too much a prisoner of his past experience. Like virtually everyone else, he couldn't yet see that the problem lay not only in U.S. policies or weak leadership, but in emerging forces leading to a very different world.

A few years later, in 1987, I would in the Root Lectures at the Council on Foreign Relations make the driving force of the microchip revolution the central focus of my remarks, laying out some of its probable globalizing effects and economic and political consequences.[239] By then, only five years after my eye-opening visit to Anhei Province, economic growth in China was becoming a significant factor in world trade and commerce. The political implications were becoming clearer, and I recall that George Ball was an attentive listener in the audience.

The Troubled Middle East

As it happened, this was also a time when my travels on government missions and private business took me regularly to the Middle East, a part of the world rapidly becoming a major new focus of U.S. foreign policy concerns. On two separate occasions, it had thrust me into the middle of two major regional crises and in direct involvement with several of the key protagonists, including the Shah of Iran and Israeli Prime Minister Menachem Begin.

Given the geopolitical accident that much of the world's petroleum reserve lies under Middle East desert soil, assuring reliable access to this vital resource has been of paramount U.S. interest for almost a century. Protecting Israel's security in a hostile environment has been a parallel U.S.-policy constant in the postwar years. The region has rarely been completely stable and at peace, yet for at least the first quarter century after World War II, as the once dominant British and French influence in the region waned, maintaining good relations with whatever feudal rulers and tribal chieftains held sway there (and keeping Soviet influence out) had succeeded without great difficulty. Occasionally, when Western interests appeared to be at risk—as in 1953 when the irascible nationalist Mohammed Mosaddeq had come to power in Iran—a combination of direct pressure and covert action had neutralized the perceived threat.

I had first visited the Middle East in 1956, spending two months on a Princeton research project in Iraq, with side trips to Syria and Lebanon, and I had made a memorable journey of discovery to the new nation of Israel. The Arab–Israeli conflict was already stirring regional emotions, though in most other respects the situation then was relatively stable and far less turbulent than in later years. In Lebanon, a complex power sharing arrangement among Muslims, Christians, and Druze was working reasonably well, and Beirut prided itself on being a tolerant, secular Levantine Paris. Iran under the Shah was firmly allied to the West, while the fledgling state of Israel was a small country still confined within its original 1948 borders.

I have never been an active Zionist, though from the beginning I have been very sympathetic to the Jewish struggle for independence. My first visit to Israel in the 1950s had left a strong impression, and I had been fascinated with the richness of the country's biblical history, archeological treasures, and, above all, the hard work, idealism, and pioneering spirit of her people.

When I went to Iraq in the summer of 1956, that World War I British concoction ruled by the pro-Western Hashemite King Faisal II was relatively calm. The Iraq of those days was poor, underdeveloped, and stuck in the past. Baghdad, where I spent much of my time, was squalid, dusty, and depressing, and Basra in the South no better. A single Baghdad hotel (well beyond the budget of a young academic) offered intermittently functioning air conditioning in some of the rooms. At the more affordable Semiramis, where I lay immobilized on my bed to escape the beastly hot afternoon hours when nothing moved outdoors, a lazy ceiling fan provided scant relief from the heat, and lizards feeding on the ubiquitous flies and mosquitos dropped on my bed to keep me awake and entertained.

Life had a kind of eternal, never-changing feel to it, and hardly anyone, least of all the oil company expatriates, realized that big changes were on the way. A visitor might occasionally sense the winds of change, but those closest could not yet feel them.

When the change did come, suddenly and without warning, it would be a rude awakening. In 1959, the monarchy was overthrown, and the Iraqi king, crown prince, and premier were killed. The British embassy was sacked, and several expatriates murdered. In neighboring Lebanon, 3,500 U.S. Marines had to intervene to quell a parallel revolt by Muslim rebels. Soon thereafter the foreign oil concessions were cancelled and the industry nationalized. Iraqis, it turned out, had no difficulty in running their own fields.

When I returned to the Middle East as treasury secretary twenty-five years later, it was to a totally different, much less stable region beset by seemingly unending upheavals and dangerous confrontations. U.S. dependence on Middle Eastern oil had grown to an alarming extent, but the control of this critical resource was now firmly in the hands of the producing states and their OPEC cartel. U.S. interests in the region were greater than ever, but relations with oil-producing countries were more fragile and complex. After several armed conflicts and intransigence on both sides, Israel's occupation of some Arab lands had led to a steady worsening of Arab–Israeli relations. Power-sharing in Lebanon had largely collapsed, while the Shah of Iran, a long-time friend of the U.S. and important figure in the region, was in trouble in his own country.

My mission for two well-publicized trips was to meet with Middle Eastern heads of state and their ministers, primarily to plead for oil price moderation and reinvestment of the region's cornucopia of petro-dollars in U.S. securities, and to lobby for support of the Arab–Israeli peace process. These encounters with Saudi royalty and assorted emirs across the Arab Peninsula were among my more memorable experiences, but my contacts with the Shah of Iran would prove the most fateful.

I met him twice—the first time in October 1977 and again in November of the next year when sporadic street riots were turning into the full-fledged revolution that would soon lead to his precipitous flight into exile. As fate would have it, I thus became the last U.S. cabinet emissary to have a face-to-face meeting with the embattled Shah in Tehran, as an accidental bit actor in ultimately futile U.S. efforts to save him—and a witness to a Washington decision-making disaster.

At least since the Nixon administration, it had been established American policy dogma to count on Israel and Iran as key U.S. allies in the Arab world. Close U.S.–Iranian relations were supposed to be the linchpin of the U.S. position in the region, and unflinching support of the Shah the key for keeping it that way. In hindsight, this policy of unquestioning support for the increasingly unpopular Iranian monarch proved to be of dubious wisdom, and would have made it difficult to salvage a reasonable post-revolution U.S.–Iranian relationship, even with more skillful diplomacy. The roots of U.S. policy errors thus go back a good many years, but the confusion and stumbles in Washington during the critical final months of the Shah's rule doomed any hope of a better outcome.

Relations between the United States and the Iranian military had always been particularly close, and ever since the Nixon years it had been a fixed element of U.S. policy to allow the Shah to purchase prodigious quantities of U.S. arms. Iran, in fact, had grown into a highly profitable market for a wide range of American products, and many influential U.S. corporate leaders doing business there were among the Shah's most ardent supporters. To them he was an enlightened ruler bent on modernizing his country, not to mention a gracious host appreciated for the extravagant hospitality he extended.

I was aware, of course, that there were others in the United States and Iran who saw the Shah quite differently. To these dissenters, he was a vainglorious and megalomaniacal tyrant undeserving of unlimited U.S. support. The main complaint of his domestic opponents, including many in the intelligentsia and the growing, better-educated middle class, was his unwillingness to tolerate any kind of meaningful political dissent. They questioned his narrow political base and his reliance on a brutal secret police apparatus, the SAVAK, to keep him in power and enforce his will. They also objected to his tolerance of pervasive corruption among a small circle of family members and privileged beneficiaries of his rule, and to his almost total isolation from key elements of the public outside the ruling classes.

Driving up to his ornate palace in the center of Tehran in 1977, I remember being intensely curious about this larger-than-life monarch, Mohammed Reza Shah Pahlavi, who called himself the Shah of Shahs. He had been the object of media fascination—and controversy—for years, and I wondered which of his two contradictory images I would find to be the more apt.

Though it was no secret that the Shah was facing growing domestic unrest, my briefing papers, supplied by the State Department, had made scant reference of it. The following year his situation had worsened radically, yet for both visits my instructions were identical: as a first item of business, deliver an unequivocal presidential message of friendship and full support. In 1977, the world oil price was high, but so was Iranian inflation, and labor unrest had cut into oil production. Popular dissatisfaction with the economy and with the Shah's dictatorial rule and SAVAK excesses had led to a string of popular protests and during the summer the Shah had found it necessary to fire his longtime prime minister and appoint a successor charged with making limited concessions to bring the situation under control.

As I was ushered into the sitting room of his palace, accompanied by U.S. ambassador Bill Sullivan and a small congressional delegation headed by Indiana Senator Dick Lugar and Illinois Congressman Henry Hyde, my first impression of the Shah was favorable. Slight in stature and elegantly dressed in Western clothes, he had greeted us cordially. His English was excellent, his smile warm and friendly, and his voice soft and modest with no sign—except for the opulence of the surroundings—of the pomposity and arrogance I had expected. Opening pleasantries having been exchanged, he graciously inquired about our accommodations and listened courteously as I delivered President Carter's message and launched into the business at hand.

A curious change in manner had abruptly come over him, however, when the time came for his response. Suddenly he raised himself ramrod straight, and launched into a monologue in an Olympian tone that brooked no interruption or contradiction. The gist of his lengthy peroration was criticism of U.S. and Western societies for their dangerous permissiveness, which, he alleged, risked their eventual disintegration. The high price of oil he considered the result of excess U.S. consumption and profligacy. President Carter's difficulties in passing remedial energy legislation was evidence of lack of will and moral lassitude, and his preoccupation with human rights almost certainly counterproductive. Much of this lecture had little to do with the specific issues I had raised and had been delivered with the air of the utter certainty of a profound world statesman. To the dissidents in Iranian streets, he had referred only fleetingly, dismissing them as unreasonable troublemakers and, in any case, well under control.

It had been an astonishing performance, all the more so because, once finished, he had sunk back into his chair and, just as abruptly, reverted to his earlier quiet and courteous manner, while promising to do his best to influence OPEC's price policies, as I had urged, and where possible to cooperate in supporting the dollar in international markets. A few more banalities having been exchanged, we took our leave in the same friendly atmosphere in which he had received us.

Dick Lugar, Henry Hyde, and I were baffled, and not quite sure what to make of it all. Bill Sullivan was less surprised. It was par for the course, he told us. The Shah was being the Shah: he could be kind one moment and overbearing the next, depending on what he thought the situation demanded.

A year later, in November 1978, again accompanied by Dick Lugar and several congressmen, I called on the Shah once more during the second of my Middle East pilgrimages. In the course of the year, things had not gone well for him. On a visit to Washington late in

1977, several hundred Iranian student protesters had become so unruly outside the White House arrival ceremony that the police had been forced to use tear gas to disperse them, but the wind had blown it back on the White House lawn—much to the distinguished visitor's embarrassment—and literally reduced the president of the United States to tears. Apparently, however, this hadn't deterred the Shah from delivering his standard lecture on Western moral weakness to the president in their private talks, while politely dismissing Carter's warning about his repressive policies and the generally unstable situation at home.[240]

Throughout 1978, the domestic situation had deteriorated further, and at the time of our visit in November it was morphing into open revolt. Iran was under martial law, riots had left hundreds dead and wounded, strikes had crippled oil production, and competing opposition groups were jockeying for position. From Paris, the leader of the religious right, Ayatollah Khomeini, was calling for the Shah's ouster.

All this was well known in Washington, yet I had once again been instructed merely to assure the Shah of "President Carter's support of him as the key person capable of leading Iran through a transition to a more broadly based and stable government." So we wondered what he would have to say to us, but we were hardly prepared for what actually happened.

When we entered his sitting room, it was immediately obvious that the Shah was a broken man and that the presidential message I had brought was of dubious relevance. Slumped in his chair, a bewildered and helpless shadow of his former self, we were treated to embarrassing silences while the Shah stared vacantly into the distance. "What can I do? No one will listen," he asked plaintively several times. "What is your advice? What does the president suggest I do?" The complete contrast to the previous year's posture of certainty and self-assurance was stunning. Here was a man obviously immobilized by fear and indecision, unable to lead and no longer in control. Under the circumstances, the ritualistic message of unspecified U.S. support we had brought him was a hollow platitude.

Did Washington understand this dire situation and the virtual certainty that the Shah was finished? Were there contingency plans for a post-Shah Iran policy? we later asked Sullivan. His answer was disturbing and hard to believe. He had reported all this for months, he told us, but there had been no constructive reaction from Washington, only contradictory messages signaling evidence of confusion and bureaucratic disagreements without practical ideas on what to do.

Something was obviously very wrong at the White House and at State. The president considered Iran our key ally in the region, and our entire position there was now at grave risk. The apparent failure to realize the Shah's desperate situation and the lack of a realistic response were hard to understand. Mystified and appalled, I sent my report to Washington and followed it up with a personal letter to the President that minced no words:

> The change in attitude and demeanor of the Shah as against a year ago was astounding . . . he gives the impression of a man unable to know what to do next . . . At best we can look forward to a lengthy period of instability and uncertainty on the Iranian scene. Indeed, even under the most favorable circumstances, it is not easy to see the personal and substantive resources at the Shah's disposal as he seeks to re-establish his authority . . . At worst, a collapse and continued disorder or worse is a distinct possibility . . . We should seek to be more active than before in maintaining contacts with the more moderate elements of the Shah's opponents in the religious, business and intellectual groups . . . and we should certainly urgently examine our contingency plans . . .[241]

Back in Washington, I immediately sought out "Zbig" Brzezinski at the White House. My report that the Shah was probably beyond redemption had clearly shocked him. He didn't trust Sullivan's recommendation to start throwing in our lot with the more moderate elements of the Shah's opposition, and he considered the State Department too ready to appease and not tough enough. What about the generals, he wanted to know, could the military take action to contain the opposition and keep the Shah on the throne? The main problem, he confessed, was that there was no one in Washington who really understood Iran, and therefore no one who could provide a hard-headed analysis with suggestions of realistic policy alternatives. After a quarter century of close U.S.–Iranian relations, this struck me as bizarre. But Zbig was clearly floundering, and so I suggested he call in George Ball for advice. George, I reminded him, had considerable knowledge of Iran, knew the Shah well, and was the kind of sober strategic thinker urgently needed.

The rest is disastrous history. Ball accepted the assignment and soon concluded—correctly, in hindsight—that the game had been lost long ago, that the Shah was beyond redemption and that further attempts to keep him in power by broadening his political base with or without the military were too late and likely to fail. A military government, in particular, was a pipe dream. The generals were weak, and their officers and men wouldn't follow them because they came from the countryside, where Khomeini's mullahs had the decisive word. Though probably too late, Ball's advice was that it was high time to reach out to others. As a long shot, perhaps an interim council of elders could take over for a time, but he wasn't optimistic.

His advice, however, had been unwelcome at the White House. It contradicted the established dogma of clinging to the Shah, and Brzezinski had quickly persuaded Carter to brush it aside. In his own post mortem years later, he voiced regret at having called in Ball in the first place, because "one should never obtain the services of an 'impartial' outside consultant . . . without first making certain in advance that one knows the likely contents of his advice," thus establishing a novel criterion for calling in expert advisors.[242]

For weeks Washington dithered, while in Iran Sullivan was at the receiving end of irrelevant questions and unrealistic instructions. Brzezinski and the State Department remained locked in bureaucratic combat over conflicting views on what to do, and as late as December 18, the president still clung to hope for the Shah.[243] A U.S. general sent to Tehran at Zbig's insistence to explore the situation with his Iranian counterparts got nowhere, much as Ball had predicted, and had to be withdrawn. Belated U.S. backing of the Shah's last premier proved equally futile. In January, the Shah finally left, and with him any hope of establishing workable relations with a post-Shah Iran.

The Iranian debacle was a serious strategic setback for the United States, with longterm consequences. For Jimmy Carter it was a political disaster.

Perhaps the demise of the Shah's rule had been inevitable. Carter inherited a dysfunctional U.S.–Iranian relationship that long antedated him. The emphasis on the U.S.–Iranian military connection and the established practice of giving the Shah virtual carte blanche to acquire vast quantities of military hardware; the resulting structural imbalance of the economy; the failure to build bridges to diverse Iranian power centers; and the exclusive support of an autocrat kept in power by a brutal police apparatus—these were all part of a policy reaching back years.[244] Yet as I watched in dismay as Washington floundered in the critical final months, it was also obvious that some of the damage to U.S. interests was the result of self-inflicted wounds, a classic case study of how history can be affected by the accidental interplay of personalities and the quality of political leadership at the top.

It should have been obvious that the Shah was a flawed leader. At heart, he was weak and insecure, forever in the shadow of a dominant father he sought to emulate, and thrust when still young into a job for which he was ill-prepared and ill-suited. Acting the role of the great statesman and arrogant monarch was probably his way of covering up his fundamental insecurities. Certainly he lacked the skills and instincts to manage the complexities of modernizing Iran, his ambitions frequently exceeded his capabilities, and his preference for surrounding himself with a small circle of family and pliant friends hurt him badly. When faced by implacable and fanatic opponents, he had no political base to fall back on and was simply overmatched.

The failures of decision making in Washington also had their roots in the personalities of the actors and their leadership failures. Bill Sullivan, Carter's ambassador in Tehran, did not speak the language and had never before served in the Middle East. In Washington, area expertise and a sophisticated understanding of Iranian affairs was surprisingly modest, and where it existed—in the Department of State or the Ball mission—it was sidelined and ignored. Neither Cy Vance, nor Zbig Brzezinski, nor Carter—the ultimate decision makers—knew much about the country.

More importantly, Iranian policy had become the focal point for fierce bureaucratic rivalries between State and the White House, a not uncommon situation but one with especially deleterious consequences in this case. The problem was that in the foreign policy field, Jimmy Carter had—unwittingly, rather than by Machiavellian design—appointed two men with incompatible personalities and very different philosophies and management styles. Cy Vance was a courteous patrician diplomat who preferred caution and negotiation over confrontation. Zbig Brzezinski, on the other hand, was a strong and skillful political operator who believed in power and delighted in using it.

In his memoirs, Brzezinski defined the differences between them in terms of, in his view, Vance's overly "litigational and contractual" approach to the conduct of foreign policy. Vance, he observed critically, preferred to "shy away from the unavoidable ingredient of force in dealing with contemporary international realities, and to have excessive faith that all issues can be resolved by compromise."[245] That wasn't Zbig's style, and it made for endless tensions and conflicts.

The relationship between them could only have worked if carefully managed, but—much as in economic policy matters—that was a skill the president lacked. He failed to appreciate the significance of the deep philosophical differences between his two advisors, did not resolve the inevitable conflicts, and failed to set the boundaries of their respective roles. Was Zbig the coordinator of foreign policy issues in the White House, the facilitator of the process of policy formulation, and the president's advisor—or was he an operational implementer, a role normally reserved to the secretary of state? The distinction was never made clear.

In the Iran crisis, the lack of clarity regarding their respective roles led to no end of trouble as Zbig sought to seize control of Iranian policy, a role which he was determined to play but for which he lacked the knowledge. The result was unending internal conflict and contradictory initiatives doomed to fail. Had the president better understood this problem, many of the missteps and much of the confusion might have been avoided.

I initially met Menachem Begin, Israel's prime minister from 1977 to 1984 and one of the most important political personalities of the period, during his visits to Washington and in courtesy calls at his Jerusalem office in the late seventies. International financial and economic issues, the usual purpose of my missions to Israel for talks with Foreign Minister Moshe Dayan or Finance Minister Simcha Ehrlich, were of limited interest to Begin, so our meetings had never been particularly substantive and rarely touched more than in passing on the Arab–Israeli and Palestinian questions he most cared about.

Though I knew something about Begin's history and formidable reputation, on these largely ceremonial occasions, he wasn't easy to get to know. On the short side and not particularly impressive in appearance, he had somewhat owlish eyes that peered out at the visitor from behind thick glasses. Contrary to the custom of most Israeli politicians, he always received me dressed formally in suit and tie, and his manner was courteous but carefully measured and reserved. The overall impression was more that of a polite, punctilious bookkeeper than of the storied freedom fighter and revolutionary leader willing to use force in the struggle for statehood, with a reputation as a relentless, charismatic politician capable of great emotional oratory. Yet in some intangible way, one sensed that below the bland and formal manner with which he received his visitor, there lurked something more formidable and complex: a considerable intellect, strong convictions, and the reservoir of tightly-wound energy of a formidable man.

In August of 1982, in a modest hotel room in Nahariya, a town just south of the Lebanese border, I would come face-to-face with these qualities under memorable circumstances. Begin had invited me to meet him there at a tense and anxious time. On June 6 he had sent Israeli forces into Lebanon for the stated purpose of establishing a twenty-five-mile buffer zone to clear the area north of the border of Palestinian raiders and the missiles they fired into Israel. The Israelis had named the operation "Peace for Galilee," but Ariel Sharon, his minister of defense (and a future prime minister) and the man in charge, had vastly expanded the mission beyond its original goals, bombed Beirut repeatedly, and pushed Israeli Defense Forces far beyond the south into the outskirts of the Lebanese capital. The move had been roundly criticized by the outside world, and Begin, under great pressure from the United States and others to stop the attacks and to pull his troops back, was having difficulty persuading Sharon to comply. Some were now calling it "Sharon's War."

Matters had evidently gotten somewhat out of hand, and when he received me in Nahariya, Begin was in a somber mood. It was, if I remember correctly, the beginning of the Sabbath, and I had come to Israel on a private visit hoping among other things to learn more about what was going on, and to ask his permission to be allowed into Lebanon to see for myself.[246]

We talked quietly for a while. I explained my reasons for wanting to make the trip, and Begin, having agreed to my request, had taken pains to stress Israel's limited objectives in Lebanon and had defended the action as essential for protecting the border. It was when he had launched into a review of the long and tortured history of the Palestinian problem that I made a comment which suddenly brought our conversation to a very dramatic turn.

"Prime Minister," I interjected at one point, "Israel is a small country in a sea of Arabs. Sooner or later it must be in your interest to make peace. The longer the problem is allowed to fester, the harder it will be—time isn't necessarily on your side. Isn't the only viable solution a formula of 'land for peace,' meaning to dismantle the West Bank settlements and return the land to the Palestinians in exchange for a viable peace settlement?"

I knew that I was venturing into dangerous territory. Three years earlier at Camp David, Begin had agreed to a peace pact with Egypt[247] and, under tenacious pressure from Jimmy Carter, signed an accord on a so-called framework for settling the Palestinian problem on largely the same lines I was suggesting. Though Carter had thought the language and understandings reached quite clear, Begin had given them a very different interpretation. Almost from the moment the ink was dry, he insisted he had not agreed to freeze or dismantle the West Bank settlements at all, nor to have committed himself to complete Palestinian autonomy. I also knew that the Carter–Begin relationship had been tense, and that the president felt misled by Begin's adamant refusal to follow through on what he considered firm commitments. The settlements had been expanded further, and far from negotiating with the Palestinians, the situation had actually deteriorated. The so-called peace process remained deadlocked. Israel had annexed the Golan Heights, Sadat had been assassinated, and Jimmy Carter was no longer in the White House. In raising the issue, I was testing whether the past three years had softened Begin's stand.

Perhaps I should have known better. I was prepared for disagreement but not for the vehemence with which he reacted to my question in a fervent fifteen- to twenty-minute lecture on biblical history. His voice was quiet and calm, yet filled with deep emotion. How could I speak of the "West Bank," he asked? Did I not know that these were the biblical lands of Samaria and Judea, two ancient Judaic regions and an integral part of Eretz Israel, the soil of the Jewish people since biblical times? "We will never surrender them," he said firmly, "they belong to the Jewish people. Nothing we agreed to at Camp David was ever meant to surrender them." The Camp David accord had referred to the "legitimate rights" of the Palestinians, but his lawyers and advisors had assured him, he said, that this was a tautology which bound him to nothing, and so he had signed it. The meaning of the goal of "full autonomy" for Palestinians had never been defined either, and was surely open to differing interpretations.

Was not the real issue for Israel how to achieve peace in the twenty-first century, rather than staking out biblical claims, I interjected at one point, but Begin would have none of it. He was a man of peace, he said, but the Holocaust had taught him that the honor of the Jewish people must be upheld at all costs, that it must be fought for if necessary, and that Israel must never again bend to the pressure or the superior power of others!

What I had expected to be a half-hour meeting had stretched out to be three times as long. Begin had done most of the talking, with force, evident deep conviction, and considerable eloquence. This was no play acting, I realized. Begin was a true believer—not merely an Israeli Jew but a fanatical Zionist, the product of Polish shtetl culture, molded by the Holocaust that had claimed the lives of his family and which he had barely escaped himself. I was familiar with such people and their feelings. I had met them before in the ghetto of Shanghai, in Israel, and occasionally in the United States. So while I did not agree with Begin, I understood him. To him, Eretz Israel had deep symbolic meaning and was the central issue from which he would never budge, where ideology and emotion rather than pragmatism and compromise counted. Convincing a man like Begin otherwise was impossible. That was how we parted.

I have often reflected on this remarkable conversation. Jimmy Carter took substantial risks and deserves much credit for his courageous exertions at Camp David on behalf of peace between Egypt and Israel and for achieving a breakthrough on the Israeli–Palestinian problem. That he failed on the latter issue does not lessen the value of what he did. It was, however, highly predictable that the negotiations with Menachem Begin on the Palestinian question were doomed, and as I listened to him in Nahariya the reasons were abundantly clear.

Carter and Begin were worlds apart in background, worldviews, convictions, and, most importantly, in their fundamental objectives. To find common ground between them on so intractable and emotional an issue as the Palestinian question would have been a near miracle. If Carter can be faulted for anything, it is that he believed that, face-to-face with a chance for peace, Begin could be persuaded by patient reasoning to compromise his bedrock goals and beliefs.[248]

The two leaders had this in common: both were zealots, though very different ones. Carter was a product of the rural South, a born-again Christian peacemaker, supremely confident of his ability to convince Begin through rational argument of the wisdom of pragmatism and compromise in the pursuit of a noble objective. He had prepared meticulously for their encounter, yet apparently failed to appreciate that the Israeli premier's character and psyche were deeply rooted and infinitely complex. A radical Zionist since childhood, Begin was profoundly affected by his early experience with anti-Semitism in Poland, the loss of his family, and his own narrow escape, and the struggle against the British for a Jewish State. Defying pressure in defense of his radical vision was second nature to him. In these matters, in Begin's mind, pragmatism and compromise were betrayal, and yielding Jewish biblical lands tantamount to surrender.

Carter had come to Camp David hoping to win agreement for the framework of a broader peace between Israel and the Palestinians. He considered freezing and giving up "West Bank" settlements, a rational compromise and a key to that objective. For Begin that would have been the betrayal of a sacred trust. He, in turn, had come determined to compromise on tactical matters but to use every means and stratagem at his disposal to concede nothing where Jewish rights to biblical lands were concerned.

Not surprisingly, the relationship between them was difficult from the start. Neither really understood the other, nor did they fully comprehend that even the words they used had different meaning in their respective minds. Carter soon complained that Begin was rigid, maddeningly unimaginative, stubborn, and legalistic, given to long emotional speechifying, unwilling to consider a broader perspective, preoccupied with words, and prone to quibbling over what Carter considered meaningless semantics. To his wife, Rosalynn, he confided that he considered the man a "psycho" and incapable of rational thought.[249]

In a private moment with Brzezinski, Begin had once exclaimed that "my right eye will fall out, my right hand will come off before I ever agree to the dismantling of a single Jewish settlement."[250] When

matter-of-fact facility in integrating the steady flow of new software tools into their daily lives. As a student and teacher in the fifties, I spent many hours in the library doing academic research, but the technology of my son's university work leaves me scratching my head. Taking good lecture notes was one of the first lessons drilled into me as a student; he simply brings his laptop and records verbatim what the professor says. I laboriously scoured the library stacks for my research, a skill my son considers largely obsolete. He searches for the book he wants on his computer, "googles" for further informational nuggets, works the networks from his laptop, "spell checks" his papers electronically, and simply emails the finished product to his professor when it is done.

What separates us is that we were born on opposite sides of the Great Divide of the electronic age, a transforming moment in history when the ever-increasing power and sophistication of microchips, software, fiber optics, and imaging began to erode old constraints of time and space. The inexorable spread of these new technologies allowed information, knowledge, capital, and services to flow instantly across the globe, thus fundamentally altering established patterns of world trade and finance and of how people the world over live and work. Not only goods became tradable, but information and services as well, thereby creating the single system of world interconnectedness, which today we call "globalism," and which gave rise to entirely new political and economic realities for mankind.

The signs that an information revolution with historic implications was under way multiplied over the course of the eighties, and as I traveled the world during that time, my corporate responsibilities and public affairs interests put me in a strategic place at the center of this process. Yet in the academy and among politicians and the general public, the realization that something unique and unprecedented was happening took hold slowly at first. I recall that as late as 1987, when I made the subject the central focus of the series of lectures I had been invited to give at the Council on Foreign Relations, it was still essentially unfamiliar territory for the audience of foreign policy experts, geopolitical thinkers and academics, generating spirited debate and a lengthy follow-up article in *Foreign Affairs*.[252] My concluding hypothesis that "with a single world market for information, production, trade, and finance, the basic notion of national sovereignty may well become obsolete and put into question the singular U.S. economic dominance on the world scene" was met with more skeptical curiosity than belief. Twenty-five years later, these predictions read like a self-evident description of the "globalized" world we have come to take for granted.

Especially in my travels behind the Iron Curtain, I had seen signs that fundamental change was in the air. In visits to the Soviet Union, I had noted the rigidities of centralized decision making, the widespread deficiency in state-of-the-art technology, the backwardness of factories, the lack of consumer products, and evidence of popular dissatisfaction with a stagnating standard of living. Behind the usual boasts and bluster of the officials I met, their realization that they were falling further and further behind the West, and their frustration over the failure to adapt to the changes needed to boost growth and improve living standards, had become apparent. Yet that the entire system would within a few years come crashing down under the pressures of technological change with cataclysmic geopolitical consequences, frankly hadn't entered my mind, any more than it had occurred to the legions of Sovietologists specializing in the study of the USSR.

As a case in point, I vividly recall a visit to the gigantic Kama River automobile manufacturing complex, the Soviets' pride and joy, where the local boss, a man named Ivanov, proudly showed me the most enormous accumulation of machine tools I had ever seen assembled in one place. So many lathes, grinders, vises, reamers, and numerical controls, etc., had been packed into one gigantic football stadium-sized hall that it reminded me of nothing so much as the annual Chicago Machine Tool Show. The machines stood there, unused or underutilized, mainly because some central planner had seen fit to order them. That the technical knowledge and management expertise to handle such sophisticated equipment, purchased at great expense in the West, was lacking had been a matter apparently overlooked by the decision makers. When I asked the harassed and chain-smoking Ivanov whether he had asked for all this gear and how he intended to use it, his response—a quizzical look and resigned shrug—spoke volumes.

In the private U.S.–USSR exchanges I chaired for some years, we had become quite conscious of the ever more insistent pleas of our Soviet counterparts for more East–West trade and technology exchanges. Western companies like mine had aggressively begun to share product development and design across national borders. Seamless communication networks humming day and night were enabling us to break down and disaggregate the product development process, and our U.S. engineers were routinely "talking" electronically to their counterparts as far away as in New Zealand, or to partner facilities in the United Kingdom, Brazil or elsewhere, with significant cost savings and productivity improvements. Knowledge was being shared, disseminated, and used in totally new ways, much as I had described it in my Root Lectures. The Soviets were shut out from all this, and they knew it.

As the eighties were ending, the new technologies were connecting the world in previously unimagined ways. The process of the globalization of human affairs was unfolding with great speed, and at the century's end no corner of the Earth would remain untouched by it. On either side of the Iron Curtain, in Asia, the Western hemisphere, and in Africa, mankind was being thrust onto a historic new path, with unimagined new opportunities but also with an entirely new set of problems and challenges. Communism was swept away as a world force, while China, India, and Brazil became important new actors on the world stage and created new geopolitical realities in ways no one had foreseen. The next century, it was clear, would be nothing like the troubled one about to draw to a close.

THE NINETIES
A New Germany

Full Circle

My life began in Germany during the first part of the twentieth century, and when I left there, still a child, I expected never to return. Yet in the nineties, a decade when the reunification of Germany was one of the seminal political events, I became reacquainted with the country of my birth under circumstances that I could not have anticipated.

The Germany in which I grew up bears little resemblance to the German Federal Republic of today. In most respects it was during mly childhood a disagreeable country, and for a long time I wanted nothing more to do with it. Prior to choosing a dissertation topic that required my visiting Germany for a time in the fifties, I had only fairly superficial knowledge about the country and a sketchy understanding of the postwar German situation. My exposure to the truncated, smaller, and very different German Federal Republic therefore surprised me and gradually changed my somewhat one-dimensional negative image, which had been colored by childhood memories of the Hitler years, wartime atrocities, and the crimes against the Jews.

There were now two Germanys—one on either side of the Iron Curtain. The Communist one in the East I visited only a few times, briefly, and its apparently seamless transition from Nazi to Communist authoritarianism (even though the heavy hand of the Soviets had much to do with it) had chilled and repelled me. East Berlin was festooned with simple-minded political slogans, the people struck me as cheerless, and the overall atmosphere of uniformity was alien and antithetical to my tastes. West Germany (FRG), however, had been an entirely different story. This was a different country altogether from the one I had remembered—officially only four years old but already a functioning democracy supported by the majority of voters, with a Constitution and a strong parliamentary majority of political parties committed to individual rights and the rule of law.

For twelve years under the Nazis every form of dissent had been ruthlessly suppressed and most opposition politicians either imprisoned or killed. That an able group of men had nevertheless emerged after the war to take charge of the key positions of political leadership at a critical and difficult time seemed a miracle.

Theodor Heuss, the fledgling Federal Republic's president, was a one-time professor of History with a clean record as a former liberal member of the old Reichstag. His solidly non-Nazi credentials and reassuring manner struck me as the right image to symbolize a new German spirit and to project it at home and abroad. The FRG emerging from the devastation of war and Allied occupation faced enormous domestic and international challenges requiring clear vision and a strong hand at the top, which was exactly what the Christian Democrats' (CDU) Chancellor Konrad Adenauer was providing. The more I saw of Adenauer, the more convinced I was that the Germans were lucky to have this formidable man leading their government during a difficult time. Many of my Social Democrat (SPD) friends disliked him, and his tolerance of former Nazis in senior positions worried me. Yet, he was what Germany needed at the time: a canny politician and effective statesman, respected on the international stage and pursuing a clear set of policies to set the FRG alongside the Western democracies in a Cold War world. His determination to set the country firmly on the side of the Western alliance was not yet universally supported, especially by the opposition, which favored a more neutralist approach with greater focus on the goal of German reunification. Adenauer, however, had the better of the arguments in the national debate—and history would prove him right. The SPD's Kurt Schumacher and, after his death, Erich Ollenhauer—

long-time SPD activists who had survived Hitler—were nevertheless effective opposition leaders.

In the twenties, during another difficult postwar time when major challenges had to be faced, it was Germany's misfortune that a dearth of effective leaders had contributed to the failure of its first experiment with democracy and opened the road to power for Hitler. As I followed the political debates in the equally challenging years of the fifties, it was clear that this time better fortune had smiled on the Germans by bringing to the fore the right kind of leadership at the right moment, including such others as Ludwig Erhard, a future chancellor, who took charge of the economy; Walter Hallstein in the chancellor's office and the future first president of the European Commission in Brussels (both of whom I would get to know well in the sixties); and strong local leaders like Max Brauer, the mayor of Hamburg, and Ernst Reuter, his opposite number in West Berlin, among others.

Not only their political leaders, but the West Germans themselves—or at least a majority—no longer fit my preconceptions. Militarism, nationalism, and pride in Germanic virtues had been supplanted by pacifism and a longing for security and peace. The success in repairing the physical destruction and the country's remarkable economic progress were impressive. And I was meeting open-minded people with political views not too different from mine, among which I had made a number of good friends. If anti-Semitism was still an issue—and I had seen signs that below the surface it still was—I had come across little direct evidence of it among the bulk of the population. When it came to the subject of Jews, what one heard above all, along with protestations of personal ignorance and innocence regarding Nazi crimes, were expressions of sympathy mixed with embarrassment and shame, but often just pained silence.

Not all my experiences had been positive, but many had. Yet, in truth, I had never felt entirely comfortable during our year's stay, because reminders of the awful past kept reappearing. Wherever I turned there had been evidence of it—physical ones, like the ruins of war, and psychological ones in the still-conflicted national psyche. I had disliked the undertone of self-pity and bitterness of many people prone to lament their cruel fate, and their adamant denial of any knowledge of the depth of chicanery against their Jewish neighbors long before they were sent off to their deaths, which I knew to be largely untrue. The widespread rehabilitation of former Nazis and their reinstatement into key jobs made me acutely uncomfortable, and that there were still fringe elements of unabashed Hitler lovers willing to defend the past scared me. It grated on me that too many Germans felt sorry for themselves. Perhaps it was too early to deal openly and honestly with the past. Perhaps the sense of loss, guilt, and shame over what had happened was still too fresh. Yet it is this—what Fritz Stern has aptly called their collective amnesia,[253] the unwillingness or inability to recognize any kind of moral responsibility for the twentieth century's worst crimes—that had bothered me most.

I had left feeling that postwar Germany was on the right track, but also that many questions about the past remained. As I returned to Princeton, my attitude toward the country of my birth had changed—mostly for the better—but remained mixed, and I assumed I would never again have truly warm feelings for Germany and Germans.

Thirty-six years later, in the evening of October 2, 1990, I was standing on the top floor of the Hotel InterContinental, on Budapester Strasse in Berlin. Edzard Reuter, the CEO of Daimler-Benz, had invited his North American advisory board to witness the historic moment of the reunification of the two Germanys—a group of U.S. business leaders and bankers including Jim Wolfensohn, a future World Bank president; Harvard economist and advisor to Ronald Reagan, Martin Feldstein; Vernon Jordan, prominent black leader and friend of presidents; and myself, among others. We had just completed a fine celebratory dinner and Reuter had led us to the InterContinental's glass-enclosed top floor from which to view the official ceremony about to unfold on the steps of the Reichstag building not far away.

Berlin was bursting at the seams with visitors from Germany

and all over the world. The atmosphere was electric, and throngs of people were roaming the streets in a festive mood. At the InterContinental, the Germans were standing shoulder to shoulder, eyes fixed on the Reichstag building which was bathed in bright lights, with a multitude of citizens massed in front of it, anxious to be a part of this momentous event that not long ago had seemed an impossible dream. The champagne had been poured, and exactly at the stroke of midnight the cheers reverberated back to us from the street, and fireworks lit the sky. At the Reichstag, a giant German flag was being raised, the big "Peace Bell" at the Schöneberg Rathaus began to chime, and church bells all over the city joined in as President von Weizsäcker and Chancellor Kohl, "the Chancellor of Unity," stepped to the microphone to proclaim a reunited single German nation.

The Germans around us were embracing and toasting each other with tears in their eyes. A few cried openly. At the Reichstag, the national anthem was being sung, and many were joining in. Left alone for a moment, we Americans were standing off to one side observing this incredible scene, when Vernon Jordan—equal parts charmer and provocateur—stepped over to me, put his arm around my shoulder and asked a question. "Well, Mike," he said, while gesturing at the people around us, "you know these Germans better than any of us. Twice before they have screwed it up. Now that they are a single nation once more, will it happen again?"

His question startled me, because my thoughts had also been on that other Germany. The InterContinental was in a part of town I knew well, around the corner from the zoo where I had often been taken as a child and not far from the other familiar landmarks of my youth: the Nollendorfplatz Café where Uncle Hellmuth had played the drums in a fake Mexican band before the Nazis shipped him off to Theresienstadt, the Fasanenstrasse synagogue I had seen smoldering the morning after Kristallnacht, the Ku'damm boulevard where Jewish store fronts had been smashed during that awful night, and the house on Duisburger Strasse from which the Levys, my uncle and aunt, had been taken and sent to their deaths.

I was glad that the obscenity of the Berlin Wall was no more, and I was happy for my German friends and wished them well. Yet with my private memories, Vernon's question had hit its mark. Now Germany would once again be the biggest and economically most powerful nation in Europe. What role would the country play in a post–Cold War world? How would the enlarged nation handle its international obligations? How would the Germans manage their domestic affairs and cope with the enormous problems to be faced? What would happen if the going got tough? All forms of overt nationalism had for years been shunned in the postwar FRG, and even patriotism had been considered politically incorrect by many. With 16 million Eastern Germans unschooled in democratic ideas added to the population mix, would all that change now? Germany's largest tabloid, the *Bild Zeitung*, had led with a banner headline reading "Germany! Lord, how Beautiful." Was it merely evidence of the moment's understandable exuberance—or an omen of things to come?

That was the core of Vernon's question, and in raising it he had not been alone. Heads of state from all over the world had sent their good wishes, but for those with special historical memories, there had also been cautionary notes. British Prime Minister Margaret Thatcher had warned against renewed German dominance. French President Mitterand had pointedly emphasized Germany's responsibility within Europe, and Israel's Yitzhak Shamir had spoken openly of Jewish "mixed feelings." How justified, I wondered, were their concerns?

Since my student days, I had visited Germany many times on business trips, and that the FRG had come a long way since my first postwar visit in the fifties was beyond doubt. Germany had become a proven Western democracy, a key member of the EU, a reliable U.S. ally, and Israel's strongest supporter in Europe. The Nazi generation had largely disappeared, and their children had long ago begun to ask the hard questions about moral responsibility for the past and the lessons to be learned that no one had wanted to face in the fifties. The FRG had actually been the only one among the war's aggressor nations with the courage to confront such painful issues openly and to make amends where possible. Only about 30,000 Jews were living in Germany again, yet the government had shown itself to be remarkably sensitive to their special needs, and in the larger cities there were again small congregations and functioning synagogues. Discussion of the Holocaust was no longer taboo and had in fact become the subject of a seemingly incessant preoccupation in the media and a required subject for study in schools. Even anti-Semitism seemed to be less of a problem than in most other countries of Europe. There was, instead, now a lively interest among the younger generation in Judaica and Jewish affairs, and though relations were still encumbered by the past, I had heard it said by some Jews—paradoxically—that Germany had become one of the best countries for a Jew in all of Europe.

As these reassuring developments had evolved over the years, my interest in and understanding of German affairs had grown, and my sympathies and respect for the country had risen to an extent that I wouldn't have thought possible in the fifties. As a student visitor I had observed events only from a distance, without direct contact with the country's political and business leadership. Over the next four decades, my corporate and U.S. government responsibilities had put me in direct touch with a good many Germans at all levels. Among others, I had formed cordial professional relations with political leaders and government officials during the Carter years, including Chancellor Helmut Schmidt, Finance Ministers Hans Matthöfer and Manfred Lahnstein, as well as Otto Graf Lambsdorff, then the minister of the economy.

The circle of my business colleagues had also steadily expanded. I had served on several German corporate boards and over the years had formed friendly relations with a good many of Germany's leading businessmen: Daimler's Edzard Reuter, Hans Merkle of Bosch, the Deutsche Bank's CEO Alfred Herrhausen, and Michael Otto, whose company was one of our major German customers, among others. Getting to know more and more Germans too young even to have been alive during the Nazi years had gradually erased the unspoken question often in my mind in the fifties—"were you a Nazi, can I trust you, and what did you do when?"

At the InterContinental that night, in the midst of my euphoric German colleagues and friends, I understood and shared their joy. Yet I was also concerned. Like most countries, the FRG faced the tough challenges of the nineties in adjusting to the impact of globalization on the domestic economy, and the cost of reunification was sure to greatly compound them. Rehabilitating the rundown infrastructure of the new *Länder* and their massive environmental degradation would weigh heavily on the federal budget. With half a million East German workers already laid off and close to 2 million working part time, unemployment was also likely to become a major issue. Folding a largely under-qualified workforce of millions into the FRG's expensive social safety net would cost billions. Having to absorb the additional 16 million inhabitants of the new *Länder*, and to manage the likely large influx of these "Ossies" moving west, would further complicate matters, with the risk of tensions and pressures on schools, the social safety net, cultural life, public peace, and tranquility. How would these Easterners feel about the differences for years to come in the standard of living between East and West, and could the inevitable demands to settle scores with the former East German Secret Police, the Stasi, be handled without major eruptions, I wondered?

In the streets, the people were happily shouting "One Volk, One Nation," but reality would surely soon overtake the good feelings. Fundamentally, I was hopeful, but the likelihood of an excruciatingly difficult period ahead was nevertheless on my mind. Could the shout of "One Volk" rekindle the old German nationalism again, and when the going got hard, might there once more be a search for scapegoats? Was there any risk that anti-Semitism might, in time, again be on the rise? All this was something I expected to follow closely from the outside.

Yet, as had happened many times in my life at critical moments when seminal political events changed twentieth century history, the wheel turned in unforeseen ways, and I would once more find myself not a distant observer from afar, but thrust squarely into the middle of the aftermath of German reunification. Thus in the last decade of the century, things had not only come full circle for the two Germanys after a half century of separation and estrangement, but in a strange way, for me as well. I had left Berlin in 1939, expecting never to return. In the nineties, a series of events would bring me back to live there again, dividing my time between homes in Princeton and Berlin.

Return to Berlin: THE JEWISH MUSEUM

A year earlier, in 1989, I had retired from Unisys and become an investment banker. Felix Rohatyn, the senior partner at Lazard Frères in New York, had been my principal banking advisor for many years at Bendix and Unisys. Not all members of his profession are equally reliable or confidence-inspiring, but with Felix I had never had any doubts. As one of the best-known and successful advisors to the top echelon of American CEOs, he had a well-deserved reputation for a first-class mind, and for his honesty, professionalism, and integrity. Trust between a CEO and his banker is the single most important ingredient of the relationship, and Felix had certainly earned it with me. His advice had always been excellent, and over time, a warm personal bond had developed between us—aided, perhaps, by our shared refugee/immigrant backgrounds. So when Felix invited me to become his partner, the lure of trying something entirely new by moving from client to the other side as advisor to CEOs had gotten the better of me, and I accepted.

My move to Lazard coincided with the death of my father in San Francisco at the age of almost 101. When he died he didn't leave me much in the way of worldly goods, except for his proudest possession—a family tree tracing the Blumenthal family roots in Brandenburg back to the seventeenth century. "There are many famous people in it," he had told me more than once, "don't lose it."

I attached little importance to it at the time, but it was this simple heirloom documenting my family's German origins that would, in short order, shape the next years of my life, and reinvolve me in German affairs more deeply than I could have imagined.

Among other assignments, my Lazard duties included assuming the chairmanship of the firm's German subsidiary in Frankfurt, and soon after my father's death we moved to Paris, in order to be closer to the various U.S.–European deals in which I had become involved. There, stimulated by the fulsome coverage of Jewish affairs in the German media, I began to take a closer look at my father's cherished family tree. At first it was mere curiosity about the "famous people" he had been so proud of—Jost Liebmann, a poor seventeenth-century Jew who became court jeweler to the Brandenburg nobility; Rahel Varnhagen, a Christian convert whose early-nineteenth-century salon was the meeting place for Berlin's intellectual elite; and the composer Giacomo Meyerbeer, one of the nineteenth century's musical giants and the special focus of Richard Wagner's anti-Semitic hatred; among others.

As I studied the lives of these ancestors, what had been idle curiosity evolved into a deeper interest in the history of German Jewry as background to their disastrous end under Hitler. Most of my life, I had known little about that history, but as I broadened my reading, the intellectual challenge of writing about it became irresistible.

The project became, in fact, a journey of discovery, and *The Invisible Wall*, published in the United States in 1998 and in German translation soon thereafter, was the result.[254]

To tackle an unfamiliar subject so removed from anything I'd ever done had involved a prodigious delving into the historical record and a good many visits to Germany. Among the numerous scholars I had met in the process, Professor Wolfgang Benz, the director of the Center for Research on Anti-Semitism at Berlin's Technical University, had been particularly helpful. It was a surprise, however, when in October of 1997, a phone call out of the blue from him reached me that would, in short order, plunge me directly into the middle of a major crisis in German–Jewish relations. Coming quickly to the point, Benz wanted to know whether I might consider "helping out" with the plans for a new Jewish Museum in Berlin, an apparently ill-starred project in considerable political trouble.

According to Benz, the museum's Israeli-born director, Amnon Barzel, had just been fired, the public and the local Jewish community were up in arms, a major crisis in Jewish–non-Jewish relations had erupted, and the city urgently needed help to put the project back on track, for which he had suggested me as a logical candidate. Would I consider it, he wanted to know. "Help, exactly how?" I asked. "Well, actually," he explained, to "take over Barzel's job for some interim period, a part-time assignment which wouldn't require moving to Berlin." My protests that I knew nothing about museums and was obviously unqualified for the assignment fell on deaf ears. The job was a lot more political than museological, he argued. Knowing that I had previously been open to public service, he had strongly recommended me to Lutz von Pufendorf, the Berlin state secretary for cultural affairs. He hoped that I would at least listen to his story.

Had I been fully aware of the depth of the Berlin Jewish Museum mess, I would almost certainly have turned him down—or done so after the two lengthy telephone conversations with Pufendorf which followed. Yet, in what was a clear case of a fool rushing in where angels fear to tread, I did the opposite and agreed to give the idea a try, based on three conditions: first, that I be given free hand to evaluate the situation on the ground; second, to be authorized, without preconditions, to make my own proposals for the kind of museum that made sense to me; and, third, in order to remain unencumbered, to work pro bono, without salary. If my proposals were not acceptable to Berlin, I told Pufendorf, there should be no hard feelings, and I would feel free to walk away. I had just ended my stint as a Lazard banker, and that is how my Jewish Museum story, and my involvement with Berlin and contemporary German affairs, began.

* * *

The fight over the Jewish Museum (JMB) had at first been strictly a Berlin issue and the sort of struggle over money and power at the heart of a lot of political in-fighting. What made this controversy so different and difficult, however, was that it came to be seen as a crisis in the German Jewish–non-Jewish relationship, one of the most sensitive issues in postwar national German life and always quick to arouse feelings of suspicion (by Jews) and guilt (by Germans). Add to this the accident of incompatible personalities, bureaucratic flim-flam, inattentive and clumsy political decision makers at the top, poor judgment plus unintended consequences, and you have all the ingredients of what made the JMB controversy so heated and complex.

The idea of establishing a Jewish Museum in Berlin to replace one the Nazis had closed in 1938 had been around for years. No one had a clear idea of exactly what such a museum would be about, and not much happened for a long time. A big budget and separate building for the small community of Jewish Berliners didn't seem appropriate, and thus arose the idea that perhaps a few rooms in the existing Berlin City Museum might be the right solution. By the early eighties, Berlin's municipal Museum Department (all German museums are state institutions) had seized on this concept and was actively promoting it for reasons of their own. The City Museum had long wanted a new building, but convincing the politicians to come up with the money had proved problematic. Since in postwar Germany Jewish citizens are always given special consideration, the city's bureaucrats assumed—not unreasonably—that if a new building incorporated a Jewish department, the budget cutters were less likely to veto it. To keep the Jewish angle linked to their building project, they pushed the somewhat specious argument that the history of Berlin and that of Berlin's Jews were two sides of the same coin and absolutely had to be depicted in a single structure, and successfully convinced Berlin's Parliament of the inherent logic of this idea. They also took to referring publicly to the entire building as a "Jewish Museum," though in fact their plan was to incorporate only a small Jewish department within it.

Even skilled bureaucrats can outsmart themselves. In 1988, the project had finally been approved, public proposals for what was vaguely described as an "independent Jewish Museum inside the Berlin Museum" were solicited, and in due time a public jury chose Daniel Libeskind's stunning, highly unusual design. Libeskind, then a relatively unknown American-Jewish architect and son of Polish Holocaust survivors, had proposed a dramatic avant-garde concept involving an exploded, jumbled-up Star of David with "voids" meant to communicate the tragic ruptures in German-Jewish life over the centuries, together with a Holocaust tower and commemorative stone garden—in other words, a design with deep Jewish symbolism. It was, to put it mildly, a daringly different approach. Eventually, when finally built, it would become one of Berlin's major architectural landmarks, and launch Daniel Libeskind's brilliant career.

What had happened was that the jurors who took the Jewish Museum label seriously had chosen a very special, very "Jewish" design for a museum actually intended only incidentally for a Jewish theme. The fall of the Berlin Wall caused yet further delays, until in 1992 the green light for construction of the Libeskind building was finally given. Eventually it would take seven years to complete it. Meanwhile, Amnon Barzel, an Israeli art historian, was hired in 1994 to run what continued to be referred to publicly as the Jewish Museum, but was in fact no more than a smallish department of the City Museum inside Libeskind's creation.

Just about everything to do with Barzel's employment went wrong from the start. The city bureaucracy wanted him to head up a small Jewish department; Barzel expected to be the director of a Jewish Museum of his own. They expected him to stick to the history of Berlin Jewry, but Barzel was more interested in modern art in general, and young Jewish artists and art themes in particular. Expecting to be a full-fledged museum director, he not unreasonably wanted independence and his own budget. Yet no such separate budget was remotely in the works—he was given virtually no staff and was allocated only minor funds. Finally, of course, he had his eye on the entire Libeskind building and was outraged to discover that "his" museum was to be restricted to some basement rooms in it.

Every aspect of his assignment was, therefore, quickly mired in disagreement, partly because of the failure to clarify the nature of his assignment and partly by the deliberate design of Berlin officials who had (as it would later be said) "played the Jewish card" in order to hoodwink the politicians with their highly questionable arguments of the logic of combining Berlin's and Jewish history, the so-called "integrated model." The resulting dustup quickly became public and progressively more nasty. At a minimum, it would have taken an unusually skillful negotiator with some knowledge of German-Jewish affairs, a feel for Berlin bureaucratic politics, empathy for Germans—and the patience of Job—to find common ground between so fundamentally conflicting objectives. Amnon Barzel, however, was quite unsuited to that task. He knew little about German history, spoke practically no German, and wasn't especially fond of Germans in general. Personally a cheerful man, in matters of tact and diplomatic subtlety he was almost totally deficient. Barzel did not negotiate or seek to clarify in private. Where he disagreed—which was on practically everything— he preferred to do battle in public and via the media—about his position, lack of autonomy, the building, the budget, the intentions of his employers, his take on German attitudes toward Jews, and even about Berlin in general. Some of his substantive complaints had merit, yet the way he went about challenging the local decision makers through the media merely infuriated them and did little to resolve any problems. The bureaucracy dug in its heels and fired back, the media had a field day, and the public took positions pro and con. Thus a local contest over money and control was allowed to escalate into what became seen even beyond German borders as a test of how Germany's capital city treated Jews. "Jewish scars reopened over Berlin Museum," the UK's *Observer* had entitled one of its reports,[255] and the nervous local political leadership was not amused.

The mayor, Eberhard Diepgen, had accepted the arguments of his officials without much thought, and for too long stuck to an atti-

tude of benign neglect. Slow to understand that he had a major political PR problem on his hands concerning one of Germany's most sensitive issues, one that raised unwanted ghosts of the past, he had sat
by as the press and public took sides, with a growing number of them
in support of the Jewish side.

Finally, however, Diepgen had had enough and in June 1997 ordered Barzel dismissed. The summary firing of the head of any local
cultural institution is always grist for the mill of local public opinion,
but removing the Jewish director—and an Israeli, at that—of what,
in the public mind, was a high-profile Jewish institution was unprecedented and immediately became a front-page sensation in Berlin and
all over the country. Far from resolving anything, the firing merely
served to raise tempers further and to heighten the criticism over
Berlin's handling of the affair.

The monkey now was squarely on the back of Senator Peter
Radunski, the CDU politician in Diepgen's cabinet in charge of
Berlin's cultural affairs, and of von Pufendorf, his deputy. Pufendorf,
however, the bearer of an old Prussian name going back to the time
of Frederick the Great, was a strong supporter of the City Museum's
interest in preserving its control over the Libeskind building. Radunski, a CDU political operative better known as the campaign manager
of Chancellor Kohl's reelection campaign than for his deep understanding of cultural matters, had for too long been content to let his
state secretary wrestle with the problem. Now he had no choice but
to grasp the nettle and quickly find a suitable, generally acceptable
successor to Barzel—someone, they hoped, who would help to calm
the waters while still allowing them to implement their plans. Somehow they concluded that in me they had found that man.

It would take a year to reach agreement on the mission of the new
Jewish Museum, its location, and how it would be managed and
financed. Within three months, as promised, I presented my recommendations, but a full nine months of tough negotiations and wran-

gling with city officials followed. The public and the media quickly lined up in support, but Berlin's bureaucrats, led by Pufendorf, stubbornly clung to their entrenched views. To their dismay, my proposal amounted to an almost total reversal of everything they had publicly advocated for years, and so the maddeningly thick-headed state secretary endlessly fought a rear-guard action with clumsy maneuvers long after the handwriting was already on the wall.

In sum, I had concluded that neither a museum dedicated to Jewish art or artists, nor one focused merely on the history of Berlin Jews, made much sense. Most of my private advisors had insisted that the very notion of "Jewish art," and the concept of Jews as a definable group of artists distinguishable from any other, were highly problematic. Historians, moreover, had pointed out that Berlin's Jews had always been an integral part of a single culture of Central European German-speaking Jewry stretching from Berlin to Vienna, Prague, and Budapest, and from every part of Germany to such distant corners in the erstwhile Austro-Hungarian empire as Czernowitz, now a part of the Ukraine. Their point was that the special role this entire group of Jewish German-speakers had played in the emergence of Germany as a modern nation, and their influence on every aspect of German life in science, art, the media, business, and finance, was the real factor of significance in understanding their place in German history, and the proper focus for a Jewish history museum in Germany's reunited capital city.

The image of a Jew in the minds of many younger Germans, few of which had ever met one, was that of a victim of Nazi crimes. This is what they remembered of their school lessons about the Holocaust, and I felt that providing them a broader historical perspective would have major benefits. Specifically, it would expand their understanding of the history of their own country by showing them that over many generations Jews had lived in Germany as a contributing minority, that all had benefitted from their participation in national life during good times, and that discrimination against them during periods of their persecution had greatly harmed everyone. I thought it would be a particularly relevant lesson underlining the importance of tolerance toward all minorities in a borderless globalized world, and a critical issue for Germany for decades to come.

Thus the approach I had proposed was that of a German history museum that would present the 2,000-year history of German-speaking Jewry from its earliest beginnings in Roman times to the present in an exciting way, including the use of interactive electronic media especially appealing to students and young people. That would require recruiting a special group of historians and museum specialists and managing them independently. It would also require much more space than a few rooms in a building dedicated to unrelated purposes. As my predecessor had insisted, albeit unsuccessfully, it meant that the entire building Daniel Libeskind had designed would be needed, as well as adequate funding of at least DM 18 to 24 million annually.

It was this that, not too surprisingly, had proved the most contentious and stubbornly resisted of all my recommendations. Yet nothing else really made any sense. Libeskind's building was deeply symbolic of the Jewish story, and using it for totally unrelated German history exhibits was unrealistic. "Frederick the Great and his Prussian soldiers don't belong in it," I stressed to the reluctant Mayor Diepgen—an argument which eventually carried the day.

Once agreement had been reached, it would take almost three more years to reconfigure the museum's interior, design the exhibition, hire staff, and get everything ready for the grand opening. The gala dinner on September 7, 2001, celebrating the official opening, was an unprecedented national event and Berlin's major newspapers exulted that "a similar parade of the prominence of the republic has never been seen before, whether in Bonn or in Berlin." Recognizing the national importance of establishing in Germany's reunited capital city what would be the largest and highest-visibility Jewish Museum in Europe, the federal government had taken over its financing and control from the city. The federal president was the main speaker, and the chancellor at the head of his cabinet, the Berlin Senate, minister-presidents of the *Länder*, Bundestag members, leaders of industry, and a phalanx of museum directors and government officials were all in attendance."[256] Daniel Barenboim had flown in the entire Chicago Symphony Orchestra to open the festivities with Mahler's *Seventh* at the Philharmonie. Easily twice as many requests for seats at the dinner as could be accommodated had poured in, and for weeks the problem of precedence and protocol—who was in and who was not—had given the museum staff sleepless nights. The guest list of notables from around the world included Henry Kissinger, New Jersey Senator Bill Bradley, a bevy of top Jewish leaders from the United States and Israel, a cardinal of the Catholic Church, the bishop of Berlin's Lutherans, and more than a dozen ambassadors. Even the mayor of Shanghai flew in for the occasion.

The contrast from the contentious atmosphere of three years earlier was extraordinary. Everyone was in excellent spirits and in a festive mood, and Germany's political establishment basked in the warm glow of international praise for having sponsored the most impressive Jewish museum in all of Europe. Jews were gratified, and the foreign guests were impressed. Yesterday's bitterest enemies in the museum controversy were smiling, and no one seemed to remember the endless quarrels of the past.

A decade after the JMB first opened its doors, it is firmly established and, with over three quarters of a million visitors annually, it is a huge success. My original intent to devote only eighteen months to it is no more than a distant memory.

Germans, especially students and young people, and tourists from all over the world come by the busloads to admire the architecture and view the exhibits. Thousands more participate in the JMB's program of lectures, concerts, and cultural events. Its archives are one of the most extensive in the Federal Republic, and the Museum Prize for Tolerance and Understanding is considered a prestigious national honor awarded annually to outstanding German and international recipients at a gala regularly attended by the German chancellor and the country's political, business and cultural leadership. Together with the separate Holocaust Memorial near the Brandenburg Gate, the JMB has become the leading component of a national network of institutions and monuments commemorating the rich history of German Jewry as well as their tragic fate.

The success of the JMB has been as extraordinary as it was unexpected—nor did I imagine my continued involvement with the museum over the last fourteen years. Along the way, the grateful German media began to endow me with almost magical powers. "He dominates the play," Berlin's *Tagesspiegel* explained[257] after the Grand Opening, and later a respected columnist in *Die Zeit* speculated that I would make an excellent mayor.[258] A book named me one of Berlin's most influential people, and to this day the media continue to solicit my views on a wide range of issues.

What explains this remarkable turnaround of the JMB project from its troubled beginnings and the overblown praise for me? A good press is a lot better than a bad one, but it's surely exaggerated, and I have no illusions that the real reason for it has much to do with me. Rather, I know that the single biggest explanation lies in the special position of Jews in Germany today, and in the surprising interest of Germans in Judaism and Jewish affairs. The story of the JMB is thus an excellent paradigm for the unique situation and turnaround in the situation of Jews in the contemporary life of the Federal Republic.

Jews and Germans Today

After almost seventy years, the Holocaust still has a profound impact on German life and on Jews and non-Jews alike.

The Nazis fanatically stoked the flames of Jew-hatred and tried hard to poison the minds of Germans with a barrage of anti-Semitic propaganda and lies. They wanted to eliminate all Jews and any trace of Jewish life on German soil, and after the war it almost seemed as if they had succeeded. Of the few who had survived, at most 12,000 to 15,000 had returned to live there.

Yet history can have a way of producing very different outcomes from what is intended by those in power. Today we know about an entirely different reality: Jewish life in Germany never totally ended and is vibrant and growing rapidly. It's a near miracle, but it is true; precise numbers are elusive, but in the second decade of the twenty-first century, upwards of 200,000 Jews again live in Germany, and the country currently has one of the fastest-growing Jewish populations in the world, already the ninth biggest and eight times as large as when I first came back in the fifties. In those days, the handful of Jews still in the country weren't much in the public eye, with scant dialogue between them and the rest of the population. Most Germans, guilt-ridden and embarrassed, had become what Wolf Lepenies has called "masters of subtle silence."[259] Two decades later there had been only limited changes. Small Jewish communities existed in some of the larger cities, but in most medium-sized and smaller towns there were none. Only sixty-seven Jews lived in the entire state of Schleswig-Holstein, for example, and with a mere forty-five synagogues and fifteen rabbis in all of Germany, the prospects for a real revival of Jewish life were still dim, all the more so because the remaining Jewish population was greatly overaged.[260] Deaths exceeded births by a factor of eight. Only 700 of the 6,000 Jews living in Berlin were less than thirty years old, twice as many throughout Germany were over fifty as below thirty, and three-quarters of Communist East Germany's Jews were over sixty.[261]

Today—after a major wave of Jewish immigration from the former Soviet Union in the nineties, active Jewish communities exist not only in all the larger cities, but also in a good many smaller towns. After a hiatus of almost three-quarters of a century, even my little hometown of Oranienburg now boasts a small community of Russian immigrant Jews and a functioning synagogue. As many as a hundred new synagogues have been built in the Federal Republic since the Wall came down. In the state of North Rhine-Westphalia alone, there are now twenty, and in a single September week of 2008, two new ones were opened to serve its 32,000 Jewish citizens. In addition to those in Berlin and Frankfurt, major new Jewish Museums have been opened in Dresden and Munich, another one is being built in Essen, and dozens of smaller towns where Jews once lived are following suit. In Berlin and in other cities there are Jewish schools, and even a seminary in Potsdam that recently graduated its first German-trained rabbi.

The land of the perpetrators of one of history's unequalled atrocities against Jews is today one of the friendliest countries anywhere outside the state of Israel in favoring and protecting Jewish life. Equally remarkable, the attitude of the majority of Germans toward Jews and their interest in Judaism has undergone a virtual sea change. There are certainly still anti-Semites in Germany—according to most studies and the estimate of the *Centralrat* (Jewish Federation) some 15 to 20 percent of the population harbor various degrees of subtle anti-Jewish sentiments. Yet that is less than in many other countries of Europe, and open expressions of anti-Semitism remain rare (excepting with the neo-Nazi fringe) and are considered the height of political incorrectness. If anything, a widespread—and to a visitor astonishing—philosemitism (love of Jews) is most often on display, and many Germans have developed a palpable fascination with all facets of Jewish life. Jews are seen as symbols of intelligence and righteousness, are treated deferentially and rarely criticized. Quite a few of Germany's major universities offer Judaic studies programs attracting large numbers of students, though job opportunities for them are limited. A single opening for a junior position at the JMB regularly generates applications from at least a hundred non-Jewish Judaic studies graduates who consider a job there a valued prize.

Bluntly put, in today's Germany, Jews and Jewishness in Germany are "in." In Berlin and other large cities there are restaurants specializing in "Jewish" food, Klezmer music is oddly popular, young Germans like to visit Israel, and some give their children Jewish names. I have run into more people in Germany who have converted to Judaism than I ever have in the United States, and I have lost count of the astounding number of Germans who proudly lay claim to partial Jewish ancestry as a kind of badge of honor.

The media mirror this interest in Jews, and the press almost obsessively features the memoirs of Jewish Holocaust survivors, or discourses on the tragic legacy of Germany's loss of its Jews. Every two weeks, my Berlin office sends me copies of such stories, a bundle of clippings rarely less than an inch thick.

Yet I worry that the present exceptional status of Jews in Germany and the tendency of large swaths of the population to idealize Jewishness may not be entirely healthy over the longer run, if a more stable German–Jewish relationship based on realism and mutual trust is to be assured. One problem is simply that many Germans still know relatively little about their Jewish fellow citizens. The problematic identity of German Jewry—how others see them and how they see themselves—is a related issue. Jews are typically seen as "different" and not fully German, as Jewish first and German second, and are, in turn, often still hesitant about a full commitment to Germany. If this perception of "otherness," endures on both sides, it could spell trouble at future moments of stress. Ironically, it is precisely their current uniquely protected and favored status that threatens to perpetuate setting Jews apart—a condition that has always been a trap for them in Germany. The willingness, furthermore, to have open and honest communication, and the courage to level with each other on sensitive issues, is still lacking on both sides. Given the painful past, this mutual reticence is understandable, and to change it won't be easy. Yet I see it as a critical prerequisite for establishing a fully normalized connection of Jews to their chosen German home.

It is surprising that, though the media constantly feature stories about Jewish subjects, many Germans remain relatively uninformed about them, and their interest in Judaism is more abstract than based on any specific knowledge. Even the better informed tend to dwell on—and to idealize—a German-Jewish past long since gone, and to speak with wistful melancholy about the Jews who formerly lived among their parents and grandparents. "It's people like you," I am often told, "who are Germany's great loss." What they have in mind are the pre-Hitler days when the greater number of the half million German Jews were well assimilated and integrated into German life, many with roots going back generations.

The reality is, however, that today's Jewish population bears little resemblance to that past. It is much less assimilated, with several ethnic, cultural, religious, and linguistic divisions, and with big differences in their sense of identity as Jews and their attitude toward Germany. Only a tiny fraction are former German Jews or their descendants, while a larger number are Polish Holocaust survivors or their children, who stayed behind after 1945. In the postwar years, it is they who dominated Jewish life in Germany and defended its interests.

By far the largest number of today's Jewish population in Germany, however—as many as 75 percemt—are recent immigrants from the former USSR. They came after 1989, mostly for economic reasons, and were admitted freely because of their claim of Jewishness. Yet though classified as Jews in the USSR, some in fact are only partly Jewish, and many have little or no real attachment to Judaism. As former Soviet citizens, they have initially shown only limited interest in German culture, and their memory of German crimes in the Soviet Union is often greater than of the Holocaust. I still remember the answer of a Jewish cab driver from Russia to my question of why, of all places, he had come to Germany. "Simple," he shot back, "it's a lot easier to make a living here than in Russia!" When I mentioned the Holocaust, he merely shrugged!

Widespread unfamiliarity with Jews and misconceptions about them could have potentially troublesome consequences. True, some of these misconceptions are merely amusing; but other implications are not. On the lighter side, many Germans assume that Jews eat only kosher food. Thus my thoroughly secular Jewish colleague, Cilly Kugelmann, was surprised to discover on a recent overseas flight that the museum official in charge of travel, who is not Jewish, had taken pains to alert the airline that a kosher meal must be served to her. Potentially more troublesome, however, is the related question of Jewish identity, and the conflation on the part of many Germans of Israel, on the one hand, and being Jewish on the other. Ignatz Bubis, the former head of the Jewish Federation in Germany, describes a particularly telling incident in this regard in his autobiography:

> "No less a person than the President of the Federal Office for Political Education . . . felt it appropriate to assure me on the occasion of a state visit by Israeli President Ezer Weizman to German Federal President Roman Herzog that "'the President' had given a splendid talk." When I allowed that President Herzog always gives splendid speeches, he replied: "I meant *your* President!"[262]

Bubis was a German citizen and not only the president of the *Zentralrat*, but also a member of the Free Democratic Party (FDP) and a well-known public figure.[263] Yet the assumption that as a Jew his first allegiance was to Israel rather than to Germany is by no means a rarity, but rather an unspoken belief of many Germans. I recall, for example, the shocked reaction of a German acquaintance to a critical comment of mine about some element of Israeli policy. Though I suspect that he agreed, he wouldn't have dared to say so, and probably considered my critique as bordering on disloyalty to "my country." It doesn't take much imagination to understand how this sets Jews apart in German eyes, with potentially troublesome consequences.

Actually, the question of identity—the reluctance to recognize minorities as full fellow citizens—is a more general German problem. The United States, for example, has always been an immigrant and multiethnic, racially and religiously diverse society. Yet, while discrimination against African-Americans, anti-Semitism, and prejudices against and between various immigrant groups at various stages of U.S. history have often been a feature of national life, the immigrants' identity as "Americans" has never been questioned once they become citizens. In Germany, that remains a problem to this day for the several million former Turkish guest workers and their families, who have lived in Germany most or all of their lives. Many are now German citizens and speak German, their children were born there and few will ever leave. In German eyes, however, they remain foreigners—*Ausländer* or, as they are now euphemistically called, people with a "migration background." A German-Turk is seen as a Turk first and a German second, which reinforces his alienation and separation from parts of normal German life, and in turn perpetuates a self-image of otherness.

German Jews are better off, yet when it comes to their identity as Germans, there are some similarities. For most Germans, a Jew is first of all a Jew—and more or less subtly, often with the best of intentions, they will let you know it. "I arrive in Berlin as an American," I sometimes tell my German audiences, "but usually I leave as a Jew." That's my way of saying that Germans will quickly signal that they are aware of my Jewishness, and that this, rather than my American nationality, defines me in their eyes. When I tell them that in the United States being Jewish in most places isn't a particularly relevant feature of one's identity as an American (outwardly observant Orthodox Jews excepted), I am never quite sure that they really grasp this; and when I tell them that I have occasionally discovered only by accident that a close colleague is also a Jew, after working with him for several months or longer, many simply cannot believe it.

In sum, my concern is that setting Jews apart as somehow different from others, even with the best of intentions, complicates the process toward a normalization of the Jewish–non-Jewish relationship which, I am convinced, is a sine qua non for a stable future for Jewish life in Germany.

The failure to speak honestly to each other is a significant barrier to normalcy and better mutual understanding. Indeed the eagerness, on the German side, to please the Jewish minority, and the reticence to speak openly or to appear to be critical on any issue involving Jews can be quite remarkable. For example, until 2007 the leaders of Berlin's Jewish Community were engaged over several years in very public and highly unattractive internecine warfare involving money and power, with vicious mutual accusations of waste and dishonesty. Since public funds were involved it would not have been surprising for the media to take a strong stand. Given that the allegations of wrongdoing were widely known and a number of dubious personalities were involved, the absence of any direct criticism in the press reports was striking. The matter would sometimes come up in my conversations with German friends, and whenever I expressed dismay over what was clearly a Berlin scandal and not merely an unappetizing Jewish family fight, their first reaction was invariably embarrassment, and then the familiar response: "You can say that—but we can't!"

It's a comment I have heard innumerable times, and most directly in connection with my involvement in the dramatic "Degussa" debate on the board of the Holocaust Memorial—the mammoth stone garden commemorating murdered Jews, in the shadow of Brandenburg Gate.

Today this remarkable monument attracts thousands of visitors every day and owes its existence to years of determined promotion by a private group of mostly non-Jewish citizens. Since it was built with public funds, a large board of some thirty members under the chairmanship of then-Bundestag President Wolfgang Thierse had been appointed to oversee its construction. A few were Jews, but the majority were non-Jewish private citizens and politicians. A handful of unaffiliated "outsiders" had been added to the mix, including me as the only non-German.

The memorial had been the subject of years of contention, and from the beginning the well-meaning Thierse had his hands full keeping order. Very late in the game, a crisis suddenly erupted when Alexander Brenner, the president of Berlin's Jewish Community, discovered that the memorial's 2,700 stones were being treated with a special coating furnished by a supplier whose name—Degussa— evokes deeply troubling Jewish memories. In Nazi times, it had been Degussa that smelted the gold extracted from the teeth of Jewish victims. Worse yet, Degussa also supplied the gas used to murder Jews, and now Brenner vehemently insisted that the Degussa contract be immediately cancelled and the large number of stones already treated, scrapped. The problem, however, was that the cost to scrap or rework them would have been prohibitive, there wasn't the money for it, and no alternate supplier was readily available.

A passionate debate followed. At least a half dozen non-Jewish members joined in fervent support of ejecting Degussa, a few others pointed out the complications without daring to oppose the idea outright, while the others sat by in embarrassed silence. No one knew what to do, and when Thierse adjourned the meeting it ended in confusion. The board was faced with a genuine dilemma but, in fact, a not unusual one. No one disputed that, except for its especially unsavory name, the Degussa of today had nothing to do with its predecessor of seventy years ago, and that in this respect the company was no different from several other suppliers and almost every major German enterprise with roots going back to the Nazi years. The successor managements are generations removed from Nazi ties, and in virtually all cases, Degussa included, they have long ago built a record of goodwill and support for Jewish causes. Acceding to Brenner's wishes would have logically required eliminating several other suppliers and put the entire initiative at risk.

When the board reconvened and the impasse continued, I eventually—with some reluctance—asked for the floor. As a Jew, the Degussa name had the same horrid ring for me, I explained, but to punish the current management which had indisputably traveled a very different road for many years struck me as unwise. After all, I argued, it was Germans who wanted the memorial to honor the victims of Nazi crimes, and these were the very German companies who had strongly supported the initiative. That had to be acknowledged. As a sympathetic outside observer, I said, I thought that the challenge for the future was for Germans and the Jewish minority to build a new and more normal relationship, and this was a small step to do so.

I had spoken for fifteen minutes, and when I finished, after a moment of uncertain silence, the ice was broken and the relief pervading the room was palpable. I was the object of lots of grateful glances, and a dozen members who hadn't spoken before screwed up their courage to support me. When Thierse polled the board, a strong majority now voted to proceed as planned. Outside the room, I heard the familiar refrain: "We always agreed, but only you could say it—we couldn't!"

Today the Holocaust Memorial is considered a great success, and the Degussa debate is long forgotten.

What all this adds up to, I believe, is this: when I was growing up in the thirties, Germany was one of the worst places in the world for a Jew. Today it is one of the best.

Among my more vivid childhood memories is the atmosphere of caution, uncertainty, and fear that held the generation of my parents in its grip. We children weren't wanted in regular German schools, yet some of the residents around the Jewish school I attended protested loudly on their street. In our apartment building in Berlin, the openly anti-Semitic neighbors intimidated us with their uniforms, swastikas, and cold stares. Many neighbors simply looked away and said nothing.

For today's Jewish Berliners, the situation couldn't be more different. There are two Jewish schools again, but the youngsters who go there do so strictly by choice—and about a third aren't Jewish at all and have freely chosen to join their Jewish classmates. As for me, these days I rent an apartment in the heart of old Berlin, and the invariably warm welcome from my neighbors is one of the reasons why I enjoy returning every couple of months.

In Nazi Germany, the Jewish population was declining and its prospects were grim. Today the welcome mat is out for a steady influx of new Jewish arrivals. There are still a lot more graves in the sprawling Jewish Weissensee cemetery than there are living Jewish Berliners, but the number of the latter is again on the rise. In addition to those from Eastern Europe who came in the nineties, there is also a regular inflow of younger Jews from the rest of the world, including—amazingly —a surprising number of Israeli-born second- and third-generation descendants of former German Jews. Asked why he had chosen the country that was once the scene of murderous crimes against Jews, Gilad Hochman, the recently-arrived Israeli twenty-six-year old grandson of a Holocaust survivor, cited the Berlin music scene and the friendly reception of the people. "My grandmother still had a number tattooed on her arm," he added, "but it's not my task to pass judgment on history. I have felt at home here from the first day."[264] Hochman is not alone: a remarkable 4,313 Israelis applied for German citizenship in 2006.

Nevertheless, for much of the more than half century since the war, the relations of those Jews who stayed behind with the Germans among whom they have chosen to live have remained ambivalent and never free of the past. Yet as shared memories become more historical than personal, the nature of the relationship of German Jews to their fellow citizens is evolving. Future generations of Germans and Jews will have to learn to live together in a less constrained, more normal atmosphere based on full mutual commitment as fellow Germans.

The special treatment of Jews in Germany is unlikely to last forever. Nor should it, because over the long run it carries with it as many seeds of trouble as it does benefits. The transition to greater normalcy will not be easy to accept for those Jews who have learned to expect— and yes, to enjoy—the uniqueness of their special position, and the material and psychological benefits that flow from it. "The 'Jewish bonus' we have enjoyed and taken advantage of is bound to fade," a Jewish leader recently confessed to me, "but there will be compensations, and I won't be altogether unhappy when it happens."

For the broader German population it will be a learning process, though ultimately a salutary one. For them the challenge is to acquire the habit of accepting all minorities in their midst as German, based on a common citizenship, Jews included. That runs counter to still deeply-ingrained German instincts. Overcoming such feelings is essential in a globalized world without borders, and Germany's demographic realities require it. Full integration of the Jewish minority is only a part of a much wider challenge that Germany faces.

The Immigrant Question

Like many Western European nations, Germany is confronted by something akin to a demographic meltdown—a steadily shrinking, rapidly aging population. Left unaddressed, this would unavoidably undermine her international competitiveness and standard of living.

Few knowledgeable observers dispute the underlying facts. While most Western European countries must deal with the common demographic reality of shrinking and aging populations, the German situation is more serious because the birth rate is among the lowest (Italy's is marginally lower) and has been declining faster than is true almost anywhere else. For the years 2000 to 2005 the average number of births per woman of child-bearing age (the fertility rate) declined in Germany from 1.58 in the seventies to 1.32, which compares unfavorably with lesser drops in much of the rest of Europe. By comparison, the U.S. fertility rate actually rose over the same period.[265]

If the recent trend is projected forward without offsetting inflows to the labor force, the consequences would be serious. Estimates are that the population would decline by a third over the next forty years, and be cut in half by the end of the century. The median age would rise from forty to about fifty by mid-century (in the United States it is closer to thirty), and the ratio of those over sixty-five to that part of the population in their productive years between twenty and sixty-four would double.[266] So large a shrinkage in the labor force relative to pensioners would put unsustainable pressure on Germany's pay-as-you-go social system, which former Chancellor Helmut Schmidt has rightly called the country's "greatest achievement of the twentieth century."[267]

The key to the postwar German *Sozialstaat* has been the high productivity of an efficient workforce, which has made Germany one of the world's great export champions. People have been Germany's most valuable resource, but a shrinking and aging population pool would put all this at risk unless major steps are taken to reverse the trend: specifically, most experts agree, a sustained national program to attract the something like 300,000 new immigrants annually required to keep the population near present levels. Absorbing so large a number of new immigrants for a good many years would be a major challenge anywhere, and especially in Germany, where the attachment to an ethnically homogeneous society is still deeply embedded in the national psyche. What is required therefore, is not only a proactive immigration policy, but also a parallel program to smooth the immigrants' path toward acceptance as full and equal citizens. The ambiguous status of German-Turks illustrates the complexity of the challenge Germany faces.

The original assumption that the Turkish guest workers, who came in the boom years of the sixties and seventis to alleviate the postwar labor shortage, would stay a while and then go home again is long since a thing of the past. Most never left and were in fact joined over the years by family members and marriage partners for their offspring. Moreover, while Germans tend to marry late (or not at all) and have few children, Turkish culture favors rather larger families. Today, the 3 million Turks are the country's largest—and most rapidly growing—ethnic minority. Their children and grandchildren are born in Germany, and an increasing number now hold German passports.

Over the years, I have come to know quite a few of them well. They are shopkeepers and restaurateurs who enrich German life in many ways, their children attend universities, some are successful professionals, and a few are active in politics. The JMB has several German-Turks on its staff, including one of my deputies, who is a valued colleague.

These, however, are still the exception. A half century later, far too many German-Turks remain the proverbial underclass, poorly integrated into German life and living in ghetto-like enclaves in the poorer sections of large cities. A disproportionate number of their children do not finish high school, have trouble finding jobs, are prone to truancy and mischief, and remain perennial outsiders.

Left to their own devices and disconnected from German life—yet in many ways already more German than Turkish—too many German-Turks remain strangers in their adopted country. The rest of the population does not accept them as real Germans, and they, resenting this identity of "otherness," cling all the more adamantly to their own language and culture. Meanwhile the public complains that they refuse to learn German, that they adhere to alien values, customs, and dress codes, and it fears their religion about which little is known or understood. Especially in difficult economic times, there is always the occasional politician, along with extremists on the left and right, who exploits such popular fears and prejudices for his own ends.

For many German-Turks, even the more assimilated, Germany is thus not a particularly welcoming environment. According to recent surveys, one in two Turks does not feel wanted in Germany and lacks a sense of belonging. In something of a vicious circle, they are expected to shed their own culture, but many resent feeling unwanted, resist the pressures for cultural conformity, and refuse assimilation for that very reason. The burden is largely placed on them, but that is a price considered too high, and so the mutual distance, rejection, and resentment continues. As one Turkish observer put it, "(Turks) . . . are stamped the eternal foreigner . . ."[268] Even those who have been born in Germany and have advanced above the others feel split in their allegiance. They argue that one can be Muslim, retain one's Turkish heritage, and be a good German too, but that the Germans make that extremely difficult. "A German passport or speaking German like a native is not enough" explains a German-Turkish lawyer and leading member of the FDP. "As long as my name is strange and I look like a Turk and am not a Christian, I'm not fully accepted."[269]

When I discuss this problem with German friends, I frequently hear an easy excuse that is as common as it is false. "Unlike you Americans," they tell me, "we are not an immigration country—it's not our tradition and so we feel differently." The reality is, however, that this claim is borne out neither by German history nor contemporary reality. Hitler's fantasies of a blond, blue-eyed German race were always a figment of his imagination, because Germany has for centuries attracted immigrants from many parts of Europe—French Huguenots in the eighteenth century, Slavs from Poland and Russia, Bohemians from the Southeast, and Jews from the East and the Mediterranean. They intermingled and intermarried with the locals over many years and, except for some of the Jews, were successfully absorbed. The postwar years, moreover, saw an even larger influx not merely of Turks, but also of Serbs, Croats, and Kosovars from the former Yugoslavia, Kurds, Iranians, and Israelis from the Near East, Italians, Poles, Russian Jews, and diverse others from a total of thirty-three additional countries.[270]

Many Germans do not seem to recognize the reality that today's foreign-born inhabitants of Germany account for 12 to 13 percent of the total population, which is just about the same as the corresponding number in that prototype of an immigration country, the United States. In Berlin, every fourth person is an immigrant, and over 40 percent of those aged six to fifteen were born outside Germany.[271] With a net inflow of 2.6 million new arrivals between 1991 and 2006, Germany in the recent past has in fact been by far the largest immigration country in the entire European Union. As a case in point, some have noted that the entire forward line of Germany's vaunted national soccer team—all are German citizens—has distinctly non-German-sounding names.

So Germany has already come a long way toward being a multiethnic society. That's a fact in daily evidence on the streets, in schools, and in all phases of everyday life. Moreover, in light of demographic trends, the need to absorb many more ethnically diverse immigrants is a certainty. The challenge Germans face in coming years is to become more proactive in managing an immigration policy in line with national needs, along with establishing high priority programs to facilitate the integration of new immigrants into national life. Retaining one's own cultural heritage and language need not be a hindrance to one's commitment to a new national identity. Indeed, such diversity is to be celebrated as a source of strength in a multiethnic society. In the United States, the classic immigration country, it has never stood in the way of the acceptance of immigrants as new Americans.

"Proud to be a Berliner"

The emergence of Berlin as one of the most interesting major capitals of Europe is part of the German reunification miracle. My early recollections of Berlin under the obscene Nazis were eminently forgettable, and its truncated, postwar successor always left me sad and nostalgic for her lost better days. So it has been all the more thrilling to be in the middle of the city's miraculous resurrection of recent years. Through the Berliners I have met, the good friends I have made, my colleagues at the JMB, and the richness of its manifold offerings and attractions, Berlin has become one of my favorite places in the world. And no one is more surprised than I.

Not long ago, I asked Lala Süsskind, then the president of Berlin's Jewish Community, whether she considered herself a German. Since many Germans think of German Jews as Jews first, I am always curious about how they themselves feel. Süsskind obviously had some difficulty with my question. She looked at me pensively for a moment, and then gave an ambiguous answer. The question was difficult to answer simply, she said, but quickly added that in any case she was truly an unconditional 100-percent Berliner. "My allegiance is to Berlin," she explained, "it's my city and my home and I feel totally a part of it!" Süsskind belongs to that generation of Jews with still vivid memories of the Holocaust, which explains her inner German identity conflicts. However her enthusiasm for Berlin was unequivocal and didn't surprise me. Indeed, I share it. For most of my life I have been an American, but I must say it clearly: I am, once again, a Berliner, too!

When the Wall came down, the contrast between the divided parts of Berlin couldn't have been greater. The Western half with amply stocked shops and well-dressed people filling restaurants and cafés belonged to an utterly different world from the Eastern side of the Wall with its Soviet bloc drabness and joyless faces. Over the almost three decades of its existence, the Wall appeared to have created not merely a physical barrier, but also a deep emotional and psychological one between the two parts of Berlin, and I remember thinking that it would take generations to bridge it. The big surprise is that it took less than one.

I often ask myself what explains the remarkably rapid transformation of two so different worlds into what is today one of the more exciting world cities and a magnet for visitors from all over. Part of the reason, I think, is that a special spirit of change, released freedom, and new possibilities quickly took hold—the Germans call it *Aufbruchstimmung*—and that many young people, including those from outside Germany, came to be a part of it. They flocked to the run-down areas of East Berlin, where rents were cheap, and rejuvenated them, physically and with new energy and drive. Today, some of these neighborhoods remind one of Soho and Greenwich Village in New York, with art galleries and rock concerts, where locals and tourists mingle in cafes and pubs till late into the night.

Berliners have an attitude and spirit I find highly appealing and which even a half century of Communism proved unable to squelch. They aren't always the most beloved among other Germans, but they are more independent-minded than many of their countrymen, and more practical and direct. They have a special sense of humor (something for which Germans aren't generally known), they don't mind telling you what they think, and they are always quick with an irreverent repartee—the famous *"Berliner Schnauze"* (trap). Recently, for example, we were about to order dinner in a restaurant when the young waitress, a typical Berliner by her accent, interrupted and insisted on first telling us about the evening's "Specials." "Go ahead," I bantered, "I'll hold my breath"—whereupon she shot back in a typical Berlin way: "Relax, Mister, you can exhale!"

Twenty years after reunification, Berlin has become a world city, a magnet for an ever-growing number of foreign visitors, and a very "livable" place with many attractions. Over the years I have lived in several major cities in Europe and in the United States. Each had its special charms. Washington is unique in America for its historic landmark buildings and monuments, San Francisco boasts surely one of the most spectacular settings of the world, and nothing can compare to the dynamism and diversity of New York. I loved the intimacy of Geneva on the shores of Lac Léman, and who could resist being seduced by the multiple attractions of Paris's culinary temples, churches, architectural gems, harmonious squares, and Gallic savoir-faire? Nevertheless, for living away from my hometowns of Princeton or New York, I would now put Berlin at the top.

Berliners have a healthy skepticism about their politicians and love to grumble, but I often advise them to count their blessings. Whether they admit it or not, they enjoy a generally high standard of living, good public services, and rich cultural offerings. Berlin may have its problems—all big cities do—but for anyone exposed to Manhattan's crowded and overstretched transportation network, Berlin's public transport sparkles by comparison. I particularly love the U-Bahn, whose trains are clean, modern, rarely overfull, and dependably on time.

Livability and people-friendliness are, in fact, the features of Berlin life I find most impressive. The city is in permanent financial straits and has one of the largest debt loads of any major German city, but, broke or not, enough money continues to be invested in infrastructure and in operations to maintain this emphasis on the comforts of daily life. The streets are well-swept, potholes are fixed, and there is plenty of attention to parks and greenery. Most major cities struggle with at least some run-down, slum-like areas, but in Berlin I know of virtually none. On weekends when the Sunday strollers are out in force, there are roller skate and bicycle races throughout town (sometimes, I think, excessively so) but pedestrians good-naturedly accept blocked-off thoroughfares to accommodate them. And the municipal building authorities, much criticized for their conservative tastes and dictatorial ways, do a better job of planning and neighborhood development than is true for most other cities I know of.

And, of course, for anyone in search of cultural stimulation, Berlin has an amazing range of offerings, an embarras de richesses in how to allocate one's leisure hours. Simon Rattle's Berlin Philharmonic is among the best orchestras in the world, and at the Staatsoper, the incredible Daniel Barenboim may be conducting Wagner or Mahler or may be doing double duty as piano soloist and conductor all at the same time. And there is always the option of walking across the Gendarmenmarkt to the Konzerthaus, where another very respectable orchestra performs. What more could a music lover ask for? I still haven't managed to work my way through all the Berlin museums, but some are my favorites, among them the remarkable Pergamon, one of the world's best, and the Neue Nationalgalerie, for its special shows. The Berggruen, with its Impressionists, is one of Berlin's special jewels.

Personally, I like some of the Berliner Ensemble's theater repertory offerings of German classics, where I have seen their excellent version of the *Threepenny Opera* at least three times. And occasionally it can be wonderful on a free afternoon to check out the art galleries around Auguststrasse in old Berlin, or in the area near the JMB and along some of the Ku'damm's side streets in the West. A lot of it is too funky and avant-garde for my tastes, but I confess that on a few occasions these excursions, as well as the Villa Grisebach's auctions, have cost me more than I had planned.

Unfortunately, not enough Berliners who can afford it dig deep enough into their own pockets to support the cultural institutions they take for granted. There is too much reliance on public funds, which, I think, is a weakness. And it would be great if Berlin's shopkeepers were allowed to decide freely when to open and close their stores. It's what most world cities do nowadays, and it's time that Berlin follows suit. Yet, when all is said and done, Berlin has never been better than it is today.

"Normal" again?

July 8, 2006, was the day before the Grand Finale of the soccer World Cup, with France slated to play Italy for the championship at Berlin's

Olympia Stadium. On a beautiful summer day, host country Germany was exuberantly celebrating what for many citizens was a once-in-a-generation experience.

Berlin was overflowing with visitors from all over the world, with a sea of more German flags displayed and joyously waved than on any previous occasion. The last time I had seen that many national flags in Berlin had been in the Nazi years, when flying the swastika was considered a civic duty, but in self-conscious postwar Germany, such patriotic displays had ever since been studiously avoided for that very reason. Yet suddenly—and astonishingly—the inhibition against outward displays of German pride appeared to have dissipated. Among the flags of the hordes of visitors—Ghanaians in native dress, Mexicans in sombreros, Japanese with rising sun hatbands and cameras at the ready, and Americans with their stars and stripes—the German colors predominated and more than held their own.

Something new—more than just soccer fever—had evidently happened to the national mood, and lots of people were commenting on it. The question going through my mind was whether it was the spirit of the moment only, or whether it was evidence of a more permanent change in the German self-image.

That day I wasn't alone in pondering the question. Henry and Nancy Kissinger had flown in for the occasion, and we had invited mutual German friends to a luncheon in their honor where the question had been debated at length. Among the guests were Kurt Biedenkopf, the longtime minister-president of Saxony, State Secretary Silberberg from the Foreign Office, Daimler executive Klaus Mangold, and Humboldt University historian Heinrich Winkler, and their wives. Kissinger is an enthusiastic soccer fan, and Barbara had decorated the dining room of our apartment with the appropriate soccer motifs (including the flags of the attendees).

As might be expected for this U.S.–German group, we had devoted the first part of the afternoon to "solving" the major political issues of the moment. Soon, however, we too had crowded around the television to watch Germany defeat Portugal for the honor of third place in the tournament. When it was over, horns were blaring in the streets below, and the television was broadcasting exuberant scenes where the national colors were being waved wildly and the cheering wouldn't stop.

It was the astute Kurt Biedenkopf who leaned over with a comment that impressed me: "So much national pride would have been unthinkable until recently," he noted with a mixture of amazement and satisfaction. "Young people would have sneered at it, and adult Germans would have been embarrassed. But now there is a new generation on the way up, we Germans have turned a corner, and no one is any longer afraid. Flags and patriotism are 'in' again; but we are starting off in the best possible way, not aggressively but in sports, and with Germany as part of Europe and a global world."

Biedenkopf was right. To be sure, German soccer fever was temporary, but it triggered something more basic that had been a long time coming. What we were witnessing was the result of a process of change acted out through successive postwar German generations. In the post-reunification nineties, Germany has become a very different country—unrecognizably different from the ugly Nazi nation of my youth but also from the traumatized, self-hating, confused, and divided one of the fifties, the striving yet still angst-ridden Cold War Germany of the Wirtschaftswunder sixties, and the angry, rebellious, internally troubled one of the seventies. In the nineties, once the Berlin Wall had come down, Germany had emerged as the largest and strongest economy in Europe. As the *New York Times*'s Roger Cohen had put it, what we had seen during the World Cup and what Biedenkopf had tried to express was the completion of the Germans', "psychological journey from denial to avowal, numbness to awakening, from tutelage to emancipation and even confrontation, from self-doubt to self-assertion."[272]

Later I would hear others say that Germany had become normal "again," yet that misstates matters. Never before in history has Germany been "normal" like this, a nation with an increasingly ethnically diverse population and an independent sense of self, but with strong allegiance to liberal principles and the rule of law. The technological revolution of the seventies and eighties ushered in the global age. All countries were deeply affected by it, but Germany arguably more profoundly than most, with the fall of the Berlin Wall and the changes in the population mix that continue to this day.

By a quirk of fate, I became an observer of this process in the nineties, and a peripheral participant in Berlin's transformation from an island city to a national capital.

At a deeply personal level, it has been the closing of a circle. For this I am grateful. It makes me hopeful for the future, and I feel privileged to have been a part of it.

NOTES

PREFACE

1. Winston Churchill, for one, well understood that individuals matter and that personal relations between political leaders can shape history. At the nadir of Britain's fortunes in World War II, when the fate of his country hung by a slender thread, everything depended on vital supplies under Lend-Lease from still-neutral America. As Churchill embarked to press his case at his first face-to-face meeting with Roosevelt, the question that most concerned him in assessing the prospects of his mission was "will he like me?" See W. Averell Harriman, *Special Envoy to Churchill and Stalin 1941–46*, Random House, New York, 1975, pg. 75.

2. Between 1960 and 1990, I was entitled to be a citizen of both East and West Germany, Israel, and the United States.

3. According to the U.S. Constitution, the line of succession runs from the Vice President to Speaker of the House, President Pro Tempore of the Senate, Secretary of State, to Secretary of the Treasury. Nominally only, however, because as a foreign-born citizen I would have been passed over for the next in line.

4. E. J. Hobsbawm, *The Age of Empire 1875–1914*, Vintage Books, New York, 1987, pg. 3.

THE THIRTIES
GERMANY IN TROUBLE: IN NAZI BERLIN

5. Their Jewish stars, Elisabeth Bergner, Max Pallenberg, the tenor Richard Tauber, Grete Mosheim, Kurt Gerron, Peter Lorre, and others, would not have as easy a time. Marlene Dietrich was a notable exception. Strongly anti-Nazi, she however was not Jewish.

6. Miraculously spared from the wartime bombing, the space is occupied by a chocolate shop today.

7. In 1920. See Bodo Harenberg (ed.), *Die Chronik Berlins*, Chronik Verlag, Dortmund, 1986, pg. 341.

8. Except, after the Berlin Wall came down, in the eastern sections of present day Berlin, where streetcars had made somewhat of a comeback under the Communists.

9. See also my chapter on Eloesser in *The Invisible Wall*, Counterpoint, Washington, 1988, pgs. 236–85.

10. For a detailed account of the Kaliski School and the role it played during its brief existence in Nazi Berlin see Busemann, Daxner, Fölling, *Insel der Geborgenheit*, Stuttgart, 1992.

11. Hugh Trevor-Roper, *Hitler's Politisches Testament*, Albrecht Kraus, Hamburg, 1981, Introduction pg. 17.

12. Ian Kershaw, *Hitler, Volume I: 1889–1936*, The Penguin Press, London, 1998, pg. xix.

13. Ibid., pg. xxi.

14. In 1938, he made the point abundantly clear to the German military's chief of staff, General Franz Halder: "You will never learn what is going on in my head," he laughed to him. "As for those who boast of being privy to my thoughts—to them I lie all the more."

15. See Max Domarus, *Hitler: Reden und Proklamationen*, Süddeutscher Verlag, München, 1965, pgs. 2236–9.

16. See Trevor-Roper, *Hitler's Politisches Testament*, pg. 64.

17. Adolf Hitler, *Monologe im Führerhauptquartier, 1941–1944. Die Aufzeichnungen Heinrich Heims.* Werner Jochmann, (ed.), Albrecht Knaus Verlag, Hamburg, 1980, pg. 99.

18. Traudl Junge, *Bis zur letzten Stunde*, Buch und Medien, München, 2002, pg. 121.

19. See Trevor-Roper, *Hitler's Politisches Testament*, pgs. 60–116.

20. Ibid, pg. 110.

21. See Henry Picker, *Hitler's Tischgespräche im Führerhauptquartier*, Ullstein, München, 2003.

22. Hermann Rauschning, *The Voice of Destruction*, GP Putnam & Sons, New York, 1940, pg. 230.

23. See Picker, *Hitler's Tischgespräche im Führerhauptquartier*, pg. 707.

24. See Ian Kershaw, *Hitler 1936–1945*, W.W. Norton & Company, New York & London, 2000, pg. 181.

25. Cited in Michael Stürmer, *Das Jahrhundert der Deutschen,* Goldmann, München, 1999, pg. 148.

26. See Anthony Eden, *Facing the Dictators*, Houghton Mifflin, Boston, 1962, pg. 27.

27. See *New York Times*, February 26, 1933 Page SM7 and March 23, pg. 1933.

28. *New York Times*, January 31, 1933, pgs. 3 & 16.

29. George A. Gordon to State Department, from Munich, May 13, 1933, pg. 20.

30. Leon Dominian, American Consul General, Stuttgart to State Department, March 31, 1933.

31. U.S. Embassy Berlin to Honorable Cordell Hull, Washington. Draft. "The Jews in Nazi Germany," pg. 33, May 30, 1933.

32. George S. Messersmith to William Phillips, U.S. Under Secretary of State, Washington, D.C. September 29, 1933.

33. William E. Dodd, Letter to President Roosevelt, November 27, 1933.

34. *New York Times*, January 31, 1933; *Time* Volume XXI, February 6, 1933; *Chicago Tribune*, February 4, 1933, pg. 12.

35. *Chicago Tribune, New York Times*, April 2, 1933.

36. See *New York Times*, March 26, 1933, pg. 28.

37. See *New York Times*, June 11, 1933, pg. E1.

38. Winston S. Churchill, *The Gathering Storm*, Houghton Mifflin, Boston, 1948, pg. 86.

39. Ibid, see Chapters 7 & 8.

40. See Paul Schmidt, *Statist auf diplomatischer Bühne, 1923–45*, Athenäum Verlag, Bonn, 1950, pgs. 318–326.

41. See Martin Gilbert, *A History of the Twentieth Century: Volume II*, Avon, New York, 1998, pgs. 14–15.

42. Churchill, *The Gathering Storm*, Chapter 6, pgs. 90–109.

43. Eugen Weber, *The Hollow Years*, W.W. Norton & Company, New York, 1994, pg. 5.

44. Hans-Heinrich Dieckhoff to the German Foreign Office, December 7, 1937, in *Akten zur deutschen auswärtigen Politik 1918–1945, Volume 1*, Baden-Baden, 1950, pg. 534.

45. See *Die Juden in Deutschland*, Wolfgang Benz, ed. CH Beck Verlag, München, pgs. 740–54.

46. Wolf-Arno Kropat, *Reichskristallnacht*, Kommission für die Geschichte der Juden in Hessen, Wiesbaden, 1997, pgs. 192–201.

47. Ibid, pgs. 185–92.

48. There is an extensive literature detailing the events of the Kristallnacht pogroms and their background. See, for example Peter Loewenberg, "The Kristallnacht as a Public Degradation Ritual," in Volume XXXII, *Leo Baeck Institute Yearbook*, 1987, pgs. 309–323. Anthony Read and David Fisher, *Kristallnacht*, Random House, New York, 1989.

49. Buffum, "Confidential Report, Anti-Semitic Onslaught in Germany as seen from Leipzig," November 21, 1938. National Archives, Washington, D.C.

50. Arthur D. Morse, *While Six Million Died*, Random House, New York, 1968, pg. 222.

51. Anthony Read & David Fisher, *Kristallnacht*, pg. 68.

52. *New York Times*, November 12, 1938, pg. 1.

53. Ibid, pg. 4.

54. These citations are similar to those in the author's *The Invisible Wall*, pgs. 360–1.

55. Avraham Barkai, *From Boycott to Annihilation*, Brandeis University Press, Hanover, New Hampshire, 1989, pgs. 152–3.

56. *Newsweek*, November 28, 1938, pg. 13.

57. Arthur Morse, *While Six Million Died,* pg. 231.

58. Saul S. Friedman, *No Haven for the Oppressed*, Wayne State University Press, Detroit, 1973, pg. 56. For a more detailed description of the failed Évian Conference, pgs. 56–70 provide a good summary.

59. Ibid., pg. 119.

60. See: "Application for restitution by victims of National Socialism," Rose-Valerie Markt Norton. February 20, 1952.

THE FORTIES
THE WAR YEARS: SHANGHAI

61. *Die Chronik Berlins*, pg. 251.

62. Bismarck, who accompanied the emperor to the inauguration in 1881, had been distinctly unimpressed, and was heard to observe skeptically that "all these railroads merely hinder traffic." Ibid.

63. For more detail, see also: Hartwig Beseler and Niels Gutschow, *Kriegsschicksale: Deutscher Architektur*, Karl Wachholtz Verlag, Berlin, 1988.

64. William L. Shirer, *20th Century Journey: The Nightmare Years 1930–1940*, Little, Brown and Company, Boston & Toronto, 1984, pg. 383.

65. See Gilbert, *A History of the Twentieth Century: Volume II*, pg. 242–3.

66. William L. Shirer, *The Rise and Fall of the Third Reich*, Simon and Schuster, New York, 1960, pg. 454.

67. Joachim C. Fest, *Hitler*, Harcourt Brace Jovanovich, New York, 1974, pg. 574.

68. Actually there were originally a total of five so-called "treaty ports" where foreigners were accorded extraterritorial rights. In addition to Shanghai these were Canton, Amoy, Foochow, and Ningpo. Only in Shanghai, however, did the occasionally amended system prevail for a hundred years.

69. F. L. Hawks-Pott, *A Short History of Shanghai*, Kelly & Walsh, Shanghai, 1928, pg. 11.

70. Ibid.

71. Cited in Marcia R. Ristaino, *Port of Last Resort*, Stanford University Press, Stanford, California, 2001, pg. 7.

72. Bernard Wasserstein, *The Secret Lives of Trebitsch Lincoln*, Yale University Press, New Haven, 1988, pg. 273.

73. See Frederic Wakeman, *The Shanghai Badlands*, Cambridge University Press, Cambridge, 1996, pg. 140 footnotes.

74. At various times in his life, Trebitsch called himself Keelan, Tandler, ITT Lincoln, Tribich Lincoln, Reverend Ignatius Timotheus Lincoln, and other variations thereof. Bernard Wasserstein's biography (see footnote 72) gives an excellent account on which I have drawn.

75. Reinhard Heydrich to Josef Meisinger, cited in Astrid Freyeisen, *Shanghai und die Politik des dritten Reiches*, Königshausen & Neumann, Würburg, 2000, pg. 468; also Wasserstein, pgs. 242–80.

76. Carl Crow, *Four Hundred Million Customers*, H. Hamilton, London, 1937.

77. A compradore was the Chinese go-between all foreign enterprises employed as indispensable for interacting with the outside Chinese world.

78. Shanghai's average monthly high in July/August is 97.2° (36.3°C) with an average humidity of 82%. Some days exceed those temperatures. In winter 43° with 76% humidity is the average low.

79. By August 1940, the relief committees had succeeded in persuading the authorities to stop unfettered refugee access by requiring each new arrival to show proof of possessing at least $400—a prohibitive sum for most. A great tragedy, but no one could have known then that, as a result, those unable to escape Germany would pay for it with their lives.

80. Ernest G. Heppner, *Shanghai Refuge*, University of Nebraska Press, Lincoln & London, 1993, pg. 41.

81. Vicki Baum, *Hotel Shanghai*, Kiepenheuer & Witsch GmbH, Köln, 1997, pg. 34.

82. In modern Shanghai, this once elegant club and the center of social life in the old French District became a part of the five-star Garden Hotel, one of present day Shanghai's finest.

83. Pidgin English, once a pervasive means of communication in old Shanghai, has almost totally disappeared. A relic of the times when foreigners ruled the roost and used it to communicate with their servants and tradesmen, only the occasional old Chinese encountered in present day Shanghai still speaks it joyfully as proof that he remembers the good old days.

84. Edgar Snow, cited in Stella Dong, *Shanghai: The Rise and Fall of a Decadent City*, William Morrow, New York, 2000. For a detailed summary of Shanghai's gangster culture see pgs. 109–130.

85. Josef von Sternberg, *Ich, Josef von Sternberg*, Belber, bei Hanover, 1967, pgs. 95ff.

86. Much of the vast race course was totally off limits to ordinary Chinese and thus Exhibit A as a symbol of colonial injustices and the blatant racism of the expatriates. After the Communists took over Shanghai, it was one of the first things that changed. Today this valuable piece of real estate has become a giant "People's Park" with gardens, restaurants, and marvelous museums.

87. There are still question marks even today, although with time enough has emerged to provide fairly solid circumstantial evidence for what had caused the authorities to move against us. See pgs. 107–112 in the text.

88. See "Minutes of the Committee for the Assistance of European Jewish Refugees in Shanghai," March 3, 1942, Jerome Agel Collection, Box 1, Folder 3, Yivo, New York.

89. At less than $4 per person a month, hardly a princely sum, but Shanghai before the war had been one of the world's cheapest places for such relief efforts.

90. Only sixteen people, including ten habitual criminals, were sentenced for crimes, and no cases of criminal violence were reported. There were sixty-five divorces during the entire Pacific War period, and twenty mothers were reported to have "sold" their babies for adoption. All in all, these are very low numbers for a community of 18,000 in a time of poverty and stress. See: Felix Grünberger, "The Jewish Refugees in Shanghai," *Jewish Social Studies*, February 1948, pg. 340.

91. For example, David Kranzler, *Japanese, Nazis & Jews*, Yeshiva University dissertation, New York, 1971; also Heppner (footnote 80 above); James R. Ross, *Escape to Shanghai*, the Free Press, New York, 1994; and many others.

92. See: *Shanghai Jewish Chronicle 1942–1945*, published in the Honkou ghetto.

93. In particular, the testimony of the former German Counsel Fritz Wiedemann. For other details, see: Kranzler, pgs. 477–504; Freyeisen, pgs. 441–475; Heppner, pgs. 104–8 and files of the American Jewish Joint Distribution Committee and HIAS.

94. Freyeisen, pg. 443.

95. Before arriving in the Far East, Meisinger had made a name for himself as an especially brutal police chief in Warsaw, responsible for the murder of thousands of Jews and Poles. For this, remembered as "the butcher of Warsaw," he was hanged in Poland after the war.

96. See Freyeisen, pg. 470. Some Shanghai Jewish community leaders have independently corroborated such accounts.

97. Kranzler, pg. 481.

98. Years later, in the early sixties, while the U.S. ambassador for trade negotiations in Geneva, I was locked in difficult negotiations with the Canadians. One day, when they complained that I was a tough negotiator, I couldn't resist telling my counterpart, Canadian Minister for Trade and Commerce Mitchell Sharp that story. "You see," I needled him joyfully, "if you had let me in, I might now be sitting on your side." His laugh had a hollow ring, but for me it was sweet revenge.

THE FIFTIES
POSTWAR USA: APPRENTICESHIP YEARS

99. Ben J. Wattenberg, *A World at Arms*, Series D, New York, 1976, pg. 164.

100. HR 0660, signed by President Eisenhower on June 29, 1956.

101. Eric Goldman, *The Crucial Decade: America 1945–55*, Knopf, New York, 1956, pg. 13.

102. In those days the terms commonly used for America's non-white minority were "negroes," or in the South, "coloreds" instead of the current "Blacks" or "African-Americans," which reflect minority members' racial pride and which are the terms used in this book.

103. Truman was of Scottish-Irish-English descent; his pioneering ancestors had moved west to Missouri from Kentucky and Virginia. Eisenhower's forebears were Pennsylvania Dutch immigrants from the Palatinate, who had gone west after the Civil War. His grandfather, Jacob, a minister among the "River Brethren," still spoke and preached in German, but in Ike's time the family had long since moved away from its German roots.

104. Goldman, pg. 291.

105. "The Cabinet: The Flavor of the New" in *Time*, January 24, 1969.

106. Times have changed. Berkeley now charges Californians a substantial $13,000 per year. Its national reputation, however, remains unimpaired.

107. John Brooks, Harper & Row, *The Great Leap*, New York, 1966, pg. 300–302.

108. Dr. Isaiah Zimmerman later became a well-known psychologist in Washington, D.C., and also claims that for his Democrat and Republican patients alike, understanding the difference between appearance and reality proved a very useful lesson.

109. Though the total endowment ranks fourth after Harvard, Yale, and Stanford, who, however, have larger student enrollments.

110. Quoted in Robert Gambee, *Princeton*, W.W. Norton, New York, 1987, pgs. 15–17.

111. Peter Fuchs (ed.), *Chronik zur Geschichte der Stadt Köln*, Volume 2, Greven, Köln, 1991, pg. 290.

112. Franz-Josef Jakobi (ed.), *Geschichte der Stadt Münster*, Volume 3, Aschendorff Verlag, Münster, 1993, pgs. 1–3, 22, 103, 109, 115.

113. *Bevölkerung und Wirtschaft 1872–1972*, published by Statistisches Bundesamt Wiesbaden, W. Kohlhammer, Stuttgart/Mainz, 1972, pg. 95.

114. Karl Hardach, *Wirtschaftsgeschichte Deutschlands im 20. Jahrhundert*, Vandenhoeck und Ruprecht, Göttingen, 1979, pg. 251.

115. Ibid., pg. 259.

116. *Der Spiegel*, No. 29, July 15, 1953.

117. *Chronik Berlin*, pg. 478.

118. See *Jahrbuch der öffentlichen Meinung*, pg. 173; also, *Der Spiegel*, Heft 10, March 3, 1954.

119. This was the first Cunarder so named, eventually succeeded by the elegant *Queen Elizabeth II* and *III* and the even larger *Queen Mary II*.

120. Maldwyn A. Jones, *The Limits of Liberty: American History 1607–1980*, Oxford University Press, New York, 1983, pg. 536.

121. Stanley I. Kutler, "Eisenhower, the Judiciary, and Desegregation: Some Reflections," in Stephen E. Ambrose and Günter Bischof (ed.), *Eisenhower: A Centenary Assessment*, Louisiana State University Press, Baton Rouge, 1995, pgs. 87–89.

122. Godfrey Hodgson, *America in Our Time*, Doubleday, New York, 1976, pg. 43.

THE SIXTIES
WASHINGTON

123. Theodore Roosevelt was some months younger when he took office in 1901, but he had been appointed after McKinley's assassination. He was forty-five when reelected in his own right three years later.

124. Theodore Sorensen, *The Kennedy Legacy*, Macmillan, New York, 1969, pg. 254.

125. Ralph Dungan served President Kennedy with distinction. After JFK's assassination LBJ appointed him U.S. ambassador to Chile, and in the Carter years, he was U.S. executive director of the Inter-American Development Bank—one of those quirks of fate, because in that job I was his boss in the Treasury.

126. George Ball, *The Past Has Another Pattern: Memoirs*, Norton, New York, 1982, pg. 170.

127. Ibid., pg. 170.

128. There are at least two probable reasons why Carter chose Cyrus Vance over Ball. For one thing, pro-Israel Jewish leaders had let it be known that they considered Ball insufficiently on Israel's side. In this they were quite wrong, though it is true that he had advocated a policy that was anathema to them—de-emphasis on shuttle diplomacy and an even-handed policy to settle the Arab–Israeli conflict based on the implementation of UN Resolution 242, both of which he considered as much in Israel's as in the United States national interest. (For a more detailed discussion, see: James A. Bill, *George Ball*, Yale University Press, New Haven, 1997, pgs. 191–2; also, "The Disenchantment of Kissinger," *Saturday Review*, June 12, 1976; and "How to Save Israel in Spite of Herself, *Foreign Affairs*, April 1977). With the benefit of hindsight and a quarter century of continuing Mideast bloodshed, Ball was once again likely more right than wrong. The second reason for Carter's passing over Ball was probably the more decisive one. Ball would have been a strong and determined foreign policy leader, unlikely to take kindly to competition with Zbigniew Brzezinski, Carter's national security advisor, who would make Vance's tenure as Secretary miserable. Whether President-Elect Carter, who had an abiding faith in his own capabilities, would have been comfortable with a strong Secretary like Ball is open to question. That Brzezinski would not have been, is not.

129. Ball, pg. 366.

130. Ibid., pg. 164.

131. Citation from his unpublished speech manuscript.

132. "TRB," *The New Republic*, March 27, 1961.

133. Henry Fairlie, *The Kennedy Promise: The Politics of Expectation*, Doubleday, Garden City, New York, 1973, pg. 13.

134. George Ball, who occasionally commented on the predilection of bureaucrats instinctively to reject any new approach or idea, called this the "giraffe question," and was fond of telling the story of a father who took his little son to the zoo, where they encountered an oddly shaped, long-necked animal. "See, that's a giraffe," said the father. To which the son responded innocently, "Why?" See James A. Bill, *George Ball*, pg. 205.

135. Martin Weil, *A Pretty Good Club: The Founding Fathers of the U.S. Foreign Service*, Norton, New York, 1978, pg. 3.

136. G. F. Kennan, "The Needs of the Foreign Service," in Joseph McLean, *The Public Service and University Education*, Princeton University Press, Princeton, 1949, pg. 97. Kennan, one of the most able and distinguished American diplomats, was a product of the Foreign Service of the twenties and thirties. He was still active when I joined the Department.

137. Frederick Van Dyne, *Our Foreign Service: The "ABC" of American Diplomacy*. The Lawyer's Cooperative Publishing Co., Rochester, New York, 1909, pg. 77.

138. James L. McCamy, *The Administration of American Foreign Affairs*, Knopf, New York, 1950, pg. 187.

139. Lamar Cecil, *The German Diplomatic Service: 1871–1914*, Princeton University Press, Princeton, 1976, pgs. 97–103.

140. Concerning "backs and necks," a vital category of American poultry exports, the U.S. ambassador to Italy had dutifully reported back to Washington on his démarche at the top in Rome. The Italian minister had listened carefully, and cabled the ambassador who had a reputation as something of a wit, but had seemed unimpressed. A possible explanation might be, he added by way of a personal aside that caused great amusement within State where his telegram was widely circulated, that this particular gentleman had the well-known reputation to be greatly more interested in "breasts and thighs," than "backs and necks."

141. See Ball, pgs. 208–222.

142. *Frankfurter Allgemeine Zeitung*, March 28, 1963, pg. 1.

143. The U.S. interest in economic development remains a critical issue to this day, though for different reasons. In the sixties, the primary political rationale, apart from commercial and humanitarian considerations, was to counter flirtations with Communism. In today's post–Cold War world, an urgent requirement is to fight the threat of terrorists who inbed themselves in economically backward "failed states." There are many factors involved here, and lack of an economic base is often, but not always, one of them. Where it exists, as for example in the Sudan, Afghanistan, and Somalia, a policy of promoting economic development should be an important element of a comprehensive strategy of improving the lot and the governance of such "failed states," thereby making them less likely safe havens for terrorists who threaten our security. (See also: Stuart E. Eizenstat, et al., "Rebuilding Weak States," *Foreign Affairs*, Vol. 84, No. 1, Jan/Feb 2005, pgs. 134–146).

144. President Kennedy's statement at the White House, March 13, 1961. See the *Department of State Bulletin*, Vol. XLIV, No. 1136, April 3, 1961, pgs. 471–78.

145. E. S. Mason, "Primary Products and Economic Development" (Round Table #3), Committee for a National Trade Policy, Inc., mimeo., Washington, D.C., January 1960.

146. "A New Coffee Pact?", *New York Times*, December 21, 1961, pg. 39.

147. "Air of Uncertainly Dominates U.N. Coffee Stabilization Talks," Special to the *New York Times*, August 15, 1962, pg. 39.

148. *Wall Street Journal* editorial, May 1, 1962.

149. *New York Times*, May 3, 1964, pg. 3.

150. Richard B. Bilder, "The International Coffee Agreement: A Case History in Negotiations," in *Law and Contemporary Problems* 28 (spring 1963), pgs. 328–391.

151. Ibid., pg. 5.

152. "Commodity Agreements," *New York Times*, March 5, 1963, pg. 6.

153. *New York Times*, May 3, 1964, pg. 3.

154. Now called the World Trade Organization (WTO).

155. *Washington Post*, May 23, 1963, pg. A23; *New York Times*, May 26, 1963, pg. 60.

156. Today these numbers seem modest. In the current "Doha Round" under the WTO, there are 142 member countries, and 32 more with observer status. That is probably one reason why trade negotiations now can last for a decade—and still fail!

157. See *New York Times*, May 17, 1963.

158. *New York Times*, November 9, 1964.

159. Ball, pgs. 199–200.

160. *New York Times*, May 21, 1963, and May 11, 1966.

THE SEVENTIES
A WORLD IN TRANSITION

161. U.S. Department of Commerce, *Statistical Abstract of the United States*, Washington, D.C., 2001, pg. 10.

162. Ibid., pg. 45.

163. Speech to Jaycees, June 27, 1967.

164. *Business Week*, February 3, 1968, pgs. 22–24.

165. In 1981, the price of oil peaked at $87 bbl in current dollars.

166. See Nicholas R. Lardy, "China: The Great New Economic Challenge," in C. F. Bergsten (ed.), *The United States and the World Economy*, Institute for International Economics, Washington, D.C., 2005, pg. 124.

167. *Fortune Magazine*, February 1976.

168. See Daniel Goleman, "What Makes a Leader?", *Harvard Business Review*, Nov/Dec 1998, for a more detailed discussion of the concept of "emotional intelligence."

169. The principal proponent of this alarmist view was the French journalist and politician, Jean-Jacques Servan-Schreiber whose widely-discussed book *Le Défi Américain* (*The American Challenge*), Denoël, Paris, 1967, expressed fears many Europeans shared in private.

170. *Fortune*, June 1975, pg. 153.

171. *Detroit Free Press*, December 15, 1975, pg. 11A.

172. *New York Times*, December 13, 1976, pg. D1.

173. *Detroit Free Press*, December 15, 1975, Pg. 11A.

174. *The Manager*, September/October 1974, pg. 8.

175. "Profit-Minded Chief at Bendix tried to set a Businessmen's Code," *The Wall Street Journal*, November 18, 1975, pg. 1.

176. Times have changed. Today Canton, now Guangzhou, boasts some of the best hotels in China, of which the White Swan is one of my favorites and a far cry from the rundown Dung Fang where I was awakened at night by rats knocking a bowl of apples off the coffee table.

177. Charles Yost, a senior retired diplomat and former U.S. ambassador to the UN, was coleader of the delegation. The late Michel Oksenberg, later President Carter's advisor on China, and professor of Chinese Studies at the University of Michigan and Stanford, was a key delegation member and fluent Chinese speaker. Jan Berris, a young woman for whom China has become a lifelong passion and who still serves as a senior officer of the National Committee, was our able delegation secretary.

178. For a good account of the underlying logic and process of a Sino–U.S. rapprochement in the early seventies see Kissinger, *The White House Years*, Chapters XVIII–XIX, Little, Brown & Company, Boston, 1979, pgs. 690–787.

179. The recollections of the meeting with Zhou are based on the (unpublished) trip notes of Jan Berris and my own records and recollections.

180. He was referring to Professor Marion Levy, a Princeton sociologist and the author of a well-known study on the Chinese family.

181. A quote attributed to Walter Robertson, a Far East expert in the U.S. Department of State.

182. Richard J. Levine, "Blumenthal Opens Discussions in Peking," *Wall Street Journal*, February 26, 1979.

183. William J. Eaton, "Blumenthal Labels China Agressor in Vietnam," *Los Angeles Times*, February 26, 1979, pg. 1.

184. Neil C. Hughes, "A Trade War with China?", *Foreign Affairs*, July/August 2005, pg. 94.

THE SEVENTIES II
THE CARTER YEARS

185. *Newsweek*, January 31, 1977, pg. 23.

186. See: Jimmy Carter, *White House Diary*, Farrar, Straus and Giroux, New York, 2010, pg. 4.

187. Carter himself has ruefully referred to his "one-week honeymoon" with Congress, which is somewhat of an exaggeration—but not much. (See: *Keeping Faith*, Bantam Books, New York, 1982, pg. 65).

188. C-SPAN Survey of Presidential Leadership, March–December 1999.

189. Remarks at Amherst College, October 26, 1963.

190. See pages 278 to 279 in the text.

191. For a more detailed report on the 21 Club affair, see: *New York Times*, July 23, 1976, pg. A1.

192. Or did so in 1976 when the Bureau of Alcohol, Tobacco, and Firearms (ATF), the Secret Service, and the U.S. Bureau of Customs were still included. They are now a part of the new Department of Homeland Security.

193. *New York Times*, December 28, 1976, pg. 1.

194. Suggested Carter Administration Agenda, pg. 12.

195. Ibid., pg. 2.

196. See Joel Havemann, "The Cabinet Band—Trying to Follow Carter's Baton," *National Journal*, July 16, 1977, pg. 1104.

197. *U.S. News & World Report*, May 9, 1977, pg. 26.

198. *Fortune*, June 1977, pgs. 98ff.

199. Quoted in Emmet John Hughes, "The Presidency vs. Jimmy Carter," *Fortune* 98, no. 11, December 4, 1978, pg. 59.

200. See also *White House Diary*, pgs. 53–4.

201. Alexander Cockburn and James Ridgeway, "Cracker Credit," *The Village Voice*, February 7, 1977, pg. 24.

202. "The Budget Chief's Balance Sheet," *Time Magazine*, May 23, 1977.

203. I had a similar obligation to sell my Bendix stock by October 31, which—though it cost me plenty—was duly accomplished.

204. See Safire columns, *New York Times*, "Carter's Broken Lance," "Boiling the Lance," "The Lance Cover-Up", July 21, 25, and August 1.

205. Though nothing had happened at the meeting, that at least was true.

206. *Time*, August 29, 1977, pg. 9.

207. Personal notes: Bert Lance Affair, August 13, 1977.

208. See *Wall Street Journal*, August 21, 1977, pg. A12.

209. In the summer of 1978, a federal grand jury indicted Lance on thirty-three counts relating to his loan practices at BNG. In a 1980 trial, he was acquitted on some counts; a mistrial was declared after the jury deadlocked on the rest, and the government dropped the case. In 1981, Bert Lance regained control of the BNG.

210. *Time*, September 12, 1977.

211. *U.S. News & World Report* Editorial, September 12, 1977, pg. 88.

212. Hugh Sidey, "Searching for that Special Formula for Leadership," *Time*, October 3, 1977, pg. 16.

213. My records show that my first formal memorandum on the subject was sent to Carter on September 10, 1977, and subsequent ones on October 18, 20, and December 14, the latter after heated but inconclusive debate in the Cabinet Economic Policy Group (EPG). Probably there were several others.

214. My memoranda to the President, March 21, 1978.

215. WMB, Personal to the President, March 21, 1978.

216. See Richard J. Levine, "The Outlook," *Wall Street Journal*, November 6, 1977, pg. 7.

217. WMB to the President, May 8, 1979.

218. Jimmy Carter "To Mike, et al.," May 15, 1979.

219. The White House: The Economic Policy Group and the Coordination of Economic Policy Making, June 1, 1979 (appendix).

220. See Carter, *Keeping Faith*, pgs. 536–7.

221. See *New York Times*, July 5, 1979, pg. 1A; July 6, 1979, pg 1A; and July 8, 1979, pg. E1.

222. Jimmy Carter, *Keeping Faith*, pgs. 115–6.

223. *New York Times*, July 8, 1979, pg. A15; *Boston Globe* Editorial, July 8, 1979; *New York Times*, July 9, 1979, pg. A17.

224. Jimmy Carter, "The Crisis of Confidence," Speech to the Nation, July 15, 1979.

225. Jimmy Carter, *Keeping Faith*, pg. 121.

226. Carter later confirmed this. See *White House Diary*, pg. 346.

227. *White House Diary*, pg. 24.

228. Ibid., pg. 71.

229. Ibid., pg. 198.

230. Ibid., pg. 131.

231. Ibid., pg. 60.

232. Ibid., pg. 214.

233. Ibid., pgs. 192–3.

234. See Fritz Stern, *Five Germanys I Have Known*, Farrar, Straus and Giroux, New York, 2006, introduction pgs. 3–11.

THE EIGHTIES
GLOBALISM

235. George W. Ball, "The Conduct of American Foreign Policy: Reflections on a Heavy Year" in *Foreign Affairs*, 59 (1981), Volume 3, pgs. 474–499.

236. Martin Gilbert, *A History of the Twentieth Century: Volume III*, William Morrow and Company, New York, 1999, pg. 556.

237. In Orlando, Florida, on March 8, 1983.

238. George W. Ball, "Reflections on a Heavy Year," *Foreign Affairs*, 1981, pgs. 474–99.

239. F.A. Root Lectures, see also: a summary of the Root Lectures I had delivered at the Council on Foreign Relations, in *Foreign Affairs* 66, no. 3 (1987/8).

240. Jimmy Carter, *Keeping Faith*, pgs. 135–137.

241. WMB for the President, November 24, 1978.

242. See Zbigniew Brzezinski, *Power and Principle*, Farrar, Straus and Giroux, New York, 1983, pgs. 370–1.

243. See Carter, *Keeping Faith*, pg. 472.

244. The literature on the history of U.S.–Iran policy in the Nixon years and thereafter, and on the causes and events surrounding the Shah's downfall is substantial and characterized by considerable controversy. For those interested see, inter alia: Amin Saikal, *The Rise and Fall of the Shah*, Princeton University Press, Princeton, 1980; William H. Sullivan, *Mission to Iran*, W.W. Norton & Co., New York, 1981; Gary Sick, *All Fall Down*, Random House, New York, 1985; James A. Bill, *George Ball*, Yale University Press, New Haven, 1997, pgs. 90–92; "Kissinger's Critique," *The Economist*, February 3 & 10, 1979; and a Ball–Kissinger exchange "Who Lost Iran," *Washington Post*, pg. A21, February 26, 1979.

245. Brzezinski, *Power and Principle*, pg. 42.

246. A request Begin granted. The following day, a military escort drove me all the way to the Cedars of Lebanon, overlooking the Mediterranean and West Beirut, and now occupied by Israeli troops, and then back again past the wretched Palestinian refugee camps of Sabra and Shatila along the coast road to Israel.

247. For which Begin and Egyptian President Anwar Sadat were awarded the Nobel Peace Prize in 1978.

248. Much has been written about the Camp David negotiations, by several of the participants and others. For those interested, see, for example, Jimmy Carter, *Keeping Faith*, pgs. 317–407; Zbigniew Brzezinski, *Power and Principle*, pgs. 234–88; Ned Temko, *To Win or to Die*, William Morrow & Co. Inc., New York, 1987, pgs. 224–32; Amos Perlmutter, *The Life and Times of Menachem Begin*, Doubleday & Co., Garden City, New York, 1987, pgs. 333–60.

249. Brzezinski, pg. 262.

250. Brzezinski, pg. 263.

251. Interview with Kissinger, December 3, 2007.

252. See W. Michael Blumenthal, "A Pluralistic World Economy and Technology Change," Root Lecture Series, Council on Foreign Relations, New York, November 30–December 3, 1987. Also *Foreign Affairs*, 1987/88, pgs. 530–550.

THE NINETIES
A NEW GERMANY
253. Fritz Stern, *Five Germanys I Have Known*, pg. 197.
254. Blumenthal, *The Invisible Wall*. In German translation, *Die unsichtbare Mauer*, Carl Hanser Verlag, München, 1999.
255. Dennis Stanton in the *Observer*, May 14, 1995. Similar stories had also appeared in several Swiss and American papers.
256. Lead in *Der Tagesspiegel*, September 11, 2001.
257. *Tagesspiegel*, December 9, 1997, pg. 25.
258. Klaus Harpprecht in *Die Zeit*, December 1997.
259. Wolf Lepenies, *The Seduction of Culture in German History*, Princeton University Press, Princeton, 2006, pg. 207.
260. For a more detailed account of the German Jewish situation in the first two postwar decades see: Leo Katcher, *Post Mortem: The Jews in Germany Today*, Delacorte Press, New York, 1968.
261. Katcher, pgs. 2–3.
262. Ignatz Bubis, *Damit bin ich noch längst nicht fertig*, Campus Verlag, Frankfurt/New York, 1996, pg. 224.
263. At one point, there were even suggestions in the media that he would make an excellent president of Germany!
264. Nicole Dolif, "Die Rückkehr der Enkel," *Berliner Morgenpost*, September 7, 2008.
265. According to UN Population Statistics.
266. See Horst Siebert, *Jenseits des sozialen Marktes: Eine notwendige Neuorientierung der deutschen Politik*, DVA, München, 2005, pgs. 219–235.
267. In a speech to the SPD Bundestagsdelegation, April 3, 2006.
268. Interview with Kerem Caliskan, *Spiegel* online, February 8, 2008.
269. Mehmet Daimagüler in *Die Zeit*, March 13, 2008, pg. 6.
270. For details, see: Statistisches Jahrbuch für die Bundesrepublik, 2007, pgs. 48 ff.
271. See *Tagesspiegel*, July 2, 2008.
272. Roger Cohen, *The Atlantic Times*, August 2006, pg. 3.

ACKNOWLEDGMENTS

I can no longer remember when the idea for this book first came to mind, but the ups and downs of my life long ago impressed upon me what became its main themes: that in history nothing is certain until it happens; that the big turn of events is largely unpredictable and, though occasionally the result of exogenous factors beyond anyone's control, that much of it is usually hostage to the chance role of individual leaders in positions of power at critical turning points. In other words, as it certainly did in the last century, leadership—good or bad—mattered a great deal in determining our individual lives and in shaping the course of history.

To illustrate this theme through my own life experiences—whether as a stateless exile and survivor, or as a witness inside the halls of economic and political power—seemed like a relatively straightforward idea when first conceived. To actually translate it into reality proved, however, more complex than I had expected. Indeed, without the encouragement, support, and assistance of a number of key helpers and important people in my life, I would almost certainly not have been able to do it.

I owe special thanks to my research assistant, Dr. Daniel Bussenius, a young German historian whose professionalism and meticulous attention to detail were of immense help to me. His diligence and energy in gathering relevant archival materials in Berlin earned him my admiration and deep gratitude.

For the work in Germany, my two ever-helpful assistants at the Jewish Museum Berlin, Margarete Sabeck and, later, Ute Kiehn, also played a much appreciated special role for which they are owed my thanks.

In the United States, it was a pleasure to work with my manuscript editor, the highly competent Sally Arteseros, whose thoughts and suggestions were always helpful.

I am especially grateful to my agent, Georges Borchardt, who worked out the publication details with the folks at The Overlook Press and provided solid and thoughtful advice on the final manuscript.

His good sense, patience, and humor were a source of much comfort to me.

The same also goes for Peter Mayer and his staff of competent professionals at The Overlook Press. To work with the ever-helpful Mark Krotov there, who made valuable suggestions on the final draft and shepherded it through the publication process with great dedication and high competence, was a real pleasure.

Last but not least, there are the two people without whom this book could not have been written.

One is Marie Santos, my longtime Princeton assistant, whose support and collaboration in writing this book was invaluable. From beginning to end, it was she who ably did everything needed to man the computer and produce the several revisions of the chapter drafts as the book took shape. She did everything to keep me afloat and moving ahead when I most needed it and was there for me from the earliest beginnings in guiding the project from a mere idea to its final reality. I owe her my very special thanks.

My wife Barbara's unfailing support on this journey of personal discovery was critical. Without her understanding and support this book could not exist. For this reason alone, plus many others she knows better than anyone, it is dedicated to her.

INDEX